BETWEEN .

Between Medieval Men argues for the importance of synoptically examining the whole range of same-sex relations in the Anglo-Saxon period, revisiting well-known texts and issues (as well as material often considered marginal) from a radically different perspective. The introductory chapters first lay out the premises underlying the book and its critical context, then emphasise the need to avoid modern cultural assumptions about both male-female and male-male relationships, and underline the paramount place of homosocial bonds in Old English literature. Part II then investigates the construction of and attitudes to same-sex acts and identities in ethnographic, penitential, and theological texts, ranging widely throughout the Old English corpus and drawing on Classical, Medieval Latin, and Old Norse material. Part III expands the focus to homosocial bonds in Old English literature in order to explore the range of associations for same-sex intimacy and their representation in literary texts such as *Genesis A, Beowulf, The Battle of Maldon, The Dream of the Rood, The Phoenix,* and *Ælfric's Lives of Saints.*

During the course of the book's argument, David Clark uncovers several under-researched issues and suggests fruitful approaches for their investigation. He concludes that, in omitting to ask certain questions of Anglo-Saxon material, in being too willing to accept the status quo indicated by the extant corpus, in uncritically importing invisible (because normative) heterosexist assumptions in our reading, we risk misrepresenting the diversity and complexity that a more nuanced approach to issues of gender and sexuality suggests may be more genuinely characteristic of the period.

Between Medieval Men

*Male Friendship and Desire in
Early Medieval English Literature*

DAVID CLARK

OXFORD
UNIVERSITY PRESS

OXFORD
UNIVERSITY PRESS

Great Clarendon Street, Oxford, OX2 6DP,
United Kingdom

Oxford University Press is a department of the University of Oxford.
It furthers the University's objective of excellence in research, scholarship,
and education by publishing worldwide. Oxford is a registered trade mark of
Oxford University Press in the UK and in certain other countries

© David Clark 2009

The moral rights of the author have been asserted

First published in 2009
First published in paperback 2013

British Library Cataloguing in Publication Data
Data available

Library of Congress Cataloging in Publication Data
Clark, David, 1977–
Between medieval men : male friendship and desire in early medieval
English literature / David Clark.
p.   cm.
Includes bibliographical references (p.   ) and index.
ISBN 978–0–19–955815–5 (acid-free paper)   1. English literature—Middle English,
1100–1500—History and criticism.   2. Male friendship in literature.   3. Desire in literature.
4. Eroticism in literature.   5. Men in literature.   I. Title.
PR275.F75C57   2009
820.9′353—dc22   2008036339

ISBN 978–0–19–955815–5 (Hbk.)
ISBN 978–0–19–967117–5 (Pbk.)

To my family and to my friends

Acknowledgements

This book originated in a paper I was invited to give for the Oxford Medieval Graduate Seminar (now the Medieval English Research Seminar) in March 2005. I would like to thank all those present for their encouraging comments and productive questions, and especially Vincent Gillespie and Heather O'Donoghue for encouraging me to pursue this project. The bulk of the book was written in the summers of 2005 and 2006 while on temporary lectureships at the University of Oxford, and was finished in the summer of 2007 after my appointment at the University of Leicester.

I am very grateful to the Readers at OUP for their invaluable comments and suggestions.

The dedicatees know who they are and how much I owe them.

Contents

Detailed Contents

Abbreviations

CCSL	Corpus Christianorum Series Latina
CH	*Ælfric's Catholic Homilies: The First Series, Text*, ed. Peter Clemoes. Oxford: Oxford University Press, 1997
EETS	Early English Text Society
Ehwald	*Aldhelmi Opera*, ed. Rudolf Ehwald. Berlin: Weidmann, 1919
Emerton	Ephraim Emerton, *The Letters of St Boniface*. New York: Octagon Books, 1973
Liddell–Scott	Henry George Liddell and Robert Scott, *A Greek-English Lexicon*, rev. Henry Stuart Jones et al. Oxford: Clarendon Press, 1968
MRTS	Medieval and Renaissance Texts and Studies
PG	*Patrologia Graeca*, 2nd ser., ed. J.-P. Migne. Paris: Migne, 1857–66
PL	*Patrologia Latina*, ed. J.-P. Migne. Paris: Migne, 1844–91

PART I

INTRODUCTORY

Introduction

Between is a preposition with a double edge. It frequently implies distance or separation, yet as often implies proximity and connection. When used of persons *between* can express antagonism (the disillusioned lover's complaint 'she came between us'), or intimacy (the gossip's murmur 'between you and me'). Indeed, like the sword that lies between Sigurd and Brynhild in some versions of their story, the word often signifies all these things at the same time. With its polyvalent quality and ambiguous connotations, the word *between* in the title of this book thus asks the reader to consider what exactly there was between medieval men at the same time as implying that there was something between them worthy of closer consideration.

Consider the following poetic representations of relationships between medieval men in, respectively, the Exeter Book *Maxims*, *Beowulf*, *The Wanderer*, and *The Battle of Maldon*:

Wretched is he who shall live alone—fate has ordained him to dwell friendless. It were better for him that he had a brother...Always shall those warriors carry arms and sleep together—let one never slander them, before death separates them.

... in his heart, firm in the bonds of his mind, a secret longing after the dear man burned within his blood.

When sorrow and sleep together bind the wretched solitary man, it seems to him in his mind that he embraces and kisses his liegelord and on his knee lays hands and head, just as often before he enjoyed the gift-seat in days of old.

He lay thane-like near to his lord...I do not wish [to go] forth, but by the side of my lord, by such a dear man, I intend to lay myself.

What do we as modern readers make of these passages? How do we interpret the intimate bonds they depict? What assumptions do we bring to our readings? A caricatured queer reading might say, 'They describe intense physical and emotional intimacy between men, therefore these men must have been lovers and we can reclaim them as our ancestors in gay history.' Conversely, a caricatured traditional reading might say 'Nonsense—these passages describe the brotherly bond that has always existed between warriors, sex has nothing to do with it.' Although these opposed interpretations are evidently extremes, they nonetheless bring out questions and issues which are seldom addressed in readings of early medieval English literature. It is clearly not useful to assume, on the one hand, that intimacy and sexual contact between men are only found in gay relationships, and, on the other, that if men had sex with one another in the past, this connects them somehow to modern gay relationships. Nevertheless, it is no more useful to assume that intimate male-male relationships in the past must of necessity have contained no erotic component. More profitable, surely, are questions such as the following: Is the comfort with and openness about male intimacy exhibited in these quotations predicated on the unimaginability of homosexual activity, or, more subtly, the cultural invisibility of homosexuality? Alternatively, does the absence of a concept of homosexuality give male relationships a latitude in terms of intimacy which might create anxiety for many modern men? Should we assume that the Anglo-Saxons had no concept of homosexuality? If they did, how did it differ from our own? How far can we assume that when we read about the concepts of longing, desire, and love in early medieval contexts that they relate in any straightforward way to their counterparts in traditional modern heterosexuality? Where should we (can we) draw the dividing line between camaraderie and erotic relations in medieval contexts?

Anglo-Saxon England was by no means a heroic warrior society such as that depicted in poems such as *Beowulf*, however. We might further ask, then, what relation these bonds between men displayed in heroic literature had to Anglo-Saxon sociocultural norms for male relationships. Moreover, these texts were produced in a religious context by scribes working in monastic scriptoria, and thus we might question how far religious and secular attitudes to same-sex friendship and sex differed.

How do we interpret this letter by the ninth-century Anglo-Saxon cleric Alcuin to Arno of Salzburg, another cleric?

I wish my eagle might fly to pray at St. Martin's, that I might there embrace his soft wings and hold him whom my soul loves, not letting him go till I bring him to my mother's house and he kisses me and we enjoy mutual love as ordained.

To the modern eye it seems homoerotic, and yet it belongs to a long tradition of poems and letters of Christian friendship—does the religious character of that tradition mitigate against any erotic feeling? How or in what way does it relate to evidence of same-sex activity in religious communities? Were official condemnations of same-sex activity in tune with actual practice in dealing with such acts? For instance, the *Colloquies* of Ælfric Bata present humorous role-plays involving situations which clearly contravene the strictures of the Benedictine Rule on homosocial intimacy and imply, or at least strongly hint at, an amused tolerance of same-sex eroticism within the monastery.

And what about the following passage from an anonymous saint's life in which a woman disguised as a man causes trouble in the monastery in which she is hiding to escape marriage?

Then because the same Smaragdus was beautiful of face, as often as the brothers came to church, then the accursed spirit sent various thoughts into their minds and they were severely tempted by his beauty, and they then at last all became angry with the abbot for bringing so beautiful a person into their monastery.

Do we see this temptation as homosexual or heterosexual, or something else? How do we interpret such passages from religious works—what lessons are they trying to instil in their audiences? What anxieties over same-sex intimacy within monastic culture might they reveal?

And the Sodomites sinned shamefully against nature, and were therefore consumed with sulphurous fire, so that their foul lust was punished with the foul sulphur.

This passage from the writings of Ælfric seems unequivocally to condemn homosexuality, but how does this fit in with the eleventh-century prayer which speaks of the 'sodomitic sins' of 'adultery, deceit, greed, faithlessness and boldness in sinning'? Do vernacular texts differ in the way they deal with the sin of Sodom from Latin texts for clerical audiences? Was there a clerical discourse of sodomy or 'the sin against nature'? Is there any evidence of an early medieval concept of homosexual identity, as opposed to a set of acts which any man (or woman) might commit?

These are the kinds of texts and issues which this book seeks to address. To do so, it proceeds on the basis of five premises, summarized briefly here and explained more fully as the discussion unfolds.[1] The first stresses the textual basis of most of our evidence; the second, the conflicting nature of that evidence, and the third, that conflicting views may coexist within a single individual's thought or writing. The fourth premise is that one should not make assumptions that a given relationship is erotic (or non-erotic) based purely on the presence or absence of genital activity, and the fifth is that, in studying relations between men in early medieval literature, we must consider both erotic and non-erotic forms of love, and leave open the question of the overlap between them. These premises are in part a response to, and are more comprehensible within, the critical context.

MEDIEVAL SAME-SEX RELATIONS: THE CRITICAL CONTEXT

Medieval Masculinities—Becoming Male in the Middle Ages—Constructing Medieval Sexuality—Conflicted Identities and Multiple Masculinities—Queering the Middle Ages—Queering Medieval Genres—these critical compilations and others provide abundant evidence that there is a flourishing and productive field

---

[1] Readers who are not interested in the theoretical underpinnings of the project may wish to skip straight to the structural outline on p. 19 below.

of medieval gender and sexuality studies. However, one of the things which these collections have in common is that they all concentrate on the Continent or on the late medieval period and contain little or nothing on Anglo-Saxon England and Old English texts.[2] Likewise transhistorical works on the history of homosexuality such as those of Greenberg and Murray have little to say about the Anglo-Saxon period, although they do discuss important evidence on same-sex relations more generally in Germanic and feudal societies.[3] Even the *Handbook of Medieval Sexuality* largely ignores the Anglo-Saxon evidence, referring only briefly to the penalties prescribed in the Anglo-Saxon penitentials in the chapter on 'Homosexuality', although in its final chapter it does consider heterosexual relations in a handful of Old English texts.[4] This privileging of male-female sexuality in the period is seen in the work of literary medievalists, too. For instance, although a 1995 article by Hugh Magennis is subtitled 'Attitudes to Sexuality in Old English Prose and Poetry', it is entirely heterosexist in outlook with little mention of non-normative sexuality, even in its discussion of the vernacular poetic version of the book of Genesis.[5] Clare Lees's 1997 article 'Engendering Religious Desire' does give some limited attention to male-male relations, but is predominantly an account of male-female sexuality in the period, albeit a stimulating and productive one.[6]

There are a couple of recent exceptions to this trend. For example, the present undertaking has much in common with the recent collection of essays in memory of Daniel Calder, *Sex and Sexuality in Anglo-Saxon England*, which comprises several illuminating separate studies of homoeroticism and friendship in individual texts or genres.[7] *Between Medieval Men* has also been influenced by Malcolm Godden's 1995 article on Anglo-Saxon literary responses to biblical sexuality, although it includes a rather wider remit of texts and takes issue with some of

[2] Clare A. Lees, ed., *Medieval Masculinities: Regarding Men in the Middle Ages*. Minnesota: University of Minnesota Press, 1994; Jeffrey Jerome Cohen and Bonnie Wheeler, eds, *Becoming Male in the Middle Ages*. New York: Garland, 1997; Karma Lochrie et al., eds, *Constructing Medieval Sexuality*. Minnesota: University of Minnesota Press, 1997; Jacqueline Murray, ed., *Conflicted Identities and Multiple Masculinities: Men in the Medieval West*. New York: Garland, 1999; Glenn Burgess and Steven F. Kruger, eds, *Queering the Middle Ages*. Minnesota: University of Minnesota Press, 2001; Tison Pugh, *Queering Medieval Genres*. New York: Palgrave Macmillan, 2005.

[3] David F. Greenberg, *The Construction of Homosexuality*. Chicago: University of Chicago Press, 1988; Stephen O. Murray, *Homosexualities*. Chicago: University of Chicago Press, 2000.

[4] Vern L. Bullough and James A. Brundage, eds, *Handbook of Medieval Sexuality*. New York: Garland, 1996.

[5] Hugh Magennis, ' "No Sex Please, We're Anglo-Saxons"? Attitudes to Sexuality in Old English Prose and Poetry', *Leeds Studies in English* 26 (1995), 1–27. On the Old English versions of Genesis, see below, Chapters 5 and 6.

[6] Clare A. Lees, 'Engendering Religious Desire: Sex, Knowledge, and Christian Identity in Anglo-Saxon England', *Journal of Medieval and Early Modern Studies* 27 (1997), 17–45.

[7] Carol Pasternack and Lisa M. C. Weston, eds, *Sex and Sexuality in Anglo-Saxon England: Essays in Memory of Daniel Gillmore Calder*. MRTS 277. Arizona Center for Medieval and Renaissance Studies, 2004. The introduction represents a very useful overview of the growth of Anglo-Saxon sexuality studies.

Godden's interpretations of the biblical material.[8] Most notably, the book owes a debt to the only other full-length study of a similar nature, Allen Frantzen's *Before the Closet: Same-Sex Love from Beowulf to Angels in America*—now, astonishingly, a decade old.[9] This valuable book contains much meticulous scholarship and many stimulating readings of early medieval texts as part of its study of attitudes to Anglo-Saxon same-sex behaviour, but, despite Frantzen's subtitle (*Same-Sex Love from Beowulf to Angels in America*), it devotes most space to the evidence of the penitentials, the broader sociohistorical context, and later appropriations and readings of the Anglo-Saxons, with two chapters only on same-sex relations in Old English literary texts.[10] It is compromised to a certain extent, too, by the way in which personal agendas creep into the work—thus Frantzen spends much time attacking the vagaries of queer theory, but ends with an avowedly speculative chapter musing on the possible relations between his own sexual experiences with men who did not identify as 'gay' and the male-male relations of the Anglo-Saxons. It remains an important study, and has influenced much of what follows, but the present book explores the literary material in more depth and takes a rather different approach to same-sex love.

As the methodology below makes clear, my work seeks to approach the texts without making rigid a priori assumptions about gender, sexuality, and the boundaries between the erotic and the non-erotic, and thus raises more provocative questions than dogmatic answers. It engages with issues such as the interrelation of religious and secular discourses of sex and the sexes, medieval concepts of friendship, subjectivity and the individual, and thus fits into the growing body of research from a similar perspective that has been published within the field of later medieval literature. This is evinced by the collections listed above, and by books such as Carolyn Dinshaw's *Getting Medieval: Sexualities and Communities, Pre-and Post Modern* (1999), Stephen Jaeger's *Ennobling Love: In Search of a Lost Sensitivity* (1999), Ruth Mazo Karras's *Sexuality in Medieval Europe: Doing unto Others* (2005), Karma Lochrie's *Heterosyncrasies: Female Sexuality When Normal Wasn't* (2005), and Richard Zeikowitz's *Homoeroticism and Chivalry* (2003).[11]

---

[8] Malcolm Godden, 'The Trouble with Sodom: Literary Responses to Biblical Sexuality', *Bulletin of the John Rylands University Library of Manchester* 77 (1995), 97–119.

[9] Allen Frantzen, *Before the Closet: Same-Sex Love from Beowulf to Angels in America*. Chicago: University of Chicago Press, 1998. See also his articles, 'Between the Lines: Queer Theory, the History of Homosexuality, and Anglo-Saxon Penitentials', *Journal of Medieval and Early Modern Studies* 26 (1996), 255–96, and 'When Women Aren't Enough', *Speculum* 68 (1993), 445–71.

[10] Indeed, he disputes the relevance of literary study to an understanding of same-sex love in the period. See Chapter 3 below for a study of what the penitentials can tell us about sexuality in the Anglo-Saxon period.

[11] Carolyn Dinshaw, *Getting Medieval: Sexualities and Communities, Pre-and Post Modern*. Durham, NC: Duke University Press, 1999; C. Stephen Jaeger, *Ennobling Love: In Search of a Lost Sensitivity*. Philadelphia: University of Pennsylvania Press, 1999; Ruth Mazo Karras, *Sexuality in Medieval Europe: Doing unto Others*. New York: Routledge, 2005; Karma Lochrie, *Heterosyncrasies: Female Sexuality When Normal Wasn't*. Minnesota: University of Minnesota Press, 2005; Richard Zeikowitz, *Homoeroticism and Chivalry: Discourses of Male Same-Sex Desire in the Fourteenth Century*. New York: Palgrave Macmillan, 2003.

However, it also fits into the wider range of critical studies of gender and sexuality in premodern periods: in early modern studies, critical collections such as Louise Fradenburg and Carla Freccero's *Premodern Sexualities* (1996); Katherine O'Donnell and Michael O'Rourke's *Love, Sex, Intimacy, and Friendship between Men, 1550–1800* (2003), and Laura Gowring, Michael Hunter, and Miri Rubin's *Love, Friendship and Faith in Europe, 1300–1800* (2005); or, in the field of Classical literature, Nancy Sorkin Rabinowitz and Lisa Auanger's collection of essays, *Among Women: From the Homosocial to the Homoerotic in the Ancient World* (2002).[12] It thus intervenes in issues and debates current to several fields of literature and various disciplines, but which are only just beginning to involve early medieval studies.

GAY, STRAIGHT, OR BI? THE CATEGORIZATION AND LABELLING OF SEXUAL IDENTITY

Labelling or categorization are activities which humans have found recurrently problematic and yet recurrently fascinating, and particularly so when it comes to human sexuality. Scholars have often claimed that homosexuality has only really existed since the end of the nineteenth century, when medical and legal discourses began the process of enshrining the separate and deviant identity known as 'the homosexual' (which in turn allowed for the creation of a complementary creature: 'the heterosexual'). However, not only has there been a more recent acknowledgment of evidence that recognizable categories of sexual identity existed prior to this point, it is also abundantly clear that, whether in the late nineteenth or the early twenty-first century, humans have never really been content with the categories of homosexual and heterosexual, however much the binary pervades modern discourse.

A discussion of modern concepts and categories of sexuality may seem a strange place to begin a book on the early medieval period. However, one of the reasons that it is imperative to maintain an awareness of the artificiality of the popular heterosexual-homosexual and male-female binaries, is precisely because much Anglo-Saxon scholarship until recently has not done so. Jonathan Ned Katz, in his book *The Invention of Heterosexuality* (1996), asserts:

Heterosexuality . . . is invented in discourse as that which is outside discourse. It's manufactured in a particular discourse as that which is universal. It's constructed in a historically specific discourse as that which is outside time. It was constructed quite recently as that which is very old: Heterosexuality is an invented tradition.[13]

---

[12] Louise Fradenburg and Carla Freccero, eds, *Premodern Sexualities*. New York: Routledge, 1996; Katherine O'Donnell and Michael O'Rourke, eds, *Love, Sex, Intimacy, and Friendship between Men, 1550–1800*. New York: Palgrave Macmillan, 2003; Laura Gowing, Michael Hunter, and Miri Rubin, eds, *Love, Friendship and Faith in Europe, 1300–1800*. New York: Palgrave Macmillan, 2005.

[13] Jonathan Ned Katz, *The Invention of Heterosexuality*. New York: Plume, 1996, p. 182.

Medieval scholars have always recognized various elements of alterity in the past. However, they have often done so without also challenging the unexamined assumptions about gender and sexuality they have taken into their work. One of the reasons perhaps that there has been little attention paid to Anglo-Saxon masculinity and Anglo-Saxon male sexuality within the flourishing discipline of medieval gender and sexuality studies, is a residual and invisible (because still normative) heterosexist bias.[14]

This book proceeds from the conviction that, since sexuality itself is a deeply problematic category, it is important to maintain an awareness that the ways in which medieval sexual acts and identities are discussed and divided and abstracted are necessarily artificial and may often be contradictory; they will certainly bear a complex relation to lived reality. A definitive account of medieval sexuality is not attempted here, indeed the feasability and desirability of such a task is questionable. The book's far more modest aim is to explore intimate relations between men in the early medieval period as depicted in Old English literature, and to show how this topic can enable us to revisit these texts with fresh eyes and to revisit our own assumptions from a new and challenging perspective.

UNDERMINING BINARIES

It is a rather amazing fact that, of the very many dimensions along which the genital activity of one person can be differentiated from that of another (dimensions that include preference for certain acts, certain zones or sensations, certain physical types, a certain frequency, certain symbolic investments, certain relations of age or power, a certain species, a certain number of participants, etc. etc. etc.), precisely one, the gender of object choice, emerged from the turn of the century, and has remained, as *the* dimension denoted by the now ubiquitous category of 'sexual orientation'.[15]

In a characteristically insightful statement from her book *Epistemology of the Closet* (1990), Eve Kosofsky Sedgwick here brings out the unnaturalness of the binary which she argues to a large extent structures modern thought—why indeed is it that, when asked about someone's sexual orientation, most people assume they are being asked whether someone is straight, gay or bisexual (the uneasy third term which both calls into question and enshrines the binary), rather than whether they are gerontophiles, size queens, or foot fetishists? In attributing the emergence of this dimension's dominance to 'the turn of the century' Sedgwick nods towards the kind of attitude popularly associated with the controversial philosopher-historian Michel Foucault—the idea that homosexuality

[14] For some further examples, see Chapter 1 below on *Wulf and Eadwacer*, *The Wife's Lament*, and *The Husband's Message*. See also the important article by James A. Schultz, 'Heterosexuality as a Threat to Medieval Studies', *Journal of the History of Sexuality* 15 (2006), 14–29.

[15] Eve Kosofsky Sedgwick, *Epistemology of the Closet*. Berkeley: University of California Press, 1990, p. 8.

(along with heterosexuality) was invented in the late nineteenth century, coming out of a legal and medical discourse of sexual inversion which entered general consciousness in the 1920s and 1930s and to some extent still holds sway today.

The assertion by Foucault most often cited on this subject is the following extract from the first volume of his never-completed *History of Sexuality*:

As defined by the ancient civil or canonical codes, sodomy was a category of forbidden acts; their author was nothing more than the juridical subject of them. The nineteenth-century homosexual became a personage—a past, a case history and a childhood, a character, a form of life...The sodomite was a backslider; the homosexual is now a species. [16]

This statement is often paraphrased in such a way as to suggest that Foucault was arguing that sexual identity was invented in the nineteenth century, and that before this there were only different sexual acts, but, although this is a convenient caricature, it in fact oversimplifies what Foucault was saying. [17]

Foucault does not actually claim to be describing what 'real people' were like or what they did, but more specifically the way their acts were discussed and put into discourse. In the medieval period, he suggests, sodomitic acts are seen as acts that are deviant and sinful quite apart from any sexual orientation any one individual might be seen to embody, but in the late nineteenth and early twentieth century, same-sex acts came to be seen as manifestations of a deviant or inverted personality. Foucault raises an important conceptual point here—there is a large question mark over the issue of to what extent a concept or concepts of homosexual identity existed prior to the creation of (in Foucault's terminology) a discourse of homosexuality.

For many years, however, research into the details and configurations of premodern sexual identities was overshadowed by the largely artificial and bar-ren debate between two opposing schools of thought on this topic known as essentialism and social constructionism. The most influential exponent of the former school is the scholar John Boswell, whose problematic but deeply learned book, *Christianity, Social Tolerance and Homosexuality* (1980), has, however, received harsh (and sometimes unfair) criticism from social constructionists. [18] Boswell restated and slightly revised his premises in his less-read 1989 article

---

[16] Michel Foucault, quoted from the translation by David Halperin in his *How to Do the History of Homosexuality*. Chicago: University of Chicago Press, 2002, p. 27; Halperin's discussion of Foucault here is extremely useful.

[17] We might note Foucault's statement, for instance, that the fact that the term sexuality does not appear till the beginning of the nineteenth century 'should be neither underestimated nor over-interpreted. It does point to something other than a simple recasting of vocabulary, but obviously it does not mark the sudden emergence of that to which "sexuality" refers.' Michel Foucault, *The Use of Pleasure: The History of Sexuality, Volume 2*, trans. Robert Hurley. Harmondsworth: Penguin, 1985, p. 3.

[18] John Boswell, *Christianity, Social Tolerance and Homosexuality: Gay People in Western Europe from the Beginning of the Christian Era to the Fourteenth Century*. Chicago: University of Chicago Press, 1980.

'Revolutions, Universals, and Sexual Categories', in which he argues that the essentialist-constructionist debate represents the recurrent conflict between realism and nominalism: between the belief that 'humans recognise real distinctions in the world around them' and the conviction that categories are 'arbitrary conventions, simply names for things that have categorical force because humans agree to use them in certain ways'.[19] A strict nominalist or social constructionist, he states, would argue that humans are fundamentally just sexual—terms such as heterosexual or homosexual, rather than describing innate types of person, in fact enable them to exist. A strict realist or essentialist would contend that humans are innately divided into different types of sexual being—different societies may have invented many different labels which are more or less appropriate, but homosexuality is a category which exists in reality and not just in discourse (p. 19). Boswell also points out, however, that few people adhere strictly to either of these positions, and in a postscript to the article he wholly rejects the idea of a debate in any real sense, since none of the participants in the controversy would actually identify themselves as essentialists, even Boswell himself.[20] For the purposes of textual study, therefore, it is less helpful to argue in abstract terms about essentialism and constructionism than to work out a productive position somewhere between the two poles.

A moderate social constructionist approach is taken by two important studies of homosexuality in a transhistorical and transcultural perspective: David Greenberg's *The Construction of Homosexuality* (1988) and Stephen Murray's *Homosexualities* (2000).[21] Both works divide homosexuality into three main types: *transgenerational*, *transgenderal*, and *egalitarian*.[22] However, both readily admit that these are analytical categories which do not accurately reflect a reality which contains much overlap between these 'types', as in Murray's concluding formulation:

> In short, there is a range of homosexualities in a society, and the dominant discourse of the predominant sexual ideology ('sexual culture') may occlude but does not preclude different kinds of relationships. There is always intracultural and intrapsychic variance, but there are also recurrent social patterns, many of which include role labels.   (p. 422)

Where Greenberg constructs modern Western homosexuality as a unified conceptual category in opposition to non-Western and premodern same-sex relationships,[23] Murray is concerned from the outset to complicate singular notions

[19] John Boswell, 'Revolutions, Universals, and Sexual Categories', in *Hidden from History: Reclaiming the Gay and Lesbian Past*, ed. Martin Duberman, Martha Vicinus, and George Chauncey, Jr. London: Meridian, 1989, pp. 17–36, at p. 18.
[20] Although he would argue that 'gay persons' (by which he means 'those whose erotic interest is predominantly directed toward their own gender') have existed in most Western societies (p. 35).
[21] See note 3 above.
[22] Greenberg, *Construction*, p. 66; Murray, *Homosexualities*, pp. 23–4. The latter contains a rather more nuanced breakdown of the three categories.
[23] As in the following comment: 'Most non-Western societies make few of these assumptions. Distinctions of age, gender, and social status loom larger. The sexes are not necessarily conceived

of 'the homosexual', whether pointing out the variety of conceptions of homosexuality prevalent today, or showing from his assessment of the premodern and non-Western evidence that, even where age or gender differences were the primary means of structuring homosexual relations, there were still examples of love between equals.

Murray's main aim in his book is to demonstrate, as he emphasizes in his introduction and reiterates four hundred pages later, 'that more than one type of homosexuality may occur in one time and place' (p. 357). This is indeed a fact of crucial importance to studies of homosexuality in different historical periods, and its recognition leads to the first premise of this book:

> *Premise 1.* Although any type of same-sex relation is potentially available in *practice* in the Anglo-Saxon period (and doubtless did exist), only certain types may have been *culturally visible*, that is recognised in popular discourse. Moreover, since we are largely dependent on accounts written by, and often for, the dominant intellectual and cultural institution of the period, the Church, we must therefore be aware of the impact of religious ideologies on literary representations and constructions of same-sex relations.[24] The gap between textual concepts and constructs of homosexuality and people's actual experience of homosexualities may be wide.

Returning to the work by Sedgwick quoted ealier, after the passage emphasizing the unnaturalness of the heterosexual-homosexual binary, Sedgwick goes on to argue that, despite the prevalence of this discourse, Western ideas of sexuality are in fact radically incoherent. She notes that the popular shared understanding of homosexual definition is surprisingly similar, whether people are heterosexual or homosexual, homophobic, or antihomophobic:

It holds the minoritizing view that there is a distinct population of persons who 'really are' gay; at the same time, it holds the universalizing views that sexual desire is an unpredictably powerful solvent of stable identities; that apparently heterosexual persons and object choices are strongly marked by same-sex influences and desires, and vice versa for apparently homosexual ones; and that at least male heterosexual identity and modern masculinist culture may require for their maintenance the scapegoating crystallization of a same-sex male desire that is widespread and in the first place internal.   (p. 85)

And this recognition that people with ironic consistency hold contradictory ideas and theories together, often with little apparent strain, seems no less relevant in approaching premodern concepts of sex and sexuality. This book's second premise, therefore, is as follows:

symmetrically. Much the same can be said of earlier periods of Western history. In medieval Catholic doctrine, the sex of one's partner was not as important as whether the sexual contact was potentially procreative' (p. 482).

[24] Compare the remarks by R. D. Fulk in 'Male Homoeroticism in the Old English *Canons of Theodore*', in Pasternack and Weston, *Sex and Sexuality*, pp. 1–34, at p. 7.

Premise 2. In the medieval as in the modern period more than one attitude to same-sex relations existed, although one may be the *dominant* discourse at any one time. For instance, the attitudes reflected in the extant texts are inevitably heavily coloured by and feed into religious discourses. However, in the medieval as in the modern period, any individual or group may hold together (with a greater or lesser degree of difficulty or anxiety) two or more conflicting notions of same-sex relations, and such tensions may be observable in written texts.[25]

It is, of course, impossible to analyse sexuality without also considering the complicating factor of gender, not merely because it has become an increasingly problematic concept in the wake of the work of gender theorists such as Judith Butler, but also because, as with sexuality, premodern notions of gender do not straightforwardly map onto our own, raising questions of exactly what we mean when we say that a premodern society's concept of homosexuality is gender differentiated.

GENDERED SEXUALITY, DISCOURSE, AND REALITY

Perhaps the most influential recent work on this subject has been that of the social historian Thomas Laqueur, whose book *Making Sex: Body and Gender from the Greeks to Freud* (1990) argues that ancient and medieval authorities viewed sexual difference through an alternative paradigm to the dominant popular paradigm in the West today of two separate, (theoretically) equal and opposite sexes.[26] Authorities influential in the ancient and medieval periods like Aristotle and Galen, Laqueur shows, worked on the principle that men and women were part of a one-sex model. Put crudely, women were anatomically the same as men, but were merely turned inside out—as Galen asserts: 'Turn outward the woman's [genital organs], turn inward (so to speak) and fold double the man's, and you will find the same in both in every respect.'[27] The medievalist Carol Clover has applied this one-sex model to the literature of medieval Scandinavia (which has many points of similarity to Old English literature), arguing that it maps onto the gender system, which leads to a binary where people are divided into men and 'not-men': that is, women, old men, male and female children, and effeminate men.[28]

---

[25] Of course, it is also possible for different groups of the same period to have differing *dominant* discourses of homosexuality, for instance, the medieval Church might maintain a dominant discourse of sinful and unnatural acts, whereas the dominant model in unconverted medieval societies might be of age-structured or gender-differentiated homosexuality.

[26] Thomas Laqueur, *Making Sex: Body and Gender from the Greeks to Freud.* Cambridge, MA: Harvard University Press, 1990.

[27] Quoted in Laqueur, *Making Sex*, p. 25.

[28] Carol J. Clover, 'Regardless of Sex: Men, Women, and Power in Early Northern Europe', *Speculum* 68 (1993), 365–88.

In connection with sexuality, this is a fascinating but also troubling concept. It is possible to argue, for instance, that this binary would allow for men to have sexual relations with male youths or effeminate men, or perhaps male slaves, without being stigmatized, since this would not affect the active partner's masculinity—in effect he would be having sex with a 'not-man'.[29] Laqueur's work offers an extremely useful analytical tool, and it is employed in modified form in Chapters 3 and 9 below. Nevertheless, it is important to draw a distinction between discursive and actual categories, since their relation seems likely to be as complex here as we saw it to be with sexuality. Indeed, it is quite possible for a two-sex model to *coexist* with a one-gender model, as Joan Cadden argues in her book *Meanings of Sex Difference in the Middle Ages: Medicine, Science, and Culture*.[30] In her study of mainly later medieval writings, Cadden shows that Laqueur somewhat oversimplifies both the views of the Ancient authorities and the extent of their adoption by medieval writers, and that from her study of the various discourses on gender and sexuality:

What emerges is not a grand synthetic scheme that captures the medieval concept of gender but rather a cluster of gender-related notions, sometimes competing, sometimes mutually reinforcing; sometimes permissive, sometimes constraining; sometimes consistent, sometimes ad hoc. The plot of this account . . . consists in the unfolding of relations among various distinct but overlapping sets of theories, values, and interests.

(pp. 9–10).

Thus, although Laqueur's concept of gender as not simply a male-female binary is extremely useful and used in what follows, it is used with certain limits and as a spur to further discussion. Laqueur and Cadden's arguments lead to:

Premise 3. As with sexuality, different concepts and discourses of gender must have coexisted in the early medieval period, although one may be

[29] The possibility that male (as well as female) slaves may have been used for sexual purposes is raised by Allen Frantzen in his 'Bede and Bawdy Bale: Gregory the Great, Angels, and the "Angli" ', in *Anglo-Saxonism and the Construction of Social Identity*, ed. Allen J. Frantzen and John D. Niles. Gainesville: University Press of Florida, 1997, pp. 17–39, at p. 24; the article appears in condensed form in chapter 7 of *Before the Closet*. Although Ruth Mazo Karras states (without adducing evidence) that sexual exploitation of male slaves was less common than that of female slaves, she concedes that it occurred with both; see her 'Desire, Descendants, and Dominance: Slavery, the Exchange of Women, and Masculine Power', in *The Work of Work: Servitude, Slavery, and Labor in Medieval England*, ed. Allen J. Frantzen and Douglas Moffat. Glasgow: Cruithne Press, 1994, pp. 16–29, esp. p. 24, nn. 9 and 10, and p. 25, n. 14. That male and female slaves were often differentiated in terms of terminology as well as treatment is shown, however, by Elizabeth Stevens Girsch, 'Metaphorical Usage, Sexual Exploitation, and Divergence in the Old English Terminology for Male and Female Slaves', in the same volume, pp. 30–54.

[30] Joan Cadden, *Meanings of Sex Difference in the Middle Ages: Medicine, Science, and Culture*. Cambridge: Cambridge University Press, 1993. See also Danielle Jacquart and Claude Thomasset, *Sexuality and Medicine in the Middle Ages*, trans. Matthew Adamson. Cambridge: Polity Press, 1988. The overlap of one-sex and two-sex models can also be seen in the 'sworn virgins' of the Balkans who are viewed as biologically female and socially male (Murray, *Homosexualities*, p. 214); see also Antonia Young, *Women Who Become Men: Albanian Sworn Virgins*. Oxford: Oxford University Press, 2000.

dominant at any one time. We may also assume that contradictory concepts may coexist within the same individual's thought and, in some cases, writings.

THE EROTIC, THE GENITAL, AND THE HOMOSOCIAL

There is one further complicating factor, however, which it is necessary to introduce into the methodology outlined above. Something which unites not only the approaches of Greenberg and Murray, but also those of the few Anglo-Saxonists who have written on same-sex relations, is their emphasis on genital contact and their desire to differentiate erotic and non-erotic relations between men.[31]

Certainly, Nancy Sorkin Rabinowitz in her introduction to *Among Women: From the Homosocial to the Homoerotic in the Ancient World*, contends that to insist on genital contact as 'proof' of homosexuality is both homophobic (in requiring proof) and masculinist (in that the only proof is a sexual act modelled on penetrative intercourse), since in heterosexual contexts the assumption of sexual significance can rest on far less stringent criteria.[32] She suggests the use of the term *homoerotic*, as one which 'suggests the possibility of desire without consummation, turns our gaze away from genital sexuality, and inscribes a more expansive field of relationships than does "homosexual" ' (3).

Nevertheless, it is true that genitality is frequently the consideration of prime importance in men's own discussion and categorization of same-sex relations, both medieval and modern. Consider the report of Murray on the complexities of male sexuality in modern Latino culture, where the division of men into *activos* (men who take the active role in sex) and *pasivos* (men who take the passive role) is rigid. Nevertheless, observers report a fear of enjoying being penetrated among Latino males, such as the young Guatemalteco who worried 'If I let him fuck me I'd probably like it and then I'd do it again, and then I'd be queer' (Murray, *Homosexualities*, p. 273). Ruth Mazo Karras describes a similar emphasis on and anxiety about penetration in her *Sexuality in Medieval Europe*, where she argues that sex was primarily seen as 'something that one person does to another' (p. 158) and that 'the dichotomy between active and passive partner

---

[31] Murray, for instance, defines male homosexuality in explicitly genital terms as follows: 'I mean contact between the penis of one male and the body of another person who was born male and/or the desire by someone born male for contact with the penis, thighs, or orifices of someone else born male.' (Murray, *Homosexualities*, p. 13.) Greenberg, too, consistently essentializes the erotic relationship as genitally expressed sexual activity (cf. *Construction of Homosexuality*, pp. 114, 258, 285), although he does recognize that erotic attraction may simply be unrecognized by one or both parties (p. 285) and that 'it may be that sexual behavior or response is not the optimal criterion for use in classification' (p. 492).

[32] Nancy Sorkin Rabinowitz, 'Introduction' in *Among Women: From the Homosocial to the Homoerotic in the Ancient World*, ed. Nancy Sorkin Rabinowitz and Lisa Auanger. Austin: University of Texas Press, 2002, pp. 1–33, at p. 3.

played a major role in the way medieval people thought about sexuality' (p. 26). Some medieval penitentials also penalise penetrative sex acts more harshly than non-penetrative ones.[33] Moreover, the young Latino man's recognition of the dangerous pleasure of being penetrated is comparable to that in medical texts widely translated in the Middle Ages such as Avicenna, where it was thought to be something to which one could become accustomed and thus lead to an exclusive desire to play the passive role in sex.[34]

Nevertheless, against any strict delimitation of the boundaries of physical and emotional intimacy there is ample evidence that physical sexual attraction for one gender without emotional involvement can coexist today with erotic involvement with the other gender that is more emotional than physical and may not be genitally expressed (cf. Murray, *Homosexualities*, p. 492 n. 23). A similarly complex picture is argued to be representative of the medieval period in the work of Karras quoted above and also in Stephen Jaeger's book *Ennobling Love*, a stimulating work which shows how male-male love and desire was encouraged and seen as ennobling and exalting in the medieval contexts he studies, as long as it did not involve sex.[35] This kind of approach seems more productive than that seen in Brian McGuire's book, *Friendship and Community: The Monastic Experience*.[36] This important work, covering the vast body of European medieval literature on friendship, deserves close attention and contains much useful material. However, McGuire clearly feels in his Epilogue that he must at least touch on the question of whether the passionate feelings described in the many texts he discusses ever found sexual expression. He entirely dismisses the possibility on the grounds that monks are celibate: 'the question of homosexual love is no more relevant in the realm of monastic friendship than that of heterosexual love. It is simply out of the question' (p. 409). Given the frequency of medieval clerical criticisms of monks and others for breaking their vows of chastity (not to mention common sense), this remark is clearly disingenous. Moreover, it privileges the genital expression of erotic desire. Although I would want to make more of a distinction between reality and discourse than Karras and Jaeger do, nevertheless their findings give weight to this book's fourth premise:

> *Premise 4.* We should not make assumptions too readily about whether a relationship is an erotic one or not, based purely on whether genital activity is involved.[37]

---

[33] See Frantzen, 'Between the Lines' (reworked as chapter 4 of *Before the Closet*).

[34] For an excellent discussion of this matter in relation to Peter of Abano, see Joan Cadden, 'Sciences/Silences: The Natures and Languages of "Sodomy" in Peter of Abano's *Problemata* Commentary', in Lochrie et al., *Constructing Medieval Sexualities*, pp. 40–57. A similar understanding of the *cinaedus* figure has also been proposed for the Classical period; cf. Halperin, *How to Do the History of Homosexuality*, pp. 32–8.

[35] See note 11 above.

[36] Brian Patrick McGuire, *Friendship and Community: The Monastic Experience 350–1250*. Cistercian Studies Series, 95. Kalamazoo, MI: Cistercian Publications, 1958.

[37] Indeed, we might want to make a distinction between the sexual and the erotic (which can include sexuality but is not limited to it).

Jaeger also advocates the application of the term *homosocial* to the relations of medieval men and thus invokes the book by Eve Kosofsky Sedgwick to which my own title alludes: *Between Men: English Literature and Male Homosocial Desire*.[38] As Jaeger remarks on the term:

> It sets sexuality to one side, eliminates its automatic inclusion, while holding it in readiness. The discourse of male-male love displays on its surface sexuality vanquished and banished. Sexual desire and sexual intercourse can infiltrate it secretly, but they do not govern it from their position of hiding. Unquestionably the texts treated here are grounded in male desire; but just as unquestionably there is something in the discourse that screens off or remains oblivious to a sexual element in this desire.   (p. 15)

And yet Sedgwick's use of the term is as part of the collocation *homosocial desire*, which she employs in pursuit of her hypothesis of 'the potential unbrokenness of a continuum between homosocial and homosexual—a continuum whose visibility, for men, in our society, is radically disrupted' (*Between Men*, p. 1).

   In our society, she explains, where there is a socially sanctioned site of homosocial desire, one often finds that this desire is normalized via homophobic discourse—homosexuality is explicitly abjected. The simplest (though rather stereotyped) analogy is the football locker-room where, we are told, manly men, so-called 'real' men, often make homophobic jokes to ward off any anxiety about their physical and emotional intimacy with other men.[39] Sedgwick hastens to clarify, however, that she does not want to suggest a genetic hypothesis—to claim that homosexual desire lies at the root of all forms of homosocial interaction. Instead, her term is 'a strategy for making generalizations about, and marking historical differences in, the *structure* of men's relations with other men' (pp. 1–2).[40]

   Sedgwick's book, although hugely influential, has been criticized from some quarters, and its main overall arguments are that the homosocial relations in early modern literature are cemented by the exchange of women (for instance, in marriage) and involve sublimated homoerotic desire.[41] Thus, the present book does not seek simply to apply Sedgwick's model to early medieval English

---

[38] Eve Kosofsky Sedgwick, *Between Men: English Literature and Male Homosocial Desire*. New York: Columbia University Press, 1985. Sharon Marcus's book *Between Women: Friendship, Desire, and Marriage in Victorian England* (Princeton: Princeton University Press, 2007) also self-consciously alludes to Sedgwick and I have found the methodology outlined in its introduction both illuminating and encouraging; my thanks to Holly Furneaux for introducing me to it.

[39] For a textbook example of this process, see Tony Cascarino, 'Boys being boys in the dressing-room helps to keep homosexuality in football's closet', *The Times*, 13 February 2006.

[40] This corresponds to and extends Katz's point that, if we avoid universalizing homosexuality *and* heterosexuality, we can ask how men 'structured their erotic relations with men, what thoughts, judgments, and physical acts of theirs we can find evidence of, and what words they used about those relations.' (Jonathan Ned Katz, ' "Homosexual" and "Heterosexual": Questioning the Terms', in *Sexualities: Identities, Behaviors, and Society*, ed. Michael S. Kimmel and Rebecca F. Plante. Oxford: Oxford University Press, 2004, pp. 44–6, at p. 46.)

[41] Compare Frantzen, 'Between the Lines', p. 295, n. 118 and the review of Sedgwick's book by G. S. Rousseau in *The Pursuit of Sodomy: Male Homosexuality in the Renaissance and Enlightenment Europe*, ed. Kent Gerard and Gert Hekma. New York: Haworth, 1989, pp. 515–29.

literature. Nevertheless, it is not necessary to adopt Sedgwick's methodology wholesale to appreciate the value of not prejudging the boundaries between and definitions of friendship, sex, desire, and love in a given historical context, which leads to this book's final and most important premise:

> *Premise 5.* In a study of relations between men in early medieval English literature, it is necessary to look at both erotic and non-erotic relationships, and indeed to leave open the questions of where platonic and erotic love part company (if indeed they can truly be said to do so), and how far sexual and emotional relations coincide.

This stance, for instance, allows one to read the intensely emotional and sometimes homoerotic letters between clerics and other religious figures without saying the feelings described are 'really' sexual, or 'really' conventional (as in Chapter 4 below).[42] And it allows one to think about the intimate relationship of warriors who sleep together without saying that this practice 'really' indicates just friendship, or 'really' must have involved no-strings-attached sex (as in Chapter 7 below).

This book attempts to avoid all such unhelpful preconceptions—to look at the various different male-male relationships we find in the literature without making a priori assumptions about whether a relationship is or is not sexual (or that the erotic can be easily distinguished from the non-erotic). It presumes neither on the one hand neatly delineated innate sexual identities nor on the other hand an undifferentiated polymorphously perverse conception of human sexuality. With this in mind, it avoids the terms *homosexual(ity)* and *heterosexual(ity)*, preferring instead to speak of *same-sex acts* and *activity*, or *male-male* and *male-female desire*, and so on.[43] While these terms may have the disadvantage of being somewhat unwieldy, it is hoped that precisely this quality will serve as a periodic reminder of the dangers of equating modern with medieval categories and concepts.

It should be remarked at this point that one major failing of this book is that it largely ignores the subject of same-sex relations between women. Quite apart from the practical issues—that including women's relations would massively extend the length of the book, and that there is even less information about women's sexual interactions with each other than about men's—it seems important at this stage in terms of methodology to consider the issues of female-female and male-male relations separately at first to determine whether and how far they *can* profitably be discussed together. Nevertheless, it is not the intention to further marginalize women in the Middle Ages and much fruitful research remains to be done in this area.[44]

---

[42] Compare Lees, 'Engendering Religious Desire', and especially 17.

[43] Though for a salutary discourse on the problems with all such terminologies, see Leila J. Rupp, 'Toward a Global History of Same-Sex Sexuality', *Journal of the History of Sexuality* 10 (2001), 287–302.

[44] See, however, E. Ann Matter, 'My Sister, My Spouse: Woman-Identified Women in Medieval Christianity', in *The Boswell Thesis: Essays on 'Christianity, Social Tolerance, and Homosexuality'*, ed. Matthew Kuefler. Chicago: University of Chicago Press, 2006, pp. 152–66; Jacqueline Murray,

THE SCOPE OF THIS BOOK

Between Medieval Men is divided into three sections. The first is 'Introductory' and consists of this introduction and Chapter 1, an analysis of three poems most often considered to be about heterosexual romantic love as a means of destabilizing at the outset assumptions often made about Old English texts, arguing that such interpretations often rest upon heterosexist and anachronistic preconceptions which are invisible because they lay implicit claim to be normative. It also reviews the arguments which claim male narrators for *Wulf and Eadwacer* and *The Wife's Lament* and the reception of these critical manoeuvres, and concludes with a call to examine more rigorously our cultural assumptions about the Anglo-Saxon period and its literature, and by acknowledging the primacy of homosocial desire.

Part II contains four chapters centred around the vexed question of 'Same-Sex Acts and Identities' in the early medieval period and attempts to uncover the range of attitudes to same-sex relations in Anglo-Saxon society, as far as it can be determined from the surviving evidence. It does this through an examination of ethnographic, penitential, and theological material, with their attendant difficulties, in order to gain a clearer insight into the sociocultural values and associations of same-sex activity.

Chapter 2 reviews the ethnographical evidence available which suggests that the pre-Migration Germanic tribes may have practised pederasty and same-sex rites of initiation, also comparing accounts of similar practices among the Celts. It explains apparently countervailing evidence from Tacitus's *Germania* by adducing the Old Norse discourse of *nið*, where only the passive partner in same-sex acts seems to have been stigmatized. It forms a pair with the following chapter which, with this heritage in mind, seeks to uncover the range of attitudes to same-sex activity in Anglo-Saxon England. Chapter 3 begins by reviewing a limited amount of evidence which suggests that the Anglo-Saxons may have had a less well-developed concept of *ergi*, and concludes that, even given the paucity of what material has survived, it is nevertheless probable that the Anglo-Saxon assumption in secular circles was that it was normal to be the insertive partner in sex with both men and women but that passivity and effeminacy were strongly stigmatized. Noting the problems of correctly interpreting the significance of legal and ecclesiastical texts as evidence for the incidence of contemporary same-sex acts and attitudes to them, this chapter emphasizes the fact that there are no extant secular legal penalties from Germanic societies, including Anglo-Saxon England. It assesses the evidence of the Anglo-Saxon penitentials, which penalize a range of same-sex acts, and discusses the obscure term *bædling* and its implications for the concept of a distinct Anglo-Saxon sexual identity.

'Twice Marginal and Twice Invisible: Lesbians in the Middle Ages', in Bullough and Brundage, *Handbook of Medieval Sexuality*, pp. 191–222. Some remarks are made about female homosociality in Chapter 9.

Chapters 4 and 5 constitute another pair of chapters, but this time the argument is that critics have been premature in finding evidence of same-sex activity. The first of these begins with a review of the biblical and patristic allusions to Sodom as a context for its study of medieval Continental and Anglo-Latin interpretations of the narrative, discussing Bede, Aldhelm, Boniface, Alcuin, and Ælfric. It shows that religious writers in Latin associate Sodom with a range of sins, and not just same-sex acts. The following chapter then constitutes a comprehensive investigation of the extant references to Sodom in Old English texts, except for *Genesis A* which is considered in Chapter 4. It divides these allusions into four categories: those using Sodom's destruction as the prime example of the punishment of sin; those where the Sodomites' behaviour exemplifies sin of an unusual gravity; those where Sodom is especially associated with sexual sin; and those in which Sodom is associated with unnatural sin. It shows that, contrary to the assumptions of many medieval scholars, not only do none of the references explicitly link Sodom to same-sex acts, but many make quite other associations with the city.

Part III of *Between Medieval Men* widens its scope from same-sex acts to a more general focus on 'Homosocial Bonds in Old English Literature': the first three chapters explore male-male relations in Old English poetic texts, and the final two bring in late Old English prose texts.

Chapter 6 investigates how homosocial bonds are constructed in the Old English poetic version of the biblical book of Genesis, starting with the treatment of the Sodomites in *Genesis A* and the contrast between their relations and the 'correct' and praiseworthy homosocial bonds between Abraham and his kinsmen and friends. It argues that, unlike other prose treatments, in *Genesis A* same-sex acts are not considered to be the primary sin of Sodom, but that they form part of a network of various forms of unsanctioned sexual desire, presented by the poet as destructive in order to promote by contrast the procreative coupling of Abraham and Sarah, the progenitors of the chosen people.

Chapter 7 focuses in on the construction of homosocial bonds, looking first at heroic male relations in *Beowulf* and *The Battle of Maldon*. It argues that the *Beowulf*-poet here as in other matters remains ambivalent, but that the *Maldon*-poet opposes what he sees as correct homosocial bonds to a cowardice stigmatized by associations with effeminacy and sexual passivity. It then contrasts the radical revaluation of masculinity and heroic passivity in *The Dream of the Rood*, paving the way for the later chapters' further analyses of vernacular religious texts which re-envision gender roles and homosocial bonds. Thus Chapter 8 analyses the repudiation of male-female sexuality in *The Phoenix* and its presentation of asexual, solitary, and spiritual reproduction. It questions how far the spiritualization of sex and gender problematizes the poem's allegorical construction of the monastic environment, and sets up a rich and paradoxical dynamic that reflects a contradictory attitude to same-sex intimacy and productive anxieties.

The ninth chapter moves into Old English prose literature to study the interaction of different constructions of homosocial desire in Ælfric's *Lives of Saints*, where same-sex relations are depicted as simultaneously natural and unnatural. Intense male loyalty inextricably fused with Christian faith is held up as an ideal in the Life of the Forty Soldiers, in contrast to male-female sexuality which is repudiated. However, there are signs of authorial anxiety over the homosocial intimacy described in the martial saints' lives. A conversion model based on homosocial community in other Lives coexists with the threat of same-sex desire, and this dynamic is compared to ways in which the eponymous transvestite protagonist of Ælfric's Life of Eugenia reflects anxieties about gender and same-sex intimacy in monastic contexts.

The final chapter then analyses at length the anonymous *Life of Euphrosyne*, which, although exhibiting some of the anxieties we find in Ælfric's work, is more open about the possibility of same-sex desire within the monastery and, as such, presents rich possibilities for transgressive readings of the text and the reappropriation of the sexual desire it seeks to exclude. The chapter continues with an examination of the *Colloquies* of Ælfric Bata, which may exhibit a pragmatic and relaxed attitude to same-sex relations more characteristic of many religious establishments not overseen by strict moralists such as Bata's tutor and namesake, Ælfric of Eynsham. It concludes by summarizing the findings of the individual chapters to characterize Anglo-Saxon England's unique literary dynamic in terms of the uneasy yet productive interaction of issues of gender and sexuality, secular and religious, individual and community.

This study makes no claim to be nobly pioneering in its approach to early medieval sexualities, nor indeed to be comprehensive in its investigation of literary representations of male relationships, but it does aim to show that provocative and productive questions still exist to be asked about sexual acts and identities in the medieval period, that traditional interpretations of texts are often coloured by cultural assumptions which are anachronistic (and often invisible precisely because they seem obvious), and that Old English texts can provide a challenging perspective on how the way in which we write and think about interpersonal relations maps onto our lived experience of friendship, sex, and everything in between.

1

A Fine Romance? *Wulf and Eadwacer, The Wife's Lament*, and *The Husband's Message*

All this is too much. Personally, I shall be content to go to the grave believing that the narrator [of *The Wife's Lament*] is a woman. But such is the ingenious desperation of some present-day critics of OE literature that (as I write in December 1970) I await with confident horror an overtly homosexual interpretation of this poem.[1]

Although this book is primarily concerned with the configurations of male-male bonds in Old English literature, this first chapter centres on three short poems which have come to be known as *Wulf and Eadwacer, The Wife's Lament*, and *The Husband's Message* (although there has been some disagreement over the appropriateness of these titles, as we shall see). These texts are all found in the Exeter Book, a tenth-century compilation housed at Exeter Cathedral Library since its donation in around 1050 by Leofric, first bishop of Exeter. They are often treated as a group, though they are not contiguous in the manuscript and there is no general agreement over whether the compilation has an underlying rationale.[2] The poems are also often considered to be examples of the Old English elegy, that notoriously slippery genre, and are frequently discussed alongside their more popular companions, *The Wanderer* and *The Seafarer*.[3] What marks out these three poems is the fact that they seem, almost uniquely in Old English literature, to explore or be based on romantic love between men and women, an emotion in which the Anglo-Saxons seem to have had little literary interest, judging from its almost complete absence in the extant corpus.[4]

---

[1] Bruce Mitchell, 'The Narrator of *The Wife's Lament*: Some Syntactical Problems Reconsidered', *Neuphilologische Mitteilungen* 73 (1972), 222–34, at 234. See below, n. 35.

[2] For a good introduction to the manuscript and its contents, see Bernard J. Muir, ed., *The Exeter Anthology of Old English Poetry: An Edition of Exeter Dean and Chapter MS 3501*. 2nd rev. edn. 2 vols. Exeter: Exeter University Press, 2000.

[3] See James W. Earl's review in *Speculum* 69 (1994), 1196–8, of Anne L. Klinck, ed., *The Old English Elegies: A Critical Edition and Genre Study*. Montreal: McGill-Queen's University Press, 1992.

[4] There is one other Old English text which contains a male-female love affair, namely the prose translation of *Apollonius of Tyre*. However, comparisons of this translation with the Latin versions show that the Old English author has consistently tried to tone down the romantic elements of the story. See Magennis, '"No Sex Please, We're Anglo-Saxons"?' though as noted in the Introduction above, p. 6, he appears to equate 'sexuality' with male-female sexuality.

It may seem rather odd to begin a book on homosocial bonds by discussing poems ostensibly about male-female love, but there are several reasons for doing so. Firstly, if we accept this characterization of their contents, then they provide a relevant contrast to representations of male-male relations—the ways in which the relationships in these poems differ from those in the other texts might have important things to tell us about the assumptions underlying the latter. Secondly, however, more than one critic has disputed the commonly accepted notions that these are poems voiced by women, or that they concern male-female sexual or romantic love, and therefore their arguments need to be assessed. Thirdly, close attention to the traditional critical interpretations of these poems reveals that they often rest on unacknowledged assumptions which are symptomatic of a wider tendency to read heterosexual norms back into Old English literature ana- chronistically. The chapter thus sets up and situates the later readings contained in this book.

Many general overviews of Old English literature view both *Wulf and Eadwacer* and *The Wife's Lament* as laments by a woman for a male lover from whom she is separated by life circumstances, and *The Husband's Message* as a love- letter from a man to a female lover from whom he has been separated. Indeed, some even see *The Husband's Message* as a reply to *The Wife's Lament*.[5] However, a characteristic that all three poems share is their enigmatic quality—like the riddles of the Exeter Book that form their immediate manuscript context, their language is allusive and tricky. In fact, all three poems have sometimes been taken to be riddles, particularly *The Husband's Message*, which has been interpreted as part of Riddle 60 (or vice versa).[6] But even more than with the riddles, with these three texts critics have often found it difficult to get any firm sense at all of what the poems are about, and perhaps because of this they have spawned dozens of different interpretations of varying ingenuity and plausibility.

Wulf and Eadwacer provides the best example of this interpretative difficulty, and it is conveniently short enough to quote in its entirety:[7]

> Leodum is minum   swylce him mon lác gife   1
> willað hy hine aþecgan   gif he on þreat cymeð
>   ungelic is ús ·
> wulf is on iege   ic on oþerre

---

[5] For a recent (inconclusive) discussion, see John D. Niles, *Old English Enigmatic Poems and the Play of the Texts*. Studies in the Early Middle Ages, 13. Turnhout: Brepols, 2006, pp. 247–50.

[6] See Earl, review of Klinck, 1197; Robert E. Kaske, 'A Poem of the Cross in the Exeter Book: "Riddle 60" and "The Husband's Message"', *Traditio* 23 (1967), 41–71; James E. Anderson, '*Deor, Wulf and Eadwacer*, and *The Soul's Address*: How and Where the Old English Exeter Book Riddles Begin', in *The Old English Elegies: New Essays in Criticism and Research*, ed. Martin Green. London and Toronto: Associated University Presses, 1983, pp. 204–30; Peter S. Baker, 'The Ambiguity of *Wulf and Eadwacer*', *Studies in Philology* 78 (1981), 39–51; Faye Walker-Pelkey, '*Frige hwæt ic hatte*: "The Wife's Lament" as Riddle', *Papers on Language and Literature* 28 (1992), 242–66.

[7] I quote from the diplomatic edition of W. S. Mackie, ed., *The Exeter Book. Part II: Poems IX–XXXII*. EETS OS 194. Oxford: Oxford University Press, 1934, p. 86.

fæst is þæt eglond   fenne biworpen   5
sindon wælreowe   weras þær on ige
willað hy hine aþecgan   gif he on þreat cymeð
        ungelice is us
wulfes ic mines widlastum   wenum dogode
þonne hit wæs renig weder   *ond* ic reotugu sæt ·   10
þonne mec se beaducafa   bogum bilegde
wæs me wyn to þon   wæs me hwæþre eac lað ·
wulf min wulf   wena me þine
seoce gedydon   þine · seldcymas
murnende mód   nales meteliste   15
gehyrest þu eadwacer   uncerne ear[*g*]ne hwelp
        bireð wulf to wuda
þæt mon eaþe toslited   þætte næfre gesomnad wæs
        uncer giedd geador · : 7

Sarah Higley's recent translation provides a good indication of most of the poem's many ambiguities:[8]

It is to my people as if one were to give them sport/gift/sacrifice.   1
They will receive/consume him if he comes into the troop/into peril.
        Different it is for us.
Wulf is on an island, I on another.
Fast is that island surrounded by fen.   5
Slaughter-fierce men are there on (the) isle.
They will receive/consume him if he comes into the troop/into peril.
        Different(ly) it is for us.
With hopes I endured/dogged the widely-laid tracks of my Wulf/wolf.
(or: I endured/dogged the wide-ranging hopes of my Wulf/wolf.)
When it was rainy weather and I sat, tearful,   10
then the battle-ready (one) surrounded me with (his) shoulders/
        boughs/forelegs/arms.
It was a joy to me to that degree; yet it was also hateful to me.
Wulf, my Wulf/wolf, expectations of you
have made me sick, your seldom-visits,
a mourning-spirit—not at all lack of food.   15
You hear, Eadwacer!/? a wolf/Wulf will bear
our wretched?/cowardly? cub to the woods.
One easily tears that which was never joined:
Our song/poem/lay/utterance together.

    [8] Sarah L. Higley, 'Finding the Man under the Skin: Identity, Monstrosity, Expulsion, and the Werewolf', in *The Shadow-Walkers: Jacob Grimm's Mythology of the Monstrous*, ed. Tom Shippey. MRTS 291. Arizona Studies in the Middle Ages and the Renaissance, 14. Tempe, AR: Arizona Center for Medieval and Renaissance Studies in collaboration with Brepols, 2005, pp. 335–78, at 371–2; cf. also Anne L. Klinck, 'Animal Imagery in "Wulf and Eadwacer" and the Possibilities of Interpretation', *Papers in Language and Literature* 23 (1987), 3–26.

As will be evident, it is very difficult to determine even the basic facts of this story. Is the possible encounter in the first two lines between the as-yet-unnamed man and the speaker's people a hostile one or a positive meeting such as a treaty? Is *Wulf* a proper noun throughout, or does it mean 'wolf', or both? Should we try to interpret the hapax legomenon *dogode* as it stands (if so, how?), or should we emend it (for instance, to *hogode* 'considered')? What is the relation between Wulf and the speaker? and Eadwacer? Indeed, is Eadwacer a personal name, or an epithet? Adding to the poem's basic interpretative difficulties (of which these are only representative examples) are its unusual formal characteristics—there appears to be a refrain (*ungelic(e) is us*), which is an extremely unusual feature in Old English poetry.[9] We have no way of knowing whether the poem is complete or fragmentary as extant, and whether a pre-existing narrative (perhaps now lost to us) lies behind it.

Given this hermeneutically challenging situation, it is perhaps not surprising that many different and often mutually exclusive explanations of the poem have been proposed, among them that it is an allusive Anglo-Saxon version of the story of Signý in the Old Norse *Vǫlsunga saga*, of the *Wulfdietrich* legend, or of the Old High German *Hildebrandslied*, or that it evokes an adulterous wife's yearning for her outlawed lover, a mother's lament for her dead son, or a dog dreaming about her canine lover, or even that it concerns a wen or tumour, or constitutes a scribal in-joke or political allegory.[10] Faced with this mass of interpretations, one has a certain amount of sympathy with Benjamin Thorpe's famous refusal to translate the poem (the only untranslated text in his 1842 edition of the Exeter Book), commenting only: 'Riddle I.—Of this I can make no sense, nor am I able to arrange the verses' (p. 527, n. to 380).[11]

Despite this multiplicity of interpretative possibilities, the adulterous version has remained the most popular one, however, and I want now to examine possible reasons for the continuing popularity of this last interpretation and what unacknowledged motivations appear to lie behind it. One set of possibilities concerns merely priority and longevity, since the original version of this interpretation was first proposed in 1888 by Henry Bradley in a review in which he suggested

---

[9] Another example is that of *Deor*, also in the Exeter Book: 'Þæs ofereode, þisses swa mæg' which can be loosely translated as 'that passed away, so may this'.

[10] For surveys of the different interpretations, see Alain Renoir, '*Wulf and Eadwacer*: A Non-Interpretation', in *Franciplegius: Medieval and Linguistic Studies in Honor of Francis Peabody Magoun, Jr.*, ed. Jess. B. Bessinger, Jr. and Robert P. Creed. New York: New York University Press, 1965, pp. 147–63; Dolores Warwick Frese, '*Wulf and Eadwacer*: The Adulterous Woman Reconsidered', in *New Readings on Women in Old English Literature*, ed. Helen Damico and Alexandra Hennessey Olsen. Bloomington and Indiana: Indiana University Press, 1990, pp. 273–91, at p. 274; Marijane Osborn, 'Reading the "Animals" of *Wulf and Eadwacer* with Hrabanus Maurus', *Medievalia et Humanistica* 29 (2003), 27–49; James J. Donahue, ' "Of this I can make no sense": *Wulf and Eadwacer* and the Destabilization of Meaning', *Medieval Forum* 4 (2004), [no page numbers], published online at <http://www.sfsu.edu/~medieval/Volume4/Donahue.html>.

[11] Benjamin Thorpe, ed. and trans., *Codex Exoniensis: A Collection of Anglo-Saxon Poetry*. London: Society of Antiquaries, 1842, p. 527 n. The text is printed as Riddle 1 on p. 380.

that the speaker is a captive woman, Wulf her outlawed lover, and Eadwacer the speaker's tyrannical husband.[12] Before this, it had been generally assumed that *Wulf and Eadwacer* was simply one of the Exeter Book riddles, and Bradley's identification of a new dramatic lyric was attractive to scholars.[13] As the first literary interpretation of the poem, then, it was likely to cast a long shadow. However, a contributing factor to its continuing popularity was the title assigned to it by early editors such as Bradley and by which it is still known. The manuscript version is of course untitled, and *Wulf and Eadwacer* had the advantage of including what were considered to be the two proper names in the poem, thus presenting at least some clue as to the text's contents. However, the inclusion of these names in the title then made it that much easier to assume that the words *wulf* and *eadwacer* do actually constitute proper names, rather than, for instance, a designation of a lupine animal or an epithet equating to 'guardian', and thus to assume that the poem concerned two men whom the speaker is torn between.

A more significant, though more complicated, factor in the continuing popularity of the adulterous version, however, is an unexamined tendency on the part of Anglo-Saxon scholars until recently to universalize certain human emotions. Consider, for instance, the following account of the poem by the ordinarily phlegmatic Bruce Mitchell:

Wulf is on one island. Eadwacer and the woman are on another. Some hold that Wulf is the lover and Eadwacer the husband, others the reverse. Who is the father of the child is not clear ... Sick with longing for Wulf, the woman sits weeping. Eadwacer comforts her and she finds his embraces pleasant and yet distasteful. *In her agony*, she cries for 'Wulf, my Wulf'. Is her cry to Eadwacer a revelation to him that she has borne a child by Wulf whom Wulf will come to claim? Or has Wulf abducted Eadwacer's son? It is not clear. *What is clear is her agony.*[14]

Mitchell is not the only scholar whose prose *Wulf and Eadwacer* causes to veer uncharacteristically toward the melodramatic. Many introductions by renowned Anglo-Saxonists to translations of the poem conclude with something like Richard Hamer's comment that: 'What is beyond doubt is that the poignancy of expression of the lady's grief emerging through all the obscurities has still power to move.'[15] A straightforward link between medieval and modern emotional expression is created—a manoeuvre seen even more clearly in Clifford Davidson's comments that 'One becomes drawn into the love *mythos* and is oneself transformed into a vicarious participant in it ... [the poem] naturally arouses our

---

[12] Henry Bradley, review of Morley's *English Writers*, *The Academy* 33 (1888), 197.
[13] For a slightly different account along similar lines, see the discussion of Gollancz below, p. 29.
[14] *The Battle of Maldon and Other Old English Poems*, trans. Kevin Crossley-Holland, ed. Bruce Mitchell. London, 1965, p. 78. Emphasis mine.
[15] *A Choice of Anglo-Saxon Verse*, trans. Richard Hamer. London: Faber and Faber, 1970, p. 83.

desire—desire to return to completeness and marital unity.'[16] S. A. J. Bradley goes so far as to comment on the poem: 'Its articulation of an apparently adulterous sexual passion is startlingly vivid, and in its seemingly frank distinction between the union of bodies and the union of hearts and minds *it is psychologically plausible.*'[17]

It is indeed very easy to reconstruct a psychologically plausible romantic narrative based on the poem—one possibility might run something like this:

A young Anglo-Saxon woman—let us call her Freawaru—is trapped in a loveless marriage to an older man whom she does not love, stuck out in the provinces on a remote island in the fens (perhaps in East Anglia).

One day a raiding party of Vikings makes an attack in the area and, although they are defeated and sail away again, they leave one of their number behind, severely wounded: a brave and handsome warrior named Wulf. Hiding out in the woods, he has no strength to escape or to hunt for food and comes close to death. However, Freawaru stumbles across his hideaway, takes pity on him and sneaks him food. Over the weeks Wulf slowly recovers, but more importantly the pair fall in love. Freawaru is racked with guilt, but Wulf is so much younger and more attractive than her inattentive husband. One day, trapped at Wulf's forest hideaway by a sudden rainstorm and feeling particularly sad about this conflict of duty and emotion, Freawaru is overcome by Wulf's importunate advances and they make love, although her pleasure is somewhat compromised by her feelings of guilt. The meetings continue but, inevitably, the lovers are discovered and Freawaru is guarded by her jealous husband from then on. Wulf escapes to another island and cannot visit without great danger. The months go by and it becomes clear that Wulf has made Freawaru pregnant. Her husband is outraged and plans to kill the bastard child as soon as it is born, but in a desperate raid Wulf manages to snatch the boy and carry him off safely to the woods, leaving Freawaru to face her inevitable fate of isolation and social ostracism with defiance.

Even if this version is a little overblown, it does nevertheless fit all the facts of the poem as extant, the point being that this version merely takes to a (somewhat flippant) extreme what is implicit in the work of many commentators and translators.

What lies behind their statements becomes clear if we return to Mitchell's remarks on the poem and his further remark that *Wulf and Eadwacer* and *The Wife's Lament* are dramatic monologues 'spoken by a woman separated from her love'. He continues: 'It will come as no surprise that Anglo-Saxon women loved their men, but we can be grateful for these variations on a universal theme.'[18] One would hardly dispute that many Anglo-Saxon women did love their male

---

[16] Clifford Davidson, 'Erotic "Women's Songs" in Anglo-Saxon England', *Neophilologus* 59 (1975), 451–62 at 458–9. Davidson argues for a genre of Anglo-Saxon 'women's songs' from the presence of female-voiced erotic Latin songs in the *Cambridge Songs*, but admits that these were copied in the middle of the eleventh century from a Continental original and are thus very late and foreign (451).

[17] *Anglo-Saxon Poetry*, ed. and trans. S. A. J. Bradley. London, 1982, p. 365. Emphasis mine.

[18] Mitchell in Crossley-Holland and Mitchell, *Battle of Maldon*, p. 78.

lovers, but there is a real problem if as scholars we take this to imply that there are no important differences in the construction of male-female relations from the Anglo-Saxon to the modern period. It is entirely anachronistic to assume that, simply because some of the elements of the poem would fit quite nicely into a modern romantic poem, that means that the poem is in fact about romantic love between a man and a woman. Mitchell goes on to talk about the difficulty in interpreting the poem, and says:

This [difficulty] is not to be wondered at. What is to be wondered at is the frequency with which, in spite of all the difficulties, the voice of the poet rings clearly across the centuries. We do not know who the woman was. But how poignant is her heart-rending cry 'Wulf, my Wulf'. *How nearly it touches us all.*   (p. 79; emphasis mine.)

Although the poem may well touch many of us in one way or another, this comment from one of the most eminent Anglo-Saxonists of the twentieth century neatly demonstrates the heterosexist bias and anachronistic presuppositions of much traditional criticism of *Wulf and Eadwacer*.

Although it is easy to reconstruct a romantic version of the poem, the text equally well fits various other interpretations, as we have seen. Alain Renoir, recognizing the inherent ambiguity of the text, opted in 1965 to make a virtue of necessity and issued a 'Noninterpretation' of the poem, revaluing the poem's uncertainties as a positive feature in their own right.[19] Patricia Belanoff pushes the implications of the poem's ambiguities even further, analysing *Wulf and Eadwacer* and *The Wife's Lament* as unique examples of the Anglo-Saxon female voice whose 'differentness' extends to their use of language. She cites the French feminist critics Cixous, Irigaray, and Kristeva, and applies to the text the implications of the link they make between female language and the body. Belanoff argues that there is a tension in the Old English poems between, on the one hand, a male symbolic language which speaks in the concrete tropes of the heroic code, and, on the other hand, a female semiotic language which emphasizes interpersonal deixis and free-floating ambiguous words and phrases. Men carry out the actions of the poem which cause the emotions of the female speakers, and the texts seek not to describe an exact situation but to evoke an intense emotion in the audience.[20]

Belanoff's argument is a powerful one in many ways—it characterizes these poems as unique texts which recover the marginalized experiences of women in a male-dominated culture. Not only this but Belanoff argues the poems also preserve a female voice and perspective on heroic society which recognizes the

[19] Renoir, '*Wulf and Eadwacer*: A Non-Interpretation', *passim*. Despite this aim, Renoir manages to 'derive the impression that [Eadwacer] might prove somewhat ungentlemanly if he were to hold Wulf in his power' (p. 159) and draws an analogy with Flaubert's *Madame Bovary* (p. 160).
[20] Patricia Belanoff, 'Women's Songs, Women's Language: *Wulf and Eadwacer* and *The Wife's Lament*', in Damico and Olsen, *New Readings on Women*, pp. 193–203.

female suffering that so often results from male violence. There are two main problems with her reading, though, however attractive to modern sensibilities.

The first is that it is open to the same criticism as the traditional adulterous interpretations—it tries to universalize the contents of the poem. Belanoff concludes her account of *Wulf and Eadwacer* and *The Wife's Lament* as follows: 'What has endured about them is a message about the value, strength, and universality of our connections to others in a world characterized by strife and alienation, both physical and emotional, from other human beings' (p. 201). Here, she subsumes the 'differentness' of the poems' language in the sameness of the emotions they evoke.[21] Belanoff is again mapping Anglo-Saxon emotions onto modern ones and vice versa. Even feminist readings, then, can fall into the universalizing trap. However, what is most significant for my purposes here is the fact that, despite scholarly emphasis on all the things that are unclear in the poem, almost all interpreters assume that *Wulf and Eadwacer* concerns a female speaker, except those who do not think it concerns a personal relationship at all.[22]

Israel Gollancz would seem to be the lone exception, judging from the comment on *Wulf and Eadwacer* in a book by Stopford Brooke, where he records: 'Mr. Gollancz has explained it, with some probability, as a little story of love and jealousy between two men, Wulf and Eadwacer.'[23] Gollancz presented the paper concerned at a meeting of the Cambridge Philological Society on 8 December 1893, and the brief report on the meeting in *The Academy* for that year tells us that scholars as eminent as Arthur Napier, Henry Bradley, W. H. Stevenson, and Walter Skeat, with typical scholarly caution, 'all accepted Mr Gollancz's proof of his interpretation as satisfactory'.[24] However, the surprising picture this gives of a nineteenth-century editor suggesting an all-male love story, and his distinguished peers accepting this version with aplomb, is sadly shattered by the fuller report of the meeting given in *The Athenaeum*, Number 3451 and the text and translation presented in Number 3452, under the heading: 'Wulf and Eadwacer: An Anglo-Saxon Monodrama in Five Acts', in which it is clear that a female speaker is thought to have committed adultery with Eadwacer in the absence of her husband Wulf, who on his return exposes their bastard child.[25]

[21] Belanoff also ignores, of course, the fact that it is not just 'female' language in Old English which is characterized by ambiguity and relational terms: *The Dream of the Rood* is just one of many examples, as Chapter 7 below argues.

[22] For instance, Norman Eliason, who interprets the poem as 'a private communication to a colleague, ruefully but playfully protesting about the mishandling of their poetry, which instead of being kept intact...has been separated.' ('On *Wulf and Eadwacer*', in *Old English Studies in Honour of John C. Pope*, ed. Robert B. Burlin and Edward B. Irving, Jr. Toronto: University of Toronto Press, 1974, pp. 225–34, at p. 228.)

[23] Stopford A. Brooke, *English Literature from the Beginning to the Norman Conquest*. rev. edn. London: Macmillan, 1898, p. 160.

[24] Report of a meeting of the Cambridge Philological Society (Friday, 8 December 1893) in *The Academy: A Weekly Review of Literature, Science, and Art* no. 1129 (Saturday, 23 December 1893), p. 572, col. 3.

[25] *The Athenaeum* No. 3451, 16 December [18]93, p. 853, col. 3 to p. 854 col. 1; *The Athenaeum* No. 3452, 23 December [18]93, p. 883, col. 3.

Nevertheless, as a retrospective tribute to the Gollancz version that never was, I offer the following, again somewhat tongue-in-cheek, alternative interpretation of *Wulf and Eadwacer*:

The speaker is a young man, Wiglaf, imprisoned on an island and socially ostracized for engaging in a sexual relationship with another man, Wulf, who has escaped to another island, but is being hunted down by their community. The speaker laments his lover's absence and remembers their first encounter on a rainy day when Wulf found Wiglaf crying and emotional comfort turned into sexual solace, a union in which pleasure was mingled with fear of the inevitable punishment to come. Faint from lack of food, Wiglaf cries out defiantly from his prison that his sickness comes rather from longing for his absent lover. The voice of his mother then intrudes as she asks her husband Eadwacer if he hears Wulf carrying their son off to safety in the woods. She describes Wiglaf unsympathetically as their *eargne hwelp* 'cowardly, or effeminate whelp'.[26] The poem finally returns to Wiglaf's lament that his and Wulf's song together is easily torn asunder, since it was never and could never be recognized as a legitimate union.[27]

What are the problems of this interpretation? It is not substantially less plausible than many of the other published interpretations, and various alternative plot elements could be imagined along similar lines. Nonetheless, the problems are twofold, and their elucidation and the ensuing discussion will help not only to delineate the difficulties with which the modern reader looking for representations of same-sex love must engage, but also what this book is and is not trying to do.

The first problem is textual. For the interpretation to work, the text must be emended. The adjective *reotugu* in line 10 as it stands is the nominative feminine singular form and thus has as its referent a female speaker. For the speaker to be male, one has to emend to *reotig* (the male adjectival form) or to *reotige* (the adverbial form). Such an emendation is relatively minor, and could be justified by explaining that the original scribe either made a genuine error and misread the letterform, or made the same assumption as many modern readers that the speaker of such a poem must be female and corrected the form accordingly. Nevertheless, an interpretation which rests on the emendation of the only surviving manuscript is shaky.

The second problem is a sociohistorical one. Alain Renoir's explicit reason for assuming that the speaker of the poem is a woman is that otherwise the statement in line 11 'would suggest a behavior suspiciously verging on homosexuality—and this topic is, to my knowledge, nonexistent in early Germanic poetry' (p. 150). One could of course point out that the topic of romantic male-female love is almost as scarce in early Germanic poetry. However, it is true that if this

---

[26] Alternatively, one could emend MS *earne* differently and have the mother refer sympathetically to their *earmne hwelp* 'poor cub'.

[27] Alternatively, the final line could refer to the ease with which the poem can be misinterpreted, because of its allusive and coded nature, necessitated to avoid censorship and thus be preserved to comfort others in a similar situation.

interpretation were accepted, it would set the poem apart as quite unique. More to the point, though, on the face of the evidence available to us today it seems improbable that the Anglo-Saxons had any concept of same-sex partnerships in the modern sense of committed unions between social equals, thus my suggested scenario flirts with anachronism of tone quite as much as the heterosexualized interpretations.[28] However laudable the aim of reclaiming past texts for modern gay audiences, to rely on deliberate anachronism is to assert that these texts have no intrinsic interest or relevance for such audiences as they stand. As explained in the Introduction, I am not primarily interested in queering Old English texts *per se* in this book, but in unravelling preconceptions, unsettling assumptions, and asking questions in order to gain a better understanding of these works on their own terms. If the above reading has any value, then, it is in highlighting the crucial importance of questioning our own cultural assumptions about Anglo-Saxon culture and literature, which may be all the more pervasive because they are invisible and unexamined.

I shall return to this idea shortly, but there is in this context one further possible interpretation to be considered: namely, that it is a poem about love between two men and by a male speaker, but that the love described is not conceived of as sexual. As we have seen from the Introduction and will see in ensuing chapters, many Anglo-Saxons seem to have been far more comfortable with same-sex intimacy than many people are today. Textual difficulties aside, is there any reason why *Wulf and Eadwacer* should not in fact represent an analogue of the moving evocation of male intimacy found in the Exeter Book *Maxims* quoted at the start of the book? This question raises issues of what levels of physical intimacy were deemed acceptable between Anglo-Saxon men, what verbal and written expressions of love and longing were considered appropriate, and how we can best negotiate the overlapping categories of the sexual, the erotic, and the affective.

Before proceeding to possible answers to these questions, let us first consider *The Wife's Lament*, concerning which heterosexist assumptions are an equally dangerous commodity, and which again has been susceptible to an incredibly diverse array of critical interpretations. As Alain Renoir summarizes, the speaker has been considered to be variously: 'a dead woman, a live man, a sorceress-elect, a mistreated wife, a minor heathen deity, and an allegorical voice yearning for the union of Christ and the Church.'[29] Like *Wulf and Eadwacer*, by far the most popular reading is that it is a dramatic elegiac monologue by a female speaker for her absent husband. However, unlike the former poem, it has received a number

[28] This evidence is discussed in the following chapters, particularly Chapter 3 where it is suggested that the Anglo-Saxons may have had a social category of the passive effeminate male.
[29] Alain Renoir, 'A Reading Context for *The Wife's Lament*', in *Anglo-Saxon Poetry: Essays in Appreciation of John C. McGalliard*, ed. Lewis E. Nicholson and Dolores Warwick Frese. Notre Dame: University of Notre Dame Press, 1975, pp. 224–41, at p. 236. On the range of possible explanatory scenarios envisaged for the poem, see also Jerome Mandel, *Alternative Readings in Old English Poetry*. New York: Peter Lang, 1987, pp. 149–50.

of critical readings in which the speaker is argued to be male. Here, rather than investigate in detail all of the poem's various interpretative difficulties, I will briefly review these interpretations, which centre on the first three lines of the text.[30]

The poem begins: 'Ic þis giedd wrece bi me, ful geomorre, | minre sylfre sið[e].' Translation of these lines is straightforward: 'I compose this song about myself, very sad/sadly, [about] my own journey.' What a translation conceals, however, is the fact that three of the words in the original—*geomorre, minre*, and *sylfre*—have a particular grammatical ending -*re*, which is usually taken to imply a female speaker.[31] In order to interpret the speaker as male, then, a scholar has in effect to make one of two decisions: either to emend the endings as scribal errors, or to explain them away as not really being feminine endings at all.

Rudolph Bambas opts for the first course of action.[32] His logic is that emendation is essential on the principle that there are three main problems with seeing the poem as a woman's lament for her husband. Firstly, Old English heroic literature seems to him generally uninterested in female experience, so *The Wife's Lament*, if genuinely presented by a female speaker, would constitute a remarkable exception to the norm. Secondly, as a female lament delivered at a feast from which women would ordinarily withdraw, it would force any Anglo-Saxon *scop* performing the poem to impersonate a woman, and 'so much mimetic capacity in the eighth or ninth century is difficult to believe in' (p. 304). He concedes that women do have speaking parts in some Old English poems, but observes that 'in these instances the woman to be quoted is first carefully identified' and finds it 'hardly credible that the audience would understand from the inflection of an adjective and two pronouns that the speaker was representing a woman'. Finally, various details in the poem, such as the talk about feud and exile, seem to him unsuitable to refer to a woman, and he finds it difficult to reconstruct a narrative behind the poem which would explain why a woman would be left alone in such a way. All these problems, according to Bambas, disappear if we remove those feminine endings.

It is certainly an elegantly simple solution. The problem with Bambas's approach, though, is that he has to make the rather implausible assumption that a scribe made three errors in a row for no apparent reason. He himself admits that this 'puts a strain on the laws of chance', but believes 'this strain is less to bear than that of understanding the poem to concern a woman' (p. 308), precisely because he finds no other instances of this kind of text.[33] Scribal corruption is

---

[30] For a sensitive recent reading, however, see Niles, *Old English Enigmatic Poems*, ch. 5.

[31] See Alistair Campbell, *Old English Grammar*. Oxford: Clarendon Press, 1959, §§638–60.

[32] Rudolph C. Bambas, 'Another View of the Old English *Wife's Lament*', *JEGP* 62 (1963), 303–9. He notes that L. L. Schücking and Émile Legouis also suggested that the poem might not be a female lament (308).

[33] Bambas asserts that, although *Wulf and Eadwacer* may be 'a feminine monologue [it] is too cryptic to be clearly intelligible' (308, n. 8).

not impossible, of course, nor intrinsically unlikely, but an argument remains less than convincing if it depends on emendation of the only extant manuscript to make the interpretation work.

Martin Stevens, however, makes the case that the text can be understood without drastic emendation to refer to a male speaker, and that 'the attribution of it to a woman speaker on grammatical grounds is at best doubtful'.[34] He concedes that the inflections are feminine, but proposes that they have 'nothing to do with the sex of the speaker', rather that they refer to 'grammatical' rather than 'natural' gender. Stevens shows that if the noun is taken to be not the masculine *sið* but the feminine *sið(ð)*, which also means 'journey', and emended to the dative *siðe*, then both *minre* and *sylfre* can be understood as dative feminine forms governed by the gender of the noun (pp. 74–9). He further argues that *geomorre* can be understood not as an adjective but as an adverb, *ful geomorre* thus meaning 'very sadly', where the final -*e* is a standard means of converting an adjective to an adverb and the doubled consonant is taken as a spelling variant rather than a geminated consonant (pp. 81–2).

If one accepts Stevens's arguments, then, there is nothing in the language of the poem which intrinsically suggests that the speaker is a woman, and there is similarly nothing in the content of the poem which suggests it either.[35] In fact, one of the problems for critics who assume that the speaker must be a woman has been the fact that the speaker repeatedly refers to concepts such as exile and feud and uses terms which seem to fit the male elegies rather than the context of a putative marital relationship.[36] For instance, the speaker describes *wonn minra wræcsiþa* 'the torment of my exile-journeys' (5), and identifies as a *wineleas wræcca* 'a friendless exile' (10a). The speaker talks about *min hlaford* 'my lord' (6a and 15a), *min freond* and *min wine* 'my friend' (47b and 50b), and *min leodfruma* 'my people's leader' (8a), rather than using terms such as *wer* 'husband'. We are also told the narrator sets out *folgað secan* 'to seek his retinue' (9b). The poem has therefore often seemed more suitable to a retainer lamenting his lost lord, in

---

[34] Martin Stevens, 'The Narrator of *The Wife's Lament*', *Neuphilologische Mitteilungen* 69 (1968), 72–90, at 73.

[35] Contrary to Marilyn Desmond's claim that Angela Lucas has 'effectively defeated' Stevens's arguments, Lucas merely demonstrates that they are not finally conclusive and that she believes the narrator to be a woman on what she admits to be 'purely subjective grounds'. See Angela M. Lucas, 'The Narrator of "The Wife's Lament"', *Neuphilologische Mitteilungen* 70 (1969), 282–97, at 296; Marilyn Desmond, 'The Voice of Exile: Feminist Literary History and the Anonymous Anglo-Saxon Elegy', *Critical Inquiry* 16 (1990), 573–90, at 574–5, n. 5. However, cf. n. 38 below. More convincing objections are raised by Bruce Mitchell, although he concedes that he finds Stevens's arguments improbable rather than impossible: Mitchell, 'The Narrator of *The Wife's Lament*' (see n. 1 above). I do not consider the issues in detail here, since the main point is not to prove that the narrator is male, but to consider the unexamined assumptions which lie behind the traditional interpretations, as explored below, and as revealed in comments such as that by Mitchell at the head of this chapter.

[36] See for instance Leonard H. Frey, 'Exile and Elegy in Anglo-Saxon Christian Epic Poetry', *JEGP* 62 (1963), 293–302.

similar terms to those we find in *The Wanderer*.[37] For instance, Bambas sees the narrator as:

a member of the entourage of a chief who is moving about in exile...the chief has undertaken a sea journey of some duration; in his selection of shipmates the narrator was not included, and he is consequently obliged to wait for the chief's return. The utter isolation of the narrator is the poet's imagined intensification of his sorrow at being deprived of the shelter of his patron.   (p. 305)

It is true that the narrator speaks of suffering the feud of *mines felaleofan* 'my very dear one' (26a), but the term *leof* 'dear one' is very frequently employed by the protagonists in heroic poems to refer to their lords, and it would be entirely anachronistic to assume that this epithet is inappropriate to male intimacy. Nevertheless, a marital relationship is assumed by editors and then reified in glosses and translations. The clearest example of anachronistic presuppositions colouring scholarly interpretation of the poem is associated with the phrase 'Frynd sind on eorþan, | leofe lifigende, leger weardiað' [Friends are on earth, dear ones living, occupy their beds] (33b–4). By translating *frynd* as 'lovers', the phrase is made to imply that in contrast to the speaker and her husband, other husbands and wives are making love in their marital beds. For instance, in an article by Jane Curry, this line forms the main justification for her assumption that the speaker is a woman, since for her the 'juxtaposition of lord, bedded lovers, and loneliness can mean little else'.[38] However, OE *freond* makes no clear distinction between 'friend' and 'lover', and friends of the same sex commonly slept in the same bed in the Anglo-Saxon period (as we saw from the Exeter Book *Maxims*), a practice indeed which continued as the norm in Europe for centuries and still often occurs today, although more hedged around with intimacy issues.

If, then, there is nothing in the language or the content of the poem that necessitates the speaker being a woman, should we therefore read the poem as a lament by a retainer for his exiled lord? Not necessarily. Some of the stronger readings of the poem are those which presuppose a female speaker, and there seems little reason further to marginalize the female voice in Old English literature.[39] Nevertheless, the male readings emphasize an important point concerning the way in which Anglo-Saxon cultural assumptions about gender and interpersonal relationships clearly differed from our own. This point is hinted at, but not explored, by Stephanie Hollis in her book *Anglo-Saxon Women and*

[37] See, for instance, Bambas, 'Another View', 305, and Jerome Mandel's extended reading of what he retitles 'The Exile's Lament', *Alternative Readings*, pp. 155–73.
[38] Jane L. Curry, 'Approaches to a Translation of the Anglo-Saxon *The Wife's Lament*', *Medium Ævum* 35 (1966), 187–98, at 189.
[39] Indeed, Marilyn Desmond makes a strong argument against critical silencing and marginalization of such voices, although her analyses of *Wulf and Eadwacer* and *The Wife's Lament* are marred by some of the same assumptions and universalizing tendencies criticized in this chapter. See Desmond, 'The Voice of Exile', pp. 574–5 and 587, and n. 34 above. My own arguments are aimed not at shoring up the 'masculinist critical tradition' (Desmond, p. 575) but at unpicking the heterosexist elements of that critical tradition.

the Church, where she states that 'The underlying relational model of *The Wife's Lament* is that of lord and retainer, more precisely, the relation of the lord and his particular intimate'.[40] Hollis expresses here the idea that the male-female relationship described in this poem is predicated on the relationship of beloved lord and faithful retainer. The corollary of this is that the primary interpersonal relationship in Old English literature is that of lord and retainer, and the one many people today see as primary, the male-female love relationship, may have been more easily comprehensible to the Anglo-Saxons as a sort of analogue of the love between lord and retainer.

This view is supported by an examination of *The Husband's Message*, the other text that is usually seen as describing romantic love. As with the other two poems, there are various textual problems, not least the fact that it is badly damaged and critics are unsure exactly where it begins and how it relates to the riddles that come just before it in the Exeter Book.[41] However, unlike *Wulf and Eadwacer* and *The Wife's Lament*, this text very clearly concerns an exiled man sending a message to a woman, his beloved *peodnes dohtor* 'chieftain's daughter' (48a), informing her with joy that she is now free to come and join him in his new homeland. Like those texts, though, the interpersonal relationship is not described in exclusively conjugal terms. It is defined in terms of promises, oaths, vows, and treaties of friendship: *treowe* (13), *wordbeotunga* (16), *freondscype* (20), *ape* (52), *wære* (53), *winetreowe* (53). The poem contains nothing one might today find particularly romantic, were one not already primed to find romance by critical introductions to the text. We are told that the lord's specific desire is to sit by his queen and share out gifts of treasure to his retainers (31–7), and that, now that he has treasures and horses and the pleasures of the mead-hall (45–8), his joy will be complete *gif he þin beneah* (49b): if he can possess his queen along with them. It is hardly a touching declaration of personal affection overall, rather it is a public declaration of a formal relationship. Here again, however, the tropes of the lord-retainer relationship provide the backdrop to the bond described.

C. S. Lewis made a notorious claim in *The Allegory of Love* about the literature of 'courtly love', asserting that:

French poets, in the eleventh century, discovered or invented, or were the first to express, that romantic species of passion which English poets were still writing about in the nineteenth. They effected a change which has left no corner of our ethics, our imagination, or our daily life untouched, and they erected impassable barriers between us and the classical past or the Oriental present. Compared with this revolution the Renaissance is a mere ripple on the surface of literature.[42]

---

[40] Stephanie Hollis, *Anglo-Saxon Women and the Church: Sharing a Common Fate*. Woodbridge: Boydell Press, 1992, p. 49.

[41] See note 4 above. For a recent reading, which interprets the speaker as a prosopopoeic ship's mast, see Niles, *Old English Enigmatic Poems*, ch. 6.

[42] C. S. Lewis, *The Allegory of Love: A Study in Medieval Tradition*. Oxford: Oxford University Press, 1936, p. 4.

This is clearly an exaggeration, and 'courtly love' itself has been increasingly subjected to scrutiny from several angles.[43] Nevertheless, it encapsulates an important point. We court trouble as modern-day readers if we assume that the Anglo-Saxons had the same primary literary interests as ourselves, or the same ways of understanding social constructs like male-female or male-male relations that are often taken for granted. In an article arguing that *Wulf and Eadwacer* is a mother's lament for her lost son, Marijane Osborn also cites Lewis's assertion and states: 'Our cultural assumption is that if someone in literature is longing for someone else, it is likely to be a case of romantic or erotic love. But this is not an assumption that an earlier audience would share.'[44] This book agrees on the importance of reassessing our cultural assumptions, but it also suggests that the distinction between erotic and platonic longing or love is not as clearly drawn in the early Middle Ages.

The chapters of Part III explore further the permutations of these intimate male relationships in Old English literature, from the devotion unto death presented as normative in *The Battle of Maldon* and the heroic relationships underpinning *Beowulf* to the radical and transformatory homosocial dynamics of *The Phoenix* and Ælfric's *Lives of Saints*. But before exploring literary representations of homosocial bonds further, it is necessary to explore the possible range of attitudes to same-sex relations in Anglo-Saxon society, and particularly to sexual relationships between men, as far as it can be determined from what material has survived. This will be achieved by an examination of ethnographic, penitential, and theological material, and, although as we shall see there are problems attendant on all these categories of text, nevertheless it is possible to gain a clearer picture of the sociocultural values and associations of same-sex acts.

---

[43] See, for instance, Jaeger, *Ennobling Love* and James A. Schultz, *Courtly Love, the Love of Courtliness, and the History of Sexuality.* Chicago: University of Chicago Press, 2006.

[44] Marijane Osborn, 'The Text and Context of *Wulf and Eadwacer*', in *The Old English Elegies: New Essays in Criticism and Research*, ed. Martin Green. London and Toronto, 1983, pp. 174–89, at 184.

PART II

SAME-SEX ACTS AND IDENTITIES

2

Germanic Pederasty: The Evidence of the Classical Ethnographers

Ethnographical evidence exists which suggests that the pre-Migration Germanic tribes may have practised pederasty and same-sex rites of initiation, a possibility supported by comparison with accounts of similar practices among the Celts. This chapter forms a pair with the following one which, with this heritage in mind, seeks to uncover the range of attitudes to same-sex activity in Anglo-Saxon England. It must be noted, though, that there are several problems with the treatment of such evidence of same-sex activity, and especially with the kinds of evidence that one is forced to use. David Greenberg discusses the problems with anthropological material on same-sex behaviour in modern so-called primitive societies as follows:

When homosexuality is discussed, it frequently receives no more than a passing reference. We may be told that it is 'common' or 'infrequent' (vague terms indeed), but nothing about who engages in it or under what circumstances. Social responses are described with equally frustrating superficiality. Typically, nothing is said about how the information was obtained. Was a report that the natives loathe homosexuality based on the testimony of a single informant, or many? Was the testimony confirmed by observing someone do something when an incident occurred? Usually, the reader has no way of knowing. To complicate matters further, some authors fail to distinguish among transvestism, homosexuality, and hermaphroditism.

To this already depressing assessment, Greenberg adds that informants often tell the observer what he or she wants to hear.[1] There are still greater problems with such material in ancient and premodern periods. The attrition of time and accident means that manuscripts survive in a relatively haphazard way, inevitably subjects such as sex are often subject to religious censorship, and until relatively recently scholarly prudery or homophobia has meant that what texts do survive are often misleadingly edited or translated, sometimes even bowdlerized, with the result that there is both scant information and limited attention to its balanced interpretation.[2] Common problems with the accounts we do possess are that they are usually from outsiders who often have a strong ideological agenda for presenting the material and who have different standards of evidence from

---

[1] Greenberg, *Construction*, p. 78.   [2] For an example, see n. 4 below.

modern ethnographers, which can render their reliability difficult to assess. The accounts can often be shown to be a mixture of eyewitness material and collated comments from earlier written accounts. It is very difficult to determine how far accounts of any one particular tribal group are representative of other related groups, and, similarly, to determine for what part of their history the information is accurate and how far cultural practices remained constant.

Even given all these caveats, however, it remains an intriguing matter of fact that the pre-Migration Germanic tribes who were the ancestors of the Anglo-Saxons are recurrently associated with institutionalized practices of pederasty and same-sex activity by Classical ethnographers; that no secular Germanic law-codes contain penalties for same-sex acts (the Visigothic code shows clear clerical influence); that, although effeminacy seems to have been stigmatized in many Germanic societies, the Norse for instance seem to have made a distinction in status between active and passive roles in same-sex activity; that the prevalence of such activities was a matter of recurrent concern for several Anglo-Saxon clerics; and that the Anglo-Saxon penitentials contain a term (*bædling*) which seems to denote a category of male associated with both effeminacy and sexual acts.

We shall take the Classical material in roughly chronological order, since any one of the texts could (and sometimes clearly did) influence any subsequent text, but leave the discussion of what might be thought to be the most important but in some ways most resistant witness, Tacitus's *Germania*, to the end. Material about the Celts is also included, for several reasons. It is sometimes unclear whether the author is discussing Celts or Germans, and confusions between the two do sometimes occur. Moreover, similarities between the accounts indicate that an author may have transferred information from one society to another, merely changing the name, or, alternatively, may have been influenced by the similarity of genuinely occurring practices to describe them in the same ways. Finally, many of these accounts have been collectively adduced by scholars as evidence for pan-Indo-European practices of pederasty and same-sex initiation rites, a practice the legitimacy of which needs to be assessed.

ETHNOGRAPHIC MATERIAL ON GERMANIC AND CELTIC TRIBES

Aristotle (Greek; 384–322 BC).[3] Aristotle is the earliest of the witnesses. In the course of a discussion of the growth of avarice in Sparta in his *Politics*, written around 350 BC, he associates esteem for wealth with female rule. He claims 'this is a common state of affairs in military and warlike races, though not among the

[3] All dates in this section represent those most commonly given in scholarly discussions, but should be considered probable and approximate only. The language of writing, dates, and explanatory material are given for the benefit of readers who may be unfamiliar with some or all of these sources. More accurate and specialized information can be found in the works footnoted.

Celts and any others who have openly accorded esteem to male homosexuality' (II. ix. 5).[4]

Posidonius (Greek; 135–51 BC). The most important of the witnesses, Posidonius's *Histories*, is unfortunately lost to us except for a few surviving fragments.[5] However, several subsequent historians cite and are clearly heavily influenced by Posidonius, and the nature and extent of this debt is assessed below. It is sometimes difficult to decide whether material comes from Posidonius, or from another Greek historian called Timaeus (345–250 BC), whose forty or so volumes of *Histories* dealing with Greece, Italy, and Sicily are now almost completely lost.[6]

Caesar (Latin; 100–44 BC). Julius Caesar's *Commentaries on the Gallic War* concern various wars occurring between 58 and 51 BC. Although Caesar is sometimes accused of deriving his information from Posidonius, whom he may well have read, Caesar spent longer in Gaul than Posidonius and visited areas the latter did not reach, thus his use of the earlier writer is certainly qualified and expanded by his own eyewitness accounts.[7] He makes no comments associating Celtic or Germanic tribes with same-sex activity, and thus is useful in this context only as negative evidence.

Diodorus Siculus (Greek; 90–30 BC). Diodorus probably drew on Posidonius, since some passages are extremely similar to the surviving fragments. His material is often used as if it faithfully reproduced the lost work, but it is very different from that of Athenaeus and Strabo, who also used Posidonius, and another possible source is Timagenes's *History*, drawn on by Ammianus (Kidd, p. 309).

In Book V, chapter xxxii, Diodorus differentiates the Celts from the Gauls on a geographical basis, but says that Romans call them all Gauls (V. xxxii. 1). He goes on to suggest they may have been the Cimmerians of ancient times who overran Asia, and that the word may have been corrupted into their present

---

[4] Trevor J. Saunders, *Aristotle. Politics. Books I and II*. Oxford: Clarendon Press, 1995, p. 42. This translation more accurately reflects the Greek original (the last clause of which could be more literally rendered 'who openly honour sex between men (συνουσα)') than earlier translations which concealed the reference to same-sex activity from non-Greek-speakers, such as the 1901 translation of J. E. C. Welldon, which renders the last phrase euphemistically as 'any others who have openly attached themselves to men'. J. E. C. Welldon, *The Politics of Aristotle*. London: Macmillan, 1901, p. 76. See Henry George Liddell and Robert Scott, *A Greek-English Lexicon*, rev. Henry Stuart Jones et al. Oxford: Clarendon Press, 1968 (hereafter Liddell-Scott), *s.v.* συνουσα (p. 1723). My thanks to Jo Quinn for her generous advice on the Greek passages in this chapter.

[5] For these, see L. Edelstein and I. G. Kidd, eds, *Posidonius*. 3 vols. Cambridge: Cambridge University Press, 1972–99.

[6] Except for Posidonius, other authors whose works are lost are referred to in the context of the extant authors who cite them.

[7] See further, I. G. Kidd, *Posidonius. II. The Commentary: (i) Testimonia and Fragments 1–149*. Cambridge: Cambridge University Press, 1988, pp. 308–10. The matter is more fully discussed in Daphne Nash, 'Reconstructing Poseidonios' Celtic Ethnography: Some Considerations', *Britannia* 7 (1976), 111–26. She argues (pp. 122–3) that Posidonius and Caesar's descriptions represent the Celts at different periods of their development, and identifies the material culture in Posidonius as belonging to the archaeological period designated as la Tène II and that in Caesar as la Tène III.

Germanic Pederasty

name of Cimbrians (V. xxxii. 4). The modern editor of the text indicates at this point in a footnote that it is indeed probable that 'the Germanic tribe of the Cimbrians who threatened Italy before 100 B.C. were belated Cimmerians who first entered Asia Minor in the seventh century B.C.',[8] thus there would seem to be some doubt as to whether this passage concerns Celts or Germans. Whichever is the case, Diodorus registers his astonishment at their preference for same-sex relations:

> Although their wives are comely, they have very little to do with them, but rage with lust, in outlandish fashion, for the embraces of males (ἐπιπλοκή). It is their practice to sleep upon the ground on the skins of wild beasts and to tumble with a catamite (συνουσία) on each side. And the most astonishing thing of all is that they feel no concern for their proper dignity, but prostitute to others without a qualm the flower of their bodies; nor do they consider this a disgraceful thing to do, but rather when anyone of them is thus approached and refuses the favour offered him, this they consider an act of dishonour.
>
> (V. xxxii. 7).

The translator rightly worries about the phrase 'with a catamite on each side'. He remarks that the Greek παρακοίτοις 'may possibly mean, "with concubines of both sexes"; but Athenaeus (13. 603 A) states that the Celts were accustomed to sleep with two boys' (p. 183). It is correct that the Greek does not make clear the sexual partners' gender.[9] However, it is not necessary to adduce Athenaeus (who might well have got his information from (mis)reading Diodorus), since it is clear from the preceding sentence that same-sex and not other-sex activity is the main focus here.[10] In fact it is the picture given by the following sentence which is more interesting, since it seems to imply a general largesse of sexual favours irrespective of rank.

Strabo (Greek; 63 BC–AD 24). It is evident from close parallels to the surviving fragments that Strabo's *Geography*, written in the early first century, made use of Posidonius, but it is clear that he also used other sources (Kidd, p. 309). He implies rather than states that the young men of the Celti (that is, the Celts) engage in same-sex acts, but emphasizes that this is 'one of the things that are repeated over and over again, namely, that not only are all the Celti fond of strife, but among them it is considered no disgrace for the young men to be prodigal of their youthful charms' (IV. iv. 6).[11] We are referred here by the editor

---

[8] C. H. Oldfather, *Diodorus of Sicily*. 12 vols. London: Heinemann, 1939, III, p. 182.
[9] παρακοτίοις might be more literally translated as 'bed-fellows'; see Liddell-Scott, *s.v.* παρακίοτοις (p. 1667). The translator's choice of the term 'catamite' gives the impression of a single, possibly older or higher-ranking active partner, with two, possibly younger or lower-ranking passive partners. Thus, the more neutral term 'male concubine' or 'bedfellow' should be preferred so as not to imply without warrant that pederasty rather than potentially egalitarian same-sex relations is at issue here.
[10] Elsewhere in Diodorus, ἐπιπλοκή also means 'sex'; see Liddell-Scott, *s.v.* ἐπιπλοκή (p. 651).
[11] Horace Leonard Jones, *The Geography of Strabo*. 8 vols. London: Heinemann, 1923, II, p. 251.

to Diodorus, but it is far from clear as we have seen that pederasty is at issue there, as is implied in this passage by the terms 'young men' (νους) and 'youthful charms' (ακμης). Strabo also informs us that the Celti practised an early form of body fascism, in that 'they endeavour not to grow fat or pot-bellied, and any young man who exceeds the standard measure of the girdle is punished', which, if true, would certainly imply a close aesthetic attention to, even sexual objectification of, young men's bodies.

Ptolemy (Greek; AD 90–168). Ptolemy's *Tetrabiblos* (or 'Four Books') is an extremely popular astrological treatise which probably drew on several earlier sources. In it he links astrology to the character and practices of the nations of the world, focusing in Book II, chapter iii on the northern nations, including the inhabitants of Britain, Gaul, Germany, Italy, Apulia, Sicily, and Spain.[12] Ptolemy asserts that, in keeping with their astrological associations, these nations are generally 'independent, liberty-loving, fond of arms, industrious, very warlike, with qualities of leadership, cleanly, and magnanimous'. He goes on:

However, because of the occidental aspect of Jupiter and Mars, and furthermore because the first parts of the aforesaid triangle are masculine and the latter parts feminine, they are without passion for women and look down upon the pleasures of love, but are better satisfied with and more desirous of association with men. And they do not regard the act as a disgrace to their paramour, nor indeed do they actually become effeminate and soft thereby, because their disposition is not perverted, but they retain in their souls manliness, helpfulness, good faith, love of kinsmen, and benevolence.

The content of the last sentence seems similar in many ways to the Diodorus passage, though the tone is rather more tolerant of the sexual preferences of these foreign nations, which Diodorus clearly sees as demeaning and dishonourable and attributes specifically to the Celts rather than to the Northern races in general. Ptolemy by contrast does not think that sex between men renders them unmanly and soft or effeminate (ανάνδροις ... καί μαλακοις).

Bardaisan (Syriac; AD 154 to 223). Although it is often attributed to Bardaisan (Romanized Bardesanes) and is certainly from his school, *The Book of the Laws of Countries* (or *The Dialogue on Fate*), one of the earliest texts of Syriac literature, is in fact now agreed to have been written by his pupil Philippus.[13] Since the work takes the form of a dialogue about fate and the laws of human nations, which are stronger than fate, it thus preserves important ethnographic material. It was given greater currency and distribution via translation into Greek as part

---

[12] F. E. Robbins, *Ptolemy. Tetrabiblos*. London: Heinemann, 1980, pp. 133 and 135.
[13] H. J. W. Drijvers, trans., *The Book of the Laws of Countries: Dialogue on Fate of Bardaiṣan of Edessa*. Assen (Netherlands): Van Gorcum, 1965.

of the *De evangelica praeparatione* (or *Praeparatio evangelica*) of Eusebius (AD 275–340).[14] Of the Northern nations, we are told that:

in the territory of the Germans and their neighbours, the boys who are handsome serve the men as wives, and a wedding feast, too, is held then. This is not considered shameful or a matter of contumely by them, because of the law obtaining among them. Yet it is impossible that all those in Gaul who are guilty of this infamy should have Mercury in their nativity together with Venus in the house of Saturn in the field of Mars and in the Western signs of the Zodiac. For regarding the men who are born under this constellation, it is written that they shall be shamefully used, as if they were women.   (p. 49)

Again, there are certain similarities to the passage in Ptolemy, but the astrological information (perhaps unsurprisingly) is rather at odds with the material there. In this section of *The Book of the Laws of Countries*, pederasty again seems to be at issue, although on a more institutionalized level, since the handsome boys are accorded the dignity of a wedding feast. However, we are later informed that 'Fate does not [prevent] the Gallic men from having sexual intercourse with one another' (p. 53), which gives a rather less hierarchized picture.

Sextus Empiricus (Greek; fl. second (and possibly third) century AD). Sextus's *Outlines of Pyrrhonism* clearly draws on many different sources. In the course of a discussion of the great variety of morals, laws, customs, and so on, he states:

For example, amongst us sodomy is regarded as shameful or rather illegal, but by the Germani, they say, it is not looked upon as shameful but as a customary thing.

(III. 199)

Thus sodomy becomes just one more example of cultural difference between nations.[15] The editor's note explains that 'amongst us' means 'amongst the Greeks' and, more narrowly, refers to the laws and customs of Athens as they apply to free adult males.[16] However, his assertion that the 'Germani' here are 'Prob. not "Germans," but a Persian tribe, *cf.* i. 152' is ill-advised. The cross-reference is to a passage where Sextus says: 'And we oppose habit to the other things, as for instance to law when we say that amongst the Persians it is the habit to indulge in intercourse with males, but amongst the Romans it is forbidden by law to do so ...' (I. 152) There is no warrant to suppose that the Germani and the Persians are the same people merely on the grounds that they engage in the same behaviour.[17] In the context of the other passages cited here which associate the Celts and the Germans with same-sex activity, it seems far more likely that

[14] Eusebius, *De evangelica praeparatione*, VI. x. 27. For Greek text (p. 222) with French translation (p. 223), see *Eusèbe de Césarée. La préparation évangélique*, ed. and trans. Édouard des Places. Paris: Cerf, 1980.

[15] αρρενομιξίας is a hapax legomenon and means 'the mixing, or plaiting, of men'; see Liddell-Scott *s.v.* αρρενομιξας (p. 246).

[16] R. G. Bury, *Sextus Empiricus*. 4 vols. London: Heinemann, 1976, I, p. 460, note b.

[17] Γερμανοις can mean 'true', but not in this context; there is no suggestion that it is also the name of a Persian tribe.

Sextus is here drawing on an earlier account of the Germans akin to that of Bardaisan.

Athenaeus (Greek; fl. AD 200). Athenaeus's *Deipnosophistae* was probably written in the early second century, and may draw on Posidonius and/or Timaeus, since, in the course of a wider discourse on pederasty, Athenaeus remarks that 'The practice of pederasty came into Greece from the Cretans first, according to Timaeus.'[18] After further discussion of where the practice may have originated, Athenaeus then remarks:

And among barbarians the Celts also, though they have very beautiful women, enjoy boys more; so that some of them often have two lovers to sleep with on their beds of animal skins. (XIII. 603)

He then goes on to cite Herodotus's idea that the Persians learned about pederasty from the Greeks, and to talk about Alexander and his love of boys. His account of the Celts' spurning of women for boys and practice of sleeping with two lovers upon animal skins is clearly indebted either to Diodorus Siculus or to a source upon which they both drew. However, the desire to associate pederasty with foreignness is either his own thought, or more likely represents a common tradition.

Ammianus Marcellinus (Latin; AD 325–91). The surviving eighteen books of Ammianus's *History* of the Roman Empire cover the period AD 353–78. In Book XXXI, chapter ix, dated AD 377, he recounts the battle between Frigeridus, Gratian's general, and the Goths and an associated tribe he calls the Taifali, led by their chieftain Farnobius who had recently received them as allies (XXXI. ix. 3).[19] Frigeridus defeated them, and sent the survivors he spared to work in the fields around Mutina, Regium, and Parma in Italy. Ammianus concludes:

We have learned that these Taifali were a shameful folk, so sunken in a life of shame and obscenity, that in their country the boys are coupled with the men in a union of unmentionable lust, to consume the flower of their youth in the polluted intercourse of those paramours. We may add that, if any grown person alone catches a boar or kills a huge bear, he is purified thereby from the shame of unchastity. (XXXI. ix. 5)

Institutionalized pederasty certainly seems to be at issue here, supported by the fact that the mention of boar and bear has been argued to point to a context of rites of inititiation into manhood. However, fuller discussion of this must follow the evidence of the final witness, Procopius.

Procopius (Greek; AD 500–65). Procopius's *History of the Wars* was written in the mid-sixth century AD, and, since Procopius took part in wars against the Goths,

---

[18] Charles Burton Gulick, *Athenaeus. The Deipnosophists.* 7 vols. London: Heinemann, 1937, VI, p. 251. παιδεραστεια means literally 'love of boys'; see Liddell-Scott *s.v.* παιδεραστεια (p. 1286).
[19] John C. Rolfe, *Ammianus Marcellinus*. 3 vols. London: Heinemann, 1958, III, p. 445. On the Taifali, and their consistent close association with the Goths, see further Ludwig Schmidt, *Die Ostgermanen*. 2nd edn. Munich: Beck, 1941; repr. (unaltered) 1969, pp. 546–8.

the descriptions here may be based on first-hand evidence. Book VI deals with
the Gothic War, and chapter xiv concerns the Eruli (or Heruli), a tribe associated
with Scandinavia.[20] We are told that, bored with peace, the people taunt their
leader Rodolphus with cowardice and effeminacy (section 11). This insults him
so much that he attacks the Lombards without provocation, resulting in his
own death and the flight of the survivors (section 22). They are forced to settle
elsewhere and eventually become neighbours and, on Justinian's accession, allies
to the Romans. However, Procopius warns, although they submit to Christian
laws and support the Romans in battle, they are nonetheless faithless. In the
standard Loeb translation of the text, we are then informed that 'they mate in an
unholy manner, especially men with asses, and they are the basest of all men and
utterly abandoned rascals. (VI. xiv. 36)[21] However, a more accurate rendering of
the second clause would be 'even with men and with asses' (ἄλλας τε και ανδρων
και όνων).

A further passage on the Eruli often cited in this context is found in Book II
(on the Persian War), chapter xxv, sections 27–8. It recounts the practice of the
Eruli in battle to fight mostly without protection:

> For the Eruli have neither helmet nor corselet nor any other protective armour, except a
> shield and a thick jacket, which they gird about them before they enter a battle. And
> indeed the Erulian slaves go into battle without even a shield, and when they prove
> themselves brave men in war, then their masters permit them to protect themselves in
> battle with shields. Such is the custom of the Eruli.   (II. xxv. 27–8)

This passage is interpreted by Greenberg (p. 243) in connection with the comment on the same-sex preferences of the Eruli to be a reference to ritual pederasty,
and he cites the analogy of present-day tribes which practise pederasty until
a youth achieves manhood through some initiation rite or trial of strength.[22]
However, before fuller discussion of this methodology, there is one final passage
which is often deemed to concern pederasty, and that is Procopius's account in
Book III on the Vandalic War of how Alaric, leader of the Visigoths, captured
Rome. After a prolonged siege and neither force nor any other device had proved
successful, we are told that he formed another plan:

> Among the youths in the army whose beards had not yet grown, but who had just come
> of age [that is, around 13–15 years old], he chose out three hundred whom he knew to be
> of good birth and possessed of valour beyond their years, and told them secretly that he

---

[20] On the Eruli, see further Schmidt, *Die Ostgermanen*, pp. 548–64. Immediately after the
passage quoted below, Procopius discusses the settlement by the Eruli of Thule, identified as either
Iceland or northernmost Scandinavia, suggesting they may be North Germanic.

[21] H. B. Dewing, *Procopius*. 6 vols. London: Heinemann, 1919, III, p. 413

[22] Slaves here thus would imply something like acolytes or initiands. Widengren shows that
terms like 'servant' and 'slave' are often used of young men and warriors, and that this is typical
of warrior-bands in Indo-European contexts. See Geo Widengren, *Der Feudalismus im alten Iran:
Männerbund, Gefolgswesen, Feudalismus in der iranischen Gesellschaft im Hinblick auf die indogermanischen Verhältnisse.* Cologne: Westdeutscher Verlag, 1969, pp. 9–44, 50 f.

was about to make a present of them to certain of the patricians in Rome, pretending that they were slaves. And he instructed them that, as soon as they got inside the houses of those men, they should display much gentleness and moderation and serve them eagerly in whatever tasks should be laid upon them by their owners.   (III. ii. 15–16)

Once the youths had lulled their putative owners into a false sense of security, they were to wait for an appointed day and, during the afternoon siesta, to proceed to the Salarian gate, kill the guards, and open the gates to their compatriots. The plan succeeds, for we are told that the youths 'by being unusually obedient to their owners, averted suspicion'. There certainly seems to be grounds for reading a sexual undertone into this episode, as Greenberg does (p. 249), although Procopius refrains from making it explicit, perhaps because this would reflect badly in his eyes on the morality and manliness of the Roman patricians lulled into a false sense of security by these compliant adolescent boys.

The above material gives ample evidence that a consistent connection is made in Classical ethnography between Germanic and Celtic tribes and same-sex activity. There are, however, various problems with assessing this material, as hinted above. The first is that later writers clearly borrow from and are influenced by earlier writers, especially Posidonius. Some scholars see this as evidence that the accounts are fictional, representing literary borrowings only.[23] The most suspicious might argue that, even if true of the Celts, the same-sex associations of the Germans are merely transferred from the earlier accounts, as a trait 'appropriate' to foreign barbarians. Similarly, some of the witnesses display strong ideological biases, and reports of same-sex activity could represent part of a standard trope of creating 'the barbarian Other', or be used as part of a favourable or unfavourable contrast with Roman or Greek society, aimed at encouraging social reform. And, finally, astrological contexts are hardly suggestive of reliability.

On the other hand, the later material does *not* consist merely of unreflective borrowings. Rather, the later historians collate various earlier written sources with oral eyewitness accounts, and some were even in a position to gain firsthand information themselves. Moreover, similarity of expression does not equate to fictionality—it may be that the similarity of practices observed led writers to describe them in similar ways, perhaps even tacitly drawing a comparison with the other tribes. And the placing of a practice in an astrological context does not necessarily mean that the practice itself was invented.

If the material itself is accepted as broadly accurate, then further problems present themselves. How admissible is it to extrapolate from these individual tribes to conclude that pederasty or institutionalized same-sex practices were a pan-Germanic, pan-Celtic, or even pan-Indo-European phenomenon? Certainly,

---

[23] For this approach to Posidonius and Caesar, see J. J. Tierney, 'The Celtic Ethnography of Posidonius', *Proceedings of the Royal Irish Academy* 60C (1960), 189–275. For a refutation, see Nash, 'Reconstructing Poseidonios' Celtic Ethnography'.

Jan Bremmer does just that, in an article which seeks to place Greek same-sexuality in its Indo-European context. He concludes that it is very likely that the Indo-Europeans favoured cross-generational same-sex practices, which were designed to make the power differential clear and to keep younger men submissive until they achieved adulthood, when they would switch roles to perpetuate the relation.[24] Greenberg goes even further, adducing contextual evidence from modern societies such as New Guinea, Hawaii, and Micronesia, where what he deems to be similar social relations are observable, and Murray systematically collates evidence of cross-generational same-sex relations in a multitude of warrior societies, ancient and modern.[25]

It is certainly true that age-differentiated same-sex practices are found across an enormous variety of societies in all periods, but it is far from certain that one can draw straightforward parallels from one to another, particularly when separated by time and distance. Moreover, it is often too easy to ignore important differences between tribes and societies, when one is looking for what connects them. Arnold Price, in his 1980 article on the Germanic warrior club, gives an excellent account of the methodological problems inherent in demonstrating even relatively limited and local propositions about only one set of warrior groups.[26] Although he does not mention same-sex practices, Price makes it clear that, while one should certainly not view tribes as mutually exclusive social groups, neither can one ignore their differentiating characteristics and variant customs (pp. 560–1). It is certainly very probable that same-sex activity *occurred* in all Germanic tribal societies to some degree, as in all known societies, and it is also probable that this was largely age differentiated. One cannot, however, assume that pederasty was *institutionalized* in all Germanic tribes.[27] Nevertheless, there is no reason to doubt that same-sex activity was an institutionalized feature of some Germanic tribal societies.

The question of whether pederasty or same-sex activity, institutionalized or otherwise, survived the Migration as rite, institution, or custom into Anglo-Saxon England is a still more complex matter, and we shall return to it shortly. First, though, we must consider the evidence of Tacitus, the most famous Classical commentor on the Germanic tribes, since it might seem to contradict the associations with same-sex practices that have just been reviewed. Tacitus's countervailing evidence can, however, as we will see, be explained by adducing

[24] Jan Bremmer, 'An Enigmatic Indo-European Rite: Paederasty', *Arethusa* 13 (1980), 279–98, at 290–1.

[25] Greenberg, *Construction*, pp. 108–15; Murray, *Homosexualities*, pp. 23–96.

[26] Arnold H. Price, 'The Role of the Germanic Warrior Club in the Historical Process: A Methodological Exposition', *Miscellanea mediaevalia* 12 (1980), 558–65, especially 558–61.

[27] There is also a question mark over whether pederasty is exclusively at issue here, since it is by no means clear from all the accounts that the sexual partners are differentiated in terms of age or rank. It is possible that the familiarity of pederasty to Greek or Roman writers or observers coloured their understanding of the societies described. It is also possible that later scholars are more comfortable with the idea of pederasty than egalitarian same-sex relations because pederasty is less disturbing to gender stereotypes and ideas about the 'manly' nature of warrior societies.

the Old Norse discourse of *níð*, where only the passive partner in same-sex intercourse seems to have been stigmatized.

THE TACITEAN EVIDENCE: *IGNAVES, IMBELLES ET CORPORE INFAMES*

In the *Germania*, completed in AD 98, Tacitus gives his Roman audience detailed geographical and sociocultural information about the tribes populating the lands beyond the Rhine and the Danube. There are many passages of interest, several of which are frequently cited in introductory works on the Anglo-Saxons and their culture.[28] Tacitus owes literary debts to earlier historical works such as Caesar's *Gallic War* (see above), the lost 104th book of the vast history of Livy (59 BC–AD 17) and the lost histories of the Roman wars in Germany of Pliny the Elder (AD 23–79). He also betrays a strong ideological bias, presenting the Germanic tribes as a pure society of noble savages clearly intended to contrast strongly with and to the shame of contemporary Romans whom he regarded as living in degenerate and effete luxury.[29] However, archaeological evidence supports many of his observations, as does the fact that several of the sociocultural phenomena he observes survive into and are recorded in the Anglo-Saxon period.[30]

Although Tacitus describes the strong homosocial bonds between a Germanic chief and his retinue—most strikingly in chapter 14, where devotion unto death is depicted as an unquestioned duty—there is little explicit comment on same-sex erotic relations. In chapter 20, Tacitus informs us that 'Late comes love to the young men, and their first manhood is not enfeebled' and that 'Sisters' children mean as much to their uncle as to their father: some tribes regard this blood-tie as even closer and more sacred than that between son and father.'[31] However, Greenberg goes too far when he concludes from the widespread evidence of the importance of the sister's son relationship that uncles are likely to have ritually

---

[28] On the problems with linking Tacitus's account of the battle practices of the Germanic tribes to the poetic account of the late tenth-century Battle of Maldon, see Rosemary Woolf, 'The Ideal of Men Dying with their Lord in the *Germania* and in *The Battle of Maldon*', *Anglo-Saxon England* 5 (1976), 63–81; Roberta Frank, 'The Ideal of Men Dying with their Lord in *The Battle of Maldon*: Anachronism or *nouvelle vague*?' in *People and Places in Northern Europe 500–1600: Essays in Honour of Peter Hayes Sawyer*, ed. Ian Wood and Niels Lund. Woodbridge: Boydell Press, 1991; repr. 1996, pp. 95–106; Steven Fanning, 'Tacitus, *Beowulf*, and the *Comitatus*', in *Haskins Society Journal* 9 (1997), 17–38; David Clark, 'Creating a Tradition: Dying with One's Lord in "The Battle of Maldon" and its Analogues' (forthcoming). On *Maldon* itself, see further Chapter 7 below.

[29] See Ronald Syme, *Tacitus*. Oxford: Clarendon Press, 1958, p. 127.

[30] Hans Jankuhn, 'Archäologische Bemerkungen zur Glaubwürdigkeit des Tacitus in der Germania', *Nachrichten der Akademie der Wissenschaften in Göttingen*, Philologisch-historische Klasse; Jahrg. 1966, 409–26, especially 425.

[31] *Tacitus. Germania*, trans. M. Hutton, rev. E. H. Warmington. London: Harvard University Press, 1970, p. 163.

sodomized their nephews.[32] It is also not possible conclusively to state that pederastic relations lie behind the description in chapter 13 of initiation into manhood. Tacitus tells us that the gift of a shield and spear marks the transition to the status of manhood, and that when a chieftain admits a young man into his retinue 'they mingle with the others, men of maturer strength and tested by long years, and have no shame to be seen among his retinue' (p. 151). The seemingly unmotivated raising of the possibility of shame has seemed suggestive to some, and it is uncertain what the phrase 'mingle with the others' connotes.[33] Nevertheless, there is not enough evidence to conclude that this passage alludes to and conceals institutionalized pederasty.

Indeed, some scholars conclude from another passage in *Germania* chapter 12 that same-sex activity was in fact stigmatized and possibly even punished with execution, in keeping with the idealizing comment by Pseudo-Quintilian that 'the Germani know nothing [about homosexual activity], and life on the Ocean is lived more purely'.[34] The passage in question concerns the nature of the death penalty among the Germans, which, Tacitus explains, differs according to the offence:

traitors and deserters are hung from trees; cowards and poor fighters and sexual perverts are plunged in the mud of marshes with a hurdle on their heads: the difference of punishment has regard to the principle that crime should be blazoned abroad by its retribution, but abomination hidden.[35]

The phrase translated 'cowards and poor fighters and sexual perverts' corresponds to the Latin *ignavos et imbelles et corpore infames*, the interpretation of which has occasioned intense debate amongst scholars. The most recent and convincing reading is that of J. B. Rives, whose explanatory note is worth quoting at length:

The Latin phrase *corpore infamis* means literally 'with a bad reputation because of (or with respect to) one's body'; Tacitus later uses it of an actor...and a variation, *mollitia corporis infamis*, 'with a bad reputation because of the effeminacy of his body', of a senator... There is little question that the phrase served as a euphemism for the *pathicus* or *cinaedus*, an effeminate man who enjoyed taking the passive sexual role with other men. Since such men were assumed to be inherently cowardly, it is likely enough that all

[32] Greenberg, *Construction*, p. 109. On this relation see also Jan Bremmer, 'Avunculate and Fosterage', *Journal of Indo-European Studies* 4 (1976), 65–78, especially 71, and, for Old English, Rolf H. Bremmer, Jr., 'The Importance of Kinship: Uncle and Nephew in "Beowulf"', *Amsterdamer Beiträge zur älteren Germanistik* 15 (1980), 21–38.
[33] See, for example, J. B. Rives, *Tacitus. Germania*. Oxford: Clarendon Press, 1999, pp. 181–2.
[34] Pseudo-Quintilian, *Declamationes maiores*, 3. 16, quoted in Rives, *Germania*, p. 174. For Latin text and French translation, see Catherine Schneider, *[Quintilien]. Le soldat de Marius (Grandes déclamations, 3)*. Cassino: Edizioni dell'Università degli Studi di Cassino, 2004, pp. 64–5. The moral purity of the Germani claimed here is clearly rhetorically necessary, since the point of the paradox created depends on the contrast between the Romans and the Germans being as stark as possible; cf. Schneider's commentary, n. 303, p. 226, and Cicero, *De inventione* I. 103.
[35] Tacitus, *Germania*, trans. Hutton, pp. 149, 151.

three of the terms Tacitus uses here denotes one class of person, rather than two separate classes of cowards and passive homosexuals.[36]

There are a few problems with this statement, since although Tacitus may well be using the phrase as a euphemism for *cinaedus*, this might be merely his own reading of the type of person rather than a genuine Germanic category. Moreover, it is possible to view cowards, effete, and sexually passive persons as of a similar overall type while still making certain distinctions between them.[37] However, it does seem convincing that this passage does concern and attach a stigma to men deemed unmanly, including those who play the passive role in sex and who are thus considered to have degraded their bodies. The question for us in this context must be: does this then conflict with the evidence assembled above associating the Germans with non-stigmatized same-sex activity? Although it would seem to at face value, in fact we should note that this passage does not necessarily stigmatize the active participant in same-sex relations, as we can see if we adduce as a context the Old Norse concept of *ergi*, as in fact Rives does, following early explanations such as that of Lily Weiser-Aall in an article from 1933 which translates as follows:

Ignavus et imbellis et corpore infamis seems to be the interpreter's clarification of the Germanic words *argr* or *ragr*, which encapsulate the three concepts. The sense in this context should be 'wholly unmanly'.[38]

OLD NORSE *NÍÐ*, *ERGI*, AND PHALLIC AGGRESSION

The concept of *níð* has attracted much attention in Old Norse studies recently. It denotes an extensive discourse in which stigma is attached to men who show themselves to be 'unmanly' by taking on the inappropriate gender role. The noun *ergi*, verb *ergjask*, and the adjective *argr* and its metathesized form *ragr* represent

[36] Rives, *Germania*, p. 174. Compare Donald J. Ward, 'The Threefold Death: An Indo-European Trifunctional Sacrifice?' in *Myth and Law Among the Indo-Europeans: Studies in Indo-European Comparative Mythology*, ed. Jaan Puhvel. Berkeley: University of California Press, 1970, pp. 123–42, at p. 127.

[37] Compare the remarks in Karras, *Sexuality in Medieval Europe*, p. 130.

[38] '*Ignavus et imbellis et corpore infamis* scheint die Erklärung des Dolmetschers vom germanichen Worte *argr* oder *ragr*, das die drei Begriffe in sich vereinigt, zu sein. Der Sinn dürfte an dieser Stelle sein, "durchaus unmännlich".' Lily Weiser-Aall, 'Zur Geschichte der altgermanischen Todesstrafe und Friedlosigkeit', *Archiv für Religionswissenschaft* 30 (1933), 209–27, at 212 n. 3; cf. Nat. Beckman, 'Ignavi et imbelles et corpore infames', *Arkiv för nordisk filologi* 52 (1936), 78–81. The connection with *argr* is also made in Wayne R. Dynes, ed., *Encyclopedia of Homosexuality*. 2 vols. London: St. James Press, 1990. The article on 'Law, Germanic' (II, pp. 687–9), however, defines *argr* as denoting 'passivity and lack of courage associated with the passive-effeminate male rather than sexual behaviour per se', in support of its claim that 'close philological analysis of the entire passage and of the phrase in question shows that Tacitus was describing a violation of military discipline, cowardice or failure to perform one's soldierly duty, and not a sexual offense' (p. 688). However, no supporting evidence is given for this distinction, which seems untenable.

the ultimate insult to a man, implying that he is not merely effeminate but specifically has been the passive partner in anal intercourse, also represented by the adjective *(sann)sorðinn* '(truly) buggered'. Indeed, under medieval Icelandic law a man accused of *níð* can kill his slanderer with legal impunity.[39]

In passages involving *níð* in the Icelandic sagas, stigma is often attached to both partners in same-sex intercourse. For instance, in chapter two of *Gísla saga Súrssonar*, a character named Holmgang-Skeggi in order to mock Kolbjǫrn, the cowardly rival suitor of Gísli's sister Þordís, tells his carpenter to carve two wooden figures of Gísli and Kolbjǫrn: *and skal annarr standa aptar en annarr, ok skal níð þat standa ávallt, þeim til háðungar* 'and one shall stand behind the other, and the shame of that will always remain to their dishonour'.[40] However, Preben Meulengracht Sørensen makes an important distinction in this episode between the shame that attaches to the man in front—that is, the shame of being *argr*, or effeminate, allowing oneself to be anally penetrated—and the shame that attaches to the man behind—that is, the shame of putting one's friend in the position of being *argr*. In *Bjarnar saga Hítdœlakappa*, where a similar episode occurs, the saga author tells us that *mæltu menn, at hvárkis hlutr væri góðr, þeira er þar stóðu, ok enn verri þess, er fyrir stóð* 'people said that neither's situation was good, of those who stood there, but still it was worse for the one standing in front'. Sørensen reads this distinction as suggesting that the active partner, or the aggressor, is disapproved of, not because he has shown effeminacy, on the contrary, in fact, but rather that he has shown himself to be uncivilized and savage by his actions, committing what we might term phallic aggression.[41] He further convincingly argues that the stigma originally attached only to the passive partner and that it is only with Christianization that the stigma is generalized from passivity and receptivity to all forms of same-sex interaction.[42]

A similar concept to Old Norse *ergi* (and indeed a cognate noun *arga*) clearly existed in sixth-and seventh-century Langobardy, which together with the Tacitean evidence suggests that it represents an element of common Germanic culture.[43] Certain forms of same-sex sexual interaction would most likely therefore be stigmatized by the Germanic ancestors of the Anglo-Saxons. However, if the stigma originally and in non-clerical contexts attaches only to the passive partner, this does not conflict with the ethnographic evidence which associates non-stigmatized same-sex activity with Germanic tribes, any more than

---

[39] See further Preben Meulengracht Sørensen, *The Unmanly Man: Concepts of Sexual Defamation in Early Northern Society*, trans. Joan Turville-Petre. Odense: Odense University Press, 1983, *passim*, and references therein.

[40] *Gísla saga* is edited in *Vestfirðinga sǫgur*, ed. Björn K. Þórólfsson and Guðni Jónsson. Íslenzk fornrit VI. Reykjavík: Hið íslenzka fornritafélag, 1943, p. 10.

[41] Sørensen, *The Unmanly Man*, pp. 57–8. On phallic aggression, see further David Clark, 'Revisiting *Gísla saga*: Sexual Themes and the Heroic Past', *JEGP* 106 (2007), 492–515.

[42] Sørensen, *The Unmanly Man*, p. 26; cf. Boswell, *Christianity, Social Tolerance, and Homosexuality*, p. 184.

[43] Rives, *Germania*, pp. 174–5.

the concept of the *cinaedus* conflicts with the evidence of widespread (though primarily age- or rank-differentiated) same-sex relations in Roman culture.[44]

Is there, however, any evidence that such a nuanced attitude survived into Anglo-Saxon England? The next chapter investigates this possibility and explores a limited amount of evidence which suggests that the Anglo-Saxons may have had a separate conceptual category for those men who exclusively enjoyed same-sex relations.

---

[44] See further, Halperin, *How to Do the History of Homosexuality, passim.*

3

Attitudes to Same-Sex Activity in Anglo-Saxon England: *earg*, the Penitentials, and OE *bædling*

The previous chapter showed a widespread association of Germanic (and Celtic) tribes with same-sex activity. As argued there, the concept of *nið* from the culturally cognate Old Norse literature can explain the apparently contradictory evidence from Tacitus that the Germans despised effeminacy; instead, this suggests that it was primarily sexual passivity that was stigmatized. The present chapter investigates the possibility that the Anglo-Saxons had a similar concept through a review of Old English terms in the semantic field of effeminacy and cowardice cognate to Old Norse *ergi* (and Langobardic *arga*). Limited though the evidence is, it suggests that the Anglo-Saxons may have had a concept of *ergi*, albeit in a less developed form. Even given the paucity of what material has survived, it is nevertheless probable that the Anglo-Saxon assumption in secular circles was that it was normal to be the insertive partner in sex with both men and women but that passivity and effeminacy were strongly stigmatized. The ramifications of the presence of the unusual term *bædling* in Old English penitential material suggest a discourse that deserves exploration, perhaps even identification as a category of sexual identity.

OLD ENGLISH *EARG, EARGIAN, EARGLICE*

A search of the Toronto Dictionary of Old English throws up around one hundred or so occurrences of the Old English adjective *earg* and its various cognates, and the range of meanings given for *earg* is representative.[1] One set is defined as 'cowardly, craven, timid (esp. in military contexts)', an example of which occurs in *The Battle of Maldon*, where the traitor Godric is called *earh*

---

[1] Antonette diPaolo Healey, ed., *Dictionary of Old English: A to G Online*. Toronto: Pontifical Institute of Mediaeval Studies, 2007. The dictionary has so far published as far as the letter <G>. Additionally, a 'Simple Search' was done of the whole corpus for words beginning with *earg-* (43×), *earh-* (45×), and *yrh-* (14×) at <http://ets.umdl.umich.edu/o/oec/> (Antonette diPaolo Healey, ed., *Dictionary of Old English Web Corpus*. Toronto: Pontifical Institute of Mediaeval Studies).

Oddan bearn 'the cowardly son of Odda' (237). Another group of meanings is 'dilatory, indolent, torpid, spiritless', as in the Old English translation of Boethius's *Consolation of Philosophy*, where Wisdom exclaims: *Eala, ge eargan 7 idelgeornan. hwy ge swa unnytte sien 7 swa aswundne* 'Alas, you indolent and idle! why are you so useless and so slothful?'[2] A third set of meanings is 'vile, wicked, depraved, base', as in the warning in *Christ II* that great expanses of the world will lament when the bright king repays them for having lived on earth *eargum dædum... leahtrum fa* 'in wicked deeds... stained with sins' (827b–8a). However, it is of course in practice impossible to make such precise distinctions. In the last instance, for example, the adjective 'slothful' would fit just as well (and is indeed the translation choice made by S. A. J. Bradley).[3] Similarly, there are numerous instances of *earg* or a cognate where there seems to be a mixture of overlapping connotations ranging from fear and cowardice through idleness and wickedness that could perhaps be summed up in the rather old-fashioned but suitably ambiguous phrase 'moral turpitude'.

What is interesting in the context of *ergi* and *nið* is that several instances of *earg* and its cognates seem to shade into a semantic field of effeminacy and base sexual desires. In the Old English translation of *Orosius*, for example, we are told about one of Hannibal's campaigns against Rome, where the Roman men do not acquit themselves well:

On þæm teoþan geare þæs þe Hannibal won on Italie, he for of Campaina þam londe oþ þrio mila to Romabyrg 7 æt þære ie gewicade þe mon Annianes hætt, eallum romanum to ðæm mæstan ege, swa hit mon on þara wæpnedmonna gebærum ongitan mehte, hu hie afyrhtede wæron 7 agælwede, þa þa wifmen urnon mid stanum wið þara wealla 7 cwædon þæt hie þa burg werian wolden, gif þa wæpnedmen ne dorsten. Þæs on mergen Hannibal gefor to þære byrig 7 beforan ðæm geate his folc getrymede þe mon hætt Collina. Ac þa consulas noldon hie selfe swa earge geþencan swa hie þa wifmen ær forcwædon, þæt hi hie binnan þære byrig werian ne dorsten, ac hie hie butan þæm geate angean Hannibal trymedon.[4]

In the tenth year from that in which Hannibal fought in Italy, he went from the land of Campania within three miles of the city of Rome and camped at the river which is called Anio, to the greatest fear of all the Romans, so that one could perceive it in the males' behaviour, how they were terrified and dismayed, when the females ran with stones toward the walls and said that they would defend the city, if the males dared not. On the following morning Hannibal went to the city and arrayed his people before the gate which is called Collina. But the consuls did not want to consider themselves so *earge* as the females had said before, that they did not dare defend themselves within the city, but they arrayed themselves outside the gate against Hannibal.

[2] *King Alfred's Anglo-Saxon Version of Boethius De Consolatione Philosophiæ*, ed. and trans. Samuel Fox. Cited from the reprint of the 1864 edition. New York: AMS Press, 1970, (XL. iv), p. 238.
[3] Bradley, *Anglo-Saxon Poetry*, p. 227.
[4] *The Old English Orosius*, ed. Janet Bately. EETS SS 6. London: Oxford University Press, 1980, IV. x. 13–23 (p. 103).

The Old English translator has strikingly altered and added to his source. First, his choice of the terms *wifmen* and *wæpnedmen* makes the gender dynamic of the episode more evident (something I have attempted to represent in my translation choices of 'males' and 'females' rather than just 'men' and 'women'). Here the base term for 'person' (*mann*) is supplemented with the element *wif* 'woman' or *wæpned* 'weaponed', implicitly criticizing the men who, far from embodying the traditional role of the man-as-martial protector embedded in the term used to describe them, run away and leave the defence to the women to make, not with weapons but with rocks. His second addition is the motives attributed to the women for their actions (that they want to take over the defence in the absence of their men) and the consuls' response to their bravery (that they are responding to the women's accusations that they are *earg*).[5]

This scene in fact contains certain elements which give it a remarkable resemblance to the well-known scenes of whetting or goading in Old Norse literature, where women taunt the male members of their family with effeminacy in order to force them to take revenge for some injury.[6] One famous episode is found in *Brennu-Njáls saga*, chapter 116, where Hildigunnr wants to force her kinsman Flosi to take blood-vengeance for the killing of her husband Hǫskuldr in addition to the legal case he is willing to prosecute. When she fails to get her way through verbal taunts alone, Hildigunnr goes to a chest and takes out the cloak which Flosi had given Hǫskuldr and which he had been wearing at his death. She throws it over Flosi, causing the congealed blood with which the cloak is saturated to shower over him, saying:

Skýt ek því til guðs ok góðra manna, at ek sœri þik fyrir alla krapta Krists þíns ok fyrir manndóm ok karlmennsku þína, at þú hefnir allra sára þeira, er hann hafði á sér dauðum, eða heit hvers manns níðingr ella.[7]

I call God and all good men to witness that I adjure you with all the powers of your Christ and your manhood and manliness, that you avenge all those wounds which [Hǫskuldr] had upon him when dead, or be called every man's *níðingr* otherwise.

Is it possible that, in the additions he has made to his source, the Old English translator is allusively incorporating a similar topos to make this Roman conflict

---

[5] Compare Bately's commentary on these lines, *Old English Orosius*, p. 290.

[6] On this subject, see for example Carol J. Clover, 'Hildigunnr's lament', in *Structure and Meaning in Old Norse Literature: New Approaches to Textual Analysis and Literary Criticism*, ed. John Lindow et al. Odense: Odense University Press, 1986, pp. 141–83; Rolf Heller, *Die literarische Darstellung der Frau in den Isländersagas*. Halle (Saale): M. Niemayer, 1958; and, with caution, Jenny Jochens, *Old Norse Images of Women*. Philadelphia: University of Pennsylvania Press, 1996. On the whetting and avenging woman, see also David Clark, 'Undermining and En-Gendering Vengeance: Distancing and Anti-Feminism in the *Poetic Edda*', *Scandinavian Studies* 77 (2005), 173–200; and idem, 'Vengeance and the Heroic Ideal in Old English and Old Norse Literature' (unpublished doctoral thesis, University of Oxford, 2003), chs 3–4.

[7] Einar Ól. Sveinsson, ed., *Brennu-Njáls saga*. Íslenzk fornrit XII. Reykjavík: Hið íslenzka forn-ritafélag, 1954, ch. 116, p. 291. On the episode, see further Clover, ibid., and William Ian Miller, 'Choosing the Avenger: Some Aspects of the Bloodfeud in Medieval Iceland and England', *Law and History Review* 1 (1983), 159–204, at 174–94.

more accessible to an Anglo-Saxon audience? Certainly, it seems altogether probable that the adjective *earge* in the episode does not mean simply 'cowardly', but carries overtones of effeminacy or unmanliness.

The adjective *earg* is also the choice of the Old English translator of the biblical book of Judges when he comments on the destruction of *ðam eorgan Sisaran 7 þam arleasan Iabine* 'the *eorg* Sisera and the faithless Jabin', where it may have seemed the appropriate term to use of Sisera because he was ignominiously killed while sleeping at the hands of a woman, Jael, who drives a tent-peg through his temple. Sisera would have seemed particularly unmanly to an Anglo-Saxon audience because he was resting in the tent after fleeing from a battle where all his men had perished, thus constituting the antithesis of the ideal lord who should lead his troops into battle and fight to the death.[8]

A further suggestive use of the term comes in the passage in the Old English translation of Boethius where Wisdom explains that wickedness degrades humanity, and that if a man has turned from good to evil, he is more a beast than a man. Covetous, belligerent, deceitful, wrathful, indolent, frivolous, and lascivious men are likened to the wolf, dog, fox, lion, bird, and pig. But, we are told, 'þone ungemetlice eargan, þe him ondræt ma þonne he þyrfe, ðu meaht hatan hara ma þonne mon' [the excessively *earg* one, who is more fearful than he need be, you may call a hare more than a man].[9] John Boswell shows that the hare is associated with same-sex behaviour and hermaphroditism in Pliny's natural history, the first-century Epistle of Barnabus and the third-century *Paedagogus* of Clement of Alexandria, an association which persisted well into the later Middle Ages.[10] It seems significant that the adjective *earg* is the one deemed appropriate for this context, although it is not possible at present to state how well-known the sexual associations of the hare would have been in Anglo-Saxon England.[11]

The evidence adduced above, however, remains only suggestive and not conclusive. The term *earg* does seem to have connotations of moral baseness, sometimes connected with dubious sexual desires, but these are not restricted to same-sex situations. For instance, in the version of the rape of Lucretia in the Old English Orosius, the rapist Tarquin is wickedest, most lustful, most hateful, and *eargast* of the wicked kings who ruled after Romulus. Moreover, *earg* can gloss Latin *adulter* 'wicked', *peccatrix* 'sinful', *luxuriosus* 'excessive, voluptuous',

---

[8] The lord-retainer dynamic in some heroic poems is explored later in Chapter 7.

[9] Fox, *King Alfred's Anglo-Saxon Version of Boethius*, XXXVII. iv, p. 192.

[10] Boswell, *Christianity, Social Tolerance, and Homosexuality*, pp. 137–43. Boswell gives a translation of the Clement passage in his Appendix II, pp. 355–9. See also Andrew Boyle, 'The Hare in Myth and Reality: A Review Article', *Folklore* 84 (1973), 313–26.

[11] The most closely contemporary association of the hare with problematic gender I have come across is the eleventh-century Gwentian code of north-east Wales, in which 'the hare is said to be incapable of legal evaluation because it is male one month and female another': cited in Beryl Rowland, 'Animal Imagery and the Pardoner's Abnormality', *Neophilologus* 48 (1964), 56–60, at 57. See also Edward Topsell, *The Historie of Four-footed Beasts*. London, 1607, cited in *The Leaping Hare*, George Ewart Evans and David Thomson. London: Faber and Faber, 1972, pp. 24–5.

and *earglice* is an equivalent in one manuscript for *muliebriter* 'womanly, effem-
inately'.[12] It therefore belongs to a wide semantic field which may not have made
clear and consistent distinctions between wickedness, cowardice, luxuriousness,
and effeminacy.

There is certainly no equivalent in Old English of the extensive and well-
defined discourse of *níð* in Old Norse. However, it is an overlooked fact deserving
of further attention that the Old English cognates of *ergi* are found in a small
number of contexts which have an important gendered or sexual element. It
is thus possible that, as with medieval Scandinavians, Anglo-Saxons may have
stigmatized sexual passivity in same-sex contexts, but did not stigmatize the active
role until the advent of Christianity, as the rest of this chapter investigates.

OLD ENGLISH *BÆDLING* AND
THE ANGLO-SAXON PENITENTIALS

As remarked in the previous chapter, no secular Germanic law-code prescribes
any penalty for same-sex acts, with the exception of the seventh-century Visigothic code, which shows clear clerical influence.[13] The Anglo-Saxon law-codes
are no exception to this trend. Therefore, since it seems unlikely that such
acts never occurred in secular society, it was not deemed important to impose
secular penalties on them. Although the ecclesiastical prohibitions and penalties
about to be considered provide evidence that same-sex acts did indeed occur in
Anglo-Saxon England, they cannot tell us how widely and how often, and the
proscriptions form merely one part of a wider condemnation of non-procreative
sexual acts. They are also unable to tell us how strictly and consistently penalties
were imposed, how far sinners actually confessed their misdeeds, how detailed
Anglo-Saxon instructions about sexual behaviour would have been, and, most
importantly, how far laymen would have associated same-sex acts with Sodom
and its inhabitants. As the following chapters show, the Old Testament city had
mixed associations even in Latin writings, and vernacular texts make even weaker
links between Sodom and same-sex activity. First, however, we shall explore in
more detail the penalties for same-sex acts in the Old English and Anglo-Latin
penitentials.

The implications of the Anglo-Saxon penitentiary material for the history of
sexuality were not widely considered until the pioneering work of Allen Frantzen,
who brought study of the penitentials from the recesses of textual scholarship to a
wider audience with the article 'Between the Lines: Queer Theory, the History of

---

[12] See Bately, *Old English Orosius*, II. ii. 1 (p. 40), and Healey, *Dictionary of Old English s .v. earg*
sense 3.b and *earglice* sense 3.

[13] See Vern L. Bullough, 'The Sin Against Nature and Homosexuality', in *Sexual Practices and
the Medieval Church*, ed. Vern L. Bullough and James Brundage. New York: Prometheus Books,
1982, pp. 55–71 at p. 59.

Homosexuality, and Anglo-Saxon Penitentials' (reworked as chapter 4 of *Before the Closet*).[14] More recently still, R. D. Fulk has devoted detailed and scholarly attention to just one of the penitentials in his essay 'Male Homoeroticism in the Old English *Canons of Theodore*'.[15]

Frantzen outlines well the problems with which scholars must grapple when dealing with the evidence of the penitentials. He reminds us that they 'are rhetorical documents, not transparent records of behavior and social standards. We do not know how they were used or whether they reflect standards actually enforced or only outline ideal standards that were never met.'[16] A further problem usually encountered when analysing penitentials, that different penitentials are not standardized and are thus difficult to compare, does not apply to the vernacular Anglo-Saxon documents because they draw on 'only two sources, Theodore's *Penitential* ... and the ninth-century *Penitential* of Halitgar of Cambrai' and they also 'borrow from one another' and thus demonstrate 'impressive conformity' (p. 270). Finally, though, it can be difficult to determine the precise significance of certain sexual acts isolated from their social contexts, and Frantzen warns that 'we cannot always separate the sexual from the social (or the literary)' (p. 271; cf. Fulk, 'Male Homoeroticism', p. 7).

Frantzen does suggest a certain degree of confidence in our ability to draw conclusions about Anglo-Saxon practice from the penitentials in his further statement that 'Their close alignment with secular law on most issues, and the frequency of calls for confession and penance in other sources, together support the argument that they were, in some form, connected to social practice.' However, even this assertion is problematic and potentially misleading, given that there are no Anglo-Saxon secular penalties for same-sex behaviour, and calls for confession and penance by their very nature can only represent clerical attitudes. Thus Frantzen's statement is only true if one understands him to be saying that the penitentiary and other evidence supports the argument that the behaviour prohibited or complained of was actually taking place. It has no bearing on non-clerical attitudes to this behaviour, except to indicate that some people at least were not dissuaded from such behaviour by the penalties and prohibitions. Indeed, in a related area, Fulk points out the comparable disparity between lay and clerical attitudes to concubinage and remarriage (Fulk, 'Male Homoeroticism', p. 4). The following discussion therefore proceeds only tentatively from an analysis of the penitentiary material to conclusions about Anglo-Saxon life and practice.

The four Anglo-Saxon penitentials, found in a handful of eleventh-century manuscripts, are designated by Frantzen with the titles: *Scriftboc*, the *Old English Penitential*, the *Old English Handbook*, and the *Canons of Theodore*. Although

---

[14] Frantzen, 'Between the Lines'. For an introduction to the penitential literature, see Frantzen's *The Literature of Penance in Anglo-Saxon England*. New Brunswick: Rutgers University Press, 1983.
[15] Fulk, 'Male Homoeroticism'.   [16] Frantzen, 'Between the Lines', p. 270.

same-sex behaviour between women is barely mentioned, the penitentials do contain several canons pertaining to sex between men, particularly sex involving young boys.[17] It is clear that any form of same-sex activity is prohibited by the Anglo-Saxon Church, along with adultery, incest, masturbation, bestiality, and other forms of sexual behaviour outside the confines of marriage, or indeed non-procreative sex within marriage. Specific forms of sexual activity are often specified, such as kissing, mutual masturbation, fellatio, interfemoral and anal intercourse.[18] What is interesting, however, are the distinctions that some of the penitentials seem to draw between the types of person involved in same-sex acts, and the penalties allotted to them. For instance, consider the following canon from *Scriftboc*:

Lytel cniht gif he byð fram maran ofðrycced in hæmede, faste VII niht; gif he him geðafige, fæste XX nihta.

If a boy is forced into sex by a bigger one, he shall fast seven nights; if he consents to it, he shall fast twenty nights.[19]

Here, non-consensual sex is seen as a sin on the part of the boy whom we would today consider to have been raped. It is not possible to deduce from this that the older aggressor is not himself subject to penance, as Frantzen claims, since the previous canons could cover his case.[20] However, his conclusion from this and another comparable canon from the *Canons of Theodore* seems plausible, that the penance is not just designed to remove the pollution of sex from him, but rather that boys are also seen as accountable for the effects of their beauty on older men (just as female beauty is seen as dangerous and culpable in innumerable patristic and medieval religious texts).[21] The social assumptions behind another

---

[17] Frantzen calculates the relative percentages of canons that concern sex acts and those that concern same-sex acts and concludes that, although the Anglo-Saxon penitentials are 'comparable to Irish and early Anglo-Latin ones in the proportion of canons they devote to sexual regulation', nevertheless the Anglo-Saxon ones are 'less concerned with homosexual acts than the earlier documents', which indicates 'either tolerance of homosexual acts or lack of concern with them' ('Between the Lines', p. 269). This is interesting, if true, but the numbers with which Frantzen is working are not statistically significant enough to give such conclusions weight. On lesbianism in the Middle Ages, see the Introduction above, n. 44.

[18] For texts and translations of all the canons concerning same-sex acts, see Frantzen, *Before the Closet*, Appendices 1 and 2, pp. 175–80.

[19] Cited in Frantzen, 'Between the Lines', p. 274, from Robert Spindler, *Das altenglische Bussbuch (sog. Confessionale Pseudo-Egberti)*. Leipzig: Tauchnitz, 1934, VI 'De iuvenis,' 7a, p. 177. The version in *Before the Closet* (p. 178) incorrectly gives a penalty of five nights instead of seven. Translation mine.

[20] As Fulk also points out, making the excellent point that 'one would not expect the "active" partner's sin to be listed in the same clause as the "passive" one's, since they are different offences' ('Male Homoeroticism,' p. 9, n. 25).

[21] Frantzen indeed appositely cites modern rape trials where the victim has sometimes been blamed for provoking his or her assaulter. Compare the *Canons of Theodore*: 'Gyf he hit mid gehadedum men do .iii. feowertigo. oðða eal gear fæste' [If he does it [i.e. interfemoral intercourse] with a man in orders, (he is to fast) for the three forty-day periods or one year]; cited in Frantzen, 'Male Homoeroticism', p. 275. See also Chapter 10 below on Euphrosyne, where the provocative

set of canons are no longer accessible to us either, but here the interpretation of the canons is even more problematic, because they seem also to involve social categories for which the modern equivalents are unclear.

The canons form part of chapter 2 of the *Canons of Theodore* (on fornication) and I give the text and translation of both the Latin and the Old English below from Fulk's article, since he is in the process of preparing what will be the standard edition. The Old English translator makes several significant alterations to his Latin source, and I discuss the most important of these, mostly relying on Fulk's interpretation of the problematic Latin text, which updates Frantzen's discussion.[22]

The Latin text

2.2. Qui sepe cum masculo aut cum pecore fornicat X annos ut peniteret iudicavit.
2.3. Item aliud. Qui cum pecoribus coierit XV annos peniteat.
2.4. Qui coierit cum masculo post XX annum XV annos peniteat.
2.5. Si masculus cum masculo fornicat X ann. peniteat.
2.6. Sodomitae VII annos peniteant et molles sicut adultera.

2.2. If a male fornicates often with a male or with livestock (Theodore) prescribed that he should do penance ten years.
2.3. On the same subject another: whoever has copulated with livestock, let him do penance fifteen years.
2.4. Whoever has copulated with a male (*coierit*, i.e. penetrated him) after his twentieth year, let him do penance fifteen years.
2.5. If a male fornicates with a male (*fornicat*, no penetration implied), let him do penance ten years.
2.6. Let Sodomites do penance seven years and molles just as an adulteress.

My understanding of these canons is as follows:

2.2. gives Theodore's penance for habitual sex (not necessarily involving penetration) between adult men and bestiality; 2.3. points out that other codifiers give a harsher penance for bestiality; 2.4. can be interpreted in two ways: (a) as allocating a harsher penance if a man penetrates another adult man (over 20 years old), implying that penetration of boys or adolescents would be punished less harshly; or (b) as allocating a harsher penance if the penetrator is over 20 years old (which fits with the lighter penalties allotted elsewhere to boys); 2.5. seems just to repeat 2.2.

More problematic are the terms *sodomitae* and *molles* in 2.6., which Fulk assumes 'refer to the penetrator and the receptor in male same-sex anal

beauty of the saint (cross-dressed and thought to be a man) results in her/him being confined to solitary quarters, and Chapter 6 on the partial attribution of the blame for the Flood to female beauty in *Genesis A*.

[22] For fuller discussions of these canons, their Latin source and their possible contexts and interpretation, see Frantzen, 'Between the Lines', pp. 276–80, and Fulk, 'Male Homoeroticism,' pp. 8–12, 22–30.

intercourse' (p. 12). He thus thinks it 'pointless to attempt to reconcile the apparent incongruity between assigning fifteen years' penance for penetrating a male (canon 4) and seven years' penance for Sodomites (canon 6)'. However, since the penance for an adulteress is also seven years [14.14], it seems to me much simpler and more satisfactory to assume that the phrase *molles sicut adultera* is essentially a rephrasing of *Sodomitae VII annos peniteant*, and that both terms refer to the passive partner in this context. This is not to say that *molles* means exactly the same thing as *sodomitae*—Fulk gives persuasive evidence that *molles* often denotes specifically sexually passive males, and *sodomitae* can elsewhere refer to both active and passive partners collectively. Rather I think it unjustified to assume that this canon distinguishes active and passive partners. The identical lighter penance also argues against the interpretation of *sodomitae* as 'penetrator' and *molles* as 'receptive partner' and in favour of their joint differentiation from the *masculus* who penetrates.

Fulk agrees with Payer that 'in the penitentials the word *sodomita* in general denotes one who engages in same-sex (and not opposite-sex) anal intercourse' (p. 13). While this may be true, it does not follow that it denotes the active partner.[23] Moreover, it is perhaps a mistake to try to differentiate these terms too neatly and consistently. The word *molles*, particularly, is used in other contexts where its range of meanings includes masturbation,[24] and it seems likely that the reason we as modern scholars find these texts confusing and difficult to align with one another is that the original writers had different concepts of what exactly was covered by these terms, or indeed made less of a distinction between concepts we find it important to differentiate, such as same-sex behaviour, masturbation, sexual indulgence, gender inversion, hermaphroditism, and eunuchism. I shall return to this idea shortly, after considering the Old English version of this text.

The Old English text

[a] Se þe mid bædlinge hæme. oþþe mid oþrum wæpnedmen. oþþe mid nytene. fæste .X. winter.

[b] On oþre stowe hit cwyð. se þe mid nytene hæme. fæste .XV. winter. 7 sodomisce .VII. gear. fæston.

---

[23] We shall also see in Chapters 4 and 5 that Fulk is unjustified in associating the semantic broadening of 'the sin of Sodom' with the early modern period (p. 16). He is led to this conclusion because he gives only limited attention to the vernacular literature concerning Sodom. His comparison of the *Canones Gregorii* seems to me inapposite, since the text is clearly corrupt and does not make sense as it stands (p. 11 n. 33).

[24] As noted in Fulk, 'Male Homoeroticism', pp. 16, n. 46, 17, n. 48. Indeed, even *sodomy* and *sodomite* were used to refer to masturbation as late as the sixteenth century: G. W. Bernard, *The King's Reformation: Henry VIII and the Remaking of the English Church*. New Haven: Yale University Press, 2005, p. 258. Thanks to Greg Walker for this reference.

[c] Gif se bædling mid bædlinge hæme .X. winter bete. hi beoð hnesclice swa forlegene.[25]

Whoever has sex with a *bædling*, or with another male, or with livestock, let him fast ten years.

In another place it says, whoever copulates with livestock, let him fast fifteen years and Sodomites seven years.

If the *bædling* has sex with a *bædling*, let him make amends for ten years. They are soft, like an adulteress.

The key question in this set of canons, clearly, is what the term *bædling* means, and we are largely dependent on informed guesswork, since it appears only four times in the extant literature, in two glossaries and two penitential texts (both based on the Latin penitential of Theodore; the first of these texts is given above). The *Dictionary of Old English* defines it cautiously as '? effeminate man ? homosexual', although as we shall see this is perhaps not cautious enough.[26] In both glosses, the word seems to have associations of effeminacy, and these associations are supplemented by the probably cognate noun *bæddel* 'hermaphrodite', which again appears only twice in a glossary.[27]

Both Frantzen and Fulk provide very detailed analyses of the possible distinctions between the Old English terms *bædling* and *sodomisce* (and possibly *hnesclice*) here and their relation to the different terms used in the Latin text: *masculus*, *sodomitae*, and *molles*. However, it seems to me that these discussions do not take enough account of the distinct possibility that the Old English translator did not fully understand the meaning of the Latin terms or the distinctions between them. I would reconstruct the translator's rationale as follows: The first clause [a] translates the Latin canon 2.2., but introduces a distinction (discussed below) between *bædling* and *wæpnedmen* not in the original (which just has *masculus*); it also omits the adverbial modifier *sepe* 'often'. The second clause [b] translates 2.3., but adds the first clause from 2.6. The translator omits 2.4.,

---

[25] Fulk, 'Male Homoeroticism,' pp. 22–3. I have omitted the last clause of the canon because, as Frantzen and Fulk indicate, the meaning of both the Latin source and the Old English translation are extremely doubtful (it is likely, as Fulk suggests, that the translator has not understood his source); the clause does not contribute significantly to the argument.

[26] Healey, *Dictionary of Old English, s.v. bædling*. For the glosses, see William G. Stryker, ed., 'The Latin-Old English Glossary in MS. Cotton Cleopatra A. III' (unpub. doctoral thesis, Stanford University, 1951), pp. 28–367—'*effeminati, molles*—bædlingas'; Robert T. Oliphaunt, ed., *The Harley Latin-Old English Glossary* [British Library MS Harley 3376]. The Hague: Mouton, 1966, p. 56, l. 405—'Cariar. *bædling' on which, see Fulk, p. 21 n. 62.

[27] *Dictionary of Old English, s.v. bæddel*. L. Kindschi, 'The Latin-Old English Glossaries in Plantin-Moretus MS. 32 and British Museum MS. Additional 32246,' (unpublished doctoral thesis, Stanford University, 1955)—'*hermafroditus*—wæpenwifestre uel scritta uel bæddel,' pp. 111–89 and '*anareporesis .i. homo utriusque generis*—bæddel,' pp. 42–105; cf. Fulk, 'Male Homoeroticism', p. 26 n. 75 and the following note on why the derivation from the verb *bædan* is problematic. Fulk suggests his own etymology on p. 27, but this is at variance with the conclusion of Richard Coates that *bæddel* is 'an *-il-* derivative' of a putative Old English adjective **badde*: 'Middle English *badde* and Related Puzzles', *North-Western European Language Evolution* 11 (1988), 91–104 at 99. My thanks to Paul Cullen for this reference.

then [c] translates 2.5., substituting *bædling* for *masculus*, and adds his version of the second half of 2.6.

The simplest interpretation of these decisions seems to me to be that the translator did not understand or think important some of the distinctions of age or type of sexual activity drawn by the Latin writer, and thus sought to reduce the canons to what he saw as their salient points, reducing unnecessary repetition. Clause [a] gives a penance of ten years to a man who has sex with another man or with a *bædling* or with cattle. The translator thus thought that just to speak of sex with a man would not quite cover the possibilities. He rightly reads the Latin clause 2.3. as presenting an alternative harsher penance for bestiality, and clearly thinks that 2.6. also represents an alternative penance (and thus that it would be clearer and more efficient to present all the alternative penances in the same place). The second alternative penalty is a lighter penance for *sodomisce* 'sodomites'. It is unclear whether he understood *sodomitae* to be synonymous with *masculus* and thus that the penance was a true alternative to the one in [a] (i.e. that canons 2.2. and 2.6. were inconsistent), or whether he thought that 2.6. was intended to make a more precise distinction between types of men, which he attempted to render more efficiently in [a] with his own distinction between the *bædling* and the *wæpnedmen*. After the puzzling omission of Latin clause 2.4., [c] translates 2.5. in such as way as to turn it into a clarification that the *bædling* of [a] is also punished for same-sex activity, and interprets the second half of 2.6. not as concerning yet another separate type of person, the *molles*, but rather as a comment about the nature of the *bædling*: they are 'soft'.

What, then, does *bædling* mean? As already indicated, canon [b] seems to me not necessarily to present a further category of 'the sodomite'. The point of the canon's inclusion is to signal that there is a difference of opinion on the appropriate length of penance for the activities of bestiality and same-sex intercourse, and not to introduce another category of person; the variation (or inconsistency) in terminology need be nothing more than elegant variation. Nevertheless, it is clearly significant that the Old English translator thinks it important to construct a difference not present in the Latin source between the *bædling* and the *oþrum wæpnedmen*, but that difference is not easy to interpret.

Oþrum wæpnedmen means literally 'another weaponed-person, or male-person', and thus the clause could imply that both the *bædling* and the *wæp-nedman* are different types of man, in opposition to the category woman (the emphasis being 'Whoever has sex with a *bædling* or *another* male'), a possibility which we shall consider shortly as the more likely option. It is just possible, however, that the phrase could imply that the *bædling* represents a different category altogether from *bædling* (the emphasis thus becoming 'Whoever has sex with a *bædling* or with another *male* person'). This could then give us a trio of *wæpnedmon* 'male-person, or man', *wifmon* 'female-person, or woman', and *bædling*, neither man nor woman, but some indeterminate gender. In this context, it would chime well with *bæddel* 'hermaphrodite', and could perhaps represent another kind of indeterminacy analogous to that of eunuchs and similarly denoted by the kind of medical and physiognomic characteristics widely discussed in the later medieval period (though not including physical lack of a penis). However, this interpretation cannot be supported without further evidence, such as further textual connections with eunuchs or hermaphrodites, about neither of which we have much information (since presumably both were rare in Anglo-Saxon England).[28] It thus seems unnecessary at present to postulate a 'third gender' for Anglo-Saxon England.

Frantzen understands the difference between *bædling* and *wæpnedmon* differently—in fact he presents several interpretative options. First, he suggests that the distinction might distinguish between men who have sex only with women and men who have sex with men as well as women (p. 278). However, there is little evidence that the Anglo-Saxons distinguished people on the basis of the gender of their sexual object choice, and, more importantly, the content of the canon clearly implies that both *bædling* and *wæpnedmon* were engaging in same-sex activity. Second, then, Frantzen suggests the terms might differentiate active and passive partners in same-sex anal intercourse. However, he then immediately dismisses this possibility in favour of a further option which he favours, the explanation of which remains unclear to me, but seems to boil down to a distinction between the *bædling* and *wæpnedmon* on the one hand ('taken together', p. 279) and, on the other, the sodomite (whom he defines as a 'womanly' man, p. 280). He then, of course, cannot explain why the *bædling* and the *wæpnedmon* should be distinguished in this way, given that they receive the same penance (p. 281).

Fulk, by contrast, is attracted to the notion that *bædling* denotes 'the male receptor in anal intercourse' (p. 24), but points out that this would not explain why a penance is specified for a *bædling* who has sex with another *bædling*. His tentative suggestion that the phrase might refer to 'turn-taking in anal intercourse' does not hold water. As he concedes, it would render the canon 'superfluous, since the penalty for penetrating a man has already been given' (p. 25). It could possibly refer to male receptors who, in the absence of a penetrator, have

---

[28] As we shall see in Chapter 9, Ælfric uses the Latin term *eunuchus*, which he then qualifies, saying *þæt synd belisnode* 'that is castrated'. This indicates the lack of a native term equivalent to *eunuchus*, but not, of course, the lack of a concept of eunuchism. Fulk ('Male Homoeroticism,' pp. 30–2) briefly discusses the 'hermaphrodite' figure of the seventh- or eighth-century *Liber Monstrorum*, the description of which may represent an in-joke about the ubiquity of feminine men whose gender ambiguity even allows them to seduce other men. See also Boswell, *Christianity, Social Tolerance, and Homosexuality*, p. 185; Peter Clemoes, *Interactions of Thought and Language in Old English Poetry*. Cambridge Studies in Anglo-Saxon England, 12. Cambridge: Cambridge University Press, 1995, p. 37. Further research is necessary in these areas. It is well known for later periods that men such as John/Eleanor Rykener, the transvestite prostitute from London tried in 1394, were able to seduce many men without their partners realizing that they were in fact men; see Karras, *Sexuality in Medieval Europe*, p. 143. It was perhaps in some men's interests to maintain an indistinctness about gender.

recourse to non-penetrative intercourse, for instance, interfemoral intercourse. However, it seems likely that more is involved here than simply sexual acts.

I think, like Fulk, that it makes sense to see the *wæpnedmon* as a 'normal' male, from whom the *bædling* is distinguished. I would also agree that, although one of the major distinctions may have been that a *wæpnedmon* was the insertive, and the *bædling* the passive partner, nevertheless the latter term involves some form of cultural identity. However, rather than the etymological arguments Fulk adduces, I would return to the context of the Classical and Norse evidence given above, and the discussion of *earg* and its cognates. Moreover, I would argue we need to rethink the gender dynamic of these canons. Frantzen and (especially) Fulk do attempt to go beyond the binary male-female opposition that constitutes the popular construction of gender today, but it is possible to push this process further by invoking Laqueur's concept of the 'one-sex model' which Clover applies to medieval Scandinavia (discussed in the Introduction above).

If we assume that the Anglo-Saxons recognized a continuum of gender, of which 'manly man' is the positive pole, the *bædling* falls neatly into place as one of a variety of examples of 'not-men', including ('normal') women, children, and unmanly men. I would postulate that the category of unmanly man, as in medieval Scandinavia, might have included old men, disabled men, and the *bædling*, who is unmanly by virtue of his submission to (or indeed preference for) being anally penetrated by other men.[29] This is not to say that the Anglo-Saxons did not see the *bædling* as a physical man, but rather to draw a distinction between his biological status and his social status. Just like women and other not-men, the *bædling* is sexually passive. However, unlike other not-men, his sexual passivity is not a *result* of his age (as with a child), or his social status (like a slave or a woman), rather his active choice of sexual passivity is the *cause* of his inferior social status.

This remains merely informed conjecture in the absence of fuller evidence, and a single term which appears only four times is not much to go on.[30] However, the above hypothesis is I think reasonable, and would account for the Anglo-Saxon translator's difficulties in rendering the Latin canons. It does nevertheless leave several questions unanswered. We might ask whether the canons (which punish all forms of same-sex behaviour) conceal a secular social dynamic in which male sexual passivity was stigmatized, but where it was seen as natural for a man to engage in sex with any other person as long as he was the active partner (as Sørensen suggests for secular Scandinavia, and as is the case in several modern

[29] Frantzen seems to reach for this notion when he suggests that the sodomite is compared to the adulteress because, just as the latter betrays a (marriage) contract (between a husband and his wife, or her father), so the sodomite betrays the (homo)social contract between manly men (p. 280).

[30] The *Encyclopedia of Homosexuality* states that OE *dyrling* has a specific sense of 'a minion, a youth favoured because of his sexual attractiveness' (I, p. 60). However, I have been unable to find a text with this sense. Given that the term is most commonly found in the religious collocations *Godes dyrling, Cristes dyrling*, it is clearly not analogous to *bædling*.

societies). There is the thorny issue of how this postulated social gender dynamic fits with the Church's attitudes to gender, and whether the Church's teachings modified societal attitudes over time. This matter is difficult to evaluate because the vast majority of our sources for the period stem from the Church itself.

It is important to emphasize that the evidence marshalled above from ethnographic sources and penitentials and from other linguistic evidence is not conclusive, either in isolation or cumulatively, but it is suggestive. It raises far-reaching issues of how gender and identity were perceived in the period and the way that men and women understood and represented their interactions in discourse. Several of the chapters that follow explore representations of male-male relations in literature in an effort to investigate these matters further. Before analysing the literature in more depth, however, it is important to explore more fully the vernacular discourse of Sodom and the Sodomites and the sin against nature, since the Old English material indicates that here, too, there is a conflict with the Latin texts. That, contrary to the assertions of Fulk and Brundage, the Anglo-Saxons did not primarily associate the story of Sodom with same-sex intercourse, rather same-sex acts were most often spoken about in religious discourse as part of a range of potential sins.

4

The Changing Face of Sodom, Part I: The Latin Tradition

The story of Sodom and Gomorrah has always fascinated and horrified its audiences, with its part shocking, part exotic account of visiting angels, attempted male rape, miraculous blindness, and a tense escape as divine fire and brimstone rains down upon the towns and their inhabitants until nothing remains but stinking, barren wasteland overlooked by the curious woman-turned-pillar of salt. However, the city of Sodom and its inhabitants are now so associated with homosexuality (or at least condemnations of homosexuality) in the popular imagination that it is sometimes difficult to credit that same-sex acts were never their primary association before the writings of Philo of Alexandria in the first century AD. Before this, the 'sin of Sodom', if there was thought to be any one specific sin, was deemed to be that of inhospitality, following biblical precedent.

This chapter, which forms a pair with the one following, shows that even after Philo, religious writers (including Anglo-Saxon clerics) associate Sodom with a range of sins, and not just same-sex acts. After a brief overview of the references to Sodom in biblical texts and Philo's treatment of the city, and a summary of its associations for the major patristic writers, the chapter discusses Sodom as it appears in Latin texts composed in or for Anglo-Saxon England by Bede, Aldhelm, Boniface, and Alcuin, focusing particularly on the latter's *Interrogationes Sigewulfi in Genesin* and the Old English translation of it produced by Ælfric. It shows that the mixed associations characteristic of the patristic tradition are reflected in the Latin tradition of Anglo-Saxon England. The following chapter explores the vernacular references to Sodom and the Sodomites. Anyone discussing these vernacular and Latin texts is deeply indebted to Allen Frantzen's *Before the Closet*, and some of what follows covers the same ground as his chapter on 'The Shadow of Sodom'. However, Frantzen's agenda of positioning same-sex desire as a 'shadow' in Anglo-Saxon England means that he does not fully consider the implications of his findings, nor is his analysis as comprehensive as that in the present and the following chapter. The evidence below indicates that most Anglo-Saxon writers do not associate Sodom exclusively (or even at all in many cases) with same-sex activity, and that furthermore the explicit associations are almost all in texts aimed at an (at least partly) educated in-house religious audience, and not in texts designed for a lay audience. By an unprecedented systematic analysis of all the vernacular references to Sodom, combined with a linguistic study of the phrase *ongean gecynd* 'against nature', the present study is able to make important modifications to current critical views of early medieval religious attitudes to sexual issues.

BIBLICAL REFERENCES TO SODOM

Genesis aside, there are a dozen or so allusions to Sodom in the Old Testament, none of which associate the Sodomites with same-sex activity. Rather, Sodom is a prime example of haughty or great sin, or of God's destruction of the wicked.[1] Indeed, the prophet Ezekiel speaks of the sin of Sodom as follows:

Behold, this was the iniquity of Sodom thy sister, pride, fulness of bread and abundance, and the idleness of her and of her daughters: and they did not put forth their hand to the needy and to the poor.   (16: 49)[2]

What is more, God is reported as telling Israel that 'thy sister Sodom herself and her daughters have not done as thou hast done and thy daughters' (16: 48).

   The New Testament emphasis is slightly different, although Sodom is again primarily an example of harsh and swift destruction of the unrepentant.[3] Nevertheless, Christ himself alludes to Sodom in the context of inhospitality, when he tells his disciples to shake the dust off their feet if anyone does not welcome them or listen to their message:

Amen, I say to you, it shall be more tolerable for the land of Sodom and Gomorrah in the day of judgment than for that city.   (Matthew 10: 15; cf. Luke 10: 12)

The only biblical allusion to Sodom which might seem to associate it with same-sex activity is the letter of Jude warning Christians against false teachers and assuring them of their punishment. Jude reminds them of how God saved Israel from Egypt, yet still destroyed those who did not trust in him, then goes on to speak of how 'the angels who kept not their principality but forsook their own habitation, he hath reserved under darkness in everlasting chains, unto the judgment of the great day' (v. 6). This verse is generally agreed to allude to an obscure passage in Genesis 6, where we are told that 'the sons of God' married 'the daughters of men' (v. 2) and had children by them who were the 'giants'

---

[1] For the main texts, see: Deuteronomy 29: 32, 32: 32; Psalm 11: 6, 107: 33–4; Isaiah 1: 9, 3: 9, 13: 19; Jeremiah 23: 14, 49: 18, 50: 40; Lamentations 4: 6; Ezekiel 16: 46–50, 53–8; Amos 4: 11; Zephaniah 2: 9. See also the book of Wisdom 10: 6–8 (regarded by medieval Christians as deutero-canonical).

[2] All biblical quotations are taken from the Douay-Rheims translation of the Vulgate, which approximates to the text which Anglo-Saxon clerics would have used. *The Holy Bible: Douay Version. Translated from the Latin Vulgate (Douay, A.D. 1609: Rheims, A.D. 1582)*. London: Catholic Truth Society, 1956.

[3] See Matthew 11: 23–4; Luke 17: 28–30; Romans 9: 29 (quoting Isaiah 1: 9); 2 Peter 2: 6–8.

or heroes of old (Hebrew *Nephilim*, v. 4). This is immediately followed by the account of the Flood, where we are told that God saw that 'the wickedness of man was great on the earth' (v. 5) and decides to destroy all but Noah. After this allusion, Jude then remarks:

As Sodom and Gomorrah and the neighbouring cities, in like manner, having given themselves to fornication and going after other flesh, were made an example, suffering the punishment of eternal fire.

Modern renderings often make this appear to be a reference to unnatural same-sex activity. However, the translation here represents the Vulgate's more literal rendering *abeuntes post carnem alteram* 'going after other flesh'.[4] It seems to be the fact that the strangers were angels, not men, that is of interest to Jude here.[5]

    This biblical tendency not to associate Sodom primarily with same-sex activity is followed by the interpretations found in the rabbinical tradition, as is made clear by Richard Kay's learned book on the sodomites of Dante's *Inferno* canto XV, which comprehensively considers the references to and interpretation of Sodom in the biblical, rabbinical, and patristic traditions.[6] It is in the works of Philo of Alexandria (20 BC to AD 40), therefore, that the Sodomites first come to be primarily associated with same-sex activity.

PHILO AND THE ASSOCIATION OF SODOM WITH SAME-SEX DESIRE

In his commentary 'On Abraham', sections XXVI and XXVII, Philo characterizes the Sodomites at length as men corrupted by 'goods in excess', establishing a link between gluttony and fornication which remained popular throughout the Middle Ages:

Incapable of bearing such satiety, plunging like cattle, they threw off from their necks the law of nature and applied themselves to deep drinking of strong liquor and dainty feeding and forbidden forms of intercourse.[7]

Philo tells us that they were so maddened with lust for women that they did not restrict themselves to adultery 'but also men mounted males without respect for

---

[4] See *The Jerusalem Bible*, ed. Alexander Jones. Standard Edition. London: Dartman, Longman & Todd, 1966, 'The New Testament', p. 423 and footnote. Romans 9: 29 (quoting Isaiah 1: 9); 2 Peter 2: 6–8.

[5] See below, p. 83, on the association of the Flood with the destruction of Sodom, and religious commentaries on Genesis 6 which depart from Jude and the apocryphal tradition in interpreting the 'Sons of God' as the descendants of Seth, rather than angels. The book of Jude is one of the many biblical books for which there is no Old English translation, but it might, of course, still have influenced learned audiences.

[6] See Richard Kay, *Dante's Swift and Strong: Essays on Inferno XV*. Lawrence: Regents Press of Kansas, 1978, chapters 8 and 9.

[7] Philo, 'On Abraham', p. 70.

the sex nature which the active partner shares with the passive', that is, he sees the same-sex acts as being originally motivated by excessive lust for women, which resulted in other men being forced to play the role of women, as he goes on to elaborate:

Then, as little by little they accustomed those who were by nature men to submit to play the part of women, they saddled them with the formidable curse of a female disease. For not only did they emasculate their bodies by luxury and voluptuousness but they worked a further degeneration in their souls and, as far as in them lay, were corrupting the whole of mankind.

Same-sex desire here, then, develops from a make-shift arrangement into a habituated perversion. Philo then refigures the destruction of Sodom as an act of 'pity for mankind' by God, who, seeing its future threatened by this sterile practice, 'gave increase in the greatest possible degree to the unions which men and women naturally make for begetting children, but abominated and extinguished this unnatural and forbidden intercourse'. An enthusiastically descriptive account of the destruction follows, concluded by an emphasis on the lasting results for the earth, since the fire 'destroyed its inherent life-power and reduced it to complete sterility to prevent it from ever bearing fruit and herbage at all. And to this day it goes on burning, for the fire of the thunderbolt is never quenched, but either continues its ravages or else smoulders.' And Philo goes on to cite as proof of the former prosperity of the country, the survival of one of the cities, surrounded by rich and fertile land.

There are two reasons for quoting Philo's account at such length. First, it was deeply influential on later writers such as Augustine and Orosius, who were in turn influential in the Anglo-Saxon period (see below, Chapter 5, pp. 96–7). Second, it makes clear just how bound up same-sex acts are with discourses of gender, nature, excess, and procreativity—for later writers' views on these subjects affect the context and the way in which they view same-sex activity. Despite Philo's clear emphasis on same-sex acts as the primary sin of the Sodomites, the picture we get from the patristic writings is much more mixed. Indeed, it is not until the end of the patristic period that the sin of Sodom is viewed as primarily sexual in nature, and even then it is not seen as exclusively to do with same-sex relations.

SODOM IN THE PATRISTIC WRITINGS: JEROME, AMBROSE, AUGUSTINE, GREGORY

Mark Jordan provides a very clear overview of the patristic situation through an account of the main comments of the four most influential Church Fathers: Jerome, Ambrose, Augustine, and Gregory the Great, all of whom were used by Anglo-Saxon religious writers. His book *The Invention of Sodomy in Christian*

Theology (1997) is mostly concerned with the period after the twelfth century, where we see the formulation and proliferation of the abstract discourse of sodomy and the 'sin against nature'.[8] Even at this point, however, same-sex activity is not the entire issue. Rather, *sodomia* is used as a term which variously embraces all sorts of sexual acts which cannot lead to procreation, just as the *peccatum contra naturam* in the later period (even in the *Summa* of Thomas Aquinas) does not equate with same-sex anal intercourse. Instead it forms a subcategory of the sin of *luxuria* (uneasily definable as lust, lechery, luxury), and is itself split into subgroups: *ratione generis* 'by reason of species' (that is, bestiality), *ratione sexus* 'by reason of sex' (that is, same-sex acts), and *ratione modi* 'by reason of manner' (that is, using any orifice or engaging in any type of sexual activity which excludes procreation).[9] What Jordan shows very clearly about the early period, however, is that 'patristic exegetes writing in Latin ... continue to speak of the inhospitality of Sodom, of its pride and arrogance, even as they speak of its association with forbidden sex' (p. 32).[10]

Jerome (*c.*347–420), for instance, claims: 'The Sodomitic sin is pride, bloatedness, the abundance of all things, leisure and delicacies.' He also associates the Sodomites with brazen sin, comparing them to princes who 'publicly proclaim [their sin] without having any shame in blaspheming'.[11] In his commentary on Genesis, he is uninterested in the Sodom narrative, commenting only that, since Lot's daughters are said to be virgins, they must only be betrothed to Lot's 'sons-in-law'.[12] Neither is there any primary link to same-sex activity in Ambrose (*c.*340–97), who according to Jordan 'identifies Sodom straightforwardly with fleshly indulgence and lasciviousness'; the Sodomites' sin is thus that of *luxuria* (p. 34).

---

[8] Mark D. Jordan, *The Invention of Sodomy in Christian Theology*. Chicago: University of Chicago Press, 1997; cf. p. 36, where he states that the first use of *sodomy* as an abstract noun is found in two Continental manuscripts of the tenth century. On sodomy in the later medieval period, see also William E. Burgwinkle, *Sodomy, Masculinity, and Law in Medieval Literature: France and England, 1050–1230*. Cambridge: Cambridge University Press, 2004.

[9] See Warren Johansson and William A. Percy, 'Homosexuality', in Bullough and Brundage, *Handbook of Medieval Sexuality*, pp. 155–89, at p. 156. This account simplifies slightly; cf. Thomas Aquinas, *Summa Theologiae: Latin Text and English Translation, Introductions, Notes, Appendices, and Glossaries*, trans. Thomas Gilby et al. 61 vols. London: Eyre & Spottiswoode, 1964–80. Second Part of the Second Part, Question 154 'Of the Parts of Lust', Article 11 'Of the Sin against Nature'. On Aquinas and homosexuality, see further, Jordan, *Invention of Sodomy*, ch. 7; Gareth Moore, 'Aquinas, Natural Law and Sexual Natures', ch. 7 in his *A Question of Truth: Christianity and Homosexuality*. London: Continuum, 2003.

[10] It is interesting in this context that the early Christians were suspected of 'cannibalism, sodomy, and promiscuity'; cf. *The First and Second Apologies. St. Justin Martyr*, trans. Leslie William Barnard. Ancient Christian Writers, 56. New York: Paulist Press, 1997, p. 195, n. 66.

[11] Jerome, *Commentaria in Hiezechielem* 5.16.48–51; *Commentaria in Esaiam* 2.3.8–9; translation in Jordan, *Invention of Sodomy*, p. 33. There is no full published translation of the commentaries.

[12] *Saint Jerome's Hebrew Questions on Genesis*, trans. C. T. R. Hayward. Oxford: Clarendon Press, 1995, p. 51.

Augustine (354–430) does explicitly identify Sodom with same-sex activity in his major work *The City of God*, stating clearly that it was destroyed as an 'ungodly city . . . For it was a place where sexual intercourse between males (*stupra in masculos*) had become so commonplace that it received the licence usually extended by law to other practices.'[13] Elsewhere, however, Sodom features more often as a symbol of human depravity more generally, and, as Jordan states, although same-sex desire is acknowledged in Augustine's work, it 'is a symptom of the madness of their fleshly appetites . . . The root sin of the Sodomites is not the desire for same-sex copulation. It is rather the violent eruption of disordered desire itself.'[14]

Finally, the attitude of Gregory the Great (*c.*540–604) is similar to that of Ambrose. In his influential *Moralia in Job*, Jordan notes that where Sodom is concerned Gregory's 'first thought is of sexual sin, not of pride or inhospitality' (p. 35). It is true that Gregory talks of *scelera carnis* 'carnal wickednesses' and *peruersa desideria ex fetore carnis* 'bad desires in the ill savour of the flesh'.[15] However, what Jordan does not draw out is that Gregory never states that these desires are same-sex in nature. Similarly, in his *Pastoral Care*, Gregory says that 'To flee from burning Sodom is to shun the sinful fires of the flesh' (cf. Jordan, p. 36), but he does not restrict this moral to same-sex activity.[16] On the contrary, in context, the chapter containing this statement is titled 'How to admonish the married and the celibate' and is concerned to encourage the unmarried to remain chaste and the married to indulge in intercourse only 'for the purpose of procreation'; Sodom for Gregory here stands for those married Christians who fail to 'shun falling into grievous sins'.[17] Sodom is certainly beginning to be associated primarily with sexual sin in the later patristic writings, but it is not same-sex sin but all forms of sexual immoderation and incontinence which are at issue.[18]

This picture of mixed associations we get from the most influential patristic writers is reflected in the extant references to Sodom and the Sodomites in Latin texts written in or for Anglo-Saxon England. It is clear that, although some writers clearly do link them with same-sex acts, others associate Sodom with both same-sex and other-sex sexual licence, or with other non-sexual sins.

---

[13] Augustine, *De civitate Dei* Bk. XVI, ch. 30; translated in *Augustine. The City of God against the Pagans*, ed. and trans. R. W. Dyson. Cambridge: Cambridge University Press, 1998, p. 743.

[14] See further his fuller discussion, *Invention of Sodomy*, pp. 34–5.

[15] Gregory of Great, *Moralia in Job* Bk. XIV, ch. 23; translated in *Morals on the Book of Job, By S. Gregory the Great, the First Pope of that Name*. 3 vols. Oxford: John Henry Parker, 1845, II, pp. 130–1. See also XIX. 46 and VI. 38.

[16] Gregory the Great, *Regula pastoralis* Pt. III, ch. 27; translated in *St. Gregory the Great. Pastoral Care*, trans. Henry Davis. London: Longmans, Green & Co., 1950, p. 189.

[17] Davis, *Pastoral Care*, pp. 189–90.

[18] For a more detailed discussion of the patristic texts, see Kay, *Dante's Swift and Strong*, chs 8 and 9.

SODOM IN MEDIEVAL LATIN TEXTS COMPOSED IN OR FOR ANGLO-SAXON ENGLAND

Bede (*c.*672–735)

Bede presents a prime example of this mixed picture in his commentary on Genesis, *In principium Genesis*.[19] He is explicit that the Sodomites 'practised the shameful act of men on men' (*masculi in masculo turpitudinem*) in his commentary on Genesis 19: 4, which earlier in his comment on Genesis 13: 13 he merely refers to as 'that unspeakable [sin]' (*illo infando*). There he emphasizes rather the interpretation of the sins of Sodom given in Ezekiel 16: 49, which he quotes. However, he then goes on to contrast the Sodomites with Lot, who 'received the angels with hospitality and was seized by them from the impious infatuation of the Sodomites'.[20] As Kay makes clear, Bede's horror at the Sodomites' behaviour is directed less at its same-sex nature *per se* than the facts that they practised their sin openly with no thought of modesty and attempted to force guests and strangers to participate in their activities (p. 231). Overall, then, Bede's perception of the Sodomites is poised between associations of inhospitality and unspeakable same-sex sin, made worse by its defiant character. We find a similar dynamic at work in the writings of Aldhelm and Boniface, neither of whom associates Sodom with same-sex activity exclusively.

Aldhelm (*c.*639–709)

Frantzen quotes Aldhelm in his poetic *De virginitate* as referring to the Sodomites in the following way: 'scortatores et molles sorde cenidos [cinaedus] qui Sodomae facinus patrabant more nefando' which he translates as 'harlots and molles [effeminate men] who were performing the act of Sodom in an unspeakable way'.[21] It thus appears to be clear that the Sodomites were engaging in same-sex intercourse. However, we have already discussed the difficulties with the term *molles* (Chapter 3 above) and, even if *cenidos* represents a form of Latin *cinaedus* as Frantzen plausibly suggests, it is still far from clear that Aldhelm understood

---

[19] Also known as the *Libri Quatuor in Principium Genesis*, this work is addressed to Bishop Acca of Hexham, in response to a request from him in AD 708, but is directed to 'a broad audience of professional churchmen' who had some Latin but who lacked Bede's facility with the patristic writings (see Roger Ray, 'What do we Know about Bede's Commentaries?' *Recherches de théologie ancienne et médiévale* 49 (1982), 5–20, at 11). Much work remains to be done on Bede's exegetical commentaries. The commentary on Genesis is edited by Charles W. Jones in *Bedæ Venerabilis Opera. Pars 2, Opera Exegetica*. CCSL, 118–21. Turnhout: Brepols, 1960–83, vol. I, *Libri quatuor in principium Genesis usque ad nativitatem Isaac et eiectionem Ismahelis adnotationum*. Jones divides Book I from the rest as an earlier work, comprising a simplified presentation of patristic acccounts of Creation, particularly Augustine's. Books II to IV are 'mature, personal, and homiletic' (Charles W. Jones, 'Some Introductory Remarks on Bede's Commentary on Genesis', *Sacris Erudiri* 19 (1969–70), 115–98, at 115.

[20] Quoted in Frantzen, *Before the Closet*, p. 194.   [21] Ibid., p. 197.

this term to denote a man who prefers being the receptive partner.[22] It does seem overwhelmingly likely that same-sex intercourse is included in this scenario, but it is not the only or even the primary sin of which the Sodomites are guilty, as the full context of the quotation above shows. After an indictment of Gluttony, Aldhelm continues, in the translation of Lapidge and Rosier:

> Drunkenness usually weakens the soul of men: for the begetter and ruler of the world after the Flood [i.e. Noah]—when the waters punished the human race with their billows—planted a vine with leafy shoot in the ditches, and drinking the nectar he shamefully exposed his private parts ... Did not Lot also, who lived generously among wicked men and as a host offered the shaded comfort of a couch and gave abundantly the comfort of food to all, when dark thunderbolts with sulphuric flashes set afire the fornicators and sodomites, softened by baseness, who were committing vile deeds of Sodom in a heinous fashion—did not he, the father, drunk, know his grown daughters in debauchery? Unknowingly he wandered into their chambers; yet he would never have done this deed, unspeakable in its perversity—unless drunk with wine, he would not have known the rights of their beds.[23]

Aldhelm clearly sees 'the vile deeds of Sodom' as including both other-sex and same-sex acts, which come under the broader heading of sins of *luxuria* along with Lot's incest, all of which are inextricably associated with sins of greed and drunkenness.

In his complementary prose *De virginitate*, Aldhelm makes no mention of Sodom or Sodomites in his extended condemnation of the vain and, one might think, effeminate 'glamorization' which he discerns in 'those of both sexes' within monasteries.[24] When he does discuss Sodom explicitly, it is merely part of a discussion of Melchisedech as a prefiguration of Christ:

> Melchisedech went out to meet the patriarch [i.e. Abraham] with his three hundred and eighteen servants bringing back his famous booty, and—after an enormous slaughter of people—bringing home the numerous spoils of the Sodomites, together with his cousin [i.e. Lot] ... [25]

The one other allusion to Sodom is in fact to Lot's wife, as an example of what happens to those who look back from the service of Christ, but the context at first reading seems suggestive, so it is worth exploring in more detail. It occurs in

---

[22] It is even less clear what his audience would have understood by these terms—many might well have understood *molles* to mean 'effeminate men', but this could be connected either to same-sex activity, or to an unmanly because immoderate interest in sex with women, or to an overly sensual self-indulgence (cf. Chapter 3 above). On the far from static understanding of *cinaedus* in the Classical period itself, the interpretation of which is presently very controversial in Classical studies, see initially Halperin, *How to Do the History of Homosexuality*, pp. 32–8.

[23] *Aldhelm: The Poetic Works*, trans. Michael Lapidge and James L. Rosier. Cambridge: Brewer, 1985, p. 158. For the Latin original, see *Aldhelmi Opera*, ed. Rudolf Ehwald. MGH Auctorum Antiquissimorum, XV. Berlin: Weidmann, 1919 (subsequently referred to as Ehwald), at p. 45.

[24] *Aldhelm: The Prose Works*, trans. Michael Lapidge and Michael Herren. Cambridge: Brewer, 1979, ch. LVIII, pp. 127–8; Ehwald, pp. 317–18.

[25] ibid., ch. LIV, p. 123; Ehwald, p. 313.

chapter XXXI, and concerns the martyr Malchus, who, having lost fervour for the monastic life was about to leave to look after his family when

he was captured by Saracen pirates and Ishmaelite robbers who were ravaging violently whatsoever was in their way, so that he was commanded to serve as a submissive slave, by a very appropriate turn of events, seeing that he who was seeking a forbidden journey homewards, was in bondage as a base slave, and he who in no way feared that loss of the woman perishing at Sodom, suffered painfully the handicap of a protracted slavery and the loathsome servitude of a master. And, while, glancing backwards, he was guiding the handle of the plough without care, the harrow pointlessly shattered among the sods of the furrowed earth; and, when, in the same place, he was forced at the point of a sword into abandoning the glories of the chastity he longed for—which he had preserved in his native land—he preferred to die transfixed cruelly by the sword rather than to defend his life by profaning the laws of chastity, fearing in no way the danger to his soul if the status of his virginity were preserved intact.   (p. 91; Ehwald, p. 270.)

In the context of this enslavement by violent pirates, one might well wonder whether Aldhelm's allusion to 'the woman perishing at Sodom' is not a hint that he thinks Malchus's degradation might well have been partly sexual. Nevertheless, if so, it is only a hint, for there is no such sense in the fuller account by Jerome, where it is also clear that the second part of the passage refers not to threatened male rape by his captors, but to a separate incident where his owner tries to force him to marry a fellow slave-woman.

Like Bede, then, Aldhelm does not associate Sodom exclusively with same-sex desire.

Boniface (*c.*672–754)

Boniface in a letter written around 746 to King Ethelbald of Mercia is often deemed to have criticized the English people for homosexuality, thus implying that it was widespread.[26] The passage in question reads:

If the English people, as is reported here and as is charged against us in France and Italy and even by the wanton heathens themselves, are scorning lawful marriage and living in wanton adultery like the people of Sodom, then we must expect that a degenerate and degraded people with unbridled desires will be produced.[27]

[26] See Greenberg, *Construction*, p. 250; Derrick Sherwin Bailey, *Homosexuality and the Western Christian Tradition*. London: Longmans, Green, 1955, p. 110, and Peter Coleman, *Christian Attitudes to Homosexuality*. London: SPCK, 1980, p. 131.

[27] 'Si enim gens Anglorum—sicut per istas provincias devulgatum est et nobis in Francia et in Italia inproperatur, et ab ipsis paganis inproperium est—spretis legalibus conubiis, adulterando et luxoriando ad instar Sodomitanæ gentis fœdam vitam vixerit, de tali commixtione meretricum, æstimandum est, degeneres populos et ignobiles et furentes libidine fore procreandos.' Translation by Ephraim Emerton, *The Letters of Saint Boniface*. New York: Octagon Books, 1973 (subsequently Emerton), LVII [73], p. 128; cf. Frantzen, *Before the Closet*, p. 197. For the Latin text, see Arthur West Haddan and William Stubbs, eds, *Councils and Ecclesiastical Documents Relating to Great Britain Ireland*. 3 vols. Oxford: Clarendon Press, 1869–78, III, pp. 350–6, at p. 354.

In Frantzen's discussion of this passage, he goes both too far and not far enough when he agrees with Boswell that there is no hint here of same-sex acts, stating rather that this refers only to adultery and lust, which must be primarily other-sex oriented because they are procreative, even if they only produce 'degenerate and degraded people'.[28] It is far from clear that *physical* offspring is what is implied by the final clause. Moreover, although it is indeed possible to see the phrase 'living in wanton adultery like the people of Sodom' as simply a restatement of 'scorning lawful marriage', it is equally possible that it means the people are giving up other-sex unions in favour of same-sex unions, or at least having unlawful sex with both men and women, and that the final phrase is metaphorical, implying that the people will become more and more corrupt. Nevertheless, if one reads the whole letter from which this extract is taken, the overwhelming probability is that the passage forms part of an extended condemnation of male-female adultery involving nuns.

The letter starts by praising Ethelbald's prowess in almsgiving but criticizing his failure to take a lawful wife and hoping that the rumours are false that he has committed the 'crime of adulterous lust' (Emerton, pp. 125–6). However, the focus then widens to report that 'these atrocious crimes are committed in convents with holy nuns and virgins consecrated to God' (p. 126), the defilement of whom is seen as even worse than ordinary adultery, since it entails defiling the brides of Christ. Boniface goes on to stress the serious nature of this sin, then to beg the king to amend his life. He follows this plea with the example of the pagans who 'punish fornicators and adulterers' (p. 127), giving a rather lurid instance of harsh punishment for adultery from Old Saxony. Boniface then repeats his plea for Ethelbald to repent and adds that 'It is time for you to have mercy upon the multitude of your people who are perishing by following the example of a sinful prince and are falling into the abyss of death' (p. 128). It is then that the passage with which we are concerned appears, followed by a comparison with the peoples of Spain, Provence, and Burgundy who 'turned thus away from God and lived in harlotry'. Boniface continues that the sin of murder is involved 'in this crime', saying that 'when those harlots, be they nuns or not, bring forth their offspring conceived in sin, they generally kill them' (p. 129). It thus seems abundantly clear that the general practice of excerpting the sentence on Sodom from its context has led scholars to misread its significance. Boniface is clearly not thinking at all here of same-sex acts, but rather associates Sodom with adultery, the sin for which he is rebuking King Ethelbald, and which is a recurrent concern in his letters, even amongst the clergy.[29]

What is most surprising in scholarly discussions of this letter, however, is that they ignore a second letter written in the same year by Boniface to Archbishop

---

[28] Frantzen, *Before the Closet*, p. 198; Boswell, *Christianity, Social Tolerance, and Homosexuality*, p. 20; Godden, 'The Trouble with Sodom', p. 99.
[29] See (in Emerton) nos XL [50], pp. 80–1; XLI [51], pp. 84, 86; LVIII [74], p. 131; cf. pp. 93, 109.

Egbert of York which confirms unequivocally the interpretation above (Emerton LIX [75], pp. 132–3). In the letter, Boniface reminds Egbert that he sent the 'letter of exhortation and admonition' to Ethelbald after submitting it to Egbert for correction. However, his other motivation was that if the Archbishop saw 'the roots of those evils' in his own people, he might be able to 'cut them down in time…and root them out completely, lest "their vine be of the vine of Sodom and of the fields of Gomorrah and their wine be the poison of dragons and the cruel venom of asps" '. One might expect this allusion to Deuteronomy 32: 32 to corroborate the interpretation that the Ethelbald letter concerns same-sex sin, were it not for the following paragraph which makes Boniface's intentions plain:

It is an evil unheard of in times past and, as servants of God here versed in the Scriptures say, three or four times worse than the corruption of Sodom, if a Christian people should turn against lawful marriage contrary to the practice of the whole world—nay, to the divine command—and should give itself over to incest, lust, and adultery, and the seduction of veiled and consecrated women.   (p. 133)

If Sodom is associated with same-sex acts at all here rather than adultery, which seems doubtful, then such acts are clearly considered to be much less serious than the male-female sexual sins Boniface enumerates.

There is in fact a reference to same-sex activity in Boniface's letter to Ethelbald (the only reference I have found in his writings), but it comes in a quotation of the Apostle Paul's First Letter to the Corinthians, chapter 6, verse 9. Boniface says that in the Apostle's

discourse and enumeration of sins he classes fornicators and adulterers together: 'Know ye not that the unrighteous shall not inherit the kingdom of God? Be not deceived: neither fornicators, nor idolaters, nor effeminate (*molles*), nor abusers of themselves with mankind (*masculorum concubitores*), nor thieves, nor covetous, nor drunkards, nor revilers, nor extortioners, shall inherit the kingdom of God.'   (p. 126)

Boniface moves immediately back to the topic of men 'found guilty of intercourse with a veiled nun consecrated to God'. Thus, although he would presumably have seen same-sex acts as sinful, he is not concerned with them here, nor does he seem to make any association at all between them and Sodom.

Alcuin (735–804)

Alcuin is a controversial figure in the context of same-sex relations. He has been claimed both as part of a homosexual clerical élite and also as a figure harshly condemnatory of same-sex acts. The former interpretation is that of John Boswell, who singles out homoerotic passages in his poetry and argues that he showed leniency toward homosexual sins.[30] Frantzen, on the other hand, criticizes Boswell for selective reading and points out that Alcuin warns that if a

---

[30] Boswell, *Christianity, Social Tolerance, and Homosexuality*, pp. 189–91 and 178, n. 31.

former student persists in the 'filthy practices of boys' his soul will 'burn in the flames of Sodom'.[31] However, although Boswell is wrong to suggest that Alcuin did not condemn same-sex activity, the evidence Frantzen adduces against his arguments is problematic and so the matter needs further discussion.

It is undeniable, on the one hand, that passages in some of Alcuin's writings display intense homosocial desire, even homoerotic imagery. Consider the following extract from a poem dedicated to Archbishop Arno of Salzburg:

> Love has penetrated my heart with its flame,
> And is ever rekindled with new warmth.
> Neither sea nor land, hills nor forest, nor even the Alps
> Can stand in its way or hinder it
> From always licking at your inmost parts, good father,
> Or from bathing your heart, my beloved, with tears.[32]

Nor is Alcuin's passion restricted to poetry. A series of letters written over the last decade of the eighth century to Arno, whom he nicknames 'the Eagle', exhibits similar feelings:

I treasure the memory of your loving friendship, holy father, longing that some day the desired time will come when I may put my longing arms around your neck. If only I could fly like Habbakuk, how quickly I would rush to embrace you and how eagerly I would kiss not only your eyes, ears and mouth but also each finger and toe not once but many times...

I wish my eagle [i.e. Arno] might fly to pray at St. Martin's, that I might there embrace his soft wings and hold him whom my soul loves, not letting him go till I bring him to my mother's house and he kisses me and we enjoy mutual love as ordained...

O if I could be spirited to you like Habbakuk! How I would fling my arms around your neck and hug you, sweet son! A whole summer day would not be too long for me to press breast to breast and lips to lips till I kissed each limb of your body in tender greeting.[33]

Nevertheless, Boswell's readings of such effusive outpourings as indicative of sexual desire have been strongly criticized. Frantzen cites Peter Dronke's placement of these letters in the 'venerable tradition of "Christian *amicitia*"' (Frantzen, *Before the Closet*, p. 198), and paraphrases with approval the following claim by Stephen Jaeger that: 'Alcuin pouvait déclarer son amour...de manière aussi directe précisément parce que plus le ton de l'expression était passionné, plus la relation était innocente' [Alcuin could declare his love in such a direct manner

---

[31] Frantzen, *Before the Closet*, p. 199.
[32] Alcuin, 'Pectus amor nostrum', in *Medieval Latin Love Poems of Male Love and Friendship*, trans. Thomas Stehling. New York: Garland, 1984, Latin text, p. 14; trans. p. 15.
[33] Translated in Stephen Allott, *Alcuin of York: His Life and Letters*. York: William Sessions, 1974; ed. by Philipp Jaffé as *Monumenta Alcuiniana*. Berlin: Weidmann, 1873. See Letters 135 (Jaffé 18); 140 (Jaffé 106); 143 (Jaffé 134); cf. 136 (Jaffé 168).

precisely because the more passionate the tone of expression, the more the relationship was innocent].[34]

However, Frantzen cites Jaeger out of context and in English paraphrase in order to allow him to go beyond Jaeger in making a straightforward separation between what is manifestly erotic language, on the one hand, and erotic feeling on the other. It seems perfectly reasonable to assume that Alcuin did not intend these passages to be understood as expressing a desire for sexual intercourse with Arno, and even that, in Jaeger's terms, the direct declaration of passionate love is predicated upon the social assumption that sexual acts between two celibate clerics are out of the question. Nevertheless, this does not equate to the absence of erotic desire, whether recognized as such or not, as indeed a fuller reading of Jaeger's work would show.[35]

It is not a matter of making a straightforward choice between Boswell's assertion of homosexuality and the view of Dronke and Frantzen that these texts express platonic friendship. It is simply not possible to say whether Alcuin's (or any other writer's) homosocial desires were the outward expression of personally recognized erotic feelings and whether those feelings were sexually expressed; nor is the question important or productive. It is perfectly possible for an individual to feel and to express homoerotic desires and yet be utterly opposed to, even repulsed by, their physical expression, just as it is possible for an individual to condemn same-sex acts and yet be homosexually active, or for that matter for an individual on the one hand to express either approval or disapproval of same-sex activity, or, on the other, to feel either arousal or disgust (or both) at the idea of same-sex contact, and yet in all these cases to refrain from such acts on the several grounds of conviction, fear, or lack of opportunity.

In this context, we might compare the following passage from the beginning of Aldhelm's prose *De virginitate*, where he makes an extended comparison of the nuns learning divine doctrine to male athletes at the gymnasium

> who eagerly win the crown of the laborious contest and the prize of the Olympic struggle by the strenuous energies of their own exertions; so that, let's say, one athlete, smeared with the ointment of some slippery liquid, strives dexterously with his partner to work out the strenuous routines of wrestlers, sweating with the sinuous writhings of their flanks in the burning centre of the wrestling-pit; another, taking the missiles of javelins and the shafts of arrows from the hidden recesses of his quiver... (ch. II, p. 60; Ehwald, p. 230)

This passage is as homoerotic as anything in Alcuin's writings, and yet, as we have already seen, Aldhelm strongly condemns both illicit same-sex and other-sex activity. There are, however, perhaps more productive questions to be asked

---

[34] C. Stephen Jaeger, 'L'Amour des rois: structure sociale d'une forme de sensibilité aristocratique', *Annales* 46 (1991), 547–71, cited in Frantzen, *Before the Closet*, pp. 199 and 340, n. 43; translation mine.

[35] See further the article cited above and his book *Ennobling Love: In Search of a Lost Sensitivity*. Philadelphia: University of Pennsylvania Press, 1999.

of authors than whether homoeroticism in their writing reflects their repressed physical desires.

There is, indeed, a productive question to be asked about whether Alcuin associates Sodom with same-sex practices, as both Frantzen and Boswell argue he does. They refer to a letter addressed to 'a dear son', in which Alcuin rebukes a former student for, according to Boswell, 'what appears to be a homosexual indiscretion' (Boswell, *Christianity, Social Tolerance, and Homosexuality*, p. 191):

What is this that I hear about you, my son, not from one person whispering in a corner but from crowds of people laughing at the story that you are still addicted to the filthy practices of boys and have never been willing to give up what you should never have done. Where is your fine education?[36]

On the one hand, Frantzen is right to criticize Boswell for his misleading omission of Alcuin's warning that the student's soul 'will burn in the flames of Sodom',[37] but on the other hand Boswell is right to point out that the fact that people are laughing at the story in public 'hardly suggests moral outrage on the part of those from whom he heard the story' (Boswell, p. 191). The key question which neither of them considers, however, is whether this letter really concerns persistence in same-sex activity. It is helpful to compare Alcuin's letter to a student he nicknames Dodo. This is a passionately tender missive, in which Alcuin even invokes Christ's words on marriage 'what God has joined, let not man separate' and applies them to his relationship with Dodo.[38] However, it is also an anxious letter, warning the recipient of the fires of hell which await him if he cannot curb the sins of desire:

Rebuke yourself instead and accept your father's entreaties, reflecting that you are always in the sight of God and the saints. Be ashamed to do before them what you shrink from doing before men, I know you believe that all will be judged: where do you think they are who did such things as the devil daily urges on you? You had the pleasures of the flesh yesterday—what remains of them today?

He goes on 'Why do you burn for what will make you burn for ever?' and invokes Ecclesiastes 11: 10 to state that 'Youth and pleasure are vanity. You have a boy's body but be a man in spirit.'[39]

[36] Allott, *Alcuin of York*, §127, p. 134.

[37] Frantzen, *Before the Closet*, p. 199. This is probably because Allott, from whom Boswell is presumably working, also omits this passage; cf. Frantzen, p. 340, n. 42.

[38] The same invocation is made in his epitaph for Paulinus of Aquileia and Arno of Salzburg (Stehling, *Medieval Latin Poems*, pp. 14–15). On Alcuin's invocation of Classical sources, including allusions which frame his love in terms of that of Nisus for Euryalus and Aeneas for Dido, see Peter Dale Scott, 'Alcuin's *Versus de Cuculo*: The Vision of Pastoral Friendship', *Studies in Philology* 62 (1965), 510–30.

[39] Letter 126 (65; 286), pp. 132–3. The marriage reference is omitted from Allott's translation, but see Adele M. Fiske, *Friends and Friendship in the Monastic Tradition*. CIDOC Cuaderno, 51. Cuernavaca, Mexico: Centro Intercultural de Documentacion, 1980, no. 8, p. 17.

It seems to me at least as likely that Alcuin is in both these texts euphemistically referring to the sin of masturbation, given the fact that this letter seems to imply that Dodo is alone when committing it, and that here and in the previous letter, he sees the sin as something one expects boys to indulge in, but which they are equally expected to grow out of.[40] It is possible that the sin is that of same-sex activity,[41] but it seems more likely that Frantzen has assumed that this is the sin concerned, partly because his interlocutor Boswell does and partly because he unwarily associates Sodom with same-sex acts rather than the more general indulgence of sexual desire.

There is, however, one text in which Alcuin is unequivocally clear that the Sodomites were punished for same-sex acts, and that is his *Interrogationes Sigewulfi in Genesin* (AD 792–6), a dialogue in which he answers Sigewulf's questions about various perplexing aspects of the biblical book of Genesis. Questions 179 to 191 deal with various aspects of the Sodom narrative, such as why three men visited Abraham but only two visited Lot (Q. 182), or why Lot's wife was turned to a pillar of salt (Q. 188). However, the relevant one for our purposes is Question 191: 'Why in the days of Noah were the sins of the world avenged with water, but those of the Sodomites were punished with fire?'[42] The response relates the opposition of water and fire to its binary opposition of sin with men and sin with women:

Because that natural sin of lust with women is condemned as if with the milder element: but this sin of lust against nature with men is punished with the sharper element of fire: and that earth cleansed with water grew green again; this one, consumed with flames, became dry with eternal barrenness.[43]

In the context of a binary opposition of deaths by sulphurous conflagration and drowning, 'milder' (*leviori*) is obviously a relative term. However, it is evident that sexual sins with women are thus seen as culpable but natural, whereas sexual sins with men are not only unnatural, but are also deserving of harsher punishment and their consequences are lasting, even eternal.

---

[40] Indeed, since masturbation is one of the sins associated with *molles* in Continental documents (Fulk, 'Male Homoeroticism', p. 16, n. 46), this should make us wary of assuming that any mention of *molles* automatically refers to men engaged in same-sex acts; cf. Chapter 3, n. 24 above.

[41] In which case the fact that Alcuin expects it of boys is interesting and might support the idea mentioned in Chapter 2 that pederasty may have been socially acceptable in some contexts because it did not disturb the gender dynamic.

[42] 'Quare diebus Noe peccatum mundi aqua ulciscitur, hoc vero Sodomitarum igne punitur?'; Alcuin's *Interrogationes et Responsiones in Genesin*, edited in *Patrologia Latina*, ed. J.-P. Migne. 221 vols. Paris: Migne, 1844–91 (hereafter cited as *PL* with volume and column number), C.515–66, at col. 543.

[43] 'Quia illud naturale libidinis cum feminis peccatum quasi leviori elemento damnatur: hoc vero contra naturam libidinis peccatum cum viris, acrioris elementi vindicatur incendio: et illic terra aquis abluta revirescit; hic flammis cremata aeterna sterilitate arescit.' (ibid.)

It is not certain whence Alcuin derived the idea of comparing the Flood and the destruction of Sodom.[44] Daniel Anlezark shows a widespread link between the Flood and the fiery destruction of the final Judgement, but makes no connection with Sodom other than to note the comparison in the *Interrogationes*, which he does not pursue.[45] However, there are some links between the two narratives in Ambrose's *De fuga saeculi* ('Flight from the World') of AD 381–4, in Chrysostom's 25th Homily on Genesis of *c*.385, in Jerome's *Adversus Jovinianum* ('Against Jovinianus') of AD 393, and in a poem by Cyprianus Gallus on Sodom of *c*.400, formerly attributed to Tertullian.[46] The sexual sin of the Sodomites and that of the 'sons of God' immediately preceding the Flood account are also compared in Jude verse 7, and the apocryphal Book of Naphtali 3: 4–5.[47] However, none of these works constructs the explicit opposition present in the Alcuin passage above, and we need perhaps look no further than Christ's description of the Second Coming in Luke 17, which he warns will be as unexpected as the destruction that came upon the people of Noah's time (vv. 26–7). He continues with a comparison to the destruction of Sodom:

Likewise as it came to pass in the days of Lot. They did eat and drink, they bought and sold, they planted and built.

And in the day that Lot went out of Sodom, it rained fire and brimstone from heaven and destroyed them all.

Even thus shall it be in the day when the Son of man shall be revealed.   (vv. 28–30)

[44] MacLean in his edition of the Old English version of the *Interrogationes*, which will be considered shortly, cites as Ælfric's additional sources for his version of this question Bede's commentary on Genesis, but the comparison of the Flood and Sodom's destruction is found in Alcuin alone.

[45] Daniel Anlezark, *Water and Fire: The Myth of the Flood in Anglo-Saxon England*. Manchester: Manchester University Press, 2006, pp. 39, 137, 156–7.

[46] Ambrose, *De fuga saeculi*, trans. Michael P. McHugh in *Saint Ambrose: Seven Exegetical Works*. Fathers of the Church, 65. Washington, DC: Catholic University of America Press, 1972—evil roams the world and 'was not sunk in that flood that encompassed the world, nor was it burned in the fire of Sodom', p. 311; Chrysostom, 25th Homily on Genesis, trans. Robert C. Hill in *Homilies on Genesis: Saint John Chrysostom*. Fathers of the Church, 74, 82, 87. Washington, DC: Catholic University of America Press, 1986–92, vol. II, p. 128; Jerome, *Adversus Jovinianum*, Bk. II, trans. W. H. Fremantle, in *The Principle Works of St. Jerome*. Select Library of Nicene and Post-Nicene Fathers, 2nd ser., vol. VI, Oxford: Parker, 1893, chs 15, 16, 18, and 22; Cyprianus Gallus, *De Sodoma*, trans. S. Thelwall as 'A Strain of Sodom' and attributed to Tertullian, in *Ante-Nicene Fathers: The Writings of the Fathers down to A.D. 325*, ed. Alexander Roberts and James Donaldson, rev. A. Cleveland Coxe. 10 vols. Peabody, MA: Hendrickson, 1994, vol. IV, (Tertullian) X. 2.

[47] See Jude 7; Book of Naphtali 3: 4–5 in *The Testaments of the Twelve Patriarchs*, trans. R. H. Charles. London: Adam and Charles Black, 1908, p. 141. There is also a comment in the First Apology of Justin Martyr, ch. 5 (second century AD), which seems to interpret the sons of God as 'evil demons' who 'both defiled women and corrupted boys' (Barnard, *First and Second Apologies. St. Justin Martyr*, ch. 5, p. 25. However, this passage is unconnected to his other references to sodomy (Apology I, ch. 28, p. 42; Apology II, ch. 12, p. 83), and his only mention of Sodom and Gomorrah (I, ch. 52) makes no references to same-sex acts, saying only that the Sodomites were 'ungodly people' (p. 60) and warning that similar sinfulness will result in destruction and a barren land (p. 61).) I am unaware of any evidence for the transmission of these texts in Anglo-Saxon England, and the dominant patristic interpretation emphasizes that the 'sons of God' are to be interpreted not as angels but as the sons of Seth; for example, Augustine, *De civitate Dei*, Bk. XV, ch. 23.

This is the passage upon which the later patristic comparisons are based, and Alcuin may well have drawn his own conclusions from this biblical juxtaposition of the two stories and the different elements used in the divine destruction of the sinful.[48] If elements of the comparison are indeed original to Alcuin, it becomes all the more interesting that an Old English translation of the *Interrogationes* of two centuries later makes certain key alterations to its source. This chapter has looked at a representative range of references to Sodom in Latin texts. With the exception of *Genesis A*—the Old English poetic version of Genesis, which receives extended treatment in Chapter 6—the following chapter investigates in detail all the extant references to Sodom in Old English texts, beginning with the Old English translation of Alcuin's *Interrogationes*.

---

[48] *De Sodoma* along with the beginning of its companion piece *De Iona* represents the closest parallel I have discovered to Alcuin's formulation, and, as we shall see below, the Ninevites are also sometimes compared with the Sodomites in Old English texts. Nevertheless, I have been unable to find any evidence that these poems were available to Alcuin, and the parallels are not exact.

5

The Changing Face of Sodom, Part II: The Vernacular Tradition

The Old English translation of Alcuin's text was produced by Ælfric of Eynsham (c.955–1010), one of the most prolific vernacular writers of the Anglo-Saxon period; it probably dates from around AD 1000 after he made his prose translation of Genesis. As well as cutting down the number of Alcuin's questions from 280 to 69, Ælfric makes some significant additions to his source, including a preface, creed, and doxology, along with material of his own invention or drawn from Bede and Isidore.[1] Sodom is discussed in Questions 66 and 67, towards the end of the work, just after a question about Abraham's extra-marital relationship, and just before one about the sacrifice of Isaac.[2] Ælfric's Question 66 reads as follows:

Hwæt gemænð þæt word þe God cwæð to Abrahame þe þam synfullum leodscipum þus: þæra Sodomitiscra hream astah up to heofenum?
Seo syn bið mid stemne þonne se gylt bið on dæde, and seo syn bið mid hreame þonne se man syngað freolice butan ælcere sceame, swilce he his yfel oþrum mannum bodige.   (p. 46)

What does that speech mean when God spoke to Abraham about the sinful people thus: the noise of the Sodomites has risen up to heaven?
The sin has a voice when the offence is in action, and the sin has a noise when the man sins freely without any shame, as if he announces his evil to other men.

This is a fairly close though not quite literal translation of Alcuin's first question about Sodom (Q. 179), and, like Jerome's comments, associates the Sodomites with flagrant and open sin. Ælfric then omits all of Alcuin's other questions on Sodom except the last one (Q. 191), quoted above:

Hwi wolde God þa ylcan Sodomitiscan mid byrnendum swæfle adydan & on Noes flode wurdon þa synfullan mid wætere gewitnode?

---

[1] *Ælfric's A-S version of Alcuini Interrogationes Sigewulfi in Genesin*, ed. G. E. MacLean in *Anglia* 6 (1883), 425–73 and *Anglia* 7 (1884), 1–59, at 425–6, 429, 471. On Ælfric, see further Chapter 9 below.

[2] MacLean notes that ending with the sacrifice of Isaac is an 'ancient division' of Old Testament history 'repeatedly used' by Ælfric, and that Bede by contrast ends with the weaning of Isaac (*Ælfric's A-S version*, p. 427, n. 1). The poem *Genesis A* also ends with the sacrifice (see further Chapter 6).

On Noes dagum gewitnode God manna galnysse mid wætere, mid liðran gesceafte, for
þan þe hi syngodan mid wifum, & þa Sodomitiscan syngodon bysmorlice ongean gecynd,
& wurdon forþi mid swæflenum fyre forswælede, þæt heora fule galnys wurde mid þam
fulan swæfle gewitnod. On Noes flode wæs seo eorðe afeormað & eft geedcucod, & on
þæra Sodomitiscra gewitnunge forbarn seo eorþe, & bið æfre unwæstmbære, & mid
fulum wætere ofergan. On Noes dagum cwæð God be þam synfullum, ne þurhwunað
min gast on þisrum mannum on ecnyssy, forþon þe hi synd flæsc. Se gast getacnað her
Godes yrre, swylce God cwæde, Nelle ic þis mennisc gehealdan to þam ecum witum,
forþam þe hi synd tyddre, ac ic wylle her on worulde him don edlean heora gedwyldes
[Alcuin, Q.97]. Nis na þus awriten be þam Sodomitiscan, þe ongean gecynd sceamlice
syngodon; forþan þe hi synd ecelice fordemede.   (p.48)

Why did God want to destroy these same Sodomites with burning sulphur, and in Noah's
Flood the sinful were punished with water?
In Noah's days God punished men's lust with water, with the milder element, because
they sinned with women, and the Sodomites sinned shamefully against nature, and were
therefore consumed with sulphurous fire, so that their foul lust was punished with the
foul sulphur. In Noah's Flood the earth was purged, and afterwards regenerated, and
in the Sodomites' punishment the earth burned up, and will be forever unfruitful, and
overspread with foul water.[3] In Noah's days God said about the sinful, 'my spirit will
not remain in these men in eternity, for they are flesh.' The spirit here signifies God's
anger, as if God said, 'I do not want to hold this race to eternal punishment, for they
are weak, but I will give them requital here in the world for their error'. It is not written
thus about the Sodomites, who shamefully sinned against nature, for they are eternally
condemned.

It is immediately obvious from a comparison that Ælfric has extended his
response to around twice the length of the Latin original, although overall he
decreases the *Interrogationes* to a quarter of their original length. He maintains
the opposition of the Flood and Sodom, on which subject Malcolm Godden
comments: 'It looks as if Ælfric was driven here by the need to polarize the Flood
against Sodom, to construct an illicit but pardonable heterosexuality as a contrast
to damnable homosexuality.'[4] However, the passage is not quite as simple as
this formulation implies. There is indeed an opposition of the drowning of the
sinful men of Noah's day and the fiery destruction of the Sodomites, but it is
significantly asymmetrical.

The sin of Noah's day is *manna galnysse* 'men's lust' and it involves sin *mid
wifum* 'with women'; the sin of the Sodomites is also *fule galnys* 'foul lust',
but where we might expect *mid werum* 'with men', we are instead told merely
that they sinned *bysmorlice ongean gecynd* 'shamefully against nature'. As we saw
above, Alcuin here explicitly distinguishes between the 'sin of lust' with women,
which is seen as somehow 'natural', and the 'sin of lust against nature with men',

---

[3] This is an expanded version of Alcuin, CXCI. Alcuin/Ælfric is drawing on Bede's *In Pent. PL*
XCI. 241; *Hexameron* IV. *PL* XCI. 178.
[4] Godden, 'The Trouble with Sodom', 102.

but Ælfric refrains from spelling this out. It may seem to be clear from the context that sex with men is what is implied, but this omission is a significant one in the light of his other allusions to Sodom, where, as we shall see, he is even more coy about the sin of Sodom. Both Godden and Frantzen note this caution, citing Ælfric's prose translation of Genesis, where he refuses explicitly to describe the Sodomites' demands for sex, saying that 'it disgraces us to tell about it openly'.[5] However, neither of these scholars considers the question of whether this caution represents a reluctance to be explicit about same-sex desire in vernacular works for lay audiences as opposed to Latin texts written with an elite ecclesiastical audience in mind.

In Ælfric's *Lives of Saints* (*c*.995), for instance, when the destruction of Sodom comes up in Ælfric's homily on the *Prayer of Moses*, assigned for Mid-Lent, the Sodomites are described as *þæs fracodostan mennisces* 'the wickedest of races'.[6] Their destruction by fire again comes in conjunction with the earlier watery destruction of the evil men in the days of Noah, but no contrast is specifically made between the two punishments, and they form part of a list of examples of God's vengeance of himself such as his punishment of the fallen angels and of Adam. Ælfric translates closely the biblical account of Abraham's bargaining with God for Sodom, but the Sodomites' demand for sex with the angels is glossed over:

God sende ða sona to ðam sceandlicum mannum twegen englas on æfen, and hi Abrahames broðor sunu Loth, mid his hiwum, alæddon of ðære byrig, and ðær næs na ma þe manful nære gemet. God sende ða fyr on merigen and fulne swefel him to, and forbærnde hi ealle and heora burga towende, and ealne þone eard mid egeslicum fyre; and ðær is nu ful wæter ðær ða fulan wunodon, and Loth se rihtwisa wearð ahred ðurh God.   (p. 298)

Then God at once sent to the shameful men two angels in the evening, and they led Abraham's brother's son Lot with his household from the town, and no more were found there who were not sinful. God then sent fire in the morning and foul sulphur to them, and burned them all up and overthrew their towns, and all the land with terrible fire; and there is now foul water where the foul ones lived, and Lot the righteous man was saved by God.

There is little difference here between the people of the Flood, who anger God *mid forligre* 'with fornication', and the Sodomites except that their fornication is premodified with the adjective 'foul', nor is there any mention of their attempt to rape the angels, or the incest of Lot's daughters. The lesson taken from their destruction has nothing to do with sexual activity; Ælfric tells us:

[5] Frantzen, *Before the Closet*, p. 212; Godden, 'The Trouble with Sodom', pp. 102–3. The Prose Genesis is discussed in detail below.
[6] *Ælfric's Lives of Saints, Being A Set of Sermons on Saints' Days formerly observed by the English Church*, ed. Walter W. Skeat. EETS OS 76 & 82 (vol. I) and 94 & 114 (vol. II), London: Trübner, 1966, I. xiii, at p. 296.

Be ðysum man mæg tocnawan þæt micclum fremiað þam læwedum mannum ða gelæredan godes ðeowas. þæt hi mid heora ðeowdome him ðingian to gode.

By this one may know that the learned servants of God greatly benefit the laity when with their service they intercede with God for them.

Elsewhere in Ælfric's work, too, as shown below, there is a reluctance to be explicit about same-sex acts apart from in texts aimed at a uniquely clerical audience. Here especially one might well wonder how many of even the pious Anglo-Saxon laity would know exactly what Ælfric was talking about.

This chapter therefore contends that it is primarily within in-house élite religious discourse that same-sexuality becomes explicitly associated with the discourse of natural and unnatural desires. However, as will be seen in later chapters, even in texts aimed at the laity or a mixed audience, same-sexuality is a haunting presence, and interacts with a destabilized gender dynamic in surprising and often contradictory ways. Returning to Ælfric's version of Alcuin's question on the destruction of Sodom, it is notable that he adds to Alcuin's text here by including a version of Alcuin's question 97 on God's pronouncement that his spirit would not remain with men for eternity. The explanation given is that he had pity on the weakness of the people of Noah's time, and spared them from *þam ecum witum* 'eternal punishment', punishing them only in this world. Ælfric draws his own conclusion from the absence of such a statement about the Sodomites, stating that they are *ecelice fordemede* 'eternally condemned' and implying that this is because they *ongean gecynd sceamlice syngodon* 'shamefully sinned against nature'. In this view, he disagrees with that of Chrysostom, who states that the Sodomites' punishment is not eternal, because they suffered so great a punishment here on earth.[7] He is thus obviously anxious to emphasize how serious their sin is; however, he still refuses to specify what sinning against nature means. It is very easy as readers positioned after Aquinas and familiar with more recent religious discourses which give only one value to 'the sin against nature' to assume that euphemisms employed in the early medieval period were equally transparent, but the evidence suggests that this is not the case; that, rather, the discourse surrounding same-sex acts is a contested and ambiguous one. Not only does Ælfric not use a vernacular expression equivalent to the nominalized and singular phrase *peccatum contra naturam* 'the sin against nature', rather qualifying the verb instead, there remains a question over how far his lay audiences would have been able to make any ready association of Sodom or its inhabitants or phrases such as *ongean gecynd* with same-sex acts.

In view, then, of the mixed associations we have seen even in the Anglo-Latin and patristic texts considered in the previous chapter, a full re-evaluation of the vernacular evidence seems due, to see how far Ælfric's attitude is reflective

---

[7] Chrysostom, 25th Homily on Genesis, in Hill, *Homilies on Genesis*, p. 128.

of those of other Old English authors. The vernacular references to Sodom divide conveniently into, and will be presented in, four broad categories. The first category comprises instances of the Sodom narrative being used as a prime example of the punishment of sin; the second cites the Sodomites' behaviour as exemplifing sin of an unusual gravity. In the third, smaller, category of texts, Sodom is especially associated with sexual sin, often as part of a condemnation of luxury or gluttony. The final category contains the few textual references to Sodom which, like the Old English *Interrogationes*, allude to unnatural sin. As will be seen, none of these references explicitly associates Sodom with same-sex acts, and many make quite other associations. Because this finding is a contentious one, the material is quoted at length to permit verification and to allow it to speak for itself as far as possible. It sets the scene for the chapters which follow, in which the complex attitudes to same-sex relations present in Old English literary texts are explored in detail.

SODOM AND THE PUNISHMENT OF SIN

Ælfric further alludes to Sodom in his *In Letania maiore* from the first series of Catholic Homilies (completed 990–4).[8] This homily was intended for the first day of Rogationtide, three days of fasting, prayer, and procession preceding Ascension Day. In the first part, Ælfric gives an account of the origins of the fast in fifth-century Vienne, following Amalarius's *Liber Officialis*; he makes the further claim that the people of Vienne were following the example of the Ninevites.[9] God's mercy on the repentant Ninevites is then contrasted with his destruction of the unrepentant Sodomites:

Þa ðurh ða gecyrrednysse þæt hi yfeles geswicon: & þurh þæt strange fæsten him gemilt-sode god. & nolde hi fordon swa swa he ær þa twa buruhwara. sodomam. et gomorram. for heora leahtrum mid heofenlicum fyre forbærnde.

Then through that conversion that they ceased from evil, and through the strict fast, God had mercy on them and did not want to destroy them just as he had burned up the inhabitants of the two cities Sodom and Gomorrah with heavenly fire for their sins.

This is one of several references to Sodom which see it as a particularly notable example of the divine punishment of sinners who refuse to repent.

[8] *Ælfric's Catholic Homilies: The First Series, Text*, ed. Peter Clemoes (= *CH I*). EETS SS 17, Oxford: Oxford University Press, 1997, XVIII, p. 318. For the date of the Catholic Homilies, see Malcolm Godden, ed., *Ælfric's Catholic Homilies. Introduction, Commentary and Glossary*. EETS SS 18. Oxford University Press, 2000, p. xxxv.

[9] The link to the Ninevites is not from Amalarius, but is paralleled in Vercelli Homily 19 and was perhaps a common tradition; cf. Godden, *Commentary*, pp. 145–7. It is also present in Jerome, *Adversus Jovinianum*, Bk. II, ch. 15; Chrysostom's 24th Homily; Cyprianus Gallus's *De Iona*; and Augustine, *De civitate Dei* XXI. xxiv. 123. For an investigation of three homilies dealing with Jonah and the Ninevites, see Paul E. Szarmach, 'Three Versions of the Jonah Story: An Investigation of Narrative Technique in Old English Homilies', *Anglo-Saxon England* 1 (1972), 183–92.

Another is found in the Blickling Homilies, a diverse collection of anonymous Old English prose texts from the end of the tenth century, of uncertain date and provenance.[10] In Homily VI 'Palm Sunday (Dominica VI in Quadragesima)', Sodom is the pre-eminent example of divine vengeance, the only one greater than the destruction of Jerusalem as punishment for the Jews' refusal to repent:

Þa he þa geseah þæt hie nænige bote ne hreowe don noldan, ah hie forþon heora yfelum þurhwunedon, Drihten þa sende on hie maran wræce þonne æfre ær ænigu oþru gelumpe, buton Sodomwarum anum.[11]

When he saw that they did not want to do any atonement or penance, but they continued on in their evil, the Lord sent upon them a greater vengeance than ever before occurred to anyone else, except to the inhabitants of Sodom alone.

Blickling Homily XIII 'Assumption of the Virgin Mary (Sancta Maria Mater Domini Nostri Iesu Cristi)' is slightly more racy, recounting legends attached to Mary and some of the disciples. In the relevant section of the homily, after being forced to convert, the leader of the Jews travels around Jerusalem where all the hostile Jews have been divinely blinded, telling his compatriots that they will be healed if they believe that Jesus is the Son of God. He finds them weeping:

ond wæron cweþende, 'Wa us la, forþon be us is nu geworden, swa swa on Sodoma byrig wæs. Þær wæs geworden þæt þær com ofer hie on fruman mycel broga ond hie wæron mid blindnesse slegene, and æfter þon þa sende Drihten fyr of heofenum ofer hie ond hie mid ealle forbærnde.'[12]

And they were saying, 'Oh woe is us! for it has now happened to us just as it was in the city of Sodom. It happened there that there came over them at first a great terror and they were struck with blindness; and after that then the Lord sent fire from heaven over them and burned them up completely.'

Here, Sodom serves as a warning to repent, which the Jews naturally heed.

An even starker reference is found in an anonymous homily on Easter Day, where Sodom is an example of one of many bad things which happened on the sixth day of the week:

And on þam sixtan dæge cain acwealde abel his broðor and on þam sixtan dæge sodoma burh and Gomorra godes englas bærndon for godes yrre mid fyres lige.[13]

---

[10] *The Blickling Homilies. Edition and Translation*, ed. and trans. Richard J. Kelly. London: Continuum, 2003, at pp. xxix, xxiii. See also *The Blickling Homilies of the Tenth Century*, ed. R. Morris. 3 vols., EETS 58, 63, 73, 1874–80; repr. in 1 vol. 1967.

[11] Kelly, *Blickling Homilies*, p. 54; Morris, *Blickling Homilies*, p. 79.

[12] Kelly, *Blickling Homilies*, p. 108, ll. 239–42; Morris, *Blickling Homilies*, p. 153.

[13] This homily has only been edited as a Columbia dissertation for the Dictionary of Old English project, thus, since the dissertation is unavailable to me, I quote from the online text in the Old English Corpus <http://ets.umdl.umich.edu/o/oec/>. See also Kenneth G. Schaefer, 'An Edition of Five Old English Homilies for Palm Sunday, Holy Saturday, and Easter Sunday' (unpublished dissertation, University of Columbia, 1972), pp. 249–59.

And on the sixth day Cain killed Abel his brother, and on the sixth day God's angels burned the cities of Sodom and Gomorrah with flames of fire because of God's wrath.

In the previous texts, the implication for contemporary Anglo-Saxon audiences must have been clear, but in a couple of homilies on the importance of observing the Sabbath rest, the homilist spells out to his audience that, should they not heed his warnings, they too will suffer the fate of Sodom.

For instance, in a homily formerly attributed to Wulfstan, the author commands the people not to work on Sunday, including especially a list of evil deeds and exempting certain good works. He then lists the punishments they will receive if they disobey, culminating in national defeat and captivity:

And syððan æfter þære earmlycan eowre geendunge, ic besence eowre sawla on susle on helle, swa swa ic hwilon dyde þa twa burh Sodomam and Gomorram, þe mid heofonlicum fyre her wurdan forbærnde, and ealle þa, þe him on eardodon, æfre byrnað on helle grunde on hatan fyre, forþan hi þone mildan god manfullice gremedon. And ealswa hit gelamp on Moyses dagum, mines gecorenan, þæt wæron twegen men, þa wæron genemnode Dathan and Abiron; hi ic besencte mid sawle and mid lichaman on hellegrund for heora oferhigde and, forþan hig spræcon bysmorlice be me and be minum sacerdum.[14]

And afterwards, after your miserable ending, I will plunge your souls into torment in hell, just as I once did to the two cities Sodom and Gomorrah, which were burned up here with heavenly fire, and all those who lived in them forever burn in hot fire in the bottom of hell, because they wickedly provoked merciful God. And likewise it happened in the days of Moses, my chosen one, that there were two men who were named Dathan and Abiron. I plunged them body and soul into the bottom of hell for their pride and because they spoke shamefully about me and about my priests.

Sodom is an example of notable and eternal punishment for general sinfulness. However, there is no mention of same-sex activity in the homily, even in its later detailing of sexual offences, and indeed the lesson for the homilist's audience would lose its force were the punishment to be due to any one particular sin.[15]

A very similar passage occurs in another homily, described by its editor as one of a group of Old English homilies built on 'a letter purporting to have been sent from heaven in order to inculcate the strict observance of Sunday'.[16] The text in question reads as follows:

---

[14] 'Sermo ad populum dominicis diebus' in *Wulfstan. Sammlung der ihm zugeschriebenen Homilien nebst Untersuchungen über ihre Echtheit*, ed. Arthur Napier. Pt. I: *Text und Varianten*. Sammlung Englischer Denkmäler in kritischen Ausgaben, 4. Berlin: Weidmann, 1883, Homily LVII.

[15] The homilist mentions the subversion of nature, but this is confined to terrible hail, unspeakable thunder, and unnatural fire (*ungecyndelic fyr*, p. 297, l. 13) which destroys.

[16] 'Be þam drihtenlican sunnandæg folces lar', ed. Napier as 'Contributions to Old English Literature 1: An Old English Homily on the Observance of Sunday,' in [W. P. Ker and A. S. Napier], eds, *An English Miscellany Presented to Dr. Furnivall in Honour of his Seventy-Fifth Birthday*. Oxford: Clarendon Press, 1901, pp. 355–62, at p. 355. See Clare A. Lees, 'The "Sunday Letter" and the "Sunday Lists"', *Anglo-Saxon England* 14 (1985), 129–51; D. G. Scragg, 'The Corpus of

Gif ge þonne elles doð butan þas forespræcenan þing, þonne swinge ic eow þam heardostan swinglan, þæt is þæt ic asette on eorðan mine feower wyrrestan domas, hungor & hæftned & gefeoht & cwelm. & ic eow gesylle to ælþeodigra handa, & ic eow fordo & besence eow, swa ic dyde Sodoman & Gomorran, & ic dyde Dathan & Abiron, þa yfelan þe wiðsocon minum naman & forsawon mine sacerdas.[17]

If you do anything else [on a Sunday] except for the aforesaid things, then I will beat you with the hardest rod, that is that I will set on earth my four worst judgements: hunger and captivity and battle and plague. And I will give you into alien hands, and I will destroy you and plunge you into fire, just as I did Sodom and Gomorrah, and I did Dathan and Abiron, those evil ones who denied my name and despised my priests.

Sodom is again an example of notable and eternal punishment for sin, and again the comparison with Dathan and Abiron occurs.[18]

In this category, too, are the extant vernacular versions of the explicit biblical references to Sodom, other than those in Genesis, which are considered below. The Old English Heptateuch contains a translation of Deuteronomy 32: 32 (but not 29: 22), of which there are also nine glossed versions in various Psalters, and the Old English translations of the Gospels give versions of Matthew 10: 15, 11: 23–4; Luke 10: 12, 17: 29. These latter texts are also glossed in the Lindisfarne and Rushworth Gospels, although the name Sodom is omitted in all the glosses except Luke 10: 12.[19]

None of the references above contains any sense that Sodom represents anything other than a town famous for generalized unrepentant sinfulness. However, the next passages contain a sense that the Sodomites were guilty of a particularly heinous act or acts.

Vernacular Homilies and Prose Saints' Lives before Ælfric', *Anglo-Saxon England* 8 (1979), 223–77, at 248, 250.

[17] Four of the homilies from the group are edited in Napier, *Wulfstan*. Napier designates them as manuscripts A (no. 45), C (no. 43), D (no. 44), and E (no. 57). B is edited in R. Priebsch, 'The Chief Sources of Some Anglo-Saxon Homilies', *Otia Merseiana* 1 (1899), 129. Napier assigns the letter F to the present homily, extant in an eleventh-century manuscript, Corpus Christi College, Cambridge 162, which constitutes a compressed version of E. Both these related texts represent a Latin original which has Peter, Bishop of Antioch, as the recipient of the letter (rather than the priest Achorius, as A and B, or the deacon Nial, as C and D), Napier, p. 356. The Sodom reference is present only in the two versions quoted here.

[18] The assocation of the destruction of Sodom and Gomorrah with that of Dathan and Abiron also occurs in Hilary of Poitier's fourth-century commentary on Psalm 67: *Sancti Hilarii Pictaviensis Episcopi Tractatus super Psalmos*, ed. J. Doignon. CCSL 61. Turnhout: Brepols, 1997, 1. 1. 22, p. 309.

[19] See the relevant verses in *The Old English Version of the Heptateuch*, ed. S. J. Crawford. EETS 160. London: Oxford University Press, 1922; repr. with additions by N. R. Ker, 1969; and *The Holy Gospels in Anglo-Saxon, Northumbrian, and Old Mercian Versions*..., ed. Walter W. Skeat. Cambridge: Cambridge University Press, 1871–87. The name Sodom is also omitted in an Old English gloss of a passage from Isidore's *Sententiae* (Bk. II, ch. xx, §1); see Regina Cornelius, ed., *Die altenglische Interlinearversion zu "De vitiis et peccatis" in der Hs. British Library, Royal 7 C. iv: Textausgabe mit Kommentar und Glossar*. Europäische Hochschulschriften: Reihe 14, Angelsächsische Sprache und Literatur, 296. Frankfurt am Main: Peter Lang, 1995, pp. 164–81. This incorporates a quotation of Isaiah 3: 9; cf. Pierre Cazier, ed., *Isidorus Hispalensis Sententiae*. CCSL, CXI. Turnhout: Brepols, 1998, 20. 1–2, pp. 135–6.

SODOM AS THE EPITOME OF EVIL

We start again with a passage from Ælfric, this time his *Sermo De Die Judicii*. The relevant parts of this homily, which is not assigned to any specific occasion and was probably composed 1002–5, are based on Luke 17: 20–37 (associating the destruction of Noah's contemporaries and Sodom) and Matthew 24 (on the Flood).[20] Although Ælfric is much influenced by Bede's commentary on Luke, Pope deems the following lines a 'free summary' of the biblical story (p. 593 n.):

Loð wæs iu gehaten sum halig Godes þegn, Abrahames broðor sunu, ær Moyses æ; se eardode þa on þam yfelan leodscipe Sodomitiscre burhware, þa wæron synfulle menn, and bysmorlice forscyldgode on sceamlicum dædum. Þa forbærnde hi God mid heora fif burhscirum mid heofonlicum fyre and hellicum swefle; ac he sende on ær twegen scinende englas to þam geleaffullan Loðe, and alædde hyne ut of þam fulan mancynne, þæt he mid him ne forwurde.   (p. 593)

A certain holy thane of God long ago was called Lot, Abraham's brother's son, before Moses's law. He lived then in the evil nation of the inhabitants of Sodom, who were sinful men, and shamefully guilty of ignominious deeds. Then God burned them up with their five boroughs with heavenly fire and hellish sulphur; but he sent beforehand two shining angels to the faithful Lot, and led him out from the foul race so that he should not perish with them.

The Sodomites are evil, shameful, and foul. However, there is no mention of what their deeds were, nor any Alcuin-like explanation of the Flood-Sodom juxtaposition. The fires of Doomsday are mentioned immediately after this passage, but they are seen as cleansing and purifying rather than associated with destruction and permanent barrenness and sterility, as in Alcuin. Indeed, as Daniel Anlezark has shown, Ælfric assumes that, although the Flood narrative would be known to his audience, the Lot story would not be known in any detail and would need explanation.[21]

Ælfric takes a similar approach in his *Letter to Sigeweard*, composed after 1005 (when he went to Eynsham as abbot) for the prominent layman Sigeweard, but clearly intended for a wider unlearned audience.[22] Sodom is mentioned as one of the significant early biblical events, but no explicit comparison is made to the Flood story.

On ðare ilcan ylde mon arerde hæðengyld wide geond þas weorld & on ðissere ylde þa yfela leoda, fif burhscira ðæs fulestan mennisces Sodomitisces eardes, mid swæflene fyre, færlice wurdon ealle forbearnde, & heora burga samod, buton Loth ane, ðe God lædde ðanon mid his þrim hiwum for his rihtwisnesse.

---

[20] *Homilies of Ælfric. A Supplementary Collection . . .*, ed. John C. Pope. 2 vols. EETS 259 & 260. London: Oxford University Press, 1967–8, II, at pp. 584–5. Clemoes, 'Chronology', pp. 238, 244.

[21] Anlezark, *Flood and Fire*, pp. 160–1.

[22] Letter to Sigeweard, reproduced as 'On the Old and New Testament', in *Heptateuch*, ed. Crawford, pp. 15–75.

In that same age one raised up idols widely throughout the world and in this age the evil peoples, five boroughs of the foulest people of the Sodomite land were suddenly completely burned up with sulphurous fire, together with their towns, except Lot alone, whom God led from there with his three householders because of his righteousness.

(p. 25)

The Sodomites are evidently seen as particularly loathsome examples of humanity in these texts. Nevertheless, in the Old English versions there is no mention of same-sex acts, or even any statement that the sins were sexual in nature.[23]

SODOM AND SEXUAL ASSOCIATIONS

The texts considered in this section are all translations or adaptations of Latin sources, and so there is the possibility that the Old English authors felt constrained by the authority of their source material to make the associations of Sodom with sexual sin that they do. However, at least one writer did not feel constrained enough to make the same-sex character of these sins explicit.

Chapter 51 of the late ninth-century translation of Gregory's Pastoral Care (*c*.590) commissioned by King Alfred represents a fairly close version of its source.[24] As seen in the previous chapter, Gregory is concerned to warn married people against having sex for any purpose other than the procreation of children.[25] The Old English translator strengthens Gregory's proscription by stating that, if the married have sex too often and too immoderately, they are not in lawful union (*ryhtum gesinscipe*), rather they are having unlawful intercourse (*unaliefedan gemengnesse*).[26] Gregory goes on to interpret Lot allegorically as an exemplar of the married state—when he fled Sodom into Zoar but did not ascend into the mountains, Gregory opines, he showed that we are to flee from 'the sinful fires of the flesh' (in the Old English version *ðone unaliefedan bryne ures lichoman* 'unlawful heat of our bodies'). However, just as Lot was

---

[23] In notable contrast to the 1623 translation of the letter: 'In this age also the wicked people of the 5 cities in the land of the filthy male-lusting Sodomites were suddenly burnt all with fire & brimstone, together with their territories; except Lot only, whom God led thence with his three women, for his righteousness.' William L'Isle of Wilburgham, *A SAXON Treatise concerning the Old and New Testament . . .* (1623); reprinted in Crawford, *Heptateuch*, at p. 25.

[24] *King Alfred's West-Saxon Version of Gregory's Pastoral Care*, ed. and trans. Henry Sweet. EETS OS 45. London: Oxford University Press, 1871. On the Alfredian translations, see Janet M. Bately, 'The Literary Prose of King Alfred's Reign: Translation or Transformation?' Inaugural Lecture in the Chair of English Language and Medieval Literature at University of London King's College, 4th March 1980, reprinted in *Old English Prose: Basic Readings*, ed. Paul E. Szarmach. New York: Garland, 2000, pp. 3–27.

[25] Davis, *Pastoral Care*, p. 189.

[26] Sweet, *Pastoral Care*, p. 397. Gregory rather makes a contrast between married sexual continence and those who do 'what is done lawfully, indeed, but is not kept under control' (Davis, *Pastoral Care*, p. 189).

unable to flee initially all the way up into the mountains, so many are unable to achieve the best life and preserve continence in marriage, that is, having sex only to produce children (Davis, *Pastoral Care*, pp. 189–90; Sweet, *Pastoral Care*, p. 399). Sodom is here clearly associated with sexual activity, but there is no hint at all in this chapter that same-sex acts are on the mind of Gregory or his translator.

It is instructive to compare another Old English translation of Gregory, this time of his Dialogues, written in the late sixth century.[27] In Dialogue IV, Gregory tells Peter that sins of the flesh are punished by foul odours, and Peter asks if this can be proved on the authority of Scripture. The Old English text represents a fairly literal translation of its source:[28]

Soðlice eac we leornodon in Genese þære bec, þæt drihten sende fyr 7 swefl samod ofer Sodoma folc, to þon þæt þæt fyr hi forbærnde, 7 se fula stenc þæs swefles hi acwealde. forþon þe hi burnon on þære unalyfdan lufe þæs gebrosniendan lichaman, hi forþon eac samod to lore wurdon in þam bryne 7 fulan stence, þæt hi ongæton on heora sylfra wite, þæt hi sealdon ær hi sylfe mid heora synlustum to þam ecan deaþe þære fulnesse.   (p. 323)

Truly we also learned in the book of Genesis, that the Lord sent fire and sulphur together over the people of Sodom to the extent that fire burned them up and the foul smell of sulphur killed them. Because they burned in that unlawful love of the corruptible body, they also therefore went to destruction together in that burning and foul smell, so that they perceived in their own punishment that they had given themselves with their sinful desires to the eternal death in that foulness.

The repetition of the idea of foulness (*se fula stenc, fulan stence, þære fulnesse*) emphasizes that the Sodomites are unusual in their degradation. However, the notion of an unlawful love of the body seen in the phrase *þære unalyfdan lufe* is, as we have seen in the Old English *Pastoral Care*, not confined to same-sex desires.[29]

The translations of Gregory represent their originals fairly faithfully, and so the omission of any clear reference to same-sex acts cannot be entirely attributed to the translator. However, the Old English Orosius is a different matter. The main source of this work is Paulus Orosius's *Historiarum adversum Paganos Libri Septem*, written in the late fifth century, but the Old English translator adds to this base text from various sources.[30] Even with these additions, however, the

[27] *Bischofs Wærferth von Worcester Übersetzung der Dialoge Gregors des Grossen*, ed. Hans Hecht. Bibliothek der Angelsächsischen Prosa, 5. Leipzig: Wigand, 1900.
[28] For Latin text and French translation, see *Grégoire le Grand. Dialogues*, ed. Adalbert de Vogüé, trans. Paul Antin. 3 vols. Paris: Cerf, 1978–80, vol. 3, IV. xxxviii, p. 138 (Latin), p. 139 (French); cf. *Saint Gregory the Great. Dialogues*, trans. Odo John Zimmermann. Washington, DC: Catholic University of America Press, 1959, p. 243.
[29] Both texts perhaps reflect an Alfredian concern to make a link between divine and secular law.
[30] Bately, *Old English Orosius*, pp. lv–lxxii.

completed translation is only two-thirds as long as the original.[31] The translation, commissioned but not made by Alfred, was probably completed in the 890s (Bately, *Old English Orosius*, pp. lxxxvi–xciii).

The chapter heading, by a different author than the rest of the text (pp. lxxxi–lxxxiii) is matter of fact about its contents, stating that it concerns: 'Hu þæt heofenisce fyr forbærnde þæt lond on þæm wæron þa twa byrig on getimbred, Sodome & Gomorre' [How heavenly fire burned up the land in which were built the two cities, Sodom and Gomorrah] (p. 1). The chapter itself reads as follows:

Ær ðam ðe Romeburh getimbred wære þusend wintra 7 an hund 7 syxtig, þæt wæstmbære land, on þæm Sodome 7 Gomorre ða byrig on wæron, hit wearð fram heofonlicum fyre forbærned, þæt wæs betuh Arabia & Palestina. Ða manigfealdan wæstmas wæron for þam swiþost ðe Iordanis seo ea ælce geare þæt land middeweard oferfleow mid fotes þicce flode, 7 hit þonne mid ðam gedynged wearð. Þa wæs þæt folc þæs micclan welan ungemetlice brucende, oð ðæt him on se miccla firenlust oninnan aweox. 7 him com of þæm firenluste Godes wraco, þæt he eal þæt land mid sweflenum fyre forbærnde. 7 seððan ðær wæs standende wæter ofer þam lande, swa hit þære ea flod ær gefleow; 7 þæs dæles se dæl se þæt flod ne grette ys gyt todæg wæstmberende on ælces cynnes blædum; 7 ða syndon swyþe fægere & lustsumlice on to seonne, ac þonne hig man on hand nymð, þonne weorðað hig to acxan.   (I. iii, pp. 22–3)

1160 years before the city of Rome was built, that fruitful land in which the cities of Sodom and Gomorrah were situated was burned up by heavenly fire; that was between Arabia and Palestine. The manifold fruits were therefore greatest in that the River Jordan each year overflowed the middle of the land with a flood a foot thick, and it was then manured with it. That people was then excessively enjoying that great prosperity until a great wicked lust grew within them, and God's vengeance came upon them for that wicked lust so that he burned up that whole land with sulphurous fire. And afterwards there was standing water over the land, as the river's flood had overflowed it; and that part of the region where the flood did not touch is still today fruitful in every kind of fruit; and they are beautiful and pleasant to look upon, but when one takes them in one's hand, they turn to ashes.

In this reworking of Orosius Bk. I, ch. 5, the translator abbreviates Orosius to a third of the original, omitting his first paragraph discussing Tacitus's comments (in the *Histories* V. vii) on the barren plains and his doubts about the stories of the divine origin of their devastation. He also omits the names of the other three of the Five Cities, but he adds the comment about the Jordan flooding.[32] In both Latin and vernacular versions, Sodom is associated with prosperity and a fertile land, the excessive enjoyment of which leads to wickedness and lust, which is punished by God with fiery destruction. However, in contrast to Orosius, who

---

[31] *Seven Books of History Against the Pagans. The Apology of Paulus Orosius*, trans. Irving Woodworth Raymond. New York: Columbia University Press, 1936, p. 23. For a translation of the Latin original of the present passage, see pp. 50–1.

[32] There is no extant written source for this comment and it has been suggested it may derive ultimately from observation (Bately, *Old English Orosius*, p. 212 n.).

emphasizes Sodom's lasting sterility and barrenness, the translator tells us that the unflooded regions are still fertile. He adds the exotic touch of fruit that seems delightful but which in practice disappoints.[33] However, a further difference (which Bately does not comment upon), is that the translator omits the explicit reference to same-sex activity present in the original, which states:

For out of abundance grew luxury, and out of luxury came such shameful passions that men rushed to commit vile practices upon their own sex without even taking into consideration place, condition, or age.[34]

This omission does not, however, necessarily reflect a squeamishness about same-sex acts alone, but rather a delicacy about sex in general, since the translator also omits the previous chapter's account of Semiramis's sins of cross-dressing, adultery, killing, and incest (pp. 49–50). Nevertheless, the overall effect of the changes is that the character of this chapter is changed from an indictment of sin to something akin to an exotic travelogue. The potential symbolism of the mysterious fruit is obvious, but the translator does not draw it out, apparently mainly interested in the motif for its own sake and not for what it might say about same-sex unions.

Like the passages from Gregory and Orosius, Ælfric's *Prayer to Moses* also associates Sodom with sexual sin, as we saw above. A final text based on a Latin original which links Sodom with illicit sexual activity is a short homily which survives only in the *Vercelli Book*, characterized by its editor as 'a general appeal to toil, harsh living and temperance'.[35] The text probably dates from the tenth century and is thought to be a more-or-less literal translation from Latin, though the exact source has not been confirmed.[36] The first section (lines 1–24) stress the importance and value of toil, citing the examples of Abel, Noah, Abraham, and other Old Testment figures. In the second section (lines 25–50), which demonstrates the penalties of idleness through biblical exempla, Sodom's inhabitants are compared to those killed in Noah's Flood as examples of how gluttony produces other sins.

Geþenceað eac þara þe in Sodome for hira unalyfedum gewilnungum forwurdon, & þara þe on Noes dagum wæron. Witodlice be ðam þe ðam yðan life lyfedon on Sodome hit

---

[33] The source of this motif is uncertain, since there are similar versions in Josephus, *Jewish War* 4. 484, Solinus, *Collectanea* 35. 8, and Augustine, *De civitate Dei* XXI. v. 27 and XXI .vi. 47. Bately claims that it comes from Josephus via Hegesippus, and that the version of Hegesippus closest in wording to the OE Orosius is Bede, *De Locis Sanctis*, PL xciv, col. 1187; see Bately, *Old English Orosius*, pp. 212–13 n.

[34] Raymond, *Seven Books*, p. 51.

[35] *The Vercelli Homilies and Related Texts*, ed. D. G. Scragg. EETS 300. Oxford: Oxford University Press, 1992, Homily VII, at p. 133.

[36] See Scragg, *Vercelli Homilies*, pp. xxxviii, 133. Samantha Zacher promises to identify the source in a forthcoming article: 'The Source of Vercelli VII: An Address to Women', in *New Readings on the Vercelli Book*, ed. Andy Orchard and Samantha Zacher (Toronto: University of Toronto Press, forthcoming).

wæs gecweden ðætte on hlafes fylnesse flowen. Þonne sio fylnes ðæs hlafes unriht wyrceð, hwæt is to cweðanne be ðam mænigfealdum smeamettum?   (p. 135)

Consider also those who perished in Sodom for their unlawful desires, and those who were in Noah's days. Certainly it was said about those who lived the easy life in Sodom that they flow in the fulness of bread [Ezekiel 16: 49]. When the fullness of the bread produces wickedness, what is there to say about the manifold delicacies?

The primary association in this extract is with *luxuria*, which here as elsewhere encompasses a fluid range of sins and which links the satisfaction of greed with the incitement of sexual desires. There is no explicit sign here that the Sodomites' desires were directed toward the same sex. In fact, what seems to be the homily's only explicit mention of same-sex acts is separated from the Sodom example by that of the men of Christ's time who were corrupted by desire for women:

Gemunað hu Esaw his dagas on ehtnesse lædde, 7 hu ða ðe ær in ryne Godes bearn wæron þurh ænlicra wifa sceawunga to fyrenlustum gehæfte on helle gehruron. Gemunað eac hu þa forwurdon þe mid wodheartnesse willan to wæpnedmannum hæmed sohton, 7 eallra Babilone 7 Egypta cyninga ealle hie swiðe ungesæliglice hira lif geendedon 7 nu syndon on ecum witum. Eac swylce þa ilcan witu syndon gearuwe þam mannum þe nu swylcum lifum lifiað swylce hie lyfedon.

Remember how Esau spent his days in persecution, and how those who were previously in the age of God's son through the contemplation of singular women bound, fallen in hell. Remember also how those perished who with madness of desire sought out sex with males, and of all the kings of Babylon and Egypt, all of them ended their lives very unhappily and now are in eternal torments. Also those same torments are ready for those men who now live such lives as they lived.

Here, the only motivation the homilist can imagine for the wish to engage in same-sex acts is 'madness of desire', and such activities will be punished by 'eternal torments'. However, the Sodomites are not the people chosen to exemplify this mad way of life, and they are grouped with those who sin with women and 'all the kings of Babylon and Egypt'.

It is notable that this passage is followed by some caustic remarks about those who clothe themselves in 'soft garments', and the words *hnesc* and *hnesclice* are repeated over and over again, making a connection between 'softness' and effeminacy which is suggestive in the close context of remarks about sex with men. The homilist expands at great length on the physical and moral weakness of women who pamper themselves with oils and perfumes and frequent washing, and the implication seems to be that men are in danger of becoming like women if they engage in similar behaviours, since the writer remarks that women who do 'lowly and heavy work . . . are more whole and stronger than the men who live in idleness'. It is thus possible that the homilist was led by an association of ideas by the mention of same-sex desire onto the topic of effeminacy and luxurious living. Nevertheless, if so it is an association that forms part only of a wider network of associations, since he is much more concerned to expatiate on the dangers of eating and drinking to excess. It would seem that in this text, same-sex desire is one of a large number of sins which result from self-indulgence—it is not possible to separate sexual sins from those involving greed: both are part of the sin of gluttony.

Thus, none of the preceding references explicitly associates Sodom with same-sex desire, and many of them more readily make other associations. One might expect the vernacular prose version of the biblical book of Genesis to depart from this pattern, and in some ways it does, in that it raises the issue of a vernacular discourse of sin against nature. However, it still betrays a concern on the part of authors writing in the vernacular to play down same-sex activity.

SODOM AND UNNATURAL SIN: THE OLD ENGLISH PROSE GENESIS

The prose translation of the first book of the Bible is at least partly by Ælfric, and all the extracts given here are unanimously accepted to be his work, completed between 992 and 1002.[37] In chapter 13, verse 13, after Lot chooses to live in Sodom, we are told 'Þa Sodomitiscan men wæron forcuðostan & swyðe synfulle ætforan Gode' [The men of Sodom were most wicked and very sinful before God']. This represents a faithful translation of the source. However, in chapter 14, verse 10, in the battle between the kings of the North and South, we are told 'Þa feollon ða cyningas on ðam gefeohte ofslagene, of Sodomam & Gomorran, þæra manfulra ðeoda, & heora geferan flugon afyrhte to muntum' [Then the kings fell slain in that battle, of Sodom and Gomorrah, of that infamous people, and their companions fled terrified to the hills]. The parenthetical comment on Sodom and Gomorrah here is an addition to the source which is neutral at this point about the cities. The passage on which Ælfric's first question above is based (Q. 66, from Alcuin Q. 179), is found in chapter 18, verses 20–1, after Abraham shows the two guests the way to Sodom:

God þa geopenode Abrahame hwæt he mid þære spræce mænde, & cwæð him to: Þæra Sodomitiscra hream & ðære burhware of Gomorra ys gemenifyld, & heora synn ys swyðe gehefegod. Ic wylle nu faran to & geseon hwæðer hi gefyllað mid weorce þone hream ðe me to com, oððe hyt swa nys, ðæt ic wite.

God then disclosed to Abraham what he meant by that speech, and said to him: 'The noise of the Sodomites and the inhabitants of Gomorrah is manifold, and their sin is made very heavy. I will now go there and see whether they fulfil in deed the noise which has come to me, or [whether] it is not so, that I may know.

---

[37] See Crawford, *Old English Heptateuch* (representing London, British Library, MS. Cotton Claudius B.IV). Clemoes accepts the following parts as Ælfric's work on a 'working basis': chs 1–3, 6–9, 12–24 (Clemoes 'Chronology', p. 224, n. 3); Godden agrees with Clemoes (*Commentary*, p. 143, n. 4.)

There is no explanatory comment here, however, and it is followed by a close translation of the interchange between Abraham and God where the patriarch persuades God to agree that he will spare Sodom if there are ten righteous people there.

Since these passages are translated so closely, it is all the more noticeable that Ælfric makes a significant omission in his translation of Genesis chapter 19. Of the 38 verses of the original, most are translated fairly literally, with only minor omissions or additions, such as the specification of Lot's relation to Abraham as his *broðor sunu* 'brother's son' (v. 1) or that he *rihtlice leofode* 'lived rightly' (v. 12). However, the account of the Sodomites' attempted rape of the angels (comprising verses 4–11) is represented only by the following sentence:

Se leodscipe wæs swa bysmorful, þæt hi woldon fullice ongean gecynd heora galnyssæ gefyllan, na mid wimmannum, ac swa fullice þæt us sceamað hyt openlice to secgenne, & þæt wæs heora hream, þæt hi openlice heora fylðe gefremedon.

The nation was so shameful, that they wanted foully against nature to fulfil their lusts, not at all with women, but so foully that it shames us to say it openly, and that was their noise, that they openly committed their filth.

There is no mention that the Sodomites wanted to have sex with the angels, or of Lot's offer of his daughters as a substitute. Malcolm Godden comments:

If Ealdorman Æthelweard, who apparently commissioned the translation, was not already familiar with the Genesis narrative he must have been baffled as to why Ælfric should interject his denunciation at that point, and puzzled about the sequence of events. For Ælfric, male homosexuality was evidently the prevailing practice at Sodom and the reason for the city's destruction, and it was a sin so appalling that it could not be described. (It is of course possible too that he was reluctant to mention Lot's questionable offer of his daughters as sexual objects.)[38]

However, there are three points to make here. Firstly, although Godden thinks that Æthelweard, and by extension the rest of the lay audience, would not have understood why the 'violent denunciation of Sodomite practices' (p. 102) was placed here, he implies that they would have understood what these practices were. However, since, as we have seen, the vast majority of references to the Sodom narrative associate it with general sinfulness, or non-specific sexual sin, it is far from certain that lay audiences would have assumed same-sex acts were at issue, rather than masturbation or bestiality or some other dimly imagined sin.[39] Secondly, it is far from certain that Ælfric thought same-sex activity was

[38] Godden, 'The Trouble with Sodom', p. 103.
[39] Compare the anecdote Frantzen prints about the Korean churchwarden who chuckled and said: 'You know, I never realized paederasty was a sin till I read the Epistle to the Romans' (*Before the Closet*, p. 300). Likewise, note Gerson's comment on masturbation that 'many adults were polluted with the sin and had never confessed it...many apologized for their ignorance, saying that they had never known such touching, whereby they did not have the desire to know women, was a

Sodom's 'prevailing practice' and 'the' single reason for its destruction, since even in texts which associate Sodom with sexual sin, this tends to be part of a wider denunciation of gluttony or *luxuria*, of which the sexual sin is a particularly advanced symptom. Thirdly, it is also less than clear that Ælfric's motivation for not describing the sin was merely its 'appalling' character. Rather, in line with his omission of Lot's offer of his daughters, the cautious cleric may have wished to gloss over events and actions which he did not want his audience to think about too closely, still less to imitate. This would fit in with the common advice to confessors in handbooks of penance not to question penitents too closely lest they tempt the innocent, as Frantzen puts it 'to commit sins they had not previously known about'.[40]

On the other hand, Godden's further point on the alterations to the incest narrative is well made. Whereas the Vulgate states that the daughters lay down with their unwary father, Ælfric says rather that he did not know *hu he befeng on hi* 'how he clasped her', which has the advantage of maintaining Lot's relative innocence while not implying an unacceptable male passivity (cf. p. 103). I am not convinced by Godden's claim that Ælfric is constructing an opposition between 'damnable and indescribable ... homosexuality' and incest which is 'illicit, forbidden, tabooed, yet heterosexual and therefore easily described and easily pardoned'. However, it does seem possible that Ælfric has in mind a less well-defined opposition of male passivity (and sterility) and (procreative) male activity, which his more well-informed audience members might pick up on.

What is even more significant, however, is the description of the sin as *ongean gecynd* 'against nature', which is the phrase Ælfric uses in his translation of the *Interrogationes*, saying that the Sodomites *syngodon bysmorlice ongean gecynd* 'sinned shamefully against nature', and repeating that they *ongean gecynd sceamlice syngodon* 'sinned against nature shamefully' (see above). Here, too, both Godden and Frantzen assume that same-sex acts are clearly implied. It is true that an obvious parallel to the phrase *syngodan mid wifum* would be *syngodan mid werum*, but by avoiding this explicit opposition Ælfric leaves the possibility open that he is referring to some other sin such as masturbation or bestiality, or more generalized sexual debauchery in which same-sex activity is included but not the exclusive component. Nevertheless, the question remains as to whether the phrase *syngodon ... ongean gecynd* is a euphemism equating with 'engaged in same-sex acts'.[41] There are only a dozen extant instances of the phrase, to which can be added a couple of references to 'unnatural sins', and a study of these yields surprising results.

---

sin.' Cited in Jeffrey Richards, *Sex, Dissidence and Damnation: Minority Groups in the Middle Ages*. London: Routledge, 1991, p. 37.

[40] Frantzen, *Before the Closet*, p. 116; cf. idem, *Literature of Penance*, p. 114.

[41] For an exploration of a different use of the term *gecynd*, see Chapter 8 below on *The Phoenix*, a poem which is deeply concerned with questions of nature and gender.

ACTS AGAINST NATURE, AND THE UNNATURAL

Ælfric provides a further couple of instances of the phrase *ongean gecynd* in his Grammar and Glossary which was produced in the 990s, designed as a teaching aid to be used with children learning Latin and English in monasteries.[42] The occurences come in the context of discussions of language. First, in the section *De personibus*, after listing the sounds animals makes, he says that men can make the same noises *ongean gecynd*, but that it is very foolish for a man to bark or bleat (p. 129). The comment appears to be original to Ælfric.[43] Secondly, in the section *Triginta divisiones grammaticae artis* ('The Thirty Divisions of Grammar'), he talks about *fabulae*, which are defined as 'þa saga, þe menn secgað ongean gecynde, þæt ðe næfre ne gewearð ne gewurðan ne mæg' [*Fabulae* are the stories which people tell against nature, that never happened or could happen] (p. 296). This derives from the anonymous compiler's additions to Priscian from Isidore, in this case from the *Etymologiae* I. xl. 1.[44] These uses strongly suggest that the phrase does not have primarily sexual connotations for Ælfric.

A further use is found in Ælfric's Homily on Philip and James (*c.*995), appointed for the feast-day of the two apostles.[45] For the latter, Ælfric's source is Eusebius's *Historia Ecclesiastica*, as translated by Rufinus in the late fourth century.[46] In the relevant section, God mercifully sends signs to persuade the Jews to convert, such as a star like a sword standing over Jerusalem, a constantly burning comet, and the following marvel:

An cu wearð gebroht. eft to ðam temple. þæt man hi geoffrode. on ða ealdan wison; Ða wolde heo cealfian. on gesihðe þæs folces. ac heo eanode lamb. ongean hire gecynde. (p. 173)

A cow was brought afterwards to the temple such that people sacrificed it in the old way. Then it wanted to calf in the sight of the people, but it gave birth to a lamb against its nature.

---

[42] For the text and a brief introduction with useful bibliography, see *Aelfrics Grammatik und Glossar: Text und Varianten*, ed. Julius Zupitza. 4th, unaltered edn with an introduction by Helmut Gneuss. Hildesheim: Weidmann, 2003; also Helmut Gneuss, *English Language Scholarship: A Survey and Bibliography from the Beginnings to the End of the Nineteenth Century*. MRTS, 125. New York: MRTS, 1996, pp. 8–13; and 'The Study of Language in Anglo-Saxon England' (The Toller Memorial Lecture 1989), *Bulletin of the John Rylands University Library of Manchester* 72 (1990), 3–32. Ælfric's sources are Donatus, Priscian, Book I of Isidore's *Etymologiae* and the anonymous *Excerptiones de Prisciano*, the last of which is the main source (ed. and trans. David W. Porter as *Excerptiones de Prisciano: The Source for Ælfric's Latin-Old English Grammar*. Cambridge: Brewer, 2002).

[43] cf. *Excerptiones*, ed. Porter, pp. 206–8.

[44] It is found in Book X, §34: 'Fabulae sunt quaedam poetarum figmenta uel histrionum, quae nec factae sunt nec fieri possunt, quiae contra naturam sunt' [Fables are certain fictions of poets or players which were neither done nor could have been done because they are contrary to nature] (Text: Porter, p. 324; trans., p. 325).

[45] *Ælfric's Catholic Homilies: The Second Series, Text*, ed. Malcolm Godden. EETS SS 5. London: Oxford University Press, 1979, Homily XVII.

[46] The first part of account is from II. xxiii, the miraculous signs are from III. viii. For the source of the quotation below, see Rufinus, *Historia Ecclesiastica*, III. viii. 3, quoted in Godden's *Commentary*, p. 511.

Along with the other signs, this speaks of God's power as Creator over his creation and over the laws of nature. Here, however, the natural order which allots offspring to animals according to their kind has been disrupted by God as a sign to the recalcitrant Jews that they are perverting the correct course of things by persisting in living according to the Old Law.

Another similar usage occurs in the Old English Life of St Nicholas, which according to its editor constitutes 'the earliest vernacular translation of the Greek and Latin *vitae* of the saint...composed at the earliest in the eleventh century'.[47] It is found in a late twelfth-century collection of various prose texts in Old English from the tenth and eleventh centuries. The present life is a close translation of a Latin life of the saint known as the *Vita de Johannis Diaconus*, but may be from an early exemplar which did not include the later accretions to the original legend (p. 49). In an exotic episode, the devil, disguised as an old woman, gives some sailors some oil prepared by sorcerers and asks them to give it to St Nicholas. While on the sea, they unexpectedly see a ship full of beautiful men, with a man very like St Nicholas in the middle. He tells them that the woman was the shameful goddess Diana, and that if they throw the oil into the sea they will see what it really is:

Hi dydon þa hwætlice eal swa heom getæht wæs; & sona swa þæt ele toc on þæt wæter, þa aras þær upp swiðe mycel fyr & seo sæ bærnde lange hwile. (Soðlice, þæt wæs ongean rihtum gecynde!) And eal swa þa scipmen þæt wunder beheoldan, þa wurdan þa scype swa fyr totwæmde ægþer fram oðren þæt heo ne mihton ofcleopigen þa oðre menn ne eac ofaxien hwæt he wære, se þe wið heom spæc. Ac ferde þa forð al swa heo ær gemynt hæfdon, & eallum þan mannum þe heo gemetton, hi tealdon hu heom gelumpan wæs.   (p. 92, ll. 315–22)

They quickly then did just as they had been instructed, and as soon as the oil touched the water there rose up a very great fire and the sea burned for a long time. (Truly, that was against true nature!) And just as the sailors saw that wonder, then the ships were separated so far from one another that they could not call out to the other men or moreover ask what he was, who spoke with them. But they then travelled on just as they had intended to before, and to all the men whom they met, they told what had happened to them.

It is true that the intervention of the devil cross-dressed as a pagan goddess raises issues of deviant gender roles, and that the effect of the oil is to separate the men from the homosocial community of the blessed.[48] However, the main interest here appears to be the exotic elements of sorcerous potions and the saint's miraculous ability to translocate.

---

[47] *The Old English Life of St Nicholas with the Old English Life of St Giles*, ed. E. M. Treharne. Leeds Texts and Monographs New Series 15. Leeds: Leeds Studies in English, 1997, at p. 2. She goes on to date it tentatively 'post-1087' (p. 51).

[48] On the devil in the *Life of Saint Nicholas*, see further chapter 3 of Peter Dendle's *Satan Unbound: The Devil in Old English Narrative Literature*. Toronto: University of Toronto Press, 2001.

Nevertheless, there is an anonymous homily on the Antichrist which also associates the devil with acts which disturb the balance of nature.[49] In the course of a description of the Antichrist's terrible doings, the anonymous homilist recounts some fearful marvels, including the following feat:

and sæ he deð on lytelre hwile beon ungemetlice and ungecyndelice swyðe astyrode, and þærrihte eftsona smylte; and mistlice gesceafta he awent of heora gecyndum: wæter he deð, þæt yrnð ongean stream; þas lyfta and windas he astyrað to ðan swiðe, þæt mannum þincð heora dead leofra, þonne ðone egesan to gehyranne.   (p. 196)

And the sea he makes in a short time to be immeasurably and unnaturally greatly stirred up, and immediately again calm. And variously he turns created things from their natures: he makes water so that it runs against the stream. He stirs up the skies and winds so greatly that death seems preferable to people than to hear the fearful thing.

As with the Life of St Nicholas, we see the devil's power over the laws of nature. However, unlike God's supension of the natural order in the Ælfric homily, which is intended to encourage repentance, the homilist implies that the Antichrist's intervention is partly motivated by the wish to terrify and partly a reflection of his own character as the inversion of all that is good. However, there is no sense in any of these texts that sexual sin is a concern.

Sexual acts do seem to be at issue in the following confessional formula, however: 'Gif hwa fullice on ungecyndelicum ðingum ongean godes gesceafte ðurh ænig ðinc hine sylfne besmite, bereowsige þæt æfre þa hwile ðe he libbe be ðam þe seo dæd sy' [If anyone foully in unnatural ways against God's creation defiles himself through anything, let him repent it always while he lives according to what the deed is]. The sentence appears three times almost identically in one manuscript of the *Poenitentiale pseudo-Egberti* (Frantzen's *Old English Penitential*), the *Old English Handbook*, and a fragment from the mid-eleventh-century manuscript London, British Library MS Cotton Tiberius A. iii, fol. 44.[50] The contexts of the first two instances are significant, however, since neither of them appears in conjunction with the canons on sex between men.

In the *Poenitentiale Pseudo-Egberti*, same-sex acts are given detailed treatment in Book II, Canon 6.[51] However, the sentence quoted above (which Raith prints

---

[49] 'De temporibus Anticristi', in Napier, *Wulfstan*, no. xlii. Although it is edited by Napier in his collection of Wulfstan's homilies, the homily is not now considered to be by Wulfstan himself; cf. *The Homilies of Wulfstan*, ed. Dorothy Bethurum. Oxford: Clarendon Press, 1957, pp. 24–49.

[50] *Die altenglische Version des Halitgar'schen Bussbuches (sog. Poenitentiale Pseudo-Ecgberti)*, ed. Josef Raith. Bibliothek der angelsächsischen Prosa, 13. Hamburg: Henri Grand, 1933, p. 69, under *Addidamenta* 'Additions'. (This text is Oxford, Bodleian Library MS Junius 121, which Ker dates to the third quarter of the eleventh century (N. R. Ker, *Catalogue of Manuscripts Containing Anglo-Saxon*. Oxford: Clarendon Press, 1957, §338, p. 412), but which probably represents a mid-tenth century original; cf. Frantzen, *Before the Closet*, p. 147.); [*Old English Handbook*], Roger Fowler, 'A Late Old English Handbook for the Use of a Confessor', *Anglia* 83 (1965), 1–34, at 25; [Fragment], A. Napier, 'Altenglische Kleinigkeiten', *Anglia* 11 (1888), 1–10, at 3, under the title *Be misdæda* 'Concerning misdeeds'. For the date, see Ker, *Catalogue*, §186, p. 240.

[51] This corresponds to fol. 6ᵛ of Oxford, Bodleian Library MS Junius 121. See Ker, *Catalogue*, §338, Helmut Gneuss, *Handlist of Anglo-Saxon Manuscripts: A List of Manuscripts and Manuscript*

under 'Addidamenta', p. 69) is found in Book IV, in a further set of canons concerning sexual sins, on fol. 86ᵛ in between a canon on sex with animals and one on masturbation.[52] Here, then, the sentence seems to function as a catch-all clause, and not to be associated with same-sex acts. Similarly, in the *Old English Handbook*, the clause does not appear together with the penances for same-sex acts (Fowler, 'Old English Handbook', p. 22, lines 164–70), but between a canon about sorcery and one about accidentally killing one's child (Fowler, p. 25, lines 267–83), sins which are unnatural because they rebel against the laws of nature or kinship bonds.[53]

Nevertheless, the *Old English Handbook* does contain a clause which juxtaposes sex with men with 'unnatural sins'. Book II opens with a Creed, followed by the following confessional formula which introduces a list of sins:

And cweðe þonne mid reowsigendum mode and eadmodlice his andetnessa to his scrifte, onbugende eadmodlice, and þus cweðe:
Ic andette ælmihtigum Gode and minum scrifte, þam gastlican læce, ealle þa synna þe me æfre þurh awirgede gastas on besmitene wurdon: oððe on dæde oððe on geþohte, oððe wið wæpmen oððe wið wifmen oððe wið ænige gesceaft, gecyndelicra sinna oððe ungecyndelicra.

And then one shall say with penitent spirit and humbly one's confessions to one's confessor, bowing humbly, and speak thus:
I confess to Almighty God and to my confessor, the spiritual physician, all those sins which ever through accursed spirits were [done] to my defilement: either in thought or in deed, either with men or with women or with any creature, of natural sins or unnatural.

However, although sins with men may well have been included under the category of 'unnatural sins', it is evident that this is not their sole or even primary association. Indeed, not only do unnatural sins have a wider remit than same-sex acts, they are also clearly *separated* from sins associated with Sodom in two late confessional prayers.

THE NATURE OF SODOMITIC SINS

The first prayer is found in a mid-tenth-century manuscript:[54]

Fragments Written or Owned in England up to 1100. Medieval and Renaissance Texts and Studies, 241. Tempe, AZ: Arizona Center for Medieval and Renaissance Studies, 2001, §644, p. 101; *Poenitentiale Pseudo-Ecgberti*, ed. Raith, pp. 18–19.

[52] Respectively, IV. 10, p. 52 and IV. 11, pp. 52–3.

[53] As befitting a collection of penitential material assembled by or at the behest of Wulfstan. See Patrick Wormald, 'Archbishop Wulfstan and the Holiness of Society', in his *Legal Culture in the Early Medieval West: Law as Text, Images and Experience*. London, 1999, pp. 225–51, at 231–40.

[54] London, British Library MS Cotton Vespasian D. xx, fol. 87; in H. Logeman, 'Anglo-Saxonica Minora', *Anglia* 11 (1888), 97–120, at 97–8. Logeman dates the manuscript to the late tenth century (97), but Ker to the mid-tenth century (Ker, *Catalogue*, §212, p. 278).

Ic ondette ealra synna cynn þe me æfre þurh owiht awiergde gæstas on besmitan oððe ic self þurh ænige unnytnesse to wo gefremede on geðohtum oððe on wordum oððe on dædum on me selfum, on sundran, oððe wið wæpned men, oððe wið wifmen, oððe wið ænige gesceafte gecyndelicra synna oððe ungecyndelicra ðara þe deofla cyn berað sawlum to besmitenesse.

Ic eom ondetta sodomiscre synne þe hie on gegyltan, þæt is geligre, leasunga, gitsunga, getreowleasnesse, yfelre recceleasnesse & ðristlæcnesse minra synna.

I confess all kinds of sins which ever through any accursed spirits defiled me, or I myself through any frivolity did in error either in word or deed to myself, singly, or with men, or with women, or with any creature, of natural sins or unnatural of those for which the devil's kind bear souls to defilement.

I am one who confesses sodomitic sins of which they are guilty, that is fornication, deceit, greed, faithlessness, evil recklessness and boldness of my sins.

As Fowler remarks, this seems to be the source of the shortened version in the *Old English Handbook*. What it reveals is that, even in late Anglo-Saxon England, there was still no straightforward link between Sodom and same-sex acts, as we can also see from the following prayer from a late-eleventh-century manuscript:[55]

Ic bidde ðe min drihten on ðæs acennedan godes naman þæt ðu mid þinre mildheortnysse on me beseoh, & þæt ðu onsend & getryme on mine heortan gedefe hreowe, & þe anddetnysse eallra minra synna ðæra ðe ic æfre gefremede wið þinne willan, & wiþ minre sawle þearfe, wið weras, oþþe wið wif, oþþe wiþ ænine man, wordum oþþe weorcum, oþþe on geðancum, þæt þu drihten on mine heortan getryme þine soðfæstnysse, & rihtne geleafan, & þinra beboda lustfullunga, & symle getruwunga on ðe.

Ic eom þe ealra anddettende, & þinum englum mid hreowe, & minum gastlicum scrifte for mine sawle & lichaman þe ic on gesingode. Ic eom anddetta sodomitiscre synne þe hig on gegylton, þæt ys geligre, leasunga & gytsunga, getrywleasnyssa & þristleasnyssa minra synna.

I entreat you my Lord in the incarnate God's name that you look upon me with your mercy, and that you send forth and strengthen in my heart proper penitence, and the confession of all my sins of those which I ever did against your will and against the need of my soul, with men or with women or with any person, in words or deeds or in thoughts, that you Lord strengthen your truth in my heart and proper belief, and delight in your commandments and always confidence in you.

I am one who confesses all to you and to your angels with penitence, and to my spiritual confessor for my soul and body in which I sinned. I am one who confesses sodomitic sins of which they are guilty, that is fornication, deceit, greed, faithlessness and boldness of my sins.

Again, the separation of sodomitic sins from same-sex acts is clear.

As suggested above, then, the vernacular evidence indicates a religious reluctance to be explicit about same-sex acts apart from in texts aimed at a uniquely clerical audience, and that it is primarily within in-house elite religious discourse

---

[55] London, British Library MS Cotton Tiberius C. i., fol. 160–1; Logeman, 'Anglo-Saxonica Mina,' p. 101; cf. Ker, *Catalogue*, §197, p. 260.

that same-sex activity becomes explicitly associated with the discourse of natural and unnatural desires. Even in late texts, Sodom is not primarily associated with same-sex sin, and even at his most explicit, in the anomalous Old English *Interrogationes*, Ælfric attempts to avoid spelling out what exactly the Sodomites were doing. It seems possible that Ælfric's increasing emphasis on condemnation of the Sodomites twinned with his reluctance to describe their deeds explicitly, reflects a concern, once his prose translation of Genesis was in the public domain, to warn those in the know in the strongest terms against same-sex activity yet not give the ignorant a new source of temptation. It is suggested in Chapters 9 and 10 below with regard to Ælfric's *Lives of Saints* and the anonymous *Life of Euphrosyne* that same-sex desire may have become an increasing source of anxiety in the period of the Benedictine Reform, particularly and unsurprisingly within the homosocial institution of the monastery, and that this is one reason why homosocial bonds become a site of tension and conflict in Ælfric's work. Same-sex sexuality is a haunting presence in some of these Lives, and interacts with a destabilized gender dynamic in surprising and often contradictory ways, perhaps facilitated by a reluctance to be specific in vernacular texts. Nonetheless, from the two late prayers just discussed, Ælfric's work clearly did not lead to a unanimous association of Sodom with uniquely sexual sin, still less same-sex activity.

The next chapter considers one final text which deals with the Sodom narrative, the vernacular poetic version of the book of Genesis itself. However, it shows that same-sex relations in this text cannot be considered in isolation from other sexual and interpersonal relations. It thus widens the scope of the book from a narrow focus on same-sex acts to male interpersonal relations more generally, and constitutes the first of a set of three chapters exploring homosocial bonds in Old English poetic texts.

PART III

HOMOSOCIAL BONDS IN OLD ENGLISH LITERATURE

6

Destructive Desire: Sexual Themes and Same-Sex Relations in *Genesis A*

> and Abrahame
> treowa sealdon,   þæt hie his torn mid him
> gewræcon on wraðum,   oððe on wæl feollan. (2036–8)[1]

and to Abraham they gave their promise that they would avenge his suffering with him upon the hostile ones, or fall in the slaughter.

The allusion to a promise of vengeance quoted here comes two-thirds of the way through the Old English poem known as *Genesis A*, a poetic reworking of the first book of the Bible up to the sacrifice of Isaac. It is not a moment that stands out in a poem that recounts the dramatic and well-known stories of the Fall, Cain's murder of Abel, the Flood, and the various adventures of Abraham, the founding father of the Israelite nation.

The passage in question is part of an expanded rendering of Genesis chapter 14, which recounts the battle between the kings of the north and the kings of the south, in particular those of Sodom and Gomorrah. In keeping with the other biblical events given heroic treatment in the poems of the Junius Manuscript, the conflict is extensively reworked as a Germanic battle, complete with beasts of battle topos and heroic diction.[2] Sodom and Gomorrah are routed, and, along with the other spoils of battle, Lot, Abraham's nephew, is taken captive. When Abraham discovers this he informs his three friends, a trio of brothers called Aner, Mamre, and Escol, who make the promise to aid Abraham in battle quoted above. The promise sets up a binary choice between vengeance and death, and evokes homosocial bonds of loyalty in a way reminiscent of

---

[1] Quotations are cited by line number from *Genesis A: A New Edition*, ed. A. N. Doane. Madison: University of Wisconsin Press, 1978). For a digital facsimile of the poem, see *A Digital Facsimile of Oxford, Bodleian Library, MS. Junius 11*, ed. Bernard J. Muir. Software: Nick Kennedy. Oxford: Bodleian Library, 2004. CD-ROM. For a recent study of the Junius manuscript and its contents, see Catherine E. Karkov, *Text and Picture in Anglo-Saxon England: Narrative Strategies in the Junius 11 Manuscript*. Cambridge: Brewer, 2001; see also the essays in *The Poems of MS Junius 11: Basic Readings*, ed. R. M. Liuzza. London: Routledge, 2002.

[2] On the heroic treatment of Genesis in *Genesis A*, see further Andy Orchard, 'Conspicuous Heroism: Abraham, Prudentius, and the Old English Verse *Genesis*', in *Heroes and Heroines in Medieval English Literature*, ed. Leo Carruthers. Cambridge: Brewer, 1994, pp. 45–58.

the vows of supreme loyalty of Byrhtnoth's retainers in *The Battle of Maldon* alluded to in the Introduction and explored in Chapter 7 below. It thus seems an entirely natural addition for an Anglo-Saxon poet to make to the biblical text. The passage takes on added significance, however, when considered in the context of the poet's version of the destruction of Sodom and Gomorrah, and this episode in its turn should not be read in isolation from the wider network of sexual themes running throughout the poem. In this poetic reworking of the biblical account, the Anglo-Saxon poet presents various forms of unsanctioned sexual desire as destructive in order to exalt contrastively the procreative coupling of Abraham and Sarah, the progenitors of God's chosen people.[3] The poem foregrounds the narrative progression towards Abraham's sacrifice of Isaac, the child of the promise, traditionally interpreted as a type of Christ's crucifixion, and it is important to read the Sodom episode in this wider context.

THE BURNING SHAME OF SODOM

One of the things that has often struck readers of the rendering of the Sodom episode in *Genesis A* is its matter-of-fact tone, where one might expect intense horror.[4] The first mention of the Sodomites in connection with sin does not specify what actions they were performing (as shown in more detail later), and God's description of their sins in the passage based on Genesis 18 does not make them sound like the sinister or monstrous sexual deviants of some later depictions of the Sodomites. God says of Sodom:

> Ic on þisse byrig   bearhtm gehyre,
> synnigra cyrm   swiðe hludne,
> ealogalra gylp,   yfele spræce
> werod under weallum habban.   forþon wærlogona sint
> folces firena hefige.   ic wille fandigan nu,
> mago ebrea,   hwæt þa men don,
> gif hie swa swiðe   synna fremmað
> þeawum and geþancum   swa hie on þweorh sprecað
> facen and inwit. (2408–16)

I hear revelry in this city, the very loud clamour of sinners, ale-wanton boasting, the troop inside the walls having evil speech together; for the crimes are heavy of the faith-breakers, of this people. I will find out now, man of the Hebrews, what those men are doing: if they commit sins so greatly in their practices and thoughts as they crookedly speak treachery and evil.

---

[3] On depictions of Abraham and Sarah's marriage throughout Old English literature, see Daniel Anlezark, 'An Ideal Marriage: Abraham and Sarah in Old English Literature', *Medium Ævum* 69 (2000), 187–210.

[4] See for example, Godden, 'Trouble with Sodom', 109.

Malcolm Godden claims of this passage that the sense overall is of 'a confident and boisterous community, with overtones of the heroic society' (110), and appositely compares the Sodomites to the drunken and badly behaved warriors in the feast at the beginning of the Old English *Judith* (15–32a). It is indeed true that the poet refrains from melodramatic condemnation of the Sodomites, and does not give us any sense here that their sins involve sexual misdemeanours. However, in the translation given in Godden's article any Modern English equivalent of the phrase *on þweorh* 'crookedly, perversely' is omitted, a term which does give a somewhat unnatural slant to the deeds God fears the Sodomites may be committing.

On its own this would not be enough to link the Sodomites to same-sex behaviour, or even to unnatural behaviour, but the description of the Sodomites' quarrel with Lot over the angels who are visiting him is much clearer in invoking the discourse of nature. The Sodomites demand that Lot hand the angels over, and:

> wordum cwædon
> þæt mid þam hæleðum hæman wolden
> unscomlice, arna ne gymden. (2459–61)

said in words that they wanted to have sex with the men shamelessly, did not care for honour.

The poet stresses that their demand is made *unscomlice* 'shamelessly', implying that they are showing an inappropriate and culpable lack of a sense of shame. The Sodomites (via the poet's coloured indirect speech) use the standard term for sex, *hæman*, thus equating same-sex with male-female intercourse.[5] Lot, however, refuses this equation, offering his virgin daughters to the Sodomites instead, saying:

> Her syndon inne unwemme twa
> dohtor mine. doð swa ic eow bidde
> —ne can þara idesa owðer gieta
> þurh gebedscipe beorna neawest—
> and geswicað þære synne. ic eow sylle þa
> ær ge sceonde wið gesceapu fremmen,
> ungifre yfel ylda bearnum. (2466–72)

Here inside are my two unblemished daughters. Do as I ask you—neither of these women yet knows intercourse through the companionship of men—and give up that sin. I will

[5] Allen Frantzen shows that the poet is following the Old Latin text of the Bible here, which states explicitly that the men demanded sex, rather than the Vulgate which states more ambiguously that the men wanted 'to know' the guests (Frantzen, *Before the Closet*, p. 221). The term *hæman* is used in penitentials and homilies for 'sexual intercourse' or 'fornication', but Shari Horner has recently argued that it is often employed in contexts where sexual violence or rape is connoted; see her 'The Language of Rape in Old English Literature and Law: Views from the Anglo-Saxon(ist)s', in Pasternack and Weston, *Sex and Sexuality*, pp. 149–81.

give them to you before you commit shame against nature, harmful evil against the sons of men.

As we shall see, the phrase *sceonde wið gesceapu fremmen* implicitly contrasts the Sodomites' behaviour with that of Adam and Eve earlier in the poem. However, even without this contrast the proposed action is clearly both shameful and unnatural. The Sodomites are continually associated throughout the poem with shame, dishonour, and sin.[6] However, it is true, as Godden points out, that the poet never explicitly indicates that same-sex activity is 'a defining characteristic of Sodomite society, or that it is what constitutes the sin of which God has heard and for which he destroys them' (111). It could be argued that in his repetition of words in the semantic fields of shame and nature, and perhaps in the phrase *on þweorh*, the poet indicates an awareness that same-sex activity equates with the 'sin against nature' of religious discourse, but from the poem alone this remains implicit, something that only an educated cleric would pick up. Moreover, as demonstrated in Chapters 4 and 5, this is a discourse that is itself not unproblematic or exclusively concerned with same-sex behaviour.

BREEDING HOPE: EXOGAMY AND ENDOGAMY IN THE ABRAHAMIC NARRATIVE

In *Before the Closet* Frantzen presents a detailed account of the Sodom episode in *Genesis A*, in which he makes the claim that 'the history of Sodom dominates the other episodes in the poem, accounting for some 700 of 2,936 lines' (p. 216). However, although it is true that several hundred lines deal with Sodom or its kings, it is misleading to imply that this equates to the episode containing the Sodomites' threatened rape of the angels and the destruction of the city, or that this episode dominates the poem. By my calculation this episode, including fitts 29, 30, and the beginning of 31, comes to 200 lines (2399–599), closer to one-seventh than a quarter of the whole poem.

It is not just a matter of numbers, though. Although it is not possible to explore *Genesis A* in full here, nevertheless, it is important to read the Sodom episode within a wider context of sexual themes in the poem. Both in the biblical Genesis and *Genesis A*, the overarching narrative is that of God's chosen people, their disobedience to him and his faithfulness to them. Emphasized in both is God's covenant with Abraham to make his descendants as numerous as the stars in the sky—it is the founding narrative of the Israelite nation. The poem as extant ends with the episode where God tests Abraham's faith by commanding him to sacrifice his only son, Isaac. When the patriarch shows that he is willing to make this ultimate sacrifice of his long-awaited child, God at the last moment substitutes a ram.

---

[6] *Genesis A* 1934–6a, 2408–16a, 2477a, 2506b, 2532a, 2533a, 2581–3a.

This might seem an odd place to end a poem, however climactic, but in the light of medieval exegesis, it seems likely that this episode was indeed originally intended to occupy the emphatic final position in the narrative. In terms of medieval typology, the sacrifice of Isaac represents a type, or a prefiguring, of Christ's crucifixion as both the Only Begotten Son of God and the Lamb of God who takes away the sins of the world.[7] It is therefore possible to use the figure of Isaac as the promised child of the covenant as a means of reading the poem as a whole, particularly its treatment of sexual themes. In this context the poem presents a normative ideal whereby the male-female procreative activity of Abraham and Sarah via divine intervention produces the promised heir. Against this norm the poem places various forms of non-ideal sexual activity, in which the activity of the Sodomites is included. In looking at the unsanctioned varieties of sexual activity, we may divide them into two groups as forms of what may be termed exogamic and endogamic relations, anthropological terms which I apply here to literature following the lead of Jane Gilbert's work on the *Gawain*-poet.[8]

As Gilbert explains, endogamy and exogamy are normally framed within anthropological discourse in exclusively heterosexual terms and are used for kinship structures, that is, they concern who can marry whom (p. 54 and n. 2). Many societies divide people into three categories of sexual availability. The first category involves endogamic relations—where the object is too close or 'too similar' to the subject. This term is usually applied to incestuous relations (that is, relations between people belonging to the same kinship group), but it is equally applicable to gender, where it disqualifies same-sex relations (that is, relations between people of the same anatomical sex). This may be called (as in Gilbert's work) extreme endogamy. The second category comprises those who are sexually available, defined in terms of degrees of kinship or sexual difference: subject and object are similar but not too similar. The third category is exogamic relations—where the object is too distant or 'too different' from the subject— this would include those who belong to a different race, or a different ontological order, such as animals, angels, or devils.[9]

---

[7] See for instance Robert P. Creed, 'The Art of the Singer: Three Old English Tellings of the Offering of Isaac', in *Old English Poetry: Fifteen Essays*, ed. Robert P. Creed. Providence, RI: Brown University Press, 1967, pp. 69–92. Creed points out the rich ambiguity of the phrase *wudu bær sunu* (l. 2887) which could be interpreted 'the son bore the wood' (Isaac carried the wood for the sacrifice); 'the wood bore the son' (Isaac was bound on the wood to be sacrificed); 'the Son bore the Cross' (Christ carried his cross to Calvary); 'the Cross bore the Son' (Christ was crucified as an atoning sacrifice). He concludes *Genesis A* 'ends with a drama that is both time-bound in the past and timeless, at once the climatic event in the life of the patriarch and a pre-enactment of the central act and ritual of Christianity' (p. 80).

[8] See Jane Gilbert, 'Gender and Sexual Transgression', in *A Companion to the* Gawain-*Poet*, ed. Derek Brewer and Jonathan Gibson. Cambridge: Brewer, 1997, pp. 53–69.

[9] See the fuller discussion in Gilbert, 'Gender and Sexual Transgression', pp. 54–6, where she also helpfully discusses the constructed nature of sexuality and the need to avoid modern assumptions in analysing relations constructed as natural or unnatural in premodern texts.

The rest of this section looks at the range of unsanctioned sexual behaviours in the Abrahamic narrative, from Abraham's marriage to Sarah and their migration with Abraham's nephew Lot to the land of Canaan at God's instruction (Doane's sections 26–41). When Abraham and Sarah pose as siblings in Egypt, for instance, exogamic relations are only narrowly avoided after Pharoah hears of Sarah's beauty and takes her for himself. In preventing this union, God prevents the exogamy of sexual relations with a member of a heathen nation (section 27a). This activity is also invoked in the section where Lot is taken captive in battle, in an addition that the poet makes to the biblical source. He sharply abbreviates the account we see in Genesis 14, omitting the unfamiliar proper names, and giving only the most essential details. However, he emphasizes the peril of the people of Sodom and Gomorrah, by adding the comment that 'sceolde forht monig | blachleor ides bifiende gan | on fremdes fæðm' (1969b–71a) [Many a pale-cheeked maiden, terrified, had to go trembling into the embrace of a stranger/foreigner]. These relations again represent negatively viewed exogamy, here forced marriage into a foreign nation.

The other examples of exogamic relations are more directly contrasted with the divinely sanctioned union, as when, immediately after God's speech promising Abraham descendants as numerous as the stars in the sky and specifically from his wife's body, Sarah decides that she knows better and gives her Egyptian maid to her husband to ensure an heir that way (sections 30–1). This exogamic union causes not only short-term trouble between Abraham and Sarah, but also long-term trouble in the form of the Ishmaelites who later continually plague Israel. The following sections clarify the place of Ishmael, the fruit of this unsanctioned union, and juxtapose his account with the institution of the rite of circumcision, the physical sign of the chosen people—a marker of the racial group against which exogamic relations can be defined.

In a similar way, the poet's version of Abraham's dealings with the foreign king Abimelech emphasizes the importance of avoiding unsanctioned unions and the narrative of Isaac, the child of the promise. As with Abraham's earlier stay in Egypt, Abraham and Sarah pose as siblings to avoid the possibility of Abraham being killed to get at his wife (section 38). In this episode, the king sends for Sarah, and the poet adds to his source the comment that 'Þa [þe] wæs ellþeodig oðre siðe, | wif abrames from were læded | on fremdes fæðm' (2630–2a) [Then, exiled for a second time, Abram's wife was taken from [her] husband into the embrace of a stranger/foreigner]. The poet emphasizes thus the parallelism with the earlier account, and the danger of exogamy into a heathen nation in both places.

In the biblical version, after Abimelech is warned by God in a dream not to take Sarah, and Abraham explains his lie, the chapter ends with two brief verses explaining that God had made all Abimelech's household infertile because of Sarah. However, the Anglo-Saxon poet greatly expands this, emphasizing the punishment and God's restoration of their fertility at Abraham's intercession.

Thus he foregrounds the fact that the attempted exogamy has resulted in the potentially normative sexual relations of Abimelech's household (being other-sex but same-nation) being made barren. Non-procreative sexual relations are implicitly viewed as purposeless, and they are contrasted with God's long-awaited fulfilment of his promise and the birth of Isaac. The poem then ends with two sections dealing with Abraham's exiling of Ishmael (the result of the unsanctioned procreative union), and the purportive sacrifice but then salvation of Isaac, the heir and fruit of the true and normative union.

The problematic and unsanctioned unions explored here are, of course, in the biblical source, but the poet has reworked them in such a way as to emphasize the contrast with the sanctioned procreative union of Abraham and Sarah. Moreover, he has also added a couple of passages to his source which foreground the terror of exogamy.

In this context, it is easy to see how the intervening sections of the narrative (sections 34–7) can be viewed as representing unsanctioned endogamy, for they concern the sins and destruction of Sodom and Gomorrah, followed by the account of Lot's incestuous union with his daughters. Incest along with same-sex activity represents extreme endogamy here, and, to a medieval society where even seven degrees of kinship represented an impediment to sexual relations, incest within the immediate family must have seemed particularly deviant to many readers. However, although it is thus possible to see how the final part of the poem represents the climax of a structured discourse where a normative divinely sanctioned union (that of Abraham and Sarah) is contrasted with various types of censured exogamic and endogamic unions, this formulation does not tell the whole story, and ignores some important elements of the poetic narrative which require closer attention.

SANCTIONED AND UNSANCTIONED
HOMOSOCIAL BONDS

The city of Sodom is first introduced in section 23 of the poem, when Lot and Abraham part company to find more room for them and their growing households, and Lot chooses the fertile land by the river Jordan where he lives within the city of Sodom. There is here a premonition of the city's coming destruction when we are told that the area

> wæs wætrum weaht   and wæstmum þeaht,
> lagostreamum leoht   and gelic godes
> neorxnawange.   on þæt nergend god
> for wera synnum   wylme gesealde
> sodoman and gomorran,   sweartan lige. (1922–6)

was refreshed with waters and covered with fruits, watered with rivers and like God's paradise, until God the Saviour, because of men's sins, gave Sodom and Gomorrah to the surging, to the black flames.

The description of its fertility and the comparison to the earthly paradise may seem to hint at the sterile 'sin against nature' which is detailed in the later episode. However, although the poet is at pains to emphasize that Lot refused to adopt the Sodomites' 'customs' and 'habits', their 'evil and sin', there is nothing in this section that states explicitly that these involve or are confined to sexual activity.

What may to the informed and alert reader indicate that same-sex activity is at least partly at issue here, is the context of this passage within the episode (comprising sections 23 to 25) which contains Lot's settlement in Sodom, the wars of the kings of the North and the South, the defeat of Sodom and capture of Lot, Abraham's rescue and meeting with Melchizedek the high priest and with the king of Sodom. This is a self-contained episode which precedes the crucial promise of God to make Abraham the father of a nation, and deserves extended analysis, since interpretations of any individual part of it will necessarily be modified in the light of this wider context.

The reason that Lot and Abraham have to find separate lands on which they and their households can live is that the lack of space in their previous dwellings causes friction between their followers: 'oft wæron teonan | wærfæstra wera weredum gemæne, | heardum hearmplega' (1896b–7a) [there were often hostilities among the people of the trustworthy men, hard strife (lit. harmful-play)]. However, Abraham is *ara gemyndig* 'mindful of honour' (1899a), and says to Lot that they as uncle and nephew should never be at enmity: 'wit synt gemagas. unc gemæne ne sceal | elles awiht nymþe ealltela | lufu langsumu' (1904–6a) [we two are kinsmen—there shall be nothing at all in common to the two of us except, quite properly, long-lasting love]. This statement is almost gnomic in its construction, emphasizing the importance of maintaining honourable homosocial bonds between kinsmen much more than the biblical original,[10] and we may compare this with the bonds of friendship between Abraham and his close companions whose promise to help him rescue Lot or die was quoted at the start of the chapter.

Throughout his narrative, Abraham is depicted as an ideal Germanic warrior leader, described with heroic epithets such as *wærfæst hæleð* 'the steadfast hero' (2026a), and his rescue of Lot, as we have seen, becomes a traditional battle-scene. We are told for instance of him and his companions: 'Rincas wæron rofe, randas wægon | forð fromlice on foldwege' (2049–50) [The warriors were brave: they bore shields forth boldly on the earth-way]. And in a passage which would

---

[10] The original has 'Let there be no quarrel, I beseech thee, between me and thee, and between my herdsmen and thy herdsmen: for we are brethren' (Genesis 13: 8).

resonate all the more strongly with an Anglo-Saxon audience who heard it after the Danegeld began to be paid, the poet asserts that

> abraham sealde
> wig to wedde   nalles wunden gold
> for his suhtrigan,   sloh and fylde
> feond on fitte. (2069b–72a)

Abraham gave war as ransom, not at all twisted gold, for his nephew; slew and felled the enemy in fight.

When Abraham brings back to the peoples of Sodom and Gomorrah their *sinc and bryda* 'treasure and brides' (2090b), *bearn* 'children' (2091a), and *mæged* 'maidens' (2092a), the poet comments:

> næfre mon ealra
> lifigendra her   lytle werede
> þon wurðlicor   wigsið ateah
> þara þe wið swa miclum   mægne geræsde. (2092b–95)

never did a man of all those living here with a small company set out more worthily on a battle-expedition of those who attacked so great a host.

It would be possible just to dismiss this episode as Anglo-Saxon hack-work— a thoughtless recasting of the biblical battle in the traditional mode of Old English battle-poetry. However, this depiction of a small band of heroic warriors, united by intense homosocial loyalty, gaining victory against the odds, also provides an implicit contrast with the inadequacies of Sodomite society, just as the Sodomite king provides a contrast to the victorious and heroic leader-figure of Abraham.

The people of Sodom are seen to be taking part in a battle against injustice— the kings of the south are revolting against the payment of tribute that the king of the Elamites has enforced for twelve years (1973–81). But they are unable to defeat their foes and indeed:

> gewiton feorh heora
> fram þam folcstyde   fleame nergan.
> secgum ofslegene   him on swaðe feollon
> æðelinga bearn,   ecgum ofþegde
> willgesiððas. (1999b–2003a)

They departed to save their lives by flight from the dwelling-place. Behind the men in their track fell the sons of nobles, their pleasant companions destroyed by sword-edge.

We have already seen how the terror of exogamy is foregrounded by the addition of a passage describing the terror of the maiden forced into the embrace of a stranger immediate before the battle, and this is reinforced after the defeat, when we are told how 'mægð siðedon | fæmnan and wuduwan, freondum beslægene, |

from hleowstole' (2009b–11a) [the maidens journeyed, the women and widows, deprived of friends, from the shelter-seat].

It is against this picture of failure and flight that the poet presents the image of Abraham and his companions, steadfast in determination to rescue Lot from these people. The contrast could hardly be stronger—Abraham fights to save his nephew and wins, the Sodomites flee the battle they are losing, even though this means their helpless womenfolk will be taken into captivity. Their treasures, womenfolk, and children are restored to them by the foreign hero, who has saved them as a by-product of his own successful agenda.

This reading of the battle gives some support to Frantzen's reading of the speeches exchanged between Abraham and the king of Sodom as fraught with irony, and intended to associate Sodom with effeminacy. However, Frantzen's argument is frequently mistaken in detail, owing to a misunderstanding of some of the language which leads him to create an inaccurate picture of what the poet is doing in these passages.

The Sodomite king's speech to Abraham is a request to be given *mennen minra leoda, þe þu ahreddest* 'the handmaidens of my nation, whom you rescued' (2126–7a) in return for which he suggests that Abraham keep the *wunden gold* 'twisted gold' (2128b), *feoh and frætwa* 'wealth [or cattle] and treasures' (2130a). The poet gives him a pathetic plea:

> læt me freo lædan
> eft on eðel   æðelinga bearn,
> on weste wic   wif and cnihtas,
> earme wydewan.   eaforan syndon deade,
> folcgesiðas   nymðe fea ane
> þe me mid sceoldon   mearce healdan. (2130b–5)

Free, let me lead the children of nobles back to their homeland, to the deserted places the women and children, [and] wretched widows. The sons are dead, the people-comrades, except a few only, those who should have held the borders with me.

Frantzen inaccurately translates *mennen* 'handmaidens' as 'men', and thus is led to think that the king is requesting the return of his warriors in opposition to the women and children of his people. He translates lines 2130b–3a in such a way as to suggest that the *æðelinga bearn* 'the children of nobles' are the Sodomite men, whom he wishes to lead back, not *with*, but *to* the women, boys, and widows who, he implies, are waiting for them at home.[11] The problems with Frantzen's interpretation of Abraham's reply to the king are more complex, but they similarly involve an oversimplification of the poet's attitude to the Sodomites.

---

[11] Compare the following page where he states: 'The warriors of Sodom have been slain, and the king now has only women (and boys) to return to' (*Before the Closet*, pp. 218–19).

Abraham in his reply refuses the offer of the gold, saying rather that the Sodomite king should take it. He does, however, reserve the share belonging to his companions Aner, Mamre, and Escol, saying:

> nelle ic þa rincas   rihte benæman
> ac hie me fulleodon   æt æscþræce,
> fuhton þe æfter frofre. (2153–5a)

I do not want to deprive the warriors of their right, for they helped me at the spear-violence, fought as a comfort for you.

Here, Abraham appears as the righteous war-leader, who magnanimously gives up his share in the spoils, but will not deprive his soldiers of their share. However, if we look at this passage in the light of his exact expressed motivation for refusing the Sodomites' gold, there seems to be more at issue. Abraham says that he does not want to take the plunder

> þy læs þu eft cweðe
> þæt ic wurde   willgesteallum
> eadig on eorðan   ærgestreonum,
> sodoma rice. (2146b–9a)

lest you afterwards say that I became blessed on earth by the pleasant companions, by the ancient treasures, by the kingdom of Sodom.

Frantzen quotes Doane's editorial note on the compound *willgesteallan* 'pleasant companions' (2147b), which Doane compares with the similar compounds *will-gebroðor* 'pleasant brothers' (971b) and *willgesweostor* 'pleasant sisters' (2608a), claiming that 'in all three places the compound in *will-ge-* has sinister and ironic overtones. Probably the poet makes Abraham reject the king of Sodom's offer in this way because of the traditional distaste for this people, even though it involves getting ahead of the story' (Doane, *Genesis A*, p. 301).

The implication is clear, as Frantzen notes, that Doane believes the poet 'looks ahead to Genesis 19 and the destruction that punished the Sodomites' sexual immorality and allows his contempt for that conduct to color his representation of the king and his defeated people' (Frantzen, *Before the Closet*, p. 218). It is indeed true that the two other *will-ge-* compounds Doane and Frantzen cite have 'ironic overtones', since *willgebroðor* is used of Cain and Abel, not normally thought of as loving brothers, and *willgesweostor* describes Lot's daughters after they seduce their drunken father and thus incestuously obtain sons. However, if (as Doane and Frantzen both suggest but do not spell out) *willgesteallan* (here and in line 2003a) carries the sly implication that the king's companionship with the Sodomites is coloured by a predilection for male-male sex, then this is at the very least complicated by the fact that the poet also refers to Abraham's own companions, Aner, Mamre, and Escol, as *willgeðoftan* 'pleasant comrades'

(2026b) just before the passage quoted at the start of this chapter where they swear loyalty unto death.

It is possible for us to read the compound *willgesteallan* as a reference to the Sodomites' same-sex activity, but if we do so, we must factor in this other homosocial relationship described in similar terms. It is implausible to suggest that Abraham and his companions are depicted as enjoying sexual relations, and thus it can only make sense to see this as the poet's attempt to construct a contrast between the two relationships, in a similar way to the way in which he contrasts the exogamic relations analysed above unfavourably with the sanctioned procreative relationship of Abraham and Sarah, and Abraham himself with the Sodomite king. In this reading we can see that Abraham is consistently associated with positively viewed homosocial relations—he speaks of the *langsamu lufu* 'long-lasting love' which is *ealltela* 'quite properly' between him and his kinsman Lot, and he and his three *willgeðoftan* exemplify the right relationship between friends and battle-allies, which we are reminded of when Abraham is careful to keep back the part of the spoil which belongs to his companions for keeping their promise to him. In contrast, the relations among the Sodomites do not lead to martial victory and glory, but to flight and the loss of their womenfolk and dependants.

It is true that this dynamic constructs the Sodomite king as less of a man than Abraham, but it is far from clear that Frantzen is correct to state that Abraham's speech 'drips with sarcasm, contempt, and ironic praise for the defeated Sodomite king, whom he calls "keeper of heroes," ... "glorious prince," ... and "protector of nobles ones"' (p. 218). It is just as easy to see these epithets as the words of a magnanimous victor, tactfully restoring some small measure of dignity to the king whose people he has had to save on his behalf. Abraham is reluctant to go down in history as the plunderer of Sodom's treasures, as we have seen, but if an ironic contrast is being drawn between Abraham and the king it is drawn by the poet and not the patriarch. Indeed, the poetic tone that comes across at this point is one of empathy for the plight of the people of Sodom, not contempt or scorn.

This interpretation is supported by the passage concerning Melchizedek, the high-priest of Sodom, before the king's interchange with Abraham. We are told that he came to Abraham with gifts and 'honorably' (2105), and 'pronounced upon him the blessing of God'. Melchizedek's speech is eloquent in its praise of Abraham and its attribution of his victory to God's personal intervention, and Abraham rewards 'the bishop of God' with a tenth of the army's booty (2120). It is hard to reconcile this event with the notion that either the poet or Abraham holds unqualified scorn for the Sodomite nation, particularly if we recall that the writer of Hebrews interprets Melchizedek as a prefiguration of Christ, 'a high priest for ever according to the order of Melchisedech'.[12] It thus seems evident

[12] Hebrews 6: 20; see further the elaboration of this typology in Hebrews chapter 7, and Doane's comments on the development of this in patristic tradition, p. 300, note to 2102. On Bede's use of this tradition, see Jones, 'Some Introductory Remarks' § III. Topics. B. Melchisedech.

that the *Genesis A* poet has a more complex attitude to the Sodomite nation than Frantzen or Doane concede.

One way of explaining this could be that the poet, contrary to the impression given by other interpreters, did not conceive of the Sodomites' desire to have sex with the angels as particularly terrible or strange. Evidence was reviewed in Chapter 2 which suggested that the Anglo-Saxons may have been familiar with male-male sex either in contemporary life or within cultural memory. Some of the Germanic tribes may have practised cross-generational sodomy, and even post-Conversion Anglo-Saxons may have retained a sense that it was perfectly manly (albeit sinful) to feel desire for boys or *bædlings* as well as for women. It seems potentially significant, then, that when the Sodomite king laments the loss of his companions, he calls them *eaforan* 'the sons, descendants' (2123), which may carry the implication of youth.

Likewise, when the angels come to Sodom, the poet tells us that they appeared as *geonge . . . men* 'young men' (2430b–1a). These two instances are not much to go on, but it may be that at least some elements in an Anglo-Saxon audience uninfluenced by the religious discourse condemning the 'sin against nature' would not have felt revulsion or surprise at the idea of men wanting to have sex with young men *per se*, or have seen the Sodomites as a nation of degenerate perverts. They might well, as we have seen, have contrasted the manliness of Abraham and the Sodomite king and their relations with their companions, but their horror at the Sodomites' desire to have sex with the angels was more likely to be at the inhospitable aggression that it signified, and the indignity that it would offer to the angels' manhood, rather than the gender of the sexual object choice in itself.[13]

However, even if this is not the case, it is undeniable that as we saw above same-sex activity is depicted in the poem as just one of many forms of undesirable sexual activity that do not lead to the correct type of procreation. We will see how this works on a lexical level shortly, but this more nuanced understanding of masculinity in the poem can help us to see the poet's version of the Flood narrative in a new light too, a narrative that, as we saw in Chapter 5, is contrasted by some Old English writers with the destruction of Sodom.

Indeed, the discourse of sanctioned procreative male-female relations and appropriate homosocial relations in contrast with unsanctioned and inappropriate relations of various kinds, may explain the poet's re-presentation of Noah's Flood as God's revenge for the union between the sons of God and the daughters of men. The biblical account in Genesis chapter 6 gives a confusing picture which was sometimes interpreted as describing miscegenation between angels (the sons of God) and humans (the daughters of man)

---

[13] The poem is often dated early (see Doane, *Genesis A*, pp. 36–7) and this might explain the lack of anxiety displayed in later writers such as Ælfric.

producing the mysterious *nephilim*, possibly giants, as offspring.[14] This forms part of a general picture of licentiousness which results in God's anger and the punishment of the world by means of the Flood. However, the Anglo-Saxon poet is unambiguous in his interpretation of the two groups involved. He makes it clear that, for him, the sons of God are the descendants of Seth, and the daughters of men are the descendants of Cain; that is, the miscegenation is between the good and the bad lines of Adam. Still further the poet presents this, in another speech attributed to God, as the joint responsibility of culpable female beauty and the devil:

> þær wifa wlite   onwod grome,
> idesa ansien   and ece feond,
> folcdriht wera   þa ær on friðe wæron. (1260–2)

The beauty of women has hostilely attacked—the countenance of females and the eternal enemy—the nation of men who before were at peace.

As Godden comments 'For God this is very much a gender war, another fall of man brought about by women with the help of the devil, just like Eden' (113). This is supported by lexical details in the passage, since *onwod* could equally be translated 'penetrated into', and *folcdriht wera* means something like 'the national army of husbands', creating an implicit gender reversal. Here it is women, not male soldiers who occupy the active, aggressive pole in the male-female binary, and the language even implies that the sexual roles have been reversed, with the women penetrating the passive men.[15] Rather than agreeing with Godden that this is a 'founding myth of heterosexual desire and its destructiveness', however, we should see the miscegenation as central here—the destructiveness of male-female sex *with the wrong kind of people*. After all, the feminine beauty of Sarah is also emphasized in the poem (e.g. lines 1846b–55), and, although this does cause trouble, her sexual union with Abraham is what enables the continuation of the chosen line. Instead, this version of the Flood provides further evidence of how masculinity must be carefully policed—throughout the Genesis narrative we are shown how easy it is to become feminized if one is not careful. Abraham, the patriarch and founder of Israel, exemplifies how to be a man in his successful maintenance through God's help of a procreative union and appropriate homosocial bonds.

---

[14] See further Doane's commentary on lines 1245b–52 (pp. 256–7), and Chapter 4 above, pp. 69–70.

[15] The assumption here, presumably, is that the passive role in sex is shameful for men, and the active role is disgraceful for women; cf. the *nið* discourse in Old Norse discussed in Chapters 2 and 3 above. Although *ergi* implies effeminacy when applied to men, it connotes nymphomania when used of women.

CREATING SHAME AND SHAMING CREATION

It was suggested earlier that Lot's plea to the Sodomites that they not *sceonde wið gesceapu fremmen* (2471) implicitly contrasts the theatened behaviour with that of Adam and Eve earlier in the poem, and that statement can now be substantiated by a brief examination of the use of the terms *sceond* (along with *sceome*) and *gesceap* throughout *Genesis A*.

Sceond and *gesceap* are employed three times each in the poem, but whereas *sceond* always means 'shame', *gesceap* can mean 'genitals', 'nature', or 'fate, decree'.[16] Judging from the rest of the poem, we would not expect *gesceapu* to be used in the Sodom episode (2471), since the poet's usual term for 'creation, created thing, the created order' is *gesceaft*.[17] The reason that *gesceapu* is chosen here, I would argue, is to associate it with the other uses of the word in the poem and to continue its association with shame. In this way, crucial events in the poem (and the biblical narrative) are linked via lexical choice, and this further supports the network of sexual themes argued for above.

The first occurrence of the term *sceond* is in line 874, when Adam and Eve have tasted the forbidden fruit and are hiding from God. Adam tells God that he is hiding because he is naked, and God replies:

> Saga me þæt, sunu min,   for hwon secest ðu
> sceade sceomiende?   þu sceonde æt me
> furðum anfenge,   ac gefean eallum
> for hwon wast þu wean   and wrihst sceome,
> gesyhst sorge   and þin sylf þecest,
> lic mid leafum,   sagast lifceare
> hean hygegeomor   þæt þe sie hrægles þearf
> nymþe ðu æppel   ænne byrgde... (873–80)

Tell me, my son, why do you seek the shadows in shame? You became ashamed before me at once, but amidst every joy why do you know woe and hide [your] shame, see sorrow and cover yourself, [your] body with leaves, [why do you] say in life-care, low and sad at heart, that there is need for raiment unless you tasted of an apple...

The alliteration in 874 binds *sceonde* to *sceomiende* and thus to *sceome* in 876, and thus associates shame with being naked and needing to cover oneself up with clothes. God then exiles the pair, and in his speech to Adam rationalizes the 'death' that tasting the apple was to bring as meaning susceptibility to disease (936–8). The poet explains the implications of this sentence for his audience

[16] More detailed discussion follows below, but the occurrences are: *gesceapu* (nominative plural, 1573) *wið gesceapu* (accusative plural, 2471); *gesceapu* (accusative plural, 2828).

[17] *gesceaft* appears in 93, 131, 171, 199, 208, 899, 1614; it also appears in three compounds: *heah-gesceaft* (4); *woruld-gesceaft* (101, 110, 863); *metod-gesceaft* (1743). It seems interesting that in all but two cases (1614 and 1743), *gesceaft* is used of the unfallen creation, or of unfallen humans (see note 18 below).

by remarking 'Hwæt, we nu gehyrað hwær us hearmstafas | wraðe onwocan and woruldyrmðo' (939–40) [Lo, we now hear how evil troubles awakened and the miseries of the world]. God then gives Adam and Eve clothes and tells them to *heora sceome þeccan* 'cover their shame' before barring Paradise to them forever. However, the poet adds a section to his source stating that God did not take away all their comfort, but rather left them as solace *hyrstedne hrof halgum tunglum* (956) 'the firmament ornamented with holy stars' and commanded the seas and land to produce the fruits of *tuddorteondra teohha gehwilcre* (959) 'each of the young-producing species'. This image of the star-studded heavens and of the breeding of progeny foreshadows God's later promise to Abraham to give him descendants as numerous as the stars in the sky and the beginning of the fulfilment of this promise in Isaac. However, this positive image is juxtaposed with the start of Adam and Eve's own immediate family, and the story of Cain and Abel, which embodies the first murder and thus shows the negative possibilities of procreation.

A second use of the term *sceond* appears in conjunction with *gesceap* in the episode where Noah gets drunk after the Flood. We are told that he falls into a drunken slumber and manages to expose himself. The poet comments that his intelligence is crippled by the drink

> þæt he ne mihte,　　on gemynd drepen,
> hine handum self　　mid hrægle wryon
> and sceome þeccan　　swa gesceapu wæron
> werum and wifum　　siððan wuldres þegn
> ussum fæder and meder　　fyrene sweorde
> on laste beleac　　lifes eðel. (1571–6)

so that he could not, dazed in mind, hide himself with his own hands with clothes and cover [his] shame *swa gesceapu wæron* for men and women after the warrior of glory locked up the home of life behind him from our father and mother with a fiery sword.

The passage is difficult to translate because the poet plays on the dual meaning of the phrase *swa gesceapu wæron* in this context. One could translate 1573–4b as 'and cover his shame as genitals were [to be covered] for men and women' or as 'and cover his shame as the fates were [that is, as was ordained] for men and women'. Whichever we choose, the sense is clear. Noah has exposed his genitals in his drunkenness and this is shameful, because it was ordained after the Fall that all men and women, like their forebears Adam and Eve, should cover their genitals, their shameful nakedness, with clothes. There is also a further implicit connection between the passage about Adam and Eve and that concerning Noah. Noah's son Cam (that is, Cham or Ham) comes in and sees his father in this predicament, but rather than showing him honour or concealing his father's disgrace (*sceonde*, 1581) from anyone else, Cam laughs and tells his brothers. They veil their faces so that they will not directly witness their father's shame and cover Noah up, and the poet tells us that they were *gode* 'good men' (1587b). When Noah awakes, he curses Cam, and we are told that his father's words have fallen heavily on him and his race ever since (1593b–7). However, in almost an inversion of the Adam and Eve passage examined above, here the negative image of bad progeny is counteracted by the image of Iafeth's descendants multiplying, indeed filling *unlytel dæl eorðan gesceafta* 'no little part of the creations of earth' (1614).[18]

Both these passages are linked lexically to the Sodom episode via the phrase *sceonde wið gesceapu fremmen*. There is some disagreement, however, as to how it should be interpreted. The grammatical form of *gesceapu* is accusative plural, and so Doane takes the phrase to mean 'do not commit shame against your natures' (*Genesis A*, p. 357). As Frantzen points out, this 'might mean either that [same-sex activity] is not their custom or that, although it is customary among them, it is against their natures anyway'—he regards the latter as 'more likely' (*Before the Closet*, p. 221). Indeed, he sees an elaborate pun in the term:

When Lot tells the Sodomites that homosexual intercourse is against their 'natures,' he could also be telling them that this act is 'against their genitals,' contrary to the natural use of their sex organs. But the act is not, ironically, 'against their fates'; given the retribution in store for the Sodomites, homosexual intercourse does not impede their fate but rather hastens it.

One could also suggest that the phrase could mean 'do not commit shame *with* your genitals', but there is a further sense possible that takes *gesceapu* to be plural in grammatical form, but singular in function—that is, the phrase could mean 'do not commit shame against nature', in the sense 'against the created order'. In this sense, as stated earlier, one might see the poet as tapping into the discourse of the 'sin against nature'. However, this is not as clear as one might think, for the usual Old English phrase for 'against nature' is *ongean gecynd* and not *wið gesceapu*, as seen in Chapter 5. It seems that, if the poet is indeed aware of this discourse, it is not an Old English discourse but perhaps the Latin that he knows and for which he is providing an equivalent. Moreover, he does not seem to associate the shameful unnatural sin or Sodom itself exclusively with same-sex activity (in line with the majority of vernacular allusions), but rather with any unsanctioned sexual activity.

To recapitulate what we have seen of the poet's lexical choices so far, the term *sceonde* is used when God asks why Adam is hiding (874), when Cam shames his drunken father Noah (1581), and in Abraham's plea to the Sodomites not to sexually abuse his guests (2471). The term *sceomu* is used when God asks why Adam is hiding (876, along with *sceomigende* in 874) and when he clothes Adam

[18] This is one of the occurrences mentioned in the previous note of *gesceaft* not being used of unfallen creation or unfallen humans. It seems significant, however, that it should be used of the good progeny of Noah who are fulfilling the creation mandate to go forth and multiply.

and Eve (942), and of Noah's drunken shame (1573). The word *gesceap* is used of Noah drunkenly uncovering his genitals in violation of the post-exilic command (1573), and also in Abraham's plea to the Sodomites.

It is the final two uses of *sceomi(g)an* and *gesceapu* which clarify the pattern in the poem. First, the verb *sceomi(g)an* is used in line 2329 where God has just explained to Abraham the covenant of circumcision which will mark out the Israelites as his Chosen People. God promises again to give Abraham and Sarah a son, Isaac, who will prosper and of whom he says *ne þearf þe þæs eaforan sceomigan* 'you will not need to be ashamed of this heir' (2329b). This promise is further emphasized by its appearance in a hypermetric couplet. Secondly, the term *gesceapu* appears in line 2828, when Abimelech asks Abraham to requite his help and make his city and people prosper, if God *se ðe gesceapu healdeð* 'who holds the fates' will grant it. This passage seems to serve primarily to motivate Abraham's dwelling in the Philistine nation and settling in Beersheba. However, it comes immediately before the putative sacrifice and then salvation of Isaac, and so perhaps additionally emphasizes God's control over this entire situation.

These passages help to make sense of the disparate uses of the terms *sceond*, *sceomu*, and *gesceap* in the poem—they support the idea put forward above that the poet is unfolding a redemptive narrative: just as Adam and Eve sinned and were sentenced by God to exile from Eden, so too their descendants sin and are under God's judgement, but this situation will be redeemed through sanctioned procreation. Original sin itself is associated with sexuality, because the Fall brings knowledge of nakedness and the necessity of covering the genitals. By the poet's use of the terms *sceond*, *sceomu*, and *gesceap* at key points in the narrative, he brings the Fall, Noah's drunken shame, and the Sodom episode into conjunction. Human progeny always has both positive and negative potentiality (Cain versus Abel, Cam versus Iapheth (there is of course no possibility of progeny at all from the Sodomites' proposed sexual acts)), but the heir of the promise, Isaac, points to the ultimate redemptive and divinely engendered progeny, Christ.

We have seen in this chapter, then, that on both a thematic and a lexical level, the Old English poet has emphasized elements of his biblical source to foreground a pattern whereby the normative and divinely sanctioned procreative union of Abraham and Sarah can be contrasted with several forms of unsanctioned exogamic and endogamic relations. The Anglo-Saxon audience is thus encouraged to be sexually orthodox, seeing the rewards of compliance in the life of Abraham and the penalties for disobedience (even accidental disobedience as with Abimelech) in the lives of others. It is also encouraged to place sexuality within a Fall and Redemption narrative where sexuality, implicitly dangerous and associated with original sin, can be redeemed through procreation, an activity implicitly related to the birth and salvific purpose of Christ himself. Accounts of the Sodom episode which fail to take account of this wider narrative structure are necessarily partial and risk creating a misleading picture of the associations of Sodom for Anglo-Saxons.

This chapter began, however, with a passage which was compared to a climactic moment in *The Battle of Maldon*, where it is seen as part of what it is to be a thane to lie beside one's lord in death. The next chapter pursues the construction of homosocial bonds in heroic literature further and investigates how such texts fit into or extend the dynamic observed so far.

7

Heroic Desire? Male Relations in *Beowulf*, *The Battle of Maldon*, and *The Dream of the Rood*

> Earm biþ se þe sceal ana lifgan,
> wineleas wunian   hafaþ him wyrd geteod;
> betre him wære þæt he broþor ahte...
> A scyle þa rincas   gerædan lædan
> ond him ætsomne swefan;
> næfre hy mon tomælde,   ær hy deað todæle.

Wretched is he who shall live alone—fate has ordained him to dwell friendless. It were better for him that he had a brother...Always shall those warriors carry arms and sleep together—let one never slander them, before death separates them.

So speaks the universalizing voice of Anglo-Saxon gnomic wisdom, evoking the utter wretchedness of being alone, which is represented here as living, not without a wife and family, but without a brother warrior, someone with whom to bear arms and to share one's bed. This lateral homosocial bond is depicted as an eternal union of equals, the gnomicist's words echoing the traditional marriage ceremony and the images and vocabulary of separation seen in Chapter 1 in *Wulf and Eadwacer* and *The Wife's Lament*. This chapter explores such intimate homosocial bonds between lords and retainers and amongst warrior equals as they are represented in some of the best-known Old English poems, starting with an analysis of *Beowulf*, followed by briefer discussions of *The Battle of Maldon*, and *The Dream of the Rood*.[1]

HOMOSOCIAL BONDS IN *BEOWULF*

In a recent article I have argued that one's understanding of the relation of the first fitt of *Beowulf* to the rest of the poem fundamentally affects one's reading of the poet's depiction of Beowulf and his attitude to the values of the society he

---

[1] The critical literature on these texts, particularly *Beowulf*, and on heroic societies and literature more generally, is now so vast that it is not possible to note or engage any more than the most immediately relevant articles and books without overburdening the footnotes and lengthening the book unacceptably.

describes, and its treatment of the lord-retainer bond is no exception.[2] The first character introduced in the poem, Scyld Scefing, seems initially to be presented as a kingly paradigm—*þæt wæs god cyning!* 'that was a good king!' (11b): forcing neighbouring nations to yield tribute, and providing an heir to ensure continuity (4–14). This heir is praised by a gnomic passage, encouraging him with costly gifts to gain retainers who will be loyal when war comes (20–5): power alone is not enough, for loyalty and social ties are indispensable, the motivation for which is *lofdædum* 'glorious deeds' (24b). Although there are several parallels between Scyld and Beowulf,[3] I have argued that it is the differences which are the more significant, and particularly the fact that the ideal presented in the prologue, whereby gifts given inspire loyalty and are repaid when war comes, manifestly fails in practice when, except for Wiglaf, Beowulf's retainers all desert him at the dragon fight. The Scyld proem seems designed as a kind of overture, the themes, gnomic statements, assumptions, and values of which are held up for scrutiny in the rest of the poem. My article contends that the themes of loyalty and treasure work together in *Beowulf* simultaneously to celebrate and to undermine the heroic way of life that Beowulf embodies, presenting an ambivalent view of the hero and indicating that a society based on the giving and receiving of treasure is doomed to feud and ultimate destruction. Here, however, I want to explore further the homosocial bonds between Beowulf and the other chief male characters in the poem, first in his capacity as a retainer and warrior to the Danish and Geatish kings Hrothgar and Hygelac, then as a king and lord himself to Wiglaf, a relationship which does seem to exemplify the gnomic ideal of the proem, and finally to discuss the relevance to these bonds of Beowulf's failure, unlike the other kings in the poem, to provide an heir.

First, let us consider the passage which describes the moving leave-taking between Hrothgar and Beowulf as the latter prepares to return home after saving Heorot from the Grendelkin who have terrorized it for so long:

> Gecyste þa   cyning æþelum god,
> þeoden Scyldinga   ðegn betstan
> ond be healse genam;   hruron him tearas
> blondenfeaxum.   Him wæs bega wen
> ealdum infrodum,   oþres swiðor,
> þæt hie seoððan no   geseon moston,
> modige on meþle.   Wæs him se man to þon leof,
> þæt he þone breostwylm   forberan ne mehte;
> ac him on hreþre   hygebendum fæst
> æfter deorum men   dyrne langað
> beorn wið blode. (1870–80)

[2] David Clark, 'Relaunching the Hero: The Case of Scyld and Beowulf Re-opened', *Neophilologus* 90 (2006), 621–42. Some paragraphs in what follows are reworked from the article, although with a different emphasis and in pursuit of a different aim. All quotations (omitting macrons) are from Fr. Klaeber, ed., *Beowulf and the Fight at Finnsburg*. 3rd edn. Boston: Heath, 1950.
[3] Clark, 'Relaunching the Hero', 623–4.

Then the good and noble king, chief of the Scyldings, kissed the best of thanes and took him by the neck; tears fell from him, from the grizzly-haired one. In him, in the old, very wise one, one of two expectations was the greater—that they would never again be able to see each other, courageous ones in a meeting. The man was so dear to him that he was not able to restrain the welling in his breast, but in his heart, firm in the bonds of his mind, a secret longing after the dear man burned within his blood.

The noble king kisses and embraces the best of retainers, tears pouring down his face because he realizes he will probably never see Beowulf again; he is old and knows that partings are often final, and he cannot restrain the wellings of sorrow in his breast, even in this public situation. What, though, should one make of the statement that in his blood Hrothgar felt *dyrne langað* 'a secret longing' for the dear man? If one saw this kind of language in a modern novel one would of course immediately associate it with illicit sexual desire. However, it is much more likely that the illicit longing here is for Beowulf to remain as Hrothgar's heir.[4] This wish is at the very least implicit when Hrothgar tells Beowulf after he kills Grendel:

> Nu ic, Beowulf, þec,
> secg betsta, me for sunu wylle
> freogan on ferhþe; heald forð tela
> niwe sibbe. Ne bið þe nænigre gad
> worolde wilna, þe ic geweald hæbbe. (946–50)

Now, Beowulf, best of men, I would like to love you as a son/have you for a son to love in my heart; maintain well henceforth [this] new kinship. There will be for you no lack of the worldly goods which I have in my control.

Hrothgar's wife, Wealhtheow, certainly seems to take this statement seriously and to find it troubling when she says that she has heard 'þæt þu ðe for sunu wolde | hererinc habban' [that you wanted to have [this] battle-warrior for a son] (1175b–6a) and urges him rather to bequeath his land and people to his kinsmen (1178b–80a). The parting between old king and younger hero in this passage should be put in the same context as the intimate vertical bonds between Beowulf and Hygelac, and later between Beowulf and Wiglaf.[5]

We are first introduced to Beowulf as *Higelaces þegn* 'Hygelac's thane' (194b) and upon arrival in Denmark he identifies himself as one of Hygelac's companions to the coastguard and the hall-guard (261, 342b–3a) and then to Hrothgar as *Higelaces mæg ond magoðegn* 'Hygelac's kinsman and young thane' (407b–8a). He proposes fighting without weapons 'swa me Higelac sie, | min mondrihten modes bliðe' [so that Hygelac, my liegelord, may be pleased with me](435b–6), and asks that if he is slain in battle that his splendid mailcoat be sent back

---

[4] Compare Frantzen, *Before the Closet*, p. 94.
[5] Vertical bonds here are those where the participants are differentiated by rank, as opposed to horizontal bonds which link social equals.

to his lord (452–4; cf. 1482–4a). Thereafter, he is regularly referred to in the early part of the poem as *mæg Higelaces* 'Hygelac's kinsman' (737a, 758b, 813b, 1530b). Although he clearly loves and respects Hrothgar, Beowulf is eager to get back to his lord (1818–20a) and is received by Hygelac with joy as he asks his *leofa Biowulf* 'dear Beowulf' (1987b) how he fared on his journey, reveals the anxiety he experienced while Beowulf was absent ('modceare | sorhwylmum seað' [with careworn heart seethed with welled-up sorrows] (1992b–3a)), and thanks God for his safe return (1997b–8). Their verbal interchanges are formal, but reveal an intimate bond—indeed, Beowulf proclaims that 'Gen is eall æt ðe | lissa gelong' [All my joys depend on you yet] (2149b–50a), and Hygelac trusts his kinsman and retainer enough to endow him with vast lands, a hall, and a throne (2195–6a), a trust that is repaid when Beowulf refuses to take the throne after Hygelac's death but maintains the kingdom for his beloved lord's heir (2369–79a). Even in old age, before his fight with the dragon, Beowulf remembers how he earned the treasures Hygelac gave him (2490) and 'symle…him on feðan beforan wolde, | ana on orde' [ever in the troop would go before him, alone at the front] (2497–8a).

Some critics have voiced criticism of Beowulf's willingness to survive his lord—alone escaping from the battlefield to return to Geatland (2367–8), rather than dying at Hygelac's side.[6] However, this stems from the dubious practice of reading Tacitean ideals into Old English literature, as Rosemary Woolf and Roberta Frank have demonstrated.[7] Rather we should attribute this to the inevitable succession of heroic society—like Scyld Scefing in the proem, Hygelac like any king must die and be replaced by his heir, just as Beowulf passes from a lord-retainer relationship where he is subordinate, to one where he occupies Hygelac's position and Wiglaf takes over his role as the young and loyal thane.[8]

For at the end of the poem, Beowulf has become an old king himself, and Wiglaf is the young hero who refuses to flee from the dragon like the rest of Beowulf's retainers. The institutional lord-retainer bond which is set up as a model at the beginning of the poem is seen signally to fail here in Beowulf's hour of need. His hand-picked band flees *en masse* and it is not Wiglaf's sworn duty that is emphasized here but rather his dual loyalty to lord and kinsman. The poet comments that 'sibb æfre ne mæg | wiht onwendan þam ðe wel þenceð' [kinship can never be turned aside at all for him who thinks rightly] (2600). He then has Wiglaf rebuke his companions for not repaying Beowulf for the gifts and armour he has given them, saying:

---

[6] For instance, W. F. Bolton, *Alcuin and Beowulf: An Eighth-Century View*. London: Edward Arnold, 1979, p. 148.

[7] See Woolf, 'Ideal of Men Dying with their Lord'; Frank, 'Ideal of Men Dying with their Lord'; Clark, 'Creating a Tradition' (forthcoming) (cf. Ch. 2, n. 28 above).

[8] The question of whether Wiglaf constitutes Beowulf's heir and the latter's failure to produce a son is considered below, pp. 137–40.

                                    God wat on mec
        þæt me is micle leofre   þæt minne lic-haman
        mid minne gold-gyfan   gled fæðmie. (2650b–2)

God knows about me, that it is much more dear to me that fire should embrace my body
with my gold-giver.

This image of a fiery communal embrace starts a process in which the poet from
here on insistently links the two warriors via interpersonal terms. Wiglaf ends
the speech just quoted with a vow, in which he promises: 'urum sceal sweord ond
helm | byrne ond beadu-scrud bam gemæne' which can be literally rendered as
'we two shall have sword and helmet, mailcoat and battle-garment in common
(to both of us)': the difficulty both of translating the sentence's confusing deictic
pronouns and of understanding how its meaning could work in practice indicates
the intimacy of the bond described. We may compare the poet's comment
when this symbiotic pair have both fatally stabbed the dragon in the belly:
'Feond gefyldan . . . | ond hi hyne þa begen abroten hæfdon, | sibæðelingas' [They
felled the enemy . . . and then they had both destroyed it, noble kinsmen]. The
term *sibæðelingas* is crucial in this passage, perfectly encapsulating their intimate
connection and the way that their identities almost merge at this crucial point in
the narrative.

It is thus possible to construct a reading of *Beowulf* as celebrating homosocial
bonds such as those between Beowulf and Hrothgar, Hygelac and Wiglaf, and
the value of the heroic way of life when everything functions correctly and men
live up to their word. Indeed, one could argue that even the ominous comment
of the poet at the end that the treasure for which Beowulf gave his life lies in
the earth even now 'eldum swa unnyt, swa hyt æror wæs' [as useless to men as it
was before] (3168) refers only to fact that it is not being used to cement societal
ties, thus strengthening his approbation of homosocial relationships. However,
as hinted earlier, my reading of the poem is much darker than this. I think the
poem undermines the value of treasure by cumulative negative association, that
it shows how, rather than functioning as an index of moral worth, it falls into the
hands of lesser warriors as battlefield loot (as in Hygelac's fatal raid on Frisia), and
fails to maintain homosocial loyalties (as with Beowulf's hand-picked retainers
in the dragon-fight).[9] Indeed, it is not just the society of the Geats that faces
certain doom at the end of the poem, but any society in which wealth must be
continually acquired and distributed, since the acquisition of treasure entails the
acquisition of enemies from whom one has taken it. The poem is framed by this
concept, from the proem in which Scyld exacts tribute from neighbouring tribes
(9–11b) to the final threat of war from the neighbouring Swedes which looms
over the Geatish people who have lost the one man who could maintain their
supremacy (3003–4). Despite all this, one could of course still argue that the

---

[9] See Clark, 'Relaunching the Hero', *passim* and especially 639 (on lines 1195b–214a) and 626–7
(on the dragon fight).

poet holds up by contrast the value of true loyalty between men, a value which shines all the more brightly against the darkness which threatens to consume it. Nevertheless, I want to consider here the possibility that the poet in fact presents homosocial bonds in an ambivalent light, as part of his general undermining and questioning of heroic ideals. In order to do so, I need to revisit Beowulf's relation to Hrothgar and his failure to provide an heir.[10]

The leave-taking scene quoted above has caused a certain amount of embarrassment to critics who view Hrothgar as a noble figure of kingly wisdom and are nonplussed by what they see as his rheumy tears and inordinate attachment to the young hero. Thomas Wright was so troubled in the 1960s by the way this passage 'turns [Hrothgar] from a stalwart if tragic king to a sentimental ancient' whose behaviour is 'neither admirable nor Teutonic', that he was driven in Chickering's words to the resort of 'contorting a number of familiar formulas' to restore the elderly king's dignity.[11] Hrothgar's behaviour in this scene has also been criticized by Mary Dockray-Miller, who sees him as a figure who exemplifies a 'growing inability to exert power over others and to enact [the] masculine heroic ethos'.[12] The same argument has been recently restated by Stacy Klein in the context of a wider argument about the gender of heroism and its links to kingship and the succession which is considered below, but Dockray-Miller's discussion of Hrothgar is fuller and thus the one evaluated here.

Drawing on Thomas Laqueur's 'one-sex model' via Carol Clover's application of it to Old Norse literature,[13] Dockray-Miller posits that the 'emotional and homoerotic nature of the farewell scene' quoted above 'shows that the "normal" male-male relationship of the *comitatus*... has broken down to the point where Hroðgar cannot find an unambiguously masculine gesture of parting from the younger man' (2). She thinks that Hrothgar tries and fails 'to be Beowulf's Father' (she capitalizes to indicate 'the psychoanalytic associations of the word') and loses masculine status by his inability to 'wield power and dominate others in the manner that Beowulf can' (2). The specifics of Dockray-Miller's argument here are unconvincing, since there is no evidence that the shedding of tears was considered feminizing in Anglo-Saxon culture, and the episode is no more (and no less) 'homoerotic' than the situation imagined in the normative Anglo-Saxon *Maxims* quoted at the start of this chapter.[14] However, I am likewise interested

---

[10] Clare Lees takes a similar approach towards the end of her article on masculinity in *Beowulf*: see 'Men and *Beowulf*', in her *Medieval Masculinities*, pp. 129–48, esp. pp. 141–2 and 144.

[11] Thomas L. Wright, 'Hrothgar's Tears', *Modern Philology* 65 (1967), 39–44, at 39; Howell D. Chickering, Jr, trans., *Beowulf: A Dual-Language Edition*. New York: Anchor Books, 1977, p. 348. For an extended analysis, see Edward B. Irving, Jr, *Rereading Beowulf*. Philadelphia: University of Pennsylvania Press, 1989, ch. 2 and especially pp. 55–6.

[12] Mary Dockray-Miller, 'Beowulf's Tears of Fatherhood', *Exemplaria* 10 (1998), 1–28, at 1.

[13] On this concept, see the Introduction above, pp. 13–14.

[14] Compare Karras, *From Boys to Men: Formations of Masculinity in Late Medieval Europe*. Philadelphia: University of Pennsylvania Press, 2003, p. 65. For a wide-ranging cultural history of weeping, see Tom Lutz, *Crying: The Natural and Cultural History of Tears*. London: Norton, 1999.

in the gender dynamics of this passage and the possible application of Laqueur's insight that masculinity is both a 'winnable and losable' attribute.

Dockray-Miller's argument rests on her analysis of two scenes in *Beowulf*, the first the leave-taking scene, to which we shall return, and the second the passage in which Hrothgar leaves Heorot to seek his bed with his wife:

> Ða him Hroþgar gewat   mid his hæleþa gedryht,
> eodur Scyldinga,   ut of healle;
> wolde wigfruma   Wealhþeo secan,
> cwen to gebeddan. (662–5)

Then Hrothgar departed with his retinue of heroes, the protector of the Scyldings, out of the hall; the war-chief wanted to seek Wealhtheow, his queen as a bed-companion.

It is not new to suggest that some irony is at work in this comment—the poet's choice of epithets, 'protector of the Scyldings', 'war-chief', seems designed to point up Hrothgar's failure to live up to his kingly roles. However, Dockray-Miller takes this further and argues that Hrothgar is here feminized by his choice of heterosexual over homosocial bonds:

to sleep in the same space as women, rather than merely to have sex with them and then go sleep in the hall with other men, is to taint oneself with effeminacy, with cowardice. Sleeping in the hall, dressed for battle, is an expression of masculinity, a form of 'male bonding' in the poem that affirms the heroic ethos. (12)

It is certainly true that, contrary to widespread modern assumptions, in several medieval contexts it is not same-sex activity which makes a man effeminate, but an overfondness for the company of women.[15] However, despite this, Dockray-Miller fails to take account of Hrothgar's status as king. To be given a separate sleeping place would surely be perceived as a marker of honour and esteem—after all, Beowulf himself is assigned a separate building to sleep in after he kills Grendel, presumably as a reward (1299b–301). There seems little evidence that the Anglo-Saxons associated the aristocracy with effeminacy; on the contrary the literature more often privileges aristocratic values and ignores the lower ranks.[16] The fact that Hrothgar gives Heorot into the hands of Beowulf (654a) may well assert the latter's greater virility and thus call the king's power into question, but this is not necessarily connected with his wish to sleep with his wife in itself.

---

[15] See the comments in Karras, *Sexuality in Medieval Europe*, p. 129; on similar attitudes in Ancient Greece and Rome see Halperin, *How to Do the History of Homosexuality*, pp. 95, 111–12.

[16] Compare Eric Gerald Stanley, 'Heroic Aspects of the Exeter Book Riddles', in *Prosody and Poetics in the Early Middle Ages: Essays in Honour of C. B. Hieatt*, ed. M. J. Toswell. Toronto: University of Toronto Press, 1995, pp. 197–218, at p. 210. Elizabeth Keiser has cast doubt on any universal correlation between aristocracy and effeminacy even for the later medieval period, where such an association does sometimes occur, showing that the Sodomites in *Cleanness* are seen as overly aggressive and masculine rather than the normative courtly model of masculinity the poem propounds. See Elizabeth E. Keiser, *Courtly Desire and Medieval Homophobia: The Legitimation of Sexual Pleasure in Cleanness and Its Contexts*. New Haven: Yale University Press, 1997, ch. 6.

Returning to the leave-taking passage, although she may be right to state that other critics gloss over the potential homoeroticism of the scene, Dockray-Miller adduces no evidence that 'The erotics [here] are intense beyond the norm of male-male social relations' (18). As she herself concedes, kissing (l. 1870) is frequent in Old English texts between men, often in religious texts, and she does not supply the reasoning behind her assertion that 'to cry, embrace, and kiss at a farewell are distinctly non-heroic gestures that indicate desperation rather than resolution' (19)—rather they would seem to anticipate the increasing mood of sorrow that increasingly dominates the poem as it unfolds. Indeed, she rather undercuts her own sense of conviction when she states that 'Nowhere else in Old English poetry do men display such overt emotions towards each other' but then immediately supplies two exceptions.[17] Furthermore, Dockray-Miller's analysis suggests that Clover's proposed gender continuum does not necessarily hold for *Beowulf*, as she shows that the Swedish king Ongentheow, although *blondenfeax* 'grey-haired' (l. 2962b) and of advancing age, nevertheless makes a heroic last stand. Old does not necessarily equal unmanly in Old English.

Hrothgar's parting from Beowulf, then, does not undermine his masculinity. However, his secret longing which is implicitly that the hero remain as his son does draw attention to the theme of sons and heirs in the poem. It is a theme emphasized from the beginning of the text, since the model of heroic society held up in the proem rests on the begetting of heirs. After Scyld Scefing forces the neighbouring tribes to pay him tribute, the poet tells us that:

> Ðæm eafera wæs   æfter cenned
> geong in geardum,   þone God sende
> folce to frofre;   fyrenðearfe ongeat
> þæt hie ær drugon   aldorlease
> lange hwile. (12–16a)

To him an heir was born afterwards, young, in the dwellings, whom God sent as a comfort for the people. He perceived their dire need, that they had endured leaderless for a long while.

Although Scyld may have arrived from nowhere, this passage suggests that the only way for a nation to avoid being 'leaderless for a long while' is for the king to beget an heir. This heir in turn has a son, the great Healfdene, whose four children include Hrothgar himself.

One of the biggest contrasts between Scyld and Beowulf is the latter's failure to provide an heir. Should one therefore interpret the tragic end of the poem as what happens when a hero grows old without engendering an heir? In this reading Beowulf would start as an active, single man whose lack of family ties is a virtue, enabling him to save the Danish community, but end as an old, single man—a heroic king who dies to save his own community but whose tragic

---

[17] *The Wanderer* 41–4 and the end of *The Battle of Maldon*. The passage from the *Maxims* quoted at the start of the chapter is just one of many similar overt displays of emotion.

failure is to leave no son to continue his protection and care. However, there are various problems with this interpretation. The first is that it would imply a recommendation of the model of society laid out in the proem, and we have already seen that other elements of that model are undermined in the body of the poem. It makes no sense for the text to hold up the different components of the heroic way of life for scrutiny, show the destructiveness of feuding, the dubious worth of treasure and the problems associated with its bestowal, but recommend the begetting of an heir to maintain this cycle. Indeed, although Hrothgar carries out this aspect of kingly duty, it does not help him against Grendel and the poet suggests that his dynasty will collapse in internecine warfare, as his nephew Hrothulf vies with his sons for power, and glorious Heorot perishes in flames (82–5 and 1164–5).[18]

A more nuanced approach to the poem's concern with dynasties is adopted by Frederick Biggs, who has recently argued that the problems of the Danish dynasty, where several potential heirs squabble over the throne, are contrasted with the problems of the Geatish dynasty, where the line is about to die out. This argument is made in support of his overall thesis that the poem seeks to explore the strengths and weaknesses of 'two models of succession, one that emphasizes the rights of a broad kin group to succeed' (which he sees as 'the older Germanic assumption'), and one which 'restricts that right primarily to sons' (viewed as 'the newer Christian ideal').[19] In Biggs's reading, Beowulf is capable of slaying monsters, but he cannot stop Hrothulf's treachery or prevent Heardred from dying: 'As another heir in the Danish court that already has too many and as a sonless king of the Geats whose ruling family has all but disappeared, Beowulf embodies both problems' (p. 741). Biggs is more interested in the Anglo-Saxon and Germanic historical and political context concerning kingship and succession than in the present study's focus on homosocial bonds, but his argument supports its suggestion that the poem questions rather than straightforwardly upholds the models of succession it portrays.

However, a further problem with the interpretation proposed above is that Wiglaf seems to be adopted as an heir by the dying Beowulf toward the end of the poem. The eponymous hero dies content and full of hope for the future, and judging from his final actions and words he clearly intends Wiglaf to be his successor. In the first speech Beowulf makes after he receives his mortal wound, he apparently laments his lack of an heir:

[18] On this, see further, Clark, 'Vengeance and the Heroic Ideal', pp. 67–8.
[19] Frederick M. Biggs, 'The Politics of Succession in *Beowulf* and Anglo-Saxon England', *Speculum* 80 (2005), 709–41, at 709 and 741; cf. also idem, '*Beowulf* and Some Fictions of the Geatish Succession', *Anglo-Saxon England* 32 (2003), 55–77. See also John M. Hill, 'Beowulf and the Danish Succession: Gift Giving as an Occasion for Complex Gesture', *Medievalia et Humanistica* 11 (1982), 177–97, especially 184–5; Stephanie J. Hollis, 'Beowulf and the Succession', *Parergon* 1 (1983), 39–54; Lees, 'Men and *Beowulf*', pp. 141–42; and Francis Leneghan ' "That Was a Good King": *Beowulf* and its Prologue' (unpublished doctoral thesis, Trinity College, Dublin, 2005).

Nu ic suna minum   syllan wolde
guðgewædu,   þær me gifeðe swa
ænig yrfeweard   æfter wurde. (2729–32)

Now to my sons I would give this war-apparel, if any inheritance-guardian had thus been granted to me.

However, Beowulf's last action is to present his young retainer with the gold torque from his neck (2809), along with his gold-ornamented helm, ring, and mailcoat (2811–12). Moreover, the following phrase 'het hyne brucan well' [commanded him to use them well] (2812) and his parting words 'Þu eart endelaf usses cynnes, | Wægmundinga' [You are the last remnant of our kin, of the Wægmundings] (2814–15) look like the ceremonial designation of an heir, or commission of a successor.[20] The critical debate over whether Wiglaf constitutes Beowulf's heir or not should therefore shift to whether Wiglaf accepts the role, and whether the poet depicts this designation as successful or not.

Certainly the poet conspicuously fails to provide Wiglaf with any ceremonial installation as leader, or with a speech encouraging the Geatish people to honour their late king by their acceptance and support of his successor, or even comforting them in their loss. The poet gives no positive indication that Wiglaf will become king, or that the Geats will continue in the peaceful existence in which Beowulf has maintained them; on the contrary, the close of the poem is occluded by elegies, laments, and prophecies of doom.[21]

As far as Wiglaf himself goes, it is clearly Beowulf who is his prime concern, not the Geatish people or the hoard, and it is his kinship ties and loyalty to the man himself which motivate the young warrior's sacrifice of his hand to aid his lord against the dragon: 'ac sio hand gebarn | modiges mannes, þær he his mæges healp' [but the brave man's hand burned as he helped his kinsman] (2697b–8; cf. 2600–1). After the fight, Wiglaf's first thought is to lave his lord's brow with water, with his own burnt hand (2720–2); he brings some of the treasure out in obedience to the specific request of his lord (2752–4), but his main concern is to get back to Beowulf while he is still alive (2783–7). As already noted, Beowulf's last action is to give his kinsman his torque and armour, apparently designating him his heir. However, the poet never has Wiglaf mention these gifts or speak in such a way as to imply that he is about to take up the reins of kingship. In his speeches to the Geats, Wiglaf tells only of Beowulf's command to construct a barrow (3096–100). Indeed, he implies that he did not think it worth Beowulf's sacrifice: 'hord ys gesceawod, | grimme gegongen; wæs þæt gifeðe to swið, | þe ðone [þeodcyning] þyder ontyhte' [the hoard is examined, | grimly obtained; that fate was too harsh which incited the [nation's king] to it] (3084–6).

---

[20] Compare Richard J. Schrader, *Old English Poetry and the Genealogy of Events*. East Lansing: Colleagues Press, 1993: Beowulf 'passes regalia to Wiglaf in lieu of a son', p. 147.

[21] This argument is in agreement with Biggs, '*Beowulf* and some Fictions', pp. 71–5; Irving, *Rereading Beowulf*, p. 117; Norman E. Eliason, 'Beowulf, Wiglaf, and the Wægmundings', *Anglo-Saxon England* 7 (1978), 95–105, at 103–4.

Contrary to the king's wishes for the treasure (to benefit his people, 2797), Wiglaf and the Geats burn the weapons and armour on the pyre (3137–40), and inter the rest of the treasure with Beowulf's ashes (3163–8). Why, then, does the poet have Beowulf die without an heir and his designated successor apparently refuse that nomination? I suggest that it is to symbolize the ultimate sterility of the heroic way of life, and heroic homosociality as part of that way of life.

It must be emphasized at the outset that the argument is not that the poet is attempting to hint that the bonds between Beowulf and Wiglaf are too close because they are sexual in nature, for instance as a clerical manoeuvre to bring them under suspicion of sodomy. That would be a possible approach in the later medieval period, perhaps, where writers like Orderic Vitalis fulminate against overly close relations between kings and courtiers and link them to sodomy.[22] However, as Chapters 4 and 5 show, the only explicit discussion of sodomy in the Anglo-Saxon corpus is confined to penitential literature and to religious texts designed for a clerical audience. If one were to see *Beowulf* as a genuine product of the Anglo-Saxon heroic past, as some suggest, then one could take a subtler approach, given the material adduced in Chapter 2 which suggests age-differentiated same-sex relations may have been a feature of Germanic society. In such a context, then, one could argue that, although it is entirely appropriate that Beowulf should move from intimate relationships with older kings such as Hygelac and Hrothgar in which he plays the subordinate and they the nurturing role to one in which he as an old king adopts the nurturing role, nevertheless this shift should be accompanied by the adoption of a wife and family, as befits a mature man.[23] However, both these approaches fall down in the face of the poem's treatment of productive dynasties, as seen above. The poem is not, then, an early medieval advert for family values. More convincing, I suggest, is the argument that the poem implies the need for a wider conception of society, one not centred solely on homosocial, kinship, or marital ties.

This approach takes a similar line to that recently advanced by Stacy Klein in her 2006 book *Ruling Women*, where, however, she devotes more space to the role of the queens and other female characters in the narrative, and where she takes the same view of Hrothgar as that of Dockray-Miller criticized above.[24] Klein thinks that *Beowulf*

> critiques and calls into question a heroic ethos of violence and vengeance... through the voices of those members of Anglo-Saxon society who were believed to be most capable of providing sound guidance and least capable of participating in the acts of militancy that were intrinsic to that ethos. (p. 91)

---

[22] Karras, *Sexuality in Medieval Europe*, p. 146, although, as Karras remarks, this is not always in opposition to sexual interest in women.

[23] Compare Karras, *From Boys to Men*, pp. 144 and 147.

[24] Stacy S. Klein, *Ruling Women: Queenship and Gender in Anglo-Saxon Literature*. Notre Dame, IN: University of Notre Dame Press, 2006 (ch. 3: '*Beowulf* and the Gendering of Heroism').

Moreover, she argues that the text (and especially Hrothgar's 'sermon') reveals 'a culture's attempts to find its way toward a new model of masculine heroism, one rooted less in external proficiency in war than in cultivation of the inner self' (p. 113). While I agree with Klein's overall attitude to the poem, I want here, however, to maintain the focus on how the poet's treatment of homosocial bonds, and particularly those involving Beowulf, contributes to this overall picture.

One of Klein's most intriguing suggestions is that Beowulf is at least partly responsible for his retainers' desertion at the dragon-fight. She links it to his decision not to take a queen and states that this 'interferes with his ability to produce the very relationships between men on which military success so heavily depended, namely, the bonds between a lord and retainers' (p. 115). Klein continues:

> In refusing to take a queen, Beowulf cuts off a crucial channel for producing loyalty among his retainers. It is little wonder that all but one of his troop . . . desert him in the final hour, fleeing to the woods in order to protect their own lives rather than that of their lord.

In this reading, then, homosocial bonds are most effective when they are supported by the figure of the Lady with the Mead Cup.[25] Nevertheless, although this idea is an attractive one, it falls down for the same reason adduced above against the argument that the tragedy at the end of *Beowulf* is the hero's failure to provide a son, namely that the poem would then implicitly endorse the model of society held up in the proem. Moreover, as Klein herself clearly shows, the kings who do take queens in *Beowulf* (such as Hrothgar) fail to provide a workable social model or induce firm ties of loyalty. I think that a better explanation can be found by refocusing attention from Beowulf's ties with other men to his own character and his aloneness.

Many critics have seen an element of the monstrous in Beowulf in his super-human strength and other epithets and qualities he shares with his adversaries, particularly Grendel.[26] However, perhaps the most striking similarity is that as a hero Beowulf is unique and acts alone. Dragland states that 'it is interesting both that the word *ânhaga* is so often applied to Grendel, and that Beowulf is *both* the hero and the solitary in the same passage.'[27] In fact, however, *anhaga* is never used of Grendel (it occurs only in line 2368), and even the nearest equivalent *angenga*, which does describe Grendel, appears only twice in *Beowulf*.[28] Rather, it is striking that, in contrast to the single use of the term *ana* to describe

---

[25] See Michael J. Enright, *Lady with a Mead Cup: Ritual, Prophecy and Lordship in the European Warband from La Tène to the Viking Age*. Blackrock, Co. Dublin: Four Courts Press, 1996.

[26] See particularly Andy Orchard, *Pride and Prodigies: Studies in the Monsters of the 'Beowulf'-Manuscript*. Cambridge: Cambridge University Press, 1995, p. 32; David Clark, 'Vengeance and the Heroic Ideal', pp. 70–2.

[27] S. L. Dragland, 'Monster-Man in *Beowulf*', *Neophilologus* 61 (1977), 606–18, at 613.

[28] *atol angengea* (165a) and *angenga* (449a).

Grendel in line 145, it is used no fewer than six times in the poem to describe Beowulf.[29]

In his first speech to Hrothgar, Beowulf vows to fight Grendel alone (424b–6a), and begs him not to refuse his request to cleanse Heorot *ana* 'alone' with his band of warriors (426b–32), and indeed it turns out to be a solitary fight in which his companions can only look on from the sidelines, just as in the fight with Grendel's mother they must wait forlorn at the mere-side for their leader's return (1602b–5a). Beowulf is the only one to escape the fatal raid on Frisia in which Hygelac is killed, described by the poet as *earm anhaga* 'wretched solitary one' (2368a), and he remembers before the dragon-fight how he always walked before his lord *ana on orde* 'alone in the front' (2498a). He refuses to allow his retainers to help in this fight saying it is no one's task *nefne min anes* 'except mine alone' (2533b), as Wiglaf ruefully recalls (2643b, 2876a).

Wiglaf, of course, does help Beowulf, but this is not allowed to detract from the text's insistence that Beowulf is 'alone' in a more existential sense—as a hero, he is exceptional and set apart, for heroism is depicted as finally a solitary occupation. Intense homosocial kinship bonds, such as those between Beowulf and Wiglaf, are seen to have value, but they are not enough in themselves, and they cannot save Beowulf. Indeed, too much focus on homosocial bonds alone may be as detrimental to society as an over-complicated network of rival claims to the succession. At the end of the poem, the various problematic models of society fall away and we are left with no clear answers, only a focus on the eponymous hero.

Neither Wiglaf nor any of the Geats can imagine a future without Beowulf, for only he could ward off attack from the Swedes and maintain the awesome achievement of fifty years' peace.[30] The ambiguity that many critics have identified in the character of Beowulf perhaps stems thus from the fact that he is mortal and dies, as all heroes must inevitably die. In Brecht's *The Life of Galileo* (written 1938–9, first produced 1943), a character asserts 'Unhappy the land that has no heroes!' but Galileo wisely replies 'No. Unhappy the land that is in need of heroes.'[31] A heroic society is utterly dependent on a supply of heroes, and it would seem from the poem (as opposed to critics' assumptions about Wiglaf's future role) that none is forthcoming. This perception of the double-edged nature of incomparable heroic stature goes a long way to explain why an Anglo-Saxon poet, writing in a society organized along very different principles, would raise a literary monument to a figure who is at once awesome

---

[29] *Beowulf* 425b, 431a, 2498a, 2643b, 2657b, 2876a; (cf. the emended line 2361b).

[30] Schrader, amongst others, agrees that the maintenance over fifty years of peace is Beowulf's major heroic achievement (*Old English Poetry*, p. 140).

[31] Bertolt Brecht, *The Life of Galileo*, trans. Desmond I. Vesey. London: Methuen, 1963, Scene Thirteen, pp. 107–8. The lines are quoted in the Simple Minds lyric, '20th Century Promised Land' (Jim Kerr, 1981).

and admirable, but also part of an ethos which belongs to the past.[32] The poem celebrates Beowulf's splendid achievements and abilities, certainly, but it also demonstrates the fragility of a heroic society which only an exceptional hero can maintain. Homosocial bonds, kinship ties, marital alliances—none of these can prevent the destruction which ultimately attends heroic society. The poem implicitly cries out for an alternative model, a different future, but it does not delineate the solution and remains ambivalent about the necessity of abandoning the past. *Beowulf*, then, is a problematic text, which raises more questions than it answers. Nevertheless, careful analysis shows that it calls into question the heroic ideals it explores, including that of loyalty between men. However, if *Beowulf* is pessimistic about the ultimate value of the intense homosocial bonds which the heroic way of life embodies, *The Battle of Maldon*, by contrast, raises them to a new and transcendent status.

HOMOSOCIAL BONDS IN *THE BATTLE OF MALDON*

The poem commemorating the Viking defeat of Byrhtnoth and the Anglo-Saxon army at Maldon in Essex in AD 991 is one of the better-known Old English texts, often translated, anthologized, quoted, and analysed.[33] This is not to say, however, that it has avoided critical controversy. Despite generations of scholarly effort, there remains no general consensus as to what degree of criticism the poet intended when he blamed Byrhtnoth's *ofermod* for his decision to grant the Vikings' cunning request for safe passage to the mainland, thus giving them *landes to fela* 'too much land'.[34] Helmut Gneuss has amply demonstrated that all other usages of *ofermod* and its cognates in Old English occur in religious contexts with negative connotations of the sin of pride, but this will not deter Byrhtnoth's defendants, since of course this does not prove the absence of a more positive secular meaning in the area of great courage.[35] One of the more ingenious solutions is that of Richard North, who suggests that the poet was deliberately playing on the ambiguity of the term, which could be read by Byrhtnoth's supporters as approbatory and his detractors as critical, and thus

---

[32] Compare Klein: 'While Beowulf's lack of progeny indeed suggests that there will never be another warrior of comparable heroic stature, it nevertheless also suggests that he is himself an anachronism. As Beowulf dies, so too will the exemplum of heroism that he so fiercely defends' (Klein, *Ruling Women*, p. 122). However, as stated above, I am not convinced by her reading of gender roles in the poem.

[33] See the collections *The Battle of Maldon: Fiction and Fact*, ed. Janet Cooper. London: Hambledon Press, 1993; *The Battle of Maldon, AD 991*, ed. Donald Scragg. Oxford: Blackwell, 1991.

[34] *Maldon* 84–90. Although *lytegian* has also sparked debate, the controversy has centred on the phrase *for his ofermode* (89b).

[35] Helmut Gneuss, '*The Battle of Maldon* 89: Byrhtnoð's *ofermod* Once Again', *Studies in Philology* 73 (1976), 117–37.

supply a solution to the problem of how to celebrate a defeat at least partly caused by a mistake in generalship.[36]

What interests me in this context, however, is the decision of some of Byrht-noth's most loyal thanes after their lord is struck down to remain and fight on to certain death on the battlefield. Not all of the retainers view their choice in this light—for many of them the poet represents the opposition as being between death and vengeance (208, 258–64), but for at least some of the warriors the option of living was destroyed when Byrhtnoth fell:

> Raðe wearð æt hilde   Offa forheawen;
> he hæfde ðeah geforþod   þæt he his frean gehet,
> swa he beotode ær   wið his beahgifan
> þæt hi sceoldon begen   on burh ridan,
> halan to hame,   oððe on here crincgan,
> on wælstowe   wundum sweltan;
> he læg ðegenlice   ðeodne gehende. (288–94)

Offa was quickly hewn down at battle; he had, however, accomplished what he promised his lord, just as he vowed before to his ring-giver that they should both ride into the stronghold, safe to their home, or perish in the host, upon the slaughter-place die from wounds; he lay thane-like near to his lord.

The distinguished literary critic Edward B. Irving, Jr, remarks of this final image that 'It would be hard to deny the very faintly sexual intensity of the image', and although one might perhaps prefer 'erotic' to 'sexual', the line does affirm an intense and intimate homosocial bond that persists in death.[37] The adverb *ðegenlice* 'like a thane' here asserts that the true mark of a retainer, what it is to be a loyal warrior, is to lie close beside one's lord, to choose death with him rather than to live and fight another day.

We know from contemporary records that Byrhtnoth and many of his retain-ers had wives and families, but, as the historian Pauline Stafford has pointed out, as far as the poem goes they might as well not exist.[38] Male-female bonds are repressed here in favour of a rhetoric which, when one steps back from its undeniable emotive force, becomes almost necrophiliac, as with the aged retainer Byrhtwold's words:

---

[36] Richard North, 'Getting to Know the General in "The Battle of Maldon"', *Medium Ævum* 60 (1991), 1–15.

[37] See Edward B. Irving, Jr, 'Heroic Role-Models: Beowulf and Others', in *Heroic Poetry in the Anglo-Saxon Period: Studies in Honor of Jess. B. Bessinger, Jr.*, ed. Helen Damico and John Leyerle. Studies in Medieval Culture, 32. Kalamazoo, MI: Medieval Institute Publications, 1993, pp. 347–72, at p. 354. On homosocial bonds in *Maldon*, see also in the same volume Joseph Harris's 'Love and Death in the *Männerbund*: An Essay with Special Reference to the *Bjarkamál* and *The Battle of Maldon*', pp. 77–114.

[38] Pauline Stafford, 'Kinship and Women in the World of *Maldon*: Byrhtnoth and His Family', in Cooper, *The Battle of Maldon*, pp. 225–35.

> fram ic ne wille,
> ac ic me be healfe   minum hlaforde,
> be swa leofan men   licgan þence. (317b–19).

I do not wish [to go] forth, but by the side of my lord, by such a dear man, I intend to lay myself.

It must be said that in the margin of the library copy of Irving's essay to which I have access, next to the 'faintly sexual' comment, a rather bold undergraduate (one assumes) has scrawled: 'this is a bag of shite.'[39] One hesitates to pursue the psychological implications of the writer's association of sexuality with the abject (another graffitist of the same margin comments 'My arse'), but the anxiety exhibited is instructive. An Old English poet of the late tenth or early eleventh century would hardly have wanted to suggest that Byrhtnoth and his men were lovers. Rather these intense examples of homosocial devotion create a discourse of personal commitment from retainer to lord. Moreover, in the contemporary political context, they clearly seek to glamorise and thus shore up the vertical bonds of loyalty which were becoming fragile owing to King Æthelred's worsening reputation and the increasingly frequent desertions of the battlefield, not by retainers, but by cowardly lords such as *ealdorman* Ælfric.[40] The heroic loyalty shown by retainers in this poem is valuable and gains those who exhibit it glory even if they should fail, and even if they should have an unworthy lord. Nevertheless, there is another point in the poem where male-male sexuality may be at issue.

In the article by Richard North mentioned above, he notes that in a later account of the battle in the twelfth-century *Liber Eliensis*, the Danes are said to have accused Byrhtnoth of cowardice if he does not dare to join battle with them, and North speculates that this might have involved OE *earh*, the cognate of ON *argr*, and thus have invoked the discourse of *níð*.[41] In this discourse, as seen in Chapter 2, the cognate noun *ergi* and verb *ergjask*, along with the adjective *argr* and its metathesized form *ragr*, denote the ultimate insult. They imply not merely that a man is cowardly, but that he is also effeminate, and specifically has been the passive partner in anal intercourse.[42] There is no reason to suppose the existence of an Anglo-Saxon *ergi* discourse in the same defined and regulated way as in Old Norse society, although the analysis in Chapter 3 revealed several interesting

---

[39] English Faculty Library, Oxford, shelfmark E73 BES.

[40] Compare the saying recorded in the Peterborough Chronicle (MS E) for 1003: 'Ðonne se heretoga wacað þonne bið eall se here swiðe gehindred' [when the general weakens, then all the army is much hindered]. The Anglo-Saxon army was hampered by leaders' desertions in 992 (Ælfric), 993 (Fræna, Godwine, Frithugist), 999 (no leader), 1003 (Ælfric), 1009 (Wulfnoth), 1010 (Thurcytel Mare's Head).

[41] North, 'Getting to Know the General', pp. 5–6. See *Liber Eliensis*, Book II, §62; trans. Janet Fairweather as *Liber Eliensis: A History of the Isle of Ely from the Seventh Century to the Twelfth, Compiled by a Monk of Ely in the Twelfth Century*. Woodbridge: Boydell Press, 2005, p. 161.

[42] See Chapter 2, pp. 51–2 and references there.

cases where the semantic field clearly includes associations of effeminacy and base sexual desires (pp. 54–8). However, as North points out:

two words in [*Maldon*] are loans, from Danish *grið* and *drengr*; two more are probably loan translations from *uppganga* and *jarl*. Therefore it is possible that... *earh* could have been used against Byrhtnoð as a loan translation of ON *ragr* 'effeminate'.[43]

That is, the Old English poet could have deliberately adopted a known Old Norse usage. Alternatively the residual sexual associations of the Old English word could have been strengthened by the more elaborate Norse usage.

The problem with North's argument is that in the poem itself, Byrhtnoth is not specifically called *earh*. North is forced to speculate that a use of the cognate noun *yrhðo* earlier in the poem was in fact moved from 'another context to which it would have been better suited' (p. 6). There is, however, no need to resort to such violent textual emendation in order to profit from North's valuable suggestion. There are two other places in the poem which explicitly invoke the semantic field of cowardice. First, after Byrhtnoth is struck down, the poet tells us that 'Þa ðær wendon forð wlance þegenas, | unearge men efston georne' [Then proud thanes went forth there, un-cowardly men eagerly hastened] (205–6); then, in his condemnation of Godric's flight from the field, Offa calls him *earh Oddan bearn* 'the cowardly son of Odda' (238a).

The Battle of Maldon is built upon oppositions—between Anglo-Saxons and Vikings, between land and sea, between standing firm and taking flight, between victory and defeat. Here, then, is another opposition which permeates the poem as we have it. At the beginning of the fragment, Offa's kinsman understands 'þæt se eorl nolde yrhðo geþolian' [that the nobleman would not tolerate cowardice] (6), makes his hawk, symbol of aristocratic peacetime pursuits, fly to the wood and steps up to the battle (7–8). Byrhtnoth avers that it would be *To heanlic* 'too shameful' (55) if the Vikings were allowed to take tribute to their ships without a fight. Even after their leader's downfall, his retainers are designated as *unearge* and are thus defined by their lack of cowardice, by what they are not (205–6). One after another they vow not to retreat one pace but to stand firm and die with their lord on the battlefield. As we have it, the poem ends with the valiant death of another Godric, and the poet is at pains to point out that he is not *earh*—'Næs þæt na se Godric þe ða guðe forbeah' [that was by no means the Godric who fled the battle] (325).

---

[43] North, 'Getting to Know the General', p. 5. Other possible Scandinavian locutions are *most* (30), *garræs* (32), *þon* (33), *hilde dælan* (33), *syllan...sylfra dom* (38), and *æschere*. See Fred C. Robinson, 'Some Aspects of the *Maldon* Poet's Artistry', in his *The Tomb of Beowulf, and Other Essays*. Oxford: Blackwell, 1993, pp. 122–37 at pp. 123–4; idem, 'Literary Dialect in *Maldon* and the Casley Transcript', in *The Tomb of Beowulf*, pp. 138–9; Marijane Osborn, 'Norse Ships at Maldon: The Cultural Context of *æschere* in the Old English Poem "The Battle of Maldon"', *Neuphilologische Mitteilungen* 104 (2003), 261–80; William Sayers, '*æschere* in *The Battle of Maldon*: Fleet, Warships' Crews, Spearmen, or Oarsmen?' *Neuphilologische Mitteilungen* 107 (2006), 199–205.

If any Anglo-Saxon poem, then, fits the dynamic described by Eve Kosofsky Sedgwick where homosocial interaction is validated and normalized by homophobic discourse, then it is *Maldon*.[44] The Norse context adduced by North gives weight to the idea that the intimate homosocial bonds elevated in the poem are constructed with reference to a repudiated effeminacy equated with sexual passivity. Manhood is constructed without reference to women and family ties, and is rather based on an ideal of competitive masculinity and the abjection of a racial and sexual other. A man's ultimate loyalty should be to the homosocial lord-retainer bond, anachronistically reworked here to echo the personal ties of the Germanic warband in aid of a propagandistic function—fight to the death, or be an effeminate coward.

So far this chapter has compared the different attitudes to homosocial bonds in two poems in which religious matters are not the prime concern, at least not explicitly.[45] I want now to compare a poem which is an unambiguously religious work with a clear didactic message, but which nevertheless is constructed around heroic homosocial bonds: *The Dream of the Rood*. The intimate relation between Christ and the Cross at its centre has much in common with those between Beowulf and Wiglaf, or Byrhtnoth and his retainers, but it radically reworks some of the assumptions which I have argued underlie those works.

HOMOSOCIAL BONDS IN *THE DREAM OF THE ROOD*

With its enigmatic start, shifting imagery and polysemy, its bold use of prosopopoeia and the complexity of its doctrinal underpinnings, *The Dream of the Rood* has been frequently mined by literary critics, and, like *Maldon*, it has remained a popular choice for anthologies, undergraduate textbooks, and collections of translations. One of the poem's most discussed features is its striking application of heroic imagery and tropes to the Crucifixion narrative, in which Christ is cast as a young hero and the Cross as his faithful retainer and the unwilling agent of his lord's death. While the Dreamer-narrator avidly listens, the Cross recounts the fateful events of the first Easter, transformed into a new and vivid context by the manipulation of traditional poetic formulae and heroic motifs. As has often been observed, the Cross's first words—'Þæt wæs geara iu, ic þæt gyta geman' [That was long ago, I remember it still] (28)—manipulate the

---

[44] See further the Introduction above, p. 17.

[45] Though there have been, of course, a range of explicitly Christian interpretations: on *Beowulf*, see particularly Margaret E. Goldsmith, *The Mode and Meaning of Beowulf*. London: Athlone Press, 1970; Bernard F. Huppé, *The Hero in the Earthly City: A Reading of Beowulf*. Binghamton, NY: State University of New York Press, 1984. For discussion of Christianity in *Maldon*, see R. Hillman, 'Defeat and Victory in "The Battle of Maldon": The Christian Resonances Reconsidered', *English Studies in Canada* 11 (1985), 385–95; N. F. Blake, 'The Battle of Maldon', *Neophilologus* 49 (1965), 332–45; J. E. Cross, 'Oswald and Byrhtnoth: A Christian Saint and a Hero who is Christian', *English Studies* 46 (1965), 93–109.

trope of the aged warrior for a new purpose.[46] The personified Rood's dilemma is often compared to that of the retainers in the 'Cynewulf and Cyneheard' episode of the *Anglo-Saxon Chronicle* entry for AD 755 who do not want ever to follow their lord's slayer. Rather than fight for his lord, he is compelled to become complicit in his death; rather than strike down his lord's enemies, he has to become their tool. Unlike *Maldon*'s warriors, the result of standing firm and resisting the urge to flee is not a heroic last stand in defence of or revenge for his beloved lord, but the experience of witnessing and abetting his painful and ignominious end.

Until recently, however, comparatively little attention has been paid to the gender dynamic at work in this text, the basic assumption apparently being that the relationship between the Cross-retainer and Christ-lord is unproblematic and relatively unremarkable. In 1997, however, the year before her article on *Beowulf* discussed above, Mary Dockray-Miller argued that the Cross is a feminized figure in the poem against which Christ's triumphal masculinity is constructed in opposition.[47] While much of her analysis is valuable, I want here to question Dockray-Miller's emphasis that Christ's masculinity is 'specifically heterosexual' (p. 1; she employs the terms *heterosexual* and *heterosexuality* no fewer than eleven times in the article). Dockray-Miller argues in contrast to traditional readings of the Cross as retainer that the Cross is a female figure to be identified with Mary rather than with Christ (pp. 7–8). From an analysis of the sexual associations of the verbs *ongyrede*, *gestigan*, *ymbclypte*, and *bifode* in the crucifixion passage, she concludes that Christ's glory and dominance is dependent on the violence and sexual aggression he directs toward the Cross, and that 'the dreamer becomes a voyeur who engages in a homosocial relationship with Christ that is mediated by the feminized cross' (p. 14). While the Cross may well be 'a dominated Other' and to an extent feminized, it is my contention that by not examining the terms on which her analysis of a masculine-feminine binary rests, Dockray-Miller is forced to the anachronistic conclusion that the central bond of the poem is 'a heterosexual rather than a homosocial relationship' (p. 7).

>   Geseah ic þa frean mancynnes
> efstan elne mycle   þæt he me wolde on gestigan.
> Þær ic þa ne dorste   ofer dryhtnes word
> bugan oððe berstan,   þa ic bifian geseah
> eorðan sceatas.   Ealle ic mihte
> feondas gefyllan,   hwæðre ic fæste stod.

---

[46] Irving compares Beowulf's speech before the dragon fight when he remembers his early martial encounters; see Edward B. Irving, Jr, 'Crucifixion Witnessed, or Dramatic Interaction in *The Dream of the Rood*', in *Modes of Interpretation in Old English Literature: Essays in Honour of Stanley B. Greenfield*, ed. P. R. Brown et al. Toronto: University of Toronto Press, 1986, pp. 101–13, at pp. 105–6.

[47] Mary Dockray-Miller, 'The Feminized Cross of *The Dream of the Rood*,' *Philological Quarterly* 76 (1997), 1–18.

> Ongyrede hine þa geong hæleð,   (þæt wæs god ælmihtig),
> strang and stiðmod.   Gestah he on gealgan heanne,
> modig on manigra gesyhðe,   þa he wolde mancyn lysan.
> Bifode ic þa me se beorn ymbclypte.   Ne dorste ic hwæðre bugan to eorðan,
> feallan to foldan sceatum,   ac ic sceolde fæste standan.
> Rod wæs ic aræred.   Ahof ic ricne cyning,
> heofona hlaford,   hyldan me ne dorste. (33b-45)[48]

Then I saw the lord of mankind hasten with great zeal in that he wanted to climb upon me. I dared not against the lord's word bend there or break when I saw the corners of the earth tremble. I could have felled all the foes, however, I stood fast. The young hero unclothed himself then—that was God Almighty, strong and resolute of heart; he ascended onto the high gallows, courageous in the sight of many when he wanted to redeem humankind. I trembled when the warrior embraced me. I dared not, however, bend to the ground, fall to the corners of the earth, but I had to stand fast. I was raised a cross. I lifted up the powerful king, lord of the heavens; I dared not bow down.

In this climactic passage, the Cross is first unambiguously identified as a cross, after the enigmatic beginning of the poem where he is described with polysemous terms such as *beam* '[light]-beam, beam [of wood]' (6, 13), and *beacen* 'beacon, symbol, standard' (6, 21), or misdirecting terms such as *treow* 'tree' (4, 14, 17, 25).[49]

Dockray-Miller shows that several verbs in the passage carry sexual connotations as well as their primary religious uses. *Gestigan* (34, 40) ordinarily refers to 'an ascent to heaven', but is used three times in *Genesis A* in contexts where 'sexuality, legitimacy, and patrimony are at issue' (p. 9), namely when Sara tells Abraham to order Hagar to ascend to his bed (2230), and then laments this action (2250a), and when Abraham explains to Abimelech why he concealed the fact that Sara used to share his bed as his wife (2716b). *Genesis A* is also the occasion for the 'only overtly sexual use of *bifian* in the extant corpus' (p. 10; *bifian* occurs in lines 36 and 42). As we saw in the previous chapter, when Lot is defeated by the kings of the north, the poet predicts that many pale-cheeked women would have to go *bifiende* 'trembling' into a stranger's embrace (1970b). Dockray-Miller states that 'The feminized cross…finds itself in a situation strikingly similar to that of the Sodomite women as they face rape' (p. 11). Perhaps surprisingly *ymbclyppan* 'to embrace' is most often used in a metaphorical sense, and there are only two concrete uses: Christ's embrace of the Cross here, and Arcestrate's embrace of Apollonius when they are reunited in the Old English version of *Apollonius of Tyre*.[50] Strangely, Dockray-Miller does not cite the clearly analogous concrete uses of the verb *clyppan*, one of which occurs in the famous

---

[48] Cited from *The Vercelli Book*, ed. George Philip Krapp. Anglo-Saxon Poetic Records, II. New York: Columbia University Press, 1932, p. 62.

[49] It is followed shortly after by the first explicit identification of *Crist* (56).

[50] *The Old English 'Apollonius of Tyre'*, ed. Peter Goolden. Oxford: Oxford University Press, 1958, p. 38, §49, l. 2.

passage in *The Wanderer* where the exile dreams of embracing and kissing his lord (41–4). Finally, *ongyrwan* 'to strip, to undress' (39) is used in the anonymous Life of Saint Mary of Egypt when Zosimus gives the saint his cloak to cover her naked body, and in the story of Saint Eufemia in the *Old English Martyrology* when the saint is stripped by her torturers.[51] Dockray-Miller asserts that 'These examples show that *ongyrede* was used in linguistic situations that were full of sexual tensions of gender, power, and naked bodies' (p. 13).

Although, as Dockray-Miller herself concedes, these sexual connotations are not the primary associations of these words, they are nevertheless present and the repeated and emphatic use of a number of such terms within a short passage means that they cannot be ignored. However, it is far from clear that one can proceed from a recognition that the relationship described is eroticized to her conclusion that the ascent of the cross here embodies 'the heterosexuality of a masculine lover coming to his feminized beloved' (p. 13) and the naturalized patriarchal opposition of dominant-masculine to subordinate-feminine (p. 15). Despite Dockray-Miller's ability to step outside contemporary and medieval patriarchy, she is unable to avoid anachronistic heterosexist assumptions, and to imagine that the character she sees as the traumatized and acquiescent victim of a violent rape (p. 14) might be male.[52] As we have seen, she even makes the explicit comparison with the Sodomite women, without it occurring to her that that particular narrative does not just contain intended sexual violence towards women.

I want to read this part of *The Dream of the Rood* both more *and* less radically, as concerning active and passive models of masculinity and a more complex gender dynamic than Dockray-Miller envisages. Rather than a cosmic rape, this poem presents a radical re-envisioning of masculinity and heroism. In a way, this is far from constituting a new reading of the text. Several critics have remarked how difficult a hero and warrior would find submitting to enforced passivity as the Cross must, summed up by Irving when he states that the Cross and the Dreamer must understand that the suffering consitutes 'the new Christian heroism of the martyr rather than the old Germanic heroism' (p. 107). Irving even goes so far as to assert that the Cross stands for 'the innocent Paradisal world of non-human nature . . . violated and appalled by man's cruelty and forced, against nature, to torture nature's own creator' (pp. 107–8), a resonant image indeed. However, he does not explicitly connect this perception to Christianity's re-envisioning of gender, inherent in the Pauline epistles' rejection of binaries such as Jew and Gentile, slave and free, male and female,

---

[51] Skeat, *Ælfric's Lives of Saints*, II, XXIIIB, p. 14; *An Old English Martyrology*, ed. George Herzfeld. EETS 116 London: Kegan Paul, Trench, Trübner, 1900, p. 172.

[52] Irving also compares the Cross to a 'shock-victim', though he does not specify the gender or link it to a sexual attack ('Crucifixion Witnessed', p. 108).

and the image of the bride of Christ, so influential throughout the Middle Ages.[53]

John Canuteson and Faith Patten, however, do draw attention to the idea of the Cross as the bride of Christ in their analyses of the poem.[54] Canuteson even remarks that 'a kind of marriage consummation takes place on the Cross' (p. 296). However, his analysis, like Dockray-Miller's, is marked by heterosexism as he states that the Cross is personified as female because 'in everything it exhibits a feminine submission'. He concedes 'This passivity is dictated by submission to God's will', but asserts 'nevertheless, one feels that he is witnessing feminine behavior' (p. 295). In a now almost incredible passage, he notes that the diction describing Christ encompasses 'all the things a woman would see and appreciate in a husband' (these things being strength, resolution, and courage) and continues 'The Cross, moreover, is demure—she trembles when she is embraced. This whole passage is simply a logical extension of the implications of the marriage of Christ and the Church. The two have now become one' (p. 296). There is clearly a certain amount of projection going on here on Canuteson's part. Patten's gender analysis is a briefer part of her argument that the Cross is to be identified with the Church, but she asserts that one element which contributes to this identification 'is the cross's sex, which seems to be female' (p. 396). In support of this statement she adduces the passage in which the Cross compares itself to Mary (90–4) and the fact that the Cross, like the Church, is the Bride of Christ. She supplements this with the passage where Christ ascends the Cross, pointing out the 'sexual imagery' and stating that 'the cross is imaged as the bride of Christ, or the Church, which, allegorically, is born from the union of Christ and the cross, that is, from the crucifixion' (p. 397). Nowhere, however, does she justify her unreflective assumption that only a female character could identify with a woman, Mary, or explore the implications of the Church being its own mother.

I would suggest, rather, that the Cross's identity in this text is an overdetermined one, in keeping with the earlier enigmatic section of the poem where it shifts identity and fluctuates between a triumphant, treasure-adorned beacon of light and an abjected, bleeding object of scorn. The Cross is both a retainer and an anti-retainer—in this topsy-turvy world where God dies and torture brings life, heroic obedience is paradoxically to slay one's lord; to be a warrior, a man, is to submit to being feminized, impotent, placed in the passive and subject position by Christ. For and in the Christ of this poem, as for the author of Galatians, there is neither male nor female, but individual men and women can, like the Cross, be a bride of Christ. In a poem constructed upon the paradox

[53] Galatians 3: 28; see further the following chapters, particularly Chapter 9.
[54] John Canuteson, 'The Crucifixion and the Second Coming in *The Dream of the Rood*', *Modern Philology* 66 (1969), 293–7; Faith Patten, 'Structure and Meaning in *The Dream of the Rood*', *English Studies* 49 (1968), 385–401.

of a Christ who is both Man and God, which revels in polysemy and shifting identities, it should perhaps not be surprising that gender is also a fluid and paradoxical characteristic. As such, however, *The Dream of the Rood* takes passive masculinity, which I have argued is abjected in *Maldon*, and revalues it as a positive and indeed heroic attribute, and thus sets forth a vision of union with Christ which anticipates the religio-erotic visions of later medieval writers such as Aelred. The following chapters explore further the re-envisioning of gender and particularly homosocial bonds in other religious texts in the vernacular.

8

Monastic Sexuality and Same-Sex Procreation in *The Phoenix*

One of the most beautiful poems in Old English, *The Phoenix* has found modern audiences consistently appreciative of its aesthetic qualities and the descriptive powers of its poet.[1] As with the homiletic endings of *The Wanderer* and *The Seafarer*, or *The Dream of the Rood*, readers are often less enamoured of the second part of the poem in which the spiritual significance of the phoenix is expounded; rather they tend to content themselves with enjoying the exotic narrative with which it begins concerning the earthly paradise and its sole inhabitant, the beautiful and unique phoenix, an account largely based on the Latin poem attributed to Lactantius (*c*.260–340).[2] Translators, too, have found this part of the poem most congenial, and many have confined themselves still more narrowly to the initial section describing the earthly paradise (lines 1–84).[3] However, critical attention, at least, was redirected toward the latter part of the poem by J. E. Cross in his influential article 'The Conception of the Old English *Phoenix*', in which he argued that, rather than a separate 'fable' followed by a spiritual explanation, *The Phoenix* was a unified poetic homily on the eponymous bird, based on the four levels of medieval exegesis.[4]

---

[1] Like the other poems discussed, it is extant in a single text only, on folios 55^v–65^v of the Exeter Book, copied *c*.970–90. See initially N. Blake, ed., *The Phoenix*. Manchester: Manchester University Press, 1964, rev. Exeter: Exeter University Press, 1990, pp. 1–2. Quotations are from this edition; translations are my own. See also Muir, *Exeter Anthology*, vols I (text) and II (commentary).

[2] Blake, *Phoenix*, pp. 17–19. Some of the correspondences of Lactantius with the Old English text are noted in Albert S. Cook and Chauncey B. Tinker, eds, *Select Translations from Old English Poetry*. Boston: Ginn, 1926, p. 144; cf. Helle Falcher Petersen, '*The Phoenix*: The Art of Literary Recycling', *Neuphilologische Mitteilungen* 101 (2000), 375–86. For a fully annotated edition and translation of Lactantius, see Mary Cletus Fitzpatrick, ed. and trans., *Lactanti De Ave Phoenice: with Introduction, Text, Translation, and Commentary*. Philadelphia: University of Pennsylvania Press, 1933. On the Anglo-Saxon poet's use of other Latin sources, see below.

[3] See, for instance, the translations by Brown, Conybeare, Hammerich, Körner, Robinson, Sims, Wright, Kennedy and Spaeth, listed in Blake, *Phoenix*, pp. 37–9.

[4] J. E. Cross, 'The Conception of the Old English *Phoenix*', in Creed, *Old English Poetry*, pp. 129–52, at p. 145. For a useful account of the four levels, see further Henri de Lubac, *Medieval Exegesis, Vol.1: The Four Senses of Scripture*, trans. Mark Sebanc. Edinburgh: Clark, 1998. Cross divides the poem as follows: on the literal level, the phoenix is a real bird in the earthly paradise (1–380), on the tropological level, the phoenix represents good Christians on earth who inhabit a nest made of good deeds (381–472), on the eschatological level, the phoenix stands for the good Christian who gains the promised land of heaven after the general resurrection and the fire of

Cross's account is ingenious and has engendered much productive further study on the sources and homiletic nature of the poem, but it has been pointed out that his analysis attributes a consistency to the poem not reflected in the text.[5] It is more profitable to see the poem as characterized by a fluid and flexible allegory, as does Joanne Spencer Kantrowitz in her article 'The Anglo-Saxon *Phoenix* and Tradition', in which, drawing on the patristic writings, she shows that in the poet's account of the phoenix's rebirth he fuses five symbols from Christian allegory: the apple, silkworm, eagle, phoenix and seed grain.[6] Kantrowitz argues that different interpretations of this passage are possible because of the range of potential spiritual significations readers could attach to each of the figures, and offers the analogy of *The Dream of the Rood* 'with its multiple meanings and kaleidoscopic imagery' (p. 13). Kantrowitz does not draw the obvious inference from her findings, however, which is that such a poem would be most accessible to a relatively learned audience such as might be found in a religious community likely to be more familiar with allegorical interpretations of the eagle and other figures. Certainly it is clear that the poet was learned, and recent research has suggested he may have used an extensive range of Latin sources.[7] This chapter argues that the poem contains several elements which make it particularly appropriate to a monastic context, and that it exhibits tensions concerning gender and same-sex relations within this context which the fluidity of the poem's allegory both enables and problematizes. It also argues that the text enshrines a radical revaluation of nature in favour of a model of sexless spiritual (same-sex) generation, but that this textual manoeuvre is complicated by anxieties around homosocial intimacy and a consequent attempt to limit the potential for subversive readings of the poem.

Judgement Day (473–543), on the typological level, the phoenix is a type of Christ after His death and resurrection (544–661).

[5] Greenfield, for instance, argues that the text does not support Cross's double interpretation of the phoenix's nest as a shelter for Christians on earth and a place to live in heaven. Moreover, he believes that Cross's neat account misrepresents 'the poem's generic expectations' and 'implies an order and structure too clean-cut for the actual poetic materials'. Stanley B. Greenfield, *The Interpretation of Old English Poems*. London: Routledge and Kegan Paul, 1972, p. 142, also pp. 11–18.

[6] Joanne Spencer Kantrowitz, 'The Anglo-Saxon *Phoenix* and Tradition', *Philological Quarterly* 43 (1964), 1–13, at 1 and *passim*. One might compare Calder's emphasis on flexibility and his statement that '*The Phoenix* is not a formal Christian allegory; rather...it is a rendering of the relationship between beauty and salvation that unites all differing allegorical perspectives in one symbolic vision' (D. G. Calder, 'The Vision of Paradise: A Symbolic Reading of the Old English *Phoenix*', *Anglo-Saxon England* 1 (1972), 167–81). The issue of beauty Calder raises is considered from a different perspective below.

[7] On the Old English poet's additional use of other Latin sources, see Kantrowitz, ibid.; Blake, *Phoenix*, pp. 20–2 (on Ambrose); E. K. C. Gorst, 'Latin Sources of the Old English *Phoenix*', *Notes and Queries* 251 (2006), 136–42 (on Dracontius, Avitus, and Corippus). See particularly, for an extended analysis of the Old English poet's use of rhetorical tropes, Jackson J. Campbell, 'Learned Rhetoric in Old English Poetry', *Modern Philology* 63 (1966), 189–201, at 194–8. More work remains to be done in this area.

A valuable analysis of *The Phoenix* in a monastic context is presented by John Bugge in his article 'The Virgin Phoenix', where he argues that resurrection is only part of the poem's theme and that it celebrates a feature of monastic spirituality 'which constitutes a guarantee of resurrection and eternal life', that is 'the strictest sexual purity', which he connects to the phoenix's 'sexlessness'.[8] There are problems with the conclusions Bugge draws from his analysis of the phoenix's indeterminate gender, which are examined in detail below. However, Patrick Conner has also proposed a monastic origin for *The Phoenix*, arguing that the second of the three booklets into which he divides the Exeter Book (which includes *The Phoenix*) represents 'a collection derived from Continental models and composed within a monastic environment before the Benedictine revolution'.[9] Although Conner's three-booklet theory has not met with universal acceptance, it provides further support for the literary evidence adduced by Bugge and supplemented by my own findings, considered below.[10] This will faciliate an understanding of *The Phoenix* as composed in a monastic context, for a monastic audience, and about the monastic vocation.

THE PHOENIX AND MONASTICISM

Bugge identifies as monastic the themes of 'Paradise as the natural homeland of the monk', of 'earthly life as an exile', of the monk as *'miles Christi*...engaged in the spiritual conflict of asceticism', and the poem's 'thoroughly eschatological emphasis' (pp. 333–7). He sees the phoenix's 'nest built of alms, good deeds, prayer, and mortification' (453–61) as symbolic of 'the monastic life itself' (p. 336). Moreover, he connects the facts that the poem speaks of praise *dæges ond nihtes* 'day and night' (478a) and that the earthly paradise contains *ne sorg ne slæp* 'neither sorrow nor sleep' (56a) to 'the monk's attitude toward vigils' (p. 337). To the phoenix's eagerness for its journey (208a) and indifference to death (368b), he compares the ascetic's longing for death, which he sees as the flipside of 'the poet's impassioned fascination with the momentous events of the

---

[8] John Bugge, 'The Virgin Phoenix', *Mediaeval Studies* 38 (1976), 332–50, at 332.

[9] Patrick W. Conner, *Anglo-Saxon Exeter: A Tenth-Century Cultural History*. Woodbridge: Boydell Press, 1993, p. 148. Conner assigns the first booklet (*Christ* I, II, and III, and *Guthlac A* and *B*) to the period of the Benedictine Reform, and the third booklet (comprising poems from the second part of *The Partridge* to the Riddles) to an intermediate, 'transitional' period. See also idem, 'Exeter's Relics, Exeter's Books', in *Essays on Anglo-Saxon and Related Themes in Memory of Lynne Grundy*, ed. Jane Roberts and Janet Nelson. London: King's College London Centre for Late Antique & Medieval Studies, 2000, pp. 117–56, which reasserts his proposition that the Exeter Book originated at Exeter against the criticisms of Richard Gameson, 'The Origin of the Exeter Book of Old English Poetry', *Anglo-Saxon England* 25 (1996), 135–85.

[10] For criticism of Conner's arguments, see Muir, *Exeter Anthology*, I, pp. 6–7 and *passim*; Richard and Fiona Gameson, [review of Conner, *Anglo-Saxon Exeter*], *Notes and Queries* 42 (1995), 228–30. Although these critics dispute Conner's reasoning from his codicological and paleographical findings, they do not contradict the idea that the poems stem from a monastic environment.

"last day" . . . [for which] the source is monastic philosophy, which was essentially eschatological' (p. 337).

It is true that not all these themes exclusively pertain to the monastery by any means—the concepts of heaven as true home and life on earth as exile are commonplace Christian themes, nor is a fascination with the End Times a uniquely monastic trait. Nevertheless, the combination of all these things is suggestive, and the comparisons Bugge makes with the Old English poetic saint's life based on the legend of the eremitical Guthlac are apposite (pp. 335–7, 343, 347–9). It seems odd, however, that Bugge makes no mention of another element which seems more obviously restricted to a monastic context, and that is the phoenix's regular singing. In a beautiful passage the poet describes how the bird flies at sunrise, singing more sweetly than anyone ever heard until the sun sets once more and the phoenix is silenced (120–45). However, he then tells us: 'Symle he twelf siþum tida gemearcað | dæges ond nihtes' [Always he marks the hours twelve times by day and night]. Far more than the later recurrence of *dæges ond nihtes* Bugge notes, the analogy with the monastic observance of the hours in this phrase is overt—and indeed seems to sit uneasily and thus more prominently against the previous descriptive passage—and it thus lends concrete support to the monastic interpretation of the other elements of the poem such as the bird's emphatic solitariness, purity, and indifference to death. In keeping with the fluidity already noted above to be characteristic of the poem, one clearly need not restrict the poem's interest solely to monks—all Christians would be expected to give alms and do good deeds, for instance (cf. 451–65), and thus a mixed audience of laypersons, clerics, and monks is envisageable, as indeed is suggested by Conner's characterization of the Exeter Book as being comprised of poems of diverse origins, brought together in the manuscript for a late tenth-century audience. However, the monastic community is indicated as a primary context for the poem and it is explored as such in what follows.[11]

THE PHOENIX: SEXLESS, ASEXUAL, ANDROGYNE?

We turn now to the question of the phoenix's gender, which has caused some critical controversy. Bugge argues from the facts that the bird's gender is unknown to men (355b–8) and that it is its own father and son and heir (374b–6), that the

---

[11] Further potential patristic allusions which would indicate a monastic environment can be found in the following studies: Judith N. Garde, *Old English Poetry in Medieval Christian Perspective: A Doctrinal Approach*. Cambridge: Brewer, 1991, ch. 8 (emphasizing the eschatological aspects of the poem); Yun Lee Too, 'The Appeal to the Senses in the Old English *Phoenix*', *Neuphilologische Mitteilungen* 91 (1990), 229–42 (exploring the relevance of the poem's imagery to patristic writings on the sacraments and ideas about the inadequacy of language to express spiritual transcendence).

'secret of its eternal viability . . . is precisely its emancipation from the deadening burden of sexual generation' (p. 339), and goes on to summarize his contention that 'the monastic poet of *The Phoenix* saw sexual purity as a prerequisite for eternal life, and that this existential *clænnes*, the sexlessness which is the true condition of the soul freed from the body, lies at the heart of . . . the poem' (p. 348). He concludes with a discussion of the Pelagian view that 'judicious asceticism, including especially the practice of celibacy, is sufficient to merit salvation and eternal life', suggesting that the *Phoenix*-poet adhered to the view he deems characteristic of early English monasticism, that 'the life which all ordinary men lead on earth . . . was a positive misfortune, tainted and degenerate' and that 'there can be no hope for the world, nor compromise with it: only absolute non-involvement with the material world allows the confident expectation of eternal life' (pp. 349 and 350).

This latter part of Bugge's argument is particularly open to question, not least because he gives no supporting evidence for the influence of Pelagianism in Anglo-Saxon England. To be sure, there are several Old English texts in which a gloomy view of earthly life is expressed—one need think no further than *The Wanderer*'s emphasis on this *læne lif*—but not only is this often not the only or dominant voice present in these texts, but they must also be set beside texts like *Widsith* or the *Maxims* which indicate a more positive, even joyful Christian acceptance of aspects of earthly existence, and which *The Phoenix* is found alongside in its extant manuscript context. Bugge may be suggesting that early monasticism was more ascetic than later religious culture, but this would seem to be at odds with the general view that monasticism became more and not less ascetic with the tenth-century Benedictine Reform. Another and more important problem, though, becomes clear from a consideration of Carol Heffernan's work on *The Phoenix*, which leads her to a very different conclusion.

Heffernan does not dispute the importance of Christological readings of the phoenix, but she puts forward evidence that various aspects of the poem also respond to a Marian reading—that the phoenix is not just the resurrected Christ and the redeemed Christian, but also represents the Virgin Mary and Mother Church.[12] She emphasizes that she is 'merely following one of two parallel lines in the poem', but asserts that 'the phoenix in the garden near the fountain that overflows twelve times yearly symbolizes the Virgin Mary as well as the maternity of the Church, and the theme of the Incarnation moves together with that of Resurrection in the drama of salvation' (p. 239). As support she cites strands of patristic tradition which stress that the phoenix, like Mary, 'conceives alone', and goes on to draw out 'three broad movements of the first half of the poem',

[12] Carol Falvo Heffernan, 'The Old English Phoenix: A Reconsideration', *Neuphilogische Mitteilungen* 83 (1982), 239–54.

namely the Virgin in the Garden (65–119), Conception (120–47), and Birth (171–257).[13]

Heffernan certainly presents ample evidence of a traditional patristic association of Mary and the Mother Church of which she is a type with the earthly paradise, and particularly the fountain of life (pp. 242–5), although her 'Conception' and 'Birth' sections are less strongly argued.[14] However, she does not address the problem that much of her argument stresses the importance of the fountain, and, in fact, her account of the role and description of the fountain is more suited to the Latin original. Lactantius speaks of a fountain 'which men call the "Fountain of Life" ', and which is 'clear, tranquil, rich in sweet waters'.[15] He goes on to describe it as 'the sacred waves' and 'the living waters'.[16] By contrast, the Old English poet employs mixed terms so that it is unclear whether a fountain or merely a stream is being described, and he certainly desacralizes and naturalizes the waters. The phoenix looks eagerly *on firgenstream* 'upon the mountain-stream' (100), and bathes *in þam burnan* 'in the brook' (107), although it is also said to be placed *æt þam æspringe* 'at the spring, fountain' (104), inhabiting *wyllestreamas* (105) which Blake translates as 'welling waters', and tasting water *brimcald* 'cold as the sea' from the *wilsuman wyllgespryngum* 'delicious wellsprings' (109–10).[17] This does not invalidate Heffernan's reading, but it does suggest that she may have rather overplayed the Marian aspects of the Old English poem.[18] Nevertheless, what I am most interested in here are Bugge and Heffernan's apparently contrasting interpretations of the phoenix's gender, since the former sees it as sexless or asexual (p. 339) and the latter thinks 'the indeterminate sexuality of the phoenix operates like the androgyne wholeness of the Church which, far from excluding the creative potential of the female, includes that of the male' (p. 239). It is my view that these interpretations are not mutually contradictory, but rather that they indicate an important tension in the poem to do with gender and sexuality, which the fluidity of the poem's allegory both enables and problematizes.[19] We need to look at the passages concerned in detail.

---

[13] Heffernan, p. 140. See also Rufinus, *Commentarius in Symbolum Apostolorum* (*PL* XXI. 350) and Albertus Magnus, *De laudibus Beatae Mariae* VII. iii. 1, both cited by Heffernan.

[14] There seems little reason to see the phoenix's nest as a reflection of the tabernacle and thus the Incarnation (p. 252), given its explicit explanation in the poem itself in terms of good works (453–61), and Heffernan herself recognizes that the second half of the poem is more difficult to link to Mary (p. 252).

[15] 'fons…quem "vivum" nomine dicunt, | perspicuus, lenis, dulcibus uber aquis'; Fitzpatrick, *Lactanti De Ave Phoenice*, p. 42, ll. 25–6; translations are Fitzpatrick's.

[16] 'pias…undas' and 'vivo…aquam'; Fitzpatrick, ibid., ll. 37–8.

[17] cf. Blake, *Phoenix*, p. 30.

[18] Compare also the account in the *Prose Phoenix* which talks unambiguously about the '*fons uite*, þæt is lifes welle' [*fons uite*, that is the Well of Life], Blake, *Phoenix*, Appendix II (a) *The Prose Phoenix*, pp. 98–100, at p. 98.

[19] For further discussion of tensions around gender and sexuality, see Chapter 9 on Ælfric's *Lives of Saints* and particularly the discussion of the possible influence of Galatians 3: 28.

THE PHOENIX AND SEXLESS (SAME-SEX) GENERATION

After a time of being praised by the rest of birdkind, the phoenix returns to the earthly paradise, young once more. The poet then tells us:

> God ana wat,
> Cyning ælmihtig   hu his gecynde bið,
> wifhades þe weres;   þæt ne wat ænig
> monna cynnes   butan Metod ana
> hu þa wisan sind   wundorlice,
> fæger fyrngesceap   ymb þæs fugles gebyrd. (355b–60)

Heffernan translates the first sentence as follows: 'God only knows, | The Almighty King, what his breed may be, | Or male or female' (p. 239); Bugge does not translate but paraphrases: 'Its gender remains a mystery to men; only the *meotod* understands…its birth or generation' (p. 339). There are several problems in translating these lines, but the following will provide a starting point for discussion:

God alone knows, Almighty King, what its nature is, [whether] of the order of a woman or a man; no one knows it of the human race, except the Creator alone, how the ways are wonderful, the fair ancient decree about that bird's birth.

This perhaps overly literal translation makes clear what more fluent renderings conceal in adapting the original to modern English idiom: that the poet employs several polyvalent terms in this statement. The key term perhaps is *gecynde*, which Heffernan translates 'breed' and Bugge 'gender', although according to Clark Hall it can carry any of the senses 'origin, generation, birth, race, species, nature, kind, property, quality, character, offspring, gender, genitalia'.[20] It is clear that the sentence overall concerns the bird's gender, but at this point the general term '(sexual) nature' is more appropriate, and several of the other senses such as 'species' or 'origin' are relevant secondary meanings in a passage which describes a bird set apart from the rest of its kind by its ability to self-replicate. Indeed, 'nature' is the only term which can embrace all the uses of *gecynd* in the poem (252, 256, 329, 356, 387), an important contextual point which we shall examine shortly.[21] However, the precise way that the poet narrows his focus

---

[20] John R. Clark Hall, *A Concise Anglo-Saxon Dictionary*. Toronto: University of Toronto Press, 1984, s.v. ± *cynd*.

[21] Blake glosses *gecynde* (356) separately as a neuter noun meaning 'sex', next to the feminine *gecynd* 'nature, kind, species' (*Phoenix*, p. 111), but this distinction is untenable: both words have the broad sense 'nature' of which 'sex' is the narrower meaning particularly relevant here. Blake's tendency to close down the possible range of meanings of a word and present a specific meaning as the 'correct' translation in support of his argument is also noticed and criticized by Cross in his review in *JEGP* 64 (1965), 153–8, and by Calder, 'The Vision of Paradise', p. 170, n. 1. The tendency is particularly marked in Blake's article, 'Some Problems of Interpretation and Translation in the OE *Phoenix*', *Anglia* 80 (1962), 50–62.

down to the bird's gender is also significant, as a comparison with the late Old English *Prose Phoenix* shows.

This text, written in a style akin to Ælfric's poetic prose, is extant in only two late manuscripts.[22] As a literary text the *Prose Phoenix* is not only very late but also immeasurably poorer in terms of both style and content than the poetic version—for instance, repeating variants of the phrase *fugel fæger, fenix gehaten* 'the beautiful bird called the phoenix' over and over again. However, it makes a useful point of comparison with the subtler rendering with which we are mainly concerned in this chapter. The relevant portion concerning the phoenix's gender reads as follows:

And næfð he nænne gemaca and nan mann ne wat hweðer hit is þe karlfugel þe cwenefugel, bute Gode ane.

And it does not have any mate and no man knows whether it is a male-bird or a female-bird, except God alone.

The element *karl*- marks the text out as late, exhibiting influence from ON *karl*.[23] However, what is particularly interesting here is the greater semantic ambiguity of the terms the author of the poetic *Phoenix* chooses in his phrase *wifhades þe weres* (357a). The first term is translated by Clark Hall as 'woman-hood' or 'female sex' (Clark Hall, s.v. *wifhad*), in keeping with the definition of -*had* as a suffix which 'usu. denotes state or condition', but it seems to me that in this particular context in a poem deriving from a monastic environment, we are justified in seeing it as a more significant compound-element, since as well as the meanings 'condition, state, nature, character, form, manner', the noun *had* can also carry the senses 'degree, rank, order, office' and especially 'holy orders' or 'holy office' (Clark Hall, s.v. *had*).[24] This potential connotation of the word is certainly strengthened by the following passage. First of all, the poet uses *had* as a noun when he tells us that it is by the bird's *had* 'nature' that it is restored

---

[22] British Library MS Cotton Vespasian D. 14, folios 166ʳ–168ʳ (V), and Corpus Christi College, Cambridge MS 198, folios 374ᵛ–377ʳ (C). V is edited in Blake, *Phoenix*, pp. 98–100; Ker dates it as s. xii med. (Ker, *Catalogue*, §209, p. 271). C is edited in A. S. Cook, *The Old English Elene, the Phoenix and the Physiologus*. New Haven: Yale University Press, 1919, pp. 128–31; Ker regards the text as a later addition in a hand of s. xi² (Ker, *Catalogue*, §48, p. 81).

[23] Indeed, the Norse connections of the text would repay further study, given the existence of two later Norse versions (Blake, *Phoenix*, pp. 100–3, where he edits the longer fifteenth-century version). Blake suggests that both Norse versions were based on the same (unknown) Latin sermon or homily from which the Old English versions were taken (p. 101). However, this is criticized by David Yerkes, who argues for the priority of the Norse account on the basis that the hapax legomena *karlfugl* and *cwenefugel* are Norse loans, and notes that the shared errors of the surviving copies means merely that neither represents the copy used by the Old English translator (who does not reproduce these errors). See David Yerkes, 'The Old Norse and Old English Prose Accounts of the Phoenix', *Journal of English Linguistics* 17 (1984), 24–8, at 26; cf. Ananya Jahanara Kabir, *Paradise, Death and Doomsday in Anglo-Saxon Literature*. Cambridge: Cambridge University Press, 2001, p. 169.

[24] See also the remarks in the following chapter, p. 193.

and rejuvenated (372–4a), which both foregrounds the word, and links it back to *gecynd*. Secondly, he then informs us:

> Bið him self gehwæðer
> sunu ond swæs fæder   ond symle eac
> eft yrfeweard   ealdre lafe. (374b–6)

It is both its own son and sweet father and always also afterwards the heir of the old remains.

This picture of sexless generation, a concept relevant to any celibate Christian, is specifically gendered masculine by the poet.[25] *The Phoenix* has often been rendered more masculine a poem in translation than the original warrants, since, despite the explicit comment on its androgynous nature, translators fail to observe the distinction made in Old English between 'grammatical' and 'natural' gender. The bird is predominantly referred to by masculine nouns such as *fenix*, *fugel*, *brid*, etc., and therefore with masculine pronouns which match this grammatical gender. However, in modern English it would be more appropriate to choose the gender neutral term 'it' which does not make the emphatic statement of gender that 'he' does, and which is misleading and inappropriate for most of the text, even concerning a bird as anthropomorphized as the phoenix is in this poem. Nevertheless, at this particular point in the text, and in contrast to Lactantius, the poet chooses in talking about the bird's self-generation to use the specifically masculine kinship terms of *sunu* and *fæder*, and this picture of a sexless but masculine generation corresponds very closely to the terms in which religious writers speak of monastic communities founded on single-sex families of fathers, brothers and sons, preserved by spiritual reproduction.[26] The bird is termed *yrfeweard* 'heir' or 'inheritance-guardian', which also makes sense in terms of a monastic community holding on to and preserving the spiritual treasures of the gospel, and the means of salvation.

This idea perhaps makes sense, too, of the intriguing phrase in the previous passage which talks of the *fæger fyrngesceap* 'the fair ancient decree' about the bird's birth, which in this context might invoke notions of monks as those chosen by God, even before the beginning of time. The poet tells us that the blessed by good works earn eternal life after death (381–6), and this is juxtaposed with the statement that God granted the phoenix that it *weorþan sceolde | eft þæt ilce þæt he ær þon wæs* 'should become again the same as it was before' (378b–9), regain its feathers after the fire (380), a picture of the refining of the flesh through fire that is disambiguated later in the poem (518–45). However, he then goes on to state:

---

[25] We may compare his original: 'ipsa sibi proles, suus est pater et suus heres, | nutrix ipsa sui, semper alumna sibi' [She is her own progeny, her own sire, and her own heir. She is her own nurse, ever foster child to herself.] Fitzpatrick, *Lactanti De ave phoenice*, p. 56, ll. 167–8; translation Fitzpatrick's.

[26] Compare the comments in the following chapter on homosocial communities and conversion models, pp. 181–4.

Þisses fugles gecynd   fela gelices
bi þam gecornum   Cristes þegnum
beacnað in burgum,   hu hi beorhtne gefean
þurh Fæder fultum   on þas frecnan tid
healdaþ under heofonum   on him heanne blæd
in þam uplican   eðle gestrynaþ. (387–92)

This bird's nature betokens a great similarity to those chosen ones of Christ's thanes on earth, how they maintain a bright joy through the Father's help in this terrible time under the heavens and secure high bliss in the upper homeland.

And this picture of soldiers of Christ, or *miles Christi*, who are chosen and divinely aided to remain joyful as they endure the nightmare of earthly existence, and who are rewarded with high bliss in the heaven that is their true home, is surely particularly suited to observers of the monastic life, in but not of the world. This interpretation is supported by the repetition of the word *gecynd*, since thus all three passages which we have been considering are linked by the concept of nature through the terms *gecynd* (356b, 387a) and *had* (357a, 372a), a concept of nature which has become associated with a monastic environment in which fleshly and mortal nature based on sexual reproduction is transcended and replaced by sexless spiritual generation which looks beyond this life to the one to come.

   The other instances of the term *gecynd* in the text provide further support for this interpretation. The account of the phoenix's rebirth after its fiery death—progressing from egg-like apple to worm to a bird resembling an eagle's hatchling, then an eagle and finally the full-fledged phoenix—is immediately followed by an extended simile where the poet likens the process of rebirth to the harvest:

Þonne bræd weorþeð
eal edniwe   eft acenned,
synnum onsundrad.   Sumes onlice
swa mon to ondleofne   eorðan wæsmas
on hærfeste,   ham gelædeð
wiste wynsume   ær wintres cyme
on rypes timan,   þy læs hi renes scur
awyrde under wolcnum;   þær hi wraðe metað,
fodorþege gefeon   þonne forst ond snaw
mid ofermægne   eorþan þeccað
wintergewædum;   of þam wæstmum sceal
eorla eadwelan   eft alædan
þurh cornes gecynd,   þe ær clæne bið
sæd onsawen,   þonne sunnan glæm,
on lenctenne   lifes tacen
weceð woruldgestreon   þæt þa wæstmas beoð,

þurh agne gecynd   eft acende
foldan frætwe;   swa se fugel weorþeð
gomel æfter gearum   geong edniwe
flæsce bifongen. (240b–59a)

Then the flesh is born again, wholly renewed, separated from sins, somewhat like when one for sustenance brings home at harvest the fruits of the earth, the pleasant feast before the coming of winter, at reaping-time lest the rain's showers spoil them under the clouds; there they find support, delight in the receiving of food when frost and snow with terrible force engulf the earth in winter garments; from the fruits shall the blessedness of noblemen be brought forth again by the nature of grain, which earlier, pure, is sown as seed, when the sun's ray, the sign of life in the spring [or Lent] wakens the world's treasure so that the fruits are born again by their own nature, the adornments of the earth; so the bird, old according to years becomes young, clothed with flesh anew.

That this passage is imbued with spiritual significance is obvious from phrases such as *eft acenned* 'born again' (241b, 256b), *synnum onsundrad* 'separated from sins' (242a), and the whole analogy of harvest with its biblical associations of resurrection. However, earlier critics have been content to see this passage as merely an allusion to Christ's resurrection, or the general resurrection of humankind. Certainly, both of these elements would be present to an audience familiar with the scriptures. In a passage taken to be a prediction of his death and resurrection, Christ says in John 12: 23–5:

But Jesus answered them, saying: The hour is come, that the Son of man should be glorified. Amen, amen I say to you, unless the grain of wheat falling into the ground die, Itself remaineth alone. But if it die, it bringeth forth much fruit.

However, he goes on to say 'He that loveth his life shall lose it; and he that hateth his life in this world, keepeth it unto life eternal', which opens the passage up from a comment on Christ's death and resurrection for the salvation of humankind to the presentation of a model for Christians to follow, an idea which is taken up by the Apostle Paul in 1 Corinthians 15: 20, where he talks of the resurrection of Christ from the dead: 'the firstfruits of them that sleep', and goes on to extend the analogy in a passage clearly alluding to Christ's pronouncement (verses 36–8, 42–4):

Senseless man, that which thou sowest is not quickened, except it die first. And that which thou sowest, thou sowest not the body that shall be; but bare grain, as of wheat, or of some of the rest. But God giveth it a body as he will: and to every seed its proper body...So also is the resurrection of the dead. It is sown in corruption, it shall rise in incorruption. It is sown in dishonour, it shall rise in glory. It is sown in weakness, it shall rise in power. It is sown a natural body, it shall rise a spiritual body.

Both these passages were popular with patristic writers, who used the seed analogy frequently (Blake, *Phoenix*, p. 78). However, the Old English poet makes original use of this topos in his justly praised extended simile.

One could merely see the details of this simile as part of the poet's fertile imagination, as decorative details only. However, in such a densely allegorical poem, it is legitimate to question whether they have a spiritual significance; to ask what these fruits which are brought home to be kept safe from the rain represent; what is the meaning of the receiving of food in winter.[27] Does the passage have to do with more than the traditional ideas of the resurrection of Christ and the Christian from death?

Blake is of the opinion that the fruits simply represent good deeds which support man on Judgement Day: 'Just as the corn which a man has stored away in the summer will provide him with sustenance in the winter, so the good deeds which a man performs on earth will be his support when he comes to face God at Doomsday' (Blake, *Phoenix*, p. 79 n.). However, several elements of this portion of the poem do not easily fit this interpretation. First of all, the assumption of an eschatological explanation of the passage does not square with the fact that the bird has not yet left for its homeland, the earthly paradise. We are told immediately afterwards that the bird waits for a time, receiving no food except *meledeawes | dæl* 'a portion of honeydew' (260b–1a) which falls in the middle of the night, upon which it nourishes itself *oþþæt* 'until' it seeks its homeland once more (259b–64). Moreover, the logic of the simile dictates against the fruits representing the Christian's good deeds. Rather, the fruits of the earth equate most easily to the reborn phoenix (240b–4a) which represents Christ or the reborn Christian. If, then, the fruits represent reborn Christians, one is justified in considering whether, rather than Judgement Day, this passage concerns the life on earth of the Christian, or more specifically the monk, after the first rebirth of conversion but before the second and final rebirth.

In this reading, the fruits represent monks as the harvest of conversion brought to a safe home (the monastery) to escape the effects of harsh weather (earthly vicissitudes and the temptations of worldly life) and to receive support and food (Christian community and the nourishment of the word of life) (242b–50a). In the rest of the simile, the grain sown as pure seed can be seen to represent the chastity and Christian life of the monk, and the sun represents God, whose divine favour awakens the seed which grows into new fruits, that is, new converts, acolytes, and novices, the 'adornments of the earth', born not of sexual intercourse but 'born again by their own nature' (250b–7a).[28] If we take

[27] Hill similarly argues for the poet's control of his material: cf. Thomas D. Hill, 'The "Synwarena Lond" and the Itinerary of the Phoenix: A Note on Typological Allusion in the Old English "Phoenix" ', *Notes and Queries* 23 (1976), 482–4.

[28] Compare Bugge, 'The Virgin Phoenix', p. 347. The use of the Sun to represent God is noted by many critics, but of course goes back to biblical imagery, e.g. Revelation 22: 5, where the light of the sun and stars is replaced by the presence of God.

on lenctenne (254a) to mean not 'in the springtime' but 'in Lent', then we have a picture of the two major festivals connected with death and resurrection—the harvest which the passage as a whole concerns, and the Lenten period which precedes the anniversary of Christ's death and resurrection and which can also be seen as the period of tribulation which the monk must observe in the world before his death into new life, or as the spiritual asceticism practised by adherents to the monastic life which produces spiritual fruit. The poet then returns to the figure of the bird once more, which although old in years becomes young, 'clothed with flesh anew' (257b–9a)—a fitting picture of the ancient Church's constant renewal by the influx of fresh converts.

The detail of the honeydew upon which the bird feeds can also be convincingly associated with the monastery, although it is often seen merely as a Classical ornithographical detail.[29] Exodus chapter 16 and Numbers chapter 11, for instance, speak of the manna which God provides during the night for the Israelites to eat in the desert, and which 'tasted like wafers made with honey'. This same association of the phoenix's honeydew with manna is made by Yun Lee Too, who suggests, however, that this may be a reference to the 'baptismal Eucharist', a drink of honey and milk representing a sort of 'baby food' for the Christian neophyte, and which could have been known in Anglo-Saxon England through texts such as Ambrose's *De Sacramentis* V. 15, resting on Christ's association of manna with the Eucharist in John 6: 31–58.[30] This is a plausible interpretation, but Too presents no other evidence that this practice was known in Anglo-Saxon England, and there is a simpler explanation of the passage's significance. In Deuteronomy 8: 3, a passage alluded to by Christ in his temptation in the desert (Matthew 4: 4), Moses comments as follows on the same incident, saying:

He afflicted thee with want, and gave thee manna for thy food, which neither thou nor thy fathers knew: to shew that not in bread alone doth man live, but in every word that proceedeth from the mouth of God.

It is thus possible that the honeydew represents the spiritual nourishment represented by the word of God, the holy scriptures upon which monks were expected to meditate daily.

These close readings, then, provide further support for the placement of the poem in a monastic context. However, they also bring to the attention another aspect of the poem, and that is its revaluation of nature—as well as articulating a world in which procreation is not sexual but spiritual and based around not the union of man and woman but a set of same-sex familial relationships, the poem destabilizes the nature of nature.

---

[29] See Blake, *Phoenix*, p. 79; Cook, *Old English Elene*, p. 116.
[30] Too, 'Appeal to the Senses', p. 234.

NATURE AND THE (UN)NATURAL IN *THE PHOENIX*

Daniel Calder's reading of the poem, already mentioned, explores the poet's use of the concept of nature in the poem, though it is nature in its sense of 'the natural world' only, and he does not consider its relation to the poem's treatment of sex and gender. He cites 'the neoplatonic bias of early medieval theology which sees the world's beauty as evidence that it was created by God, the supreme artist', and the following illustrative passage from the writings of Augustine:

For God is a great artisan in great things in such a way that he is not less in small things: these small things are to be measured not by their own greatness (for there is none), but by the wisdom of their maker.[31]

Calder points out the poet's repetition of the term *frætwe* which means both 'fruits' and 'ornaments' (p. 170), the association of paradise with jewels through the description of the sun on several occasions as a gem (921, 183a, 208b, 289a), and the phoenix's own artificiality, with its rich colouring, its eye like a gemstone, and its beak which shines like glass or a gem (291–304). He supplements these observations with a close reading of the poem in which he argues that the phoenix building its nest represents man's pursuit of his own salvation by good works, as he 'transcends the natural world rooted in mutability and reaches out toward the exemplary art of paradise with its resplendent vision of grace' (p. 176).

Calder's emphasis on the importance of beauty in the poem is a welcome corrective to attitudes such as Blake's which see the descriptions of the phoenix as a distraction from the allegory which is the important feature and centre of the poem.[32] It has also been supplemented by readings which bring out the complexity of the poet's aesthetic sense, such as Yun Lee Too's exploration of the sensual imagery of the text, Stevick's account of the poem's internal mathematical proportions which he attributes to aesthetic aims, and Anderson's recent attempt to interpret *The Phoenix* as 'a synaesthetic poem' through detailed linguistic analysis.[33] However, it seems to me that alongside a reading of the poem as an encouragement for the Christian to take example from the phoenix and perform good works in the hope of salvation and resurrection to eternal life,

---

[31] 'Deus autem ita est artifex magnus in magnis, ut minor non sit in parvis: quæ parva non sua granditate (nam nulla est), sed artificis sapientia metienda sunt.' Augustine, *De civitate Dei*, PL XLI. 335, quoted in Calder, 'The Vision of Paradise', p. 169. On ideas of divine and human artifice, see further Calder, *passim*, and Umberto Eco, *Art and Beauty in the Middle Ages*, trans. Hugh Bredin. New Haven: Yale University Press, 1986, esp. pp. 88, 93, 108.

[32] cf. Blake, 'Some Problems', 56–7.

[33] Too, 'Appeal to the Senses'; R. D. Stevick, 'Mathematical Proportions and Symbolism in *The Phoenix*', *Viator* 11 (1980), 95–121; Earl R. Anderson, 'Old English Poets and their Latin Sources: Iconicity in *Caedmon's Hymn* and the *Phoenix*', in *The Motivated Sign: Iconicity in Language and Literature 2*, ed. Olga Fischer and Max Nänny. Amsterdam: Benjamins, 2001, pp. 109–32.

it is possible to explore the recalcitrant elements of the text and the tensions that it exhibits. Indeed, the very fluidity of the poem's allegorical dynamic with its generation of multiple meanings and overdetermination of concepts such as nature paradoxically engenders the seeds of counter-readings within the text, observable as anxieties on the part of the poet.

Indeed, Calder himself recognizes the presence of one kind of tension in the text when he says that: 'Eden may be a vision of nature crystallized into art, but earth itself has its *frætwe*. The dichotomy sets up a moral tension...The ornaments of the earth may direct the soul towards the idea of paradise and heaven or they may seduce that soul into the belief that their art is 'all it needs to know' on earth' (p. 177). What I want to suggest, however, is that a different tension is exhibited in the text as a result of the conjunction of the poem's overdetermination of the concept of nature and its revisioning of gender through the indeterminate figure of the phoenix. That the poet's desire to replace the earthly model of male-female intercourse with sexless spiritual generation is complicated by an anxiety that speaking in such a way of the relational dynamic of the monastery might be misinterpreted and linked to notions of pederasty and other same-sex activity with which the monastic lifestyle was regularly associated in the early Middle Ages.

The links between monasticism and pederasty are well delineated by V. A. Kolve in his densely documented study: 'Ganymede/*Son of Getron*: Medieval Monasticism and the Drama of Same-Sex Desire.'[34] Most of his study concerns the later Middle Ages, after the publication of Peter Damian's *Book of Gomorrah* which fulminates against the continual danger in monasteries of 'not only sex between boys or youths of the same age, but what he considered the worst of all possible clerical sins, the corruption of spiritual sons by ecclesiastical fathers', a type of pederasty he regarded as tantamount to incest.[35] However, as we have already seen from the discussion of the penitentials in Chapter 3, pederasty and other forms of same-sex activity were certainly a concern in Anglo-Saxon England. I am aware of no evidence that the term Ganymede or the figure of the hare were employed in Anglo-Saxon religious circles as euphemisms for or hints at same-sex predilections, as Boswell shows that they were on the Continent and in later England, although the passage from Boethius quoted in Chapter 3 may suggest that this kind of discourse was not unknown.[36] However, that pederasty was certainly a continuing concern within early monasticism is demonstrated by several passages in patristic texts, and that it was a particular concern for religious communities in late Anglo-Saxon England is suggested by comments in

[34] *Speculum* 73 (1998), 1014–67.
[35] V. A. Kolve, 'Ganymede/*Son of Getron*: Medieval Monasticism and the Drama of Same-Sex Desire', *Speculum* 73 (1998), 1014–67, at 1028.
[36] Boswell, *Christianity, Social Tolerance, and Homosexuality*, ch. 9, esp. p. 253; cf. Chapter 3, p. 57 above.

tenth-century English religious texts and in the text which formed the basis for the religious reforms of this period, *The Benedictine Rule*.

In *De renuntiatione saeculi*, a Greek text attributed to Basil (*c*.330–79), for instance, we find several warnings about the dangers associated with young monks.[37] The author urges monks young 'in either body or mind' to avoid the 'companionship of other young men' like they would 'a flame', continuing: 'For through them the enemy has kindled the desire of many, and then handed them over to eternal fire, hurling them into the vile pit of the five cities under the pretence of spiritual love.'[38] Here, pederasty is linked unambiguously to the punishment of the Sodomites by the mention of the 'five cities'. The author goes on to suggest ways of avoiding such temptation.

Similar advice is found in Basil's *Sermo Asceticus* (*PG* XXXII. 880):

Sit in a chair far from such youth; in sleep do not allow your clothing to touch his but, rather, have an old man between you. When he is speaking to you or singing opposite you, look down as you respond to him, so that you do not by gazing at his face take the seed of desire from the enemy sower and bring forth harvests of corruption and loss. Do not be found with him either indoors or where no one can see what you do, either for studying the prophecies of Holy Scriptures or for any other purpose, no matter how necessary.[39]

However, the author of *De renuntiatione saeculi* despairs of the efficacy even of such heroic precautions:

It is frequently the case with young men that even when rigorous self-restraint is exercised, the glowing complexion of youth still blossoms forth and becomes a source of desire to those around them. If therefore, anyone is youthful and physically beautiful, let him keep his attractiveness hidden until his appearance reaches a suitable state.   (Ibid., p. 159)

The onus is thus shifted to the possessor of such dangerous beauty, who must conceal it until his appearance is no longer attractive, one assumes because of the ageing process.

The troubling notion here of culpable beauty provides yet another perspective on the presentation of beauty in *The Phoenix*, which as we saw above, Calder already views as ambivalent, capable of both positive and negative effects. But there is also another link to the poem in Basil's use of seed and harvest imagery in his *Sermo Asceticus* where he speaks of the danger to the unwary monk of even looking upon a young monk. He warns that by gazing at his face, the monk may 'take the seed of desire from the enemy sower and bring forth harvests of

[37] For a brief discussion of the authorship, see Boswell, *Christianity, Social Tolerance, and Homosexuality*, p. 159, n. 94; volume XXXI of *Patrologia Graeca*, 2nd ser., ed. J.-P. Migne. 166 vols. Paris: Migne, 1857–66 (hereafter cited as *PG* with volume and column number).

[38] Quoted in Kolve, 'Ganymede', 1028, n. 39.

[39] Basil, *Sermo Asceticus* (*PG* XXXII. 880); quoted in Boswell, *Christianity, Social Tolerance, and Homosexuality*, p. 160.

corruption and loss'. The language of procreation and harvest are fused here in a way strikingly similar to the textual dynamic set up by the Old English writer.

I am not aware of evidence of textual transmission of these comments of Basil in Anglo-Saxon England. However, it is in such a conceptual context that one must view the advice of the tenth-century English *Regularis concordia*, designed to regulate monastic relations. In the Foreword, the author lays down strict rules about contact between older and younger monks:

In the monastery moroever let neither monks nor abbot embrace or kiss, as it were, youths or children; let their affection for them be spiritual, let them keep from words of flattery, and let them love the children reverently and with the greatest circumspection. Not even on the excuse of some spiritual matter shall any monk presume to take with him a young boy alone for any private purpose but, as the Rule commands, let the children always remain under the care of their master. Nor shall the master himself be allowed to be in company with a boy without a third person as witness.[40]

As the phrase 'as the Rule commands' indicates, the author of this text is writing in accord with the Benedictine Rule, which was introduced to Anglo-Saxon monasteries as part of the tenth-century Benedictine reforms. Chapter 22 of the Rule makes detailed provision about sleeping arrangements:

Let them [i.e. the monks] sleep each one in a separate bed. Let their beds be assigned to them in accordance with the date of their conversion, subject to the abbot's dispositions. If it be possible, let them all sleep in one place; but if their numbers do not allow of this, let them sleep by tens or twenties, with seniors to supervise them. There shall be a light burning in the dormitory throughout the night. Let them sleep clothed and girt with girdles or cords, but not with their belts, so that they may not have their knives at their sides while they are sleeping, and be cut by them in their sleep. Being clothed they will thus always be ready, and rising at the signal without any delay may hasten to forestall one another to the Work of God; yet this with all gravity and self-restraint. The younger brethren shall not have their beds by themselves, but shall be mixed with the seniors. When they rise for the Work of God, let them gently encourage one another, on account of the excuses to which the sleepy are addicted.[41]

The idea of males sleeping together, seen as totally natural in the Exeter Book *Maxims* discussed in the Introduction and Chapter 7, is hedged around with rules here, one effect of which, surely, is to create a sense of what might occur were they not in place.[42] Chapter 10 explores a text from Anglo-Saxon England which displays a rather different, though equally pragmatic, attitude to pederastic relations within the monastery. However, I want now to return to *The Phoenix*

---

[40] *Regularis concordia Anglicae nationis monachorum sanctimonialiumque: The Monastic Agreement of the Monks and Nuns of the English Nation*, trans. Thomas Symons. London: Nelson, 1953, §11, pp. 7–8; cf. Kolve, 'Ganymede', p. 1028.

[41] *The Rule of St Benedict*, trans. Justin McCann. London: Sheed and Ward, 1952, 1976.

[42] One could perhaps argue along the lines of the Laqueurian one-sex model, however, that this is precisely because boys are not really 'men', but are assimilated to the 'not-men' part of the spectrum, hence their danger and the need to control access to them.

and consider it as a poem designed to speak to a monastic audience well aware of the possibility and temptation of same-sex activity.

In many ways the indeterminate gender of the phoenix is ideally suited to the representation of a monk, given their call to renounce the desires of the flesh, and the monastic ideals of transcending gender and sexuality. As other commentators have shown, the fruit which Adam and Eve tasted in Eden—identified in *The Phoenix* as an apple (403a)—is strongly associated with sexual desire and sin in early Christian thought.[43] That the poet wanted to emphasize the phoenix's escape from original sin and sexual desire is suggested by his use of the apple as a motif in the poem. He emphasizes that the taste of the forbidden apple brought lasting harm to Adam and Eve's descendents, in that they had to give up paradise to dwell *in þas deaðdene* 'in this valley of death' (416). However, when Judgement Day comes, he describes how the world will be destroyed by fire—flame shall receive *eorðan æhtgestreon* 'the earth's treasures' and *æppelde gold | gifre forgripeð* 'shall greedily swallow the appled gold' (506–7a), where the adjective *æppelde* refers to the colour and texture of gold objects but clearly creates a link to the ur-apple the eating of which impelled the course of human history which ends with this Judgement and fire. However, it is at this point (*Þonne*, 508b) that the poet states that the sign of the phoenix (*fugles tacen*, 510b) will be revealed to humankind at the general resurrection (508b–14a), the same phoenix which grew from *æples gelicnes* 'the likeness of an apple' (230b), unsusceptible to the original sin which renders every other creature mortal. In the context argued for above, the poem thus seems to set up a functional opposition between humans marred by sin, seen in the sexual union of man and woman, and those who renounce such earthly desires and follow the way of the phoenix, thus earning resurrection to eternal life. However, if this opposition is indeed present it is, of course, an asymmetrical one, since it balances the physical procreation between man and woman which produces physical offspring with the spiritual procreation performed by the monk who is both solitary and in a community of brothers, that is, sex is balanced against not-sex, presence against absence. It seems to me that this asymmetry if meditated upon is a troubling and unstable one for someone who is part of such a community, particularly a community where same-sex intimacy is circumscribed and where other men are seen as a potential source of sexual temptation. The monk like the phoenix is called to be leader of his kind but also to live apart from the world; he is called to renounce sexual desire and yet to be spiritually fruitful. Even more than the idea of nature as divine artifice destabilizes the sense of what is natural, the phoenix as a model of the transcendence of sexuality and gender radically destabilizes the sense of what human relations entail, and it is my view that the spectre of same-sex desire (that sex which is not one, or at least not-there)

---

[43] Bugge, 'The Virgin Phoenix', pp. 341–3; Too, 'The Appeal to the Senses', pp. 231–2.

hovers around these moments of the poem and motivates some of the poet's choices.

One may take the poet's emphasis on purity and chastity, for instance—the phoenix is *se clæna* 'the pure one' (167b), its nest is clean (226b), its nest-building is compared to the holy man's seeking of prayer *clænum gehygdum* 'with pure thoughts' (459a), and its resurrected body to those which the blessed receive once more *leahtra clæne* 'clean from sins' (518b) and clothed with which they raise a song like that of the phoenix, *clæne ond gecorene* 'chosen and pure' (541a). However, the most interesting use of the term comes in the extended harvest simile discussed above, where the phoenix's rebirth is compared to the regeneration of *clæne* 'pure' seed (252b). As well as associating the bird with the figure of the monk, this passage may also represent an attempt to naturalize what might otherwise seem unnatural, to liken the spiritual procreation of the monk to a natural even vegetative process, and with the addition of that seemingly unmotivated adjective *clæne* to ward off any anxiety that such procreation will be even for a moment thought of in an 'impure' context or connected to contemporary concerns about unspiritual non-procreative physical contact between monks.[44] Such an anxiety on the part of the poet may also explain the way he deals with the opposition he found in Lactantius between past destructions of the earth by fire and water.

The Latin poem tells us that the phoenix's grove in the earthly paradise is eternally green, and that, when the world was set aflame by Phaeton's chariot, the place was inviolate, just as it was saved when the rest of the world was submerged in the flood-waters of Deucalion (lines 8–15). Like the other Classical references in the Latin, these allusions to Phaeton and Deucalion are transformed by the Old English poet. He expands the Latin poet's three lines on Deucalion into the following account:

> Swa iu wætres þrym
> ealne middangeard,   mereflod þeahte
> eorþan ymbhwyrft,   þa se æþela wong
> æghwæs onsund   wið yðfare
> gehealden stod   hreora wæga
> eadig unwemme   þurh est Godes. (41b–6)

When long ago the water's might, the flood, engulfed the whole of the middle-earth, the orbit of the earth, then the noble plain, in every way unharmed by the rush of the flood, stood protected from the fierce waves, blessed, inviolate, by God's grace.

By the mere omission of the name Deucalion and the mention of 'God's grace', this becomes straightforwardly interpretable as a reference to the biblical flood of

---

[44] Bugge, too, thinks that the poet chose this term to invoke 'the mystery of sexless generation', though as part of a very different argument (p. 347).

Noah.[45] However, the poet's treatment of the Phaeton allusion is rather different. He translates Lactantius's comment on the eternally green nature of the wood, omitting only the information that it is sacred to Phoebus (33–8a), then he repeats that *Næfre brosniað | leaf under lyfte* 'Never will a leaf wither under the sky' (38b-40a), but adds

> ne him lig sceþeð
> æfre to ealdre,   ærþon edwenden
> worulde geweorðe. (40b–1a)

nor will fire harm them ever and always before the change comes upon the world.

The Flood passage then intervenes, but is immediately followed by the promise that the land

> bideð swa geblowen   oð bæles cyme,
> Dryhtnes domes   þonne deaðræced,
> hæleþa heolstorcofan   onhilden weorþað. (47–9)

will abide, thus in bloom, until the coming of the fire, the judgement of the Lord, when the halls of the dead, the heroes' chambers of darkness, will be opened.

The notion of a great conflagration of the past from which the land was exempted has become a brief statement that fire *will* not harm the leaves of the wood, and then a stark image of future fiery destruction at Judgement Day. It is true that one could view this change as motivated by the poet's clear interest in eschatological issues.[46] However, it is worth considering what the poet's other options were, and it is clear that the only major biblical fire which would be an appropriate equivalent here would be the destruction of Sodom, which as we saw in Chapter 4, Ælfric and Alcuin wrote of as a parallel to the Flood. It is not possible to draw conclusions based solely on negative evidence, but it seems likely that, if this comparison did occur to the poet, he would certainly have been reluctant to invoke a narrative which, even if not exclusively linked to same-sex desire, would raise rather too many problematic associations for the same-sex procreative model represented by the phoenix, given both the internal anxieties and the external accusations endured by contemporary monastic establishments.

Calder rightly states that *The Phoenix* is centred on a basic tension, that paradise and the phoenix 'both are and are not symbols of the heavenly world' (p. 179). However, the arguments presented here extend the observation to contend that the tension is far more radical than Calder suggests— that the paradoxes of nature and artifice, of solitariness and community, of sexless sex and same-sex procreation, both profoundly express the paradoxical position of the monk on earth on the one hand, and, on the other, also

---

[45] Noah is explicitly referred to in the *Prose Phoenix* (cf. Blake, *Phoenix*, p. 98).
[46] Compare Garde, *Old English Poetry*, ch. 8, *passim*.

evoke the anxiety that such a revisioning of essential worldly concepts might be misinterpreted; the possibility of subversive readings of the poem which must be circumscribed to maintain the absence of that sex which is not and must not be there. The following chapter explores further the productive tensions within Old English religious texts over gender and sexuality in monastic contexts.

9

Saintly Desire? Same-Sex Relations in Ælfric's *Lives of Saints*

Ælfric's *Lives of Saints* follow up his two series of *Catholic Homilies*, and it is probable that most of the Lives were written prior to 1002, since the preface addresses Ælfric's patron Æthelweard, who died in 1002 at the latest. Therefore, they are generally dated as a collection between 992 and 1002.[1] Some of the Lives are clearly intended to fill in gaps left in the *Catholic Homilies*, or to supply a demand on the part of his earlier audiences for more on certain saints, such as St Martin. However, the prefaces also mention the motivation of providing accounts of saints whom monks rather than the laity honoured.[2] The question of Ælfric's intended audience is a complex and controversial one, but recent criticism broadly concurs with Mary Clayton's assertion that he wrote 'for a mixed audience' and that, although 'aiming primarily at instructing the lay people' through vernacular preaching, Ælfric also included 'passages and sometimes whole texts that relate more to the religious elements in the congregation', and his works will also have been used for private devotional reading.[3] The Old English Preface of the *Lives of Saints* collection is addressed specifically to the secular nobleman Æthelweard and notes that the texts were requested by his son Æthelmær, but Ælfric clearly anticipates a wider audience in the Latin Preface

[1] See Godden, *Ælfric's Catholic Homilies. Introduction, Commentary and Glossary*, pp. xxi, xxiii, xxvi, xxxv; P. A. M. Clemoes, 'The Chronology of Ælfric's Works', in *The Anglo-Saxons: Studies in Some Aspects of their History and Culture presented to Bruce Dickins*, ed. Peter Clemoes. London: Bowes & Bowes, 1959, pp. 212–47, at pp. 220, 222, 243. On the Ælfric canon and chronology, see also Pope, *Homilies of Ælfric: A Supplementary Collection*, I, pp. 136–50.
[2] See Skeat, *Ælfric's Lives of Saints*, I, pp. 2 (Latin) and 4 (Old English). All citations are taken from this edition and are hereafter cited by page number within the text. I have occasionally repunctuated the original; all translations are my own. I have only discussed Ælfric's Latin sources in detail where the exact source has been identified. It is generally agreed that the ultimate sources have most often been filtered through an intermediate source similar to the Cotton-Corpus Legendary, but more work in this area needs to be done. See Patrick H. Zettel, 'Saints' Lives in Old English: Latin Manuscripts and Vernacular Accounts: Ælfric', *Peritia* 1 (1982), 17–37; Peter Jackson and Michael Lapidge, 'The Contents of the Cotton-Corpus Legendary', in *Holy Men and Holy Women: Old English Prose Saints' Lives and Their Contexts*, ed. Paul E. Szarmach. New York: State University of New York Press, 1996, pp. 131–46. See also Mechthild Gretsch, *Ælfric and the Cult of Saints in Late Anglo-Saxon England*. Cambridge Studies in Anglo-Saxon England, 34. Cambridge: Cambridge University Press, 2005, pp. 1–20.
[3] See Mary Clayton, 'Homiliaries and Preaching in Anglo-Saxon England', *Peritia* 4 (1985), 207–42; corrected reprint in Szarmach, *Old English Prose*, pp. 151–98, at p. 189.

and in his directive in the Old English Preface that any copies should accurately reflect his original text (2–6).[4]

This chapter explores the interdependent construction of gender and sexuality in the *Lives of Saints*, and explores the complex and contradictory discourse which characterizes these texts, a discourse which both affirms and undermines the gender binary, at the same time as it manifests a sense of ambivalence about same-sex relations. We saw in Chapter 5 how Ælfric is reluctant to discuss same-sex activity explicitly, even in texts not aimed at the laity, and this reluctance is still more apparent in the Lives. Nevertheless, at the same time as homosocial bonds are seen to be a crucial aspect of the religious community, the spectre of same-sex desire is a haunting presence which interacts with a destabilized gender dynamic in surprising and often contradictory ways.

WARRING SAINTS AND SAINTLY WARFARE

Ælfric's Life of the Forty Soldiers (Skeat XI) begins with his motivation for relating it. It is *þæt eower geleafa þe trumre sy, þonne ge gehyrað hu þegenlice hi þrowodon for criste* 'that your faith may be the firmer when you hear how nobly they suffered for Christ' (238). The adverb *þegenlice* literally means 'thane-like' or 'in the manner of a thane' and the choice cuts to the heart of what Ælfric is doing in this life. The word appears, as we have seen in Chapter 7, in *The Battle of Maldon* when the poet speaks about Offa's vow to his lord Byrhtnoth, namely that

> hi sceoldon begen   on burh ridan,
> halan to hame,   oððe on here crincgan,
> on wælstowe   wundum sweltan;
> he læg ðegenlice   ðeodne gehende. (291–4)

they should both ride into the stronghold, safe to their home, or perish in the host, upon the slaughter-place die from wounds; he lay thane-like near to his lord.

---

[4] See Hugh Magennis, 'Ælfric's *Lives of Saints* and Cotton Julius E.vii: Adaptation, Appropriation and the Disappearing Book', in *Imagining the Book*, ed. Stephen Kelly and John J. Thompson. Turnhout: Brepols, 2005, pp. 99–109, at p. 100; E. Gordon Whatley, '*Pearls before Swine*: Ælfric, Vernacular Hagiography, and the Lay Reader', in *Via Crucis: Essays on Early Medieval Sources and Ideas in Memory of J. E. Cross*, ed. Thomas N. Hall et al. Morgantown: West Virginia University Press, 2002, pp. 158–84, at 173–84. On the subsequent transmission and reuse of Ælfric's material, see Joyce Hill, 'The Dissemination of Ælfric's *Lives of Saints*: A Preliminary Survey', in Szarmach, *Holy Men and Holy Women*, pp. 235–59; idem, 'The Preservation and Transmission of Ælfric's Saints' Lives: Reader-Reception and Reader-Response in the Early Middle Ages', in *The Preservation and Transmission of Anglo-Saxon Culture: Selected Papers from the 1991 Meeting of the International Society of Anglo-Saxonists*, ed. Paul E. Szarmach and Joel T. Rosenthal. Studies in Medieval Culture, 40. Kalamazoo: Medieval Institute Publications, 1997, pp. 405–30; Mary Swan and Elaine Treharne, eds, *Rewriting Old English in the Twelfth Century*. Cambridge Studies in Anglo-Saxon England, 30. Cambridge: Cambridge University Press, 2000, *passim*.

Seen in this context, Ælfric's use of the term carries a complex set of implications. It takes it for granted that it is the duty of a thane to suffer for his lord, and that his audience will have that duty encoded in their world-view. It also assumes that the way a thane suffers for his secular lord equates on some level with the way the forty soldiers suffered for their divine Lord. Further, though, there is an implied relation between the forty soldiers and the listening audience—the tale is related 'that *your* faith may be the firmer': the soldiers' faith as shown in their actions is to inspire the audience members to stronger faith themselves.

One could conflate these two relationships and see the passage as thus implying that the relation of secular followers to their lord in some way equates to that of Christians to their divine Lord. This is of course a straightforward comparison, and one that is made in the New Testament and in patristic writings fairly frequently. The relation of thane and audience member in this context would thus be taken as a metaphorical one—just as thanes suffer physically for their lord in battle, so Christians suffer for their Lord in spiritual battle with demons and unbelievers, whether that suffering is spiritual, mental, or physical torture. However, it is a mistake to elide the mediating term in the binary relation between the secular thane and the Christian audience member constructed in that scenario. The forty soldiers are both Christians *and* 'thanes', and the loyalty they display in this text is not just to their Lord, but also a lateral bond of loyalty to their comrades. They represent a homosocial community, and same-sex bonds are crucial to the ideological force of this text, as we shall see if we look at the story in more detail.[5]

The forty are a community of Christian soldiers living piously within the Roman army under the anti-Christian emperor Licinius and a cruel judge called Agricola, who commands all soldiers to offer sacrifices to the gods. When the forty refuse, Agricola has them seized and brought to the idol-sacrifice, where he

cwæð mid olecunge þæt hi æþele cempan wæron, and on ælcum gefeohte fæstræde him betwynan, and symle sigefæste on swiþlicum gewinne: 'Æteowiað nu forði eowre anrædnysse, and eow sylfe underþeodað þæra cyninga gesetnyssum, and geoffriað þam godum ærþam þe gebeon getintregode.' (240)

said with flattery that they were noble champions and in each battle constant to each other, and always victorious in violent conflict: 'Show now therefore your unanimity, and subject yourselves to the king's decrees and make offerings to the gods before you are tortured.'

Agricola links their military prowess as 'noble champions' who are 'always victorious' with their 'constancy' to each other. He then attempts to use that bond of loyalty between equals and the threat of torture to get them to act as he wishes—the two acts of submission he requires (subjection to the king, and

---

[5] On the wider aspects of Ælfric's warrior saints, including a brief discussion of the Forty Soldiers, see Hugh Magennis, 'Warrior Saints, Warfare, and the Hagiography of Ælfric of Eynsham', *Traditio* 56 (2001), 27–51, esp. 45–8.

abasement before the gods) are sandwiched between the direct threat ('before you are tortured') and the indirect threat: 'Show . . . your unanimity', which may imply that non-compliance will not be unanimous, that at least one of their number will succumb under torture and break the unity of their group.

Ælfric then starkly opposes the judge and his captives through alliterative juxtaposition, as *þa Cristenan* 'the Christians' speak to *ðam cwellere* 'the murderer', in a reply which carefully reverses the terms of Agricola's discourse:

> Oft we oferswiðdon swa swa þu sylf wistest
> ure wiðerwinnan on gehwylcum gewinne
> þa þa we fuhton for ðam deadlicum kynincge,
> ac us gedafenað swyðor mid geswince to campigenne
> for þam undeadlicum cynincge and þe oferswiðan. (240)

We have often, as you yourself know, overcome our adversaries in every battle when we fought for the mortal king, but it is more fitting for us to fight with great effort for the immortal king and overcome you.

The term *deadlicum* can mean both 'deadly' and 'mortal', and so the choice of it and its counterpart *undeadlicum* brings out the contrast between the earthly ruler who has the power to kill but is nonetheless doomed to die, and the heavenly king whose service may bring physical death but guarantees spiritual life. In the soldiers' unanimous retort, speaking as if with one voice, their loyalty to the earthly king is clearly set against their loyalty to their heavenly lord which transcends all earthly allegiances. At the same time, however, the personal deixis firmly corrects the implication in Agricola's speech that to remain unified they must submit to him (and thus the emperor and the gods)—they will 'fight with great effort (literally, 'toil, struggle')' together for God.

The dynamic in this passage is replicated later when the soldiers again appear before Agricola:

> Hi þa ealle feowertig ætforan him stodon, þa began se dema eft hi herigan, cwæð þæt heora gelican næron on þæs caseres lande, ne swa geherede ne him swa leofe, gif hi noldon awendan þa lufe to hatunge. Þa cwædon þa halgan þæt hi hine hatodon for his geleafleaste and lufedon heora drihten.   (242)

When they stood all forty before him, then the judge began to praise them again, said that their like could not be found in the emperor's land, not so praised nor so dear to him—if they would not change that love to hatred. Then the holy ones said that they hated him for his unbelief and loved their Lord.

Once more Agricola flatters them: the soldiers are unique ('their like could not be found') and the emperor loves them—refusing to bow to the idols and persisting in faith is figured as actively forcing his love to turn into hatred. However, the forty throw this emotive language back in Agricola's face: they 'hate' him and 'love' only their *drihten* 'lord', the original's lack of capitalization creating a

momentary ambiguity and reminding us of the earlier passage where secular and
divine kings are contrasted.

Back in prison and awaiting the decision of a higher official, one of the forty,
named Quirio (the only soldier who is named), encourages the others, reminding
them how Christ has saved them in martial conflict before:

Hwilon we wæron on micclum gewinne, and eall ure folc mid fleame ætwand, buton we
feowertig þe on þam feohte stodon, biddende georne ures drihtnes fultum, and sume we
afligdon sume feollan ætforan us, and ure an næs gederod fram ealre þæra meniu.   (242)

Once we were in a great battle and all our people escaped by flight, except we forty who
stood firm to the fight, asking earnestly for our Lord's help, and some we put to flight,
some fell before us, and not one of us was hurt by all that multitude.

This reads rather like *Maldon* with a happy ending, or a Christianized version of
a heroic encounter such as those in the 'Cynewulf and Cyneheard' episode, but
the difference here is that it is a hyperbolic heroic encounter, where the hero is
God: the forty's primary action is to 'stand firm' and to ask for God's help.[6] It is
then that they put the enemy to flight, killing some, and the sign of this divine
enabling is the miraculous lack of wounds received by the few faithful soldiers
among a 'multitude'.

The saints' intransigence, bolstered by this past experience of divine favour, is
punished severely. They are pushed naked into a frozen lake and kept there all
night, with the temptation of a basin of warm water set nearby, where they may
get warm if they renounce their faith. It is only now that the group's unity is
threatened:

Þa eargode heora an for þam ormætum cyle, awearp his geleafan and wolde hine baðian
on þam wlacum wætere and wende fram his geferum, ac he gewat sona swa he þæt wæter
hrepode, and wearð seo wearmnys him awend to deaðe. (248)

Then one of them turned coward because of the excessive cold, threw away his faith and
wanted to bathe himself in the lukewarm water and turned from his companions; but he
passed away as soon as he touched the water, and the warmth was turned for him into
death.

This apostasy is clearly seen as a lack of faith (he 'threw away his faith'), but
it is also seen as cowardice (*eargode*) and as disloyalty to his friends: he 'turned
from his companions', and this idea is repeated in the others' response to their
erstwhile comrade's action:

Þa gesawon þa oðre hu þam anum getimode, and sungon þysne sang swylce of anum
muðe: 'Ne yrsa ðu drihten us on ðysum deopum flodum, ne þin hatheortnys on þysser
ea ne sy. Se þe hine ascyrede for þyssere scearpnysse fram us, his lima synd toslopena and

---

[6] We might thus compare the Cross in *The Dream of the Rood*; see Chapter 7 above.

he sona losode. We nellað drihten næfre fram þe twæman, oð þæt ðu us gelyffæste þe to lofe drihten'.   (248)

Then the others saw how it fell out for that one, and sang this song as if from a single mouth:
'Be not angry with us, Lord, in these deep floods, nor let Your wrath be in this water. That one who separated himself from us because of this sharpness—his limbs are relaxed and he perished at once. We, Lord, want never to part from You, until You quicken us, Lord to Your praise.'

The remaining thirty-nine soldiers sing a song to God 'as if from a single mouth', and they see the apostasy as an act of separation—the icy cold meant that he 'separated himself from us', and this decision was punished by death. However, his death leads the rest to affirm that they want 'never to part from You'—there is thus a fascinating confluence here between maintaining faith and remaining part of the homosocial community. The trope of life as death and death as life is repeated ('until You quicken us, Lord'), and this continues to the end of the story, as, to receive spiritual life from God, they accept death together, represented physically in the image of all their bones being collected after their death and being laid together, indistinguishably, in a shrine (254).

There is more to the text than this, however. Together with the play on life and death, there is another play on heat and cold: the thirty-nine pray that God will not let his *hatheortnys* 'wrath', or more literally 'hot-heartedness' be in the water. The icy coldness of the physical water in which they are immersed is seen as preferable to the punitive 'heat' of God's anger. We may be reminded of several biblical elements here—the waters of baptism, the fires of hell, perhaps also the lukewarm nature of the church at Laodicea whom God wanted to spit out of his mouth (Revelation 3: 15–16)—and these associations all may play a part. However, there are two other words which carry ambiguous connotations: as shown in Chapter 3, *eargode* may carry associations with effeminacy. Moreover, the term *toslopena* 'relaxed', can also mean 'loose' or 'dissolute'.[7] We might ask, then, whether this passage subtly implies that the soldier who was unable to bear the torture was cowardly because of a moral laxity bound up with ideas of substandard masculinity and sexuality. Alternatively, we might see the choice of words as dictated by an anxiety on Ælfric's part created by the intensity of the homosocial bonds which characterize the group and which become almost synonymous with maintaining Christian faith.[8]

Another of the Lives of Saints contains a moment which seems very like the *Maldon* passage quoted at the start of this section, and a similar homosocial dynamic to those texts analysed above, namely Ælfric's account of the Maccabees (Skeat XXV), based on the apocryphal text concerning Judas Maccabeus and his companions. The part in question comes when Judas with his brothers has

---

[7] Clark Hall, *Concise Anglo-Saxon Dictionary, s.v. toslopena*.
[8] This issue is explored further in the final section below and Chapter 10.

become established as a champion of the Jews. Various battles ensue against the heathen, who generally flee before the God-fearing Jews despite their greater numbers. However, like any champion, Judas must eventually fall. We are told that

Hi comon ða færlice mid gefohte to iudan, and his geferan eargodon butan eahta hund mannum þe him mid fuhton wið þone feondlican here. Þa cwædon his geferan þæt hi fleon woldon, forðan þe heora werod wæs gewanod mid þam fleame, and woldon heom beorgan wið þone breman here.

Þa andwyrde iudas swa swa he eall cene wæs:

'Ne ge-wurðe hit na on life þæt we alecgan ure wuldor mid earhlicum fleame ac uton feohtan wið hi, and gif god swa foresceawað we sweltað on mihte for urum gebroðrum butan bysmorlicum fleame'

… and feollan ða on twa healfe on þam gefeohte manega, and iudas eac feoll and þa oðre ætflugon.   (110)

[The enemy] then came suddenly in battle against Judas, and his companions turned coward except for eight hundred men who fought with him against the hostile army. Then his companions said that they would flee because their company was diminished by the flight [of the others], and would save themselves from the raging army.

Then Judas answered, since he was completely brave:

'Let it never happen while we are alive that we lay down our glory with cowardly flight, but let us fight against them, and if God so foreordains it, we shall die in our might for our brothers without shameful flight.'

… and then many fell on both sides in the battle, and Judas fell also, and the others fled.

The sudden attack of the enemy causes most of the army to 'turn coward' (*eargodon*), but Judas uses the spectre of cowardice, which again may carry associations with effeminacy and stigmatized same-sex activity, to present a stark choice: life can be assured by flight, but this is cowardly and shameful (*earhlicum* and *bysmorlicum*). The only viable option is to fight in the full knowledge that this may mean death, if God so 'foreordains it'. Moreover, although Judas sees the outcome as being in God's hands, he envisages with equanimity the possibility of dying 'for our brothers'. Glory entails victory with one's comrades, or death with one's comrades, whichever fate is ordained by God.

In these two military Lives, then, homosocial desire between peers is constructed as natural, and as inextricably bound up with participation in the faith community. There may be signs of authorial anxiety, however, created by the spectre of male sexual intimacy, and we shall explore this further shortly. In several of the other Lives, however, homosocial bonds are an important theme, and the faith community itself is constructed and spreads on a same-sex model of conversion. The following section discusses this model in the Lives of Crysanthus and Daria, Julian and Basilissa, Constantia/Gallicanus, and Agatha.[9]

---

[9] These Lives have been discussed extensively from the point of view of Ælfric's views on women, chaste marriage, and virginity. In addition to specific references below, the following works should supplement the present discussion with its narrower focus on homosociality: Catherine Cubitt,

THE HOMOSOCIAL CONVERSION DYNAMIC

This model of conversion is seen most strikingly in the Life of Crysanthus and Daria (Skeat XXXV). After a series of failed attempts to persuade his son of the delights of sex with women, Crysanthus's father finds a heathen maiden called Daria, who is both beautiful and *uðwitegunge snoter* 'learned in philosophy' (382). Despite this, she has no more success than any of her predecessors, for, after Crysanthus points out to her the misdeeds and foolishness of the pagan gods, she converts to Christianity, and the couple enter into a chaste marriage.[10] We are told that many others were converted by their manner of life:

> Cnihtas gecyrdon þurh crisantes lare
> and mædenu þurh darian manega to drihtne
> forlætenum synscipe and geswæsum lustum. (384)

The youths were converted through Crysanthus's teaching and the maidens through Daria's, many [people] to the Lord, having abandoned marriage and sweet desires.

Ælfric thus sets up a same-sex conversion dynamic, where both youths and maidens give up sexual pleasures in favour of a life devoted to the Lord through the teaching of an inspiring model of their own sex.

This dynamic thus constructs a model of marriage whereby refraining from sex actually results in fruitfulness—not the physical engendering of heirs, but spiritual reproduction, as we can see more clearly in the Life of Julian and Basilissa (Skeat IV). There, after their chaste marriage, Julian sets up a monastery for himself and a nunnery for his wife:

> He wearð þa fæder ofer fæla muneca
> and basilissa modor ofer manega mynecena.
> and hi þa gastlican werod under gode gewyssodon
> on dæghwamlicre lare to heora dryhtnes wyllan. (94)

He then became father over many monks, and Basilissa mother over many nuns, and they guided the spiritual host under God through daily teaching to their Lord's will.

'Virginity and Misogyny in Tenth- and Eleventh-Century England', *Gender and History* 12 (2000), 1–32; Leslie A. Donovan, 'The Gendered Body as Spiritual Problem and Spiritual Answer in the Lives of Women Saints', in her *Women Saints' Lives in Old English Prose*. Cambridge: Brewer, 1999, pp. 121–34; Shari Horner, 'The Violence of Exegesis: Reading the Bodies of Ælfric's Female Saints', in *Violence against Women in Medieval Texts*, ed. Anna Roberts. Gainesville, FL: University of Florida Press, 1998, pp. 22–43; Lees, 'Engendering Religious Desire', See also the comments in the section on Eugenia below and the following chapter on Euphrosyne.

[10] On chaste marriage and for a more detailed discussion of this Life, see further Robert K. Upchurch, 'The Legend of Chrysanthus and Daria in Ælfric's *Lives of Saints*', *Studies in Philology* 101 (2004), 250–69; cf. idem, 'Virgin Spouses as Model Christians: The Legend of Julian and Basilissa in Ælfric's *Lives of Saints*', *Anglo-Saxon England* 34 (2005), 197–217; idem, *Ælfric's Lives of the Virgin Spouses*. Exeter: University of Exeter Press, 2007, esp. pp. 1–47. I am not yet convinced by Horner's reading of Crysanthus's torture, where she suggests the hard rods of his torturers which soften as they strike him represent 'thwarted male sexuality'; Horner, 'Language of Rape', p. 175.

In these two Lives, spiritual procreation is predicated on the *absence* of physical union between man and woman—it is a sort of parthenogenesis that is firmly same-sex oriented and is thus similar to the dynamic explored earlier in *The Phoenix*. Moreover, the family that results is also imaged as a spiritual army under the divine Leader's command, an image which thus further undermines the primacy of the physical family by foregrounding the notion of a homosocial community that is based on unity of purpose, not genetic connection.[11]

Another text which clearly brings out these themes is the story attributed to Terentianus which is appended to the Life of St Agnes (Skeat VII).[12] In this story a general called Gallicanus woos the emperor Constantine's daughter Constantia, who was baptized and received the veil at the end of the Life of Agnes. The emperor is troubled because he knows his daughter would rather die than have a husband. She, however, tells her father to say that she will accept Gallicanus after he has conquered the Scythians in war, and if he gives her his daughters Attica and Arthemia as companions until the nuptials are prepared. As a parallel to this female homosocial community, she wishes Gallicanus to take her faithful fellow Christians, John and Paul, with him on his expedition:

> þæt hi mine þeawas magon him secgan
> and ic ðurh his dohtra his þeawas oncnawe. (188)

so that they can tell him my ways and through his daughters I may understand his ways.

At first sight, this seems an equal transaction—Constantia and Gallicanus will get to know each other's likes and dislikes, understand the other's point of view. However, since *þeawas* can mean not only 'habits, customs' but also 'morals, virtues', there seems to be a pun here which hints at the reality of the situation. Constantia intends not that the two of them should get to know each other and reach a compromise, but that she should convert Gallicanus's daughters, and that John and Mark should convert the general himself. This is confirmed in her prayer that God will *geðeod* 'unite' Gallicanus to faith in him, and open the hearts of him and his daughters

> þæt hi þe anne lufian and eorðlice ðing ne gewilnion
> and mid beornendre lufe to þinum brydbedde becumen. (188)

that they will love only you and will not desire earthly things, and come with burning love to your bridal bed.

---

[11] The social disruption of conversion is figured towards the end of the life in a very strong image when Martianus calls out to Julian: 'Eala þu iuliane, þe awendest minne sunu | swa þæt he min ne ræcð ne eac þære meder' (108) [Alas, Julian, you change/pervert my son so that he pays no heed to me or to his mother]. See further Upchurch, 'Virgin Spouses as Model Christians' 201–2; Dabney Anderson Bankert, 'Reconciling Family and Faith: Ælfric's *Lives of Saints* and Domestic Dramas of Conversion', in Hall, *Via Crucis*, pp. 138–57.

[12] For an extended reading of the Lives of Agnes and Constantia/Gallicanus, and the argument that they are paired deliberately in order to encourage a historicized reading of different views on virgin martyrdom, see Bankert, 'Reconciling Family and Faith'.

While Gallicanus is away, the desired conversion duly occurs, and on his return he reveals his newfound faith and vow of chastity to the emperor, who informs him in turn of his daughters' conversion. There is general rejoicing, and we are told that the daughters continued in virginity till death and that Gallicanus freed 5,000 men and gave his riches to the poor. However, there then follows a very interesting passage where we are told that Gallicanus himself goes to live with a holy man called Hilarion *mid sumum his mannum þe hine ne mihton forlætan* 'with some of his men who could not abandon him' (192). That a convert should retire into communion with a holy man to learn more of and be established in the faith is not unusual. However, the comment about his men indicates that the homosocial conversion dynamic is not constructed in opposition to the previous homosocial bonds established between Gallicanus and his soldiers prior to conversion—the conversion of Gallicanus's men, it is implied, is inextricably bound up with their desire to remain close to their general. As such, their relationship bears a strong resemblance to that of the Forty Soldiers we explored above. In Ælfric's *Lives of Saints*, male-female and familial relations may be broken and re-established in a new way, but where male-male bonds are concerned there is only continuity. The faith community is thus represented as affirming and deepening homosocial relations.

Most of the versions of homosocial community we have seen in Ælfric's *Lives* are viewed positively, but he does describe a negative version in the Life of Agatha (Skeat VIII), which qualifies this pattern. In the Life, an evil governor called Quintianus hears of Agatha's *drohtnunge* 'conduct' and desires her for himself. Since before this point all we know about Agatha is that she is a noble Sicilian maiden who is *snotor and gelyfed* 'wise and faithful', we must assume that this is what he wants in a woman, or that he sees her chastity as a challenge. What is interesting, though, is that he does not attempt to seduce her himself or through his soldiers. Rather he has Agatha taken to *anum fulum wife* 'a foul woman' (196) called Aphrodosia. Her name is clearly intended to be reminiscent of Aphrodite, the Greek goddess of sexual love, and we are told that she is *sceandlic on þeawum* 'shameful in morals/practices'. Not only this but she has nine daughters, *nahtlice and fracode* 'wicked and base', who are to be Agatha's society for a month so that she can learn Aphrodosia's *þeawas*, and that *hire mod awende þurh þæra myltestrena forspennincgæ* 'her mind may change through the prostitutes' enticements'. The diction here might make one think that physical seduction is what is being proposed, especially since *awendan* can also mean 'to pervert'. However, Agatha is quite clear that it is the prostitutes' *word* 'words' which are *winde gelice* 'like wind', but which, despite their quantity, cannot *afyllan min fæstræde geþanc* 'defile my steadfast purpose'. Nevertheless, the terms used to describe the exertions of Agatha's temptresses are indeed striking. The phrase *mod awendan* 'change/pervert the mind' is repeated of Aphrodosia, and when she finally admits defeat we are told that she saw *þæt heo þære femnan mod | gebigan ne mihte mid hyre bismorfullum tihtincgum* 'that she could not bend/debase the virgin's mind with her shameful enticements'. There may be here the suggestion of deviant sexuality for those clerical readers alert to such things. Certainly, this is an unusual use of the female homosocial community to 'pervert' a woman into consenting to male sexual desire (lines 32–4), which contrasts with Ælfric's treatment of male homosocial communities analysed above. Overall, however, Ælfric's narratives generally work to naturalize the homosocial dynamic of conversion.

EUGENIA AND THE (DE)NATURALIZATION OF TRANSVESTISM

From a consideration of positive and negative versions of homosocial communities, we turn now to a text which complicates the notion of a gender binary which underlies these communities, namely Ælfric's Life of Eugenia (Skeat II). This Life has attracted a comparatively large amount of critical attention, owing to its protagonist's status as one of a group of what Paul Szarmach has termed medieval 'transvestite saints', since they don masculine apparel in order to escape marriage and live chastely in monasteries.[13] Ælfric begins his narrative by saying that anyone who wishes may hear how Eugenia *ðurh mægðhad mærlice þeah | and þurh martyrdom þisne middaneard oferswað* 'through virginity gloriously prospered, and through martyrdom overcame this world' (24). The motivation thus for listening to the tale, and implicitly for writing it, is to encourage virginity (or at least chastity) in his audience, presumably to the point of death. Other possible motivations will be considered later, but it is certainly true, as other critics such as Gopa Roy and Paul Szarmach have pointed out, that Ælfric in translating his Latin source for this Life made every effort to focus primarily on the merits of virginity and resistance to worldly desires.[14] However, the ensuing discussion aims to show that Ælfric's attempt to de-eroticize the story is not as successful as these critics have made out, and that the central protagonist's act of

---

[13] Paul E. Szarmach, 'Ælfric's Women Saints: *Eugenia*', in Damico and Olsen, *New Readings on Women*, pp. 146–57. The review of Szarmach's article in the *Old English Newsletter* (25 (1992), 56) challenges his use of the term *transvestite*, on the dubious grounds that the reviewer's dictionary defines transvestism 'primarily as the abnormal desire to dress in the clothes of the opposite sex— and this definition does not really fit Eugenia, since the text stresses no abnormal desires on her part but rather her need for a disguise in order to live the life of a monk'. Leaving aside the question of why the writer is privileging a clearly outdated dictionary definition (though this fairly represents the current *OED* definition), one may observe that s/he is missing the point. Eugenia is not a real person, but a figure in a narrative, and the issue is what Ælfric has done with her cross-dressing behaviour, whether this is figured as normal or abnormal, and how this behaviour fits in with the gender dynamics of his text. In the present chapter, a further issue is also the audience's potential response to the transvestite figure.

[14] Szarmach, 'Ælfric's Women Saints'; Gopa Roy, 'A Virgin Acts Manfully: Ælfric's *Life of St Eugenia* and the Latin Versions', *Leeds Studies in English* NS 23 (1992), 1–27.

transvestism in fact destabilizes the sexless and genderless dynamic Ælfric tries to establish.

It is easy to summarize the crucial elements of this Life. Eugenia is the daughter of Philip, the Roman ruler of Alexandria. She is sent to school to be educated in *woruld-wysdome* 'secular wisdom', but, in addition to secular learning, Eugenia comes across the Apostle Paul's teaching. She converts to Christianity and in order to escape marriage, gets her two faithful servants to disguise her as a man and enters a monastery, with the complicity of a bishop, where she lives for many years. On the death of the abbot, the monks choose her as his replacement, a role which Eugenia reluctantly accepts. Later she cures a wealthy widow, Melantia, of a sickness, but becomes the object of the widow's sexual desire. When Eugenia repudiates Melantia's advances, in an ironic turn of events, the widow denounces her to Philip as an attempted rapist. At the trial, Melantia's servants back up their mistress's story, but Eugenia reveals her innocence by baring her breasts to her father, and explains how her present situation came about. This revelation impels the second part of the narrative in which Philip converts to Christianity and becomes a bishop but is murdered by his imperial replacement. Eugenia moves to Rome where she converts a heathen maiden called Basilla, and the two women continue the work of evangelism together. When Basilla refuses a pagan suitor, she is sentenced to death by the emperor, who also condemns all Christians who refuse to recant. Eugenia herself is asked to sacrifice to Diana, but instead destroys the temple of the goddess through prayer. After surviving attempts to kill her by drowning and scalding, Eugenia is visited in prison and sustained by Christ himself, who tells her that she will be brought to heaven on the day of his birth. After her martyrdom, Eugenia appears to her mother, adorned with gold, to assure her that she herself will join both Eugenia and Philip shortly and share their bliss with the saints.

What this summary does not fully indicate is the unusual sexual and gender dynamic of Ælfric's narrative. As Paul Szarmach shows very effectively, Ælfric works to make Christianity synonymous with virginity in the Life. For instance, he precedes the emperor's command that all Christians recant on pain of death with his command that Basilla submit to her suitor's desires, and follows it with the statement that Basilla would not choose any other bridegroom than Christ and was thus *gemartyrod for hyre mægðhade* 'martyred for her virginity' (46). Similarly, when the other Christians are killed, Ælfric observes that they were never *þurh wif besmytene* 'defiled by women', but rather lived in *clænnysse* 'purity' to the end of their lives *mid mycclum geleafan* 'with great faith'. In both these instances, faith and chastity become inseparable concepts. From the very beginning of the Life, however, the text's presentation of sexuality is complicated by the further dimension of gender. We see this when Eugenia reveals her attraction to the Christian faith to her two servants, who, we are carefully told, are both *eunuchi þæt synt belisnode* 'eunuchs, that is castrated' (28), and who are loyal and faithful to their mistress. We are then told:

Þa nam eugenia hi on sundorspræce
het hi gebroðra and bæd þæt hi
hyre fæx forcurfon on wæpmonna wysan
and mid wædum gehiwodon swylce heo cniht wære
wolde ðam cristenan genealecan
on wærlicum hiwe þæt heo ne wurde ameldod. (28)

Then Eugenia took them into private conversation, called them brothers and asked that they cut her hair in the manner of a man and transform her with clothes as if she were a boy; she wanted to approach the Christians in manly guise so that she would not be revealed.

In his discussion of this passage, Szarmach sees it as setting up a gender binary where maleness is coded positive and femaleness coded negative. He cites Vern L. Bullough's remark that female cross-dressing has proved acceptable in early Christian society despite Old Testament sanctions of the practice because it is read as the manifestation of a healthy desire to become a man: 'a normal longing not unlike the desire of a peasant to become a noble'.[15] However, in this text at least, the gender dynamic is more complex. Ælfric carefully states Eugenia's wish to have her hair cut *on wæpmonna wysan* 'in the manner of a man', where *wæpmonn* is a shortened version of *wæpnedmonn*, literally 'weaponed-person', where, as we saw in Chapter 3, the weapon may be seen as both literal (a sword or spear) and metaphorical (a penis). The word thus simultaneously foregrounds Eugenia's maleness and lack of the physical attribute which would make her a man.[16] Ælfric then tells us that she wishes to *be mid wædum gehiwodon* 'transformed with clothes' not into a man, but *swylce heo cniht wære* 'as if she were a boy'—again the text simultaneously invokes maleness but emphasizes that this is a masquerade, her maleness rests only in her clothes, and the comparison to a boy again hints at her lack: just as a boy lacks the secondary sexual characteristics of a mature man, so Eugenia lacks the physical attributes which make maleness genuine. This is summed up when we are told that she wanted to approach the Christians *on wærlicum hiwe*—Szarmach translates this as 'in the garb of a man', but *wærlicum* is in fact an adjective, which could be translated as 'male',

---

[15] Szarmach, 'Ælfric's Women Saints', p. 148, quoting Vern L. Bullough, 'Transvestites in the Middle Ages: A Sociological Analysis', *American Journal of Sociology* 79 (1974), 1381–94, at 1392; repr. with modifications in *Sexual Practices and the Medieval Church*, ed. Vern L. Bullough and James Brundage. Buffalo, NY: Prometheus Books, 1982, pp. 43–54.

[16] That Ælfric was aware of this association is perhaps shown by an anecdote in his Life of Martin (Skeat XXXI) in which the saint rebukes a monk who is tempted to bring back his former wife to serve as his assistant and companion. The monk assures Martin that they will remain chaste and it will not harm his monkhood (*munuchade*), but the saint, on ascertaining that the monk had previously been in battle as a soldier, asks him 'Gesawe þu ænig wif þa ðu wære on gefeohte | feohtan forð mid eow atogenum swurde?' [When you were in battle, did you see any woman fight alongside you with drawn sword?] (286). Here in secular terms, then, a woman is one who lacks a sword and thus cannot fight—and yet by the metaphorical transference of ideas and the context of sexual temptation, we understand that a woman cannot help in a man's spiritual battle precisely because he *does* have a sword/penis.

'masculine', or, as the present translation has it, 'manly' or 'manlike'; this fits in with the ambiguity in *hiwe* which could refer concretely to the clothes, or invoke more subtly the concept of disguise, seeming, masquerade.

What we must question, though, is whether (to use a modern designation) Eugenia is a Female-to-Male transvestite at all, or rather something subtly but crucially different. We are told that Eugenia, in speaking to her servants, *het hi gebroðra* 'called them brothers', that is, placed them on a level with her despite her superior status and rank and their lack of sexual organs, which would have marked them out not only as different but also as inferior, as 'lacking men'. Immediately after the passage analysed above, the eunuchs and Eugenia are designated as *ða þry* 'these three', and, when later Eugenia tells the bishop they wish to convert, she again designates them as equals, saying that *we ðry gebroðra* 'we three brothers' not only wish to turn from heathen ways to Christ but also *we nellað nates hwon us næfre totweman* 'we do not want by any means ever to be separated'. The interpersonal deixis here is reminiscent of that in the Life of the Forty Soldiers, and brings out the unity of this group, which is surely based not on their shared masculinity, but their shared lack. In a sense all three of them are masquerading as men—they look like men, their hair and clothes mark them out as men, but none of them possesses the physical attribute metaphorically inherent in the term *wæpnedmonn*: they thus constitute a profoundly queer homosocial community. Szarmach notes the presence of the eunuchs and comments that 'Eugenia's sexual inversion to male and to (brother-) eunuch and her accompanying social change can only obliterate her sexual identity' (p. 148), but he glosses over the way that maleness is in fact problematized by the text in this passage, raising questions about exactly how gender identity can be defined. As noted in Chapter 3, there is little information about eunuchs and attitudes to them in Anglo-Saxon England.[17] However, I want to explore Eugenia's contradictory gender status as woman/eunuch/celibate man further to argue that her Life exhibits anxieties around gender on the part of Ælfric, thus opening up the text to transgressive readings on the part of resistant audiences and providing a means of accessing other attitudes to same-sex relations which Ælfric would surely have abhorred.

Ælfric's Latin source explicitly invokes the famous passage from Galatians chapter 3, verse 28, saying that *beatus Paulus...dicat quod apud Deum non sit discretio masculi et femine: omnes enim in Christo unum sumus* 'the blessed Paul...says that in the Lord there is no distinction between male and female,

[17] On eunuchs (and anxiety about masculinity) in antiquity and at other times and places in the Middle Ages, however, see: Matthew Kuefler, *The Manly Eunuch: Masculinity, Gender Ambiguity, and Christian Ideology in Late Antiquity*. Chicago: University of Chicago Press, 2001; Shaun Tougher, 'Images of Effeminate Men: The Case of Byzantine Eunuchs', in *Masculinity in Medieval Europe*, ed. D. M. Hadley. London: Longman, 1999, pp. 89–100; idem, 'Holy Eunuchs! Masculinity and Eunuch Saints in Byzantium', in *Holiness and Masculinity in the Middle Ages*, ed. P. H. Cullum and Katherine J. Lewis. Toronto: University of Toronto Press, 2004, pp. 93–108; and his edited collection, *Eunuchs in Antiquity and Beyond*. London: Classical Press of Wales, 2002.

for we are all one in Christ'.[18] Szarmach argues that Ælfric omitted any explicit reference to the Galatians passage in his version because he saw its content as too complex to present, 'including notions of the resurrection of the body and the beatified state, while the idea of preservation of virginity is a simple enough concept to relate' (p. 154). Nonetheless, he deems that it is this biblical verse 'and its complex view of sexuality that is operating in the deep structure of Ælfric's *Life*', as the 'un-womanned' Eugenia and the 'un-manned' companions join in a community of 'three sexless saints [who] anticipate on earth the state in heaven' (p. 155). However, Szarmach's argument fails to take into account the fact that Eugenia is precisely *not* 'un-womanned', for in what is perhaps the climactic moment of the narrative (perhaps in more than one way, as we shall later consider) Eugenia is very definitely a woman in physical terms: the moment when she proves her innocence of Melantia's charge of rape. This revelation of her true identity is not in fact the first one in the text, however. As soon as Eugenia has been transformed into the likeness of a man, the text introduces Bishop Helenus, to whom Eugenia's identity is revealed by God. When she is brought to him, desiring conversion, Helenus takes her aside and tells her *gewislice* 'certainly' that *heo man ne wæs* 'she was not a man' (28). He allows her to continue in her disguise, baptizing her secretly, after which we are told that she remained in the monastery *mid wærlicum mode þeah þe heo mæden wæs* 'with a manly mind, though she was a maiden' (30). We as an audience are never allowed to forget that Eugenia is male in appearance only—that is, until she is appointed as abbot over the monastery.

    After the appointment, the text tells us that God grants Eugenia the ability to heal sickness and cast out demons. However, these healings are passed over in favour of recounting at length what occurs after the wealthy widow Melantia is cured of a long-standing fever. We are told that the widow afterwards often came to Eugenia *mid leasum mode | to þam wlytegan mædene, wende þæt heo cniht wære* 'with a false mind to the beautiful maiden; she thought that she was a boy' (32), and that, when she perceived that Eugenia cared nothing for her gifts or suggestions, then *wearð heo mid yfele eall afylled | and gebræd hi seoce mid bysmorfullum geþance* 'she became wholly filled with evil and pretended she [was] sick with shameful intent'. When Eugenia visits her, she speaks to her *sweartan geþohtas* 'dark thoughts' which constitute the revelation that not only is she wealthy but she and her husband had no intercourse during their marriage (*unc næs gemæne*); she claims to be greatly enamoured of Eugenia (*min mod awend mycclum to ðe*) and offers herself and her property, with the parting shot that:

> Ic wene þæt hit ne sy unrihtwisnysse ætforan gode
> þeah ðe þu wifes bruce and blysse on life. (34)

I think that it would not be unrighteousness before God, though you enjoyed a wife and happiness in life.

[18] See Gopa Roy, 'A Virgin Acts Manfully', p. 8, trans. p. 9.

Eugenia at first responds calmly to this *olecunge* 'flattery, blandishment', speaking in general terms of the deceitful nature of worldly desires and the sorrowful end of bodily lusts, but when *seo myltestre* 'the whore' attempts to embrace her and wants to tempt her to *bismorlicum hæmede* 'shameful adultery', Eugenia retorts *to ðære sceande* 'to that one's shame' that she is truly:

> galnysse ontendnyss and gramena mæge,
> þeostra gefæra and mid sweartnysse afylled,
> Deaðes dohtor and deofles fætels. (34)

incitement to lust and kinswoman of wrath [or the devil], companion of darkness and filled with blackness, Death's daughter and the devil's vessel.

At the righteous fury of Eugenia's outburst (emphasized by the triple alliteration), the rejected Melantia is then *micclum ofsceamod* 'greatly ashamed'. Thinking that Eugenia will reveal (*ameldian*) the conversation, she hurries to Philip (as chief ruler of Alexandria) and accuses Eugenia of attempted rape, which she calls *þæt bysmor* 'that shame/shameful act' (36). When Philip confronts Eugenia (ironically *his agenre dohtor* 'his own daughter' as the text helpfully reminds us), she states calmly that she can quite easily clear herself of the accusation, but mercifully demands that Philip swear not to condemn her false accuser (*seo lease wrægistre*). After all Melantia's servants have sworn that their mistress' account is true, Eugenia (designated here as *seo æþele fæmne* 'the noble woman', 38) explains that she had wanted

> hi sylfe bediglian
> and criste anum hyre clænnysse healdan
> on mægðhade wuniende mannum uncuð
> and forðy underfænge æt fruman þa gyrlan
> wærlices hades and wurde geefsod. (38)

to conceal herself and maintain her purity for Christ alone, dwelling in virginity, unknown to men, and therefore at the beginning took up the clothes of a manly order and was sheared.

After her speech Eugenia tears open her robes and reveals her breast to Philip, announcing her identity as his child and saying that *for cristes lufe* 'for the love of Christ' she abandoned all her family *and middaneardlice lustas swa swa meox forseah* 'and scorned earthly desires as filth'.

A reconciliation scene then follows, but there is no happy ending for Melantia, whom Eugenia had wanted to be spared. Ælfric tells us that

> crist sylf asende swægende fyr
> ufan of heofonum þæt menn onhawoden
> to melantian botle and hit mid ealle forbernde
> swa þæt ðær næs to lafe nanðing þe hyre wæs. (40)

Christ Himself sent forth a roaring fire down from the heavens so that people beheld it to Melantia's house and completely consumed it so that there was nothing left that was hers.

What this fairly close account of the Melantia narrative conceals is that there is in fact evidence of some dispute on the part of the scribes who copied this text as to how to refer to Eugenia during this crucial scene. The text quoted and translated above follows British Library MS. Cotton Julius E. vii. However, the partially burnt and destroyed manuscript British Library MS. Cotton Otho B. x preserves two leaves from the text of the Life of Eugenia, starting at the death of the abbot who preceded Eugenia and ending when Christ sends the fire which consumes Melantia's household.[19] Most of the differences between the two texts are merely orthographical, but the Otho scribe consistently makes alterations to the pronouns or phrases describing Eugenia so as to refer to her as a man or to avoid her female identity.

In the sentence *beclypte seo myltestre þæt clæne mæden | and wolde hi gebygan to bismolicum hæmede* (34) the Otho scribe substitutes *þone abbod* for *þæt clæne mæden*, and *hine* for *hi*. When Philip tells his servants to fetch Eugenia, the Julius scribe has *het hi gefæccan* where the Otho scribe reads *het gefeccan þone abbod* (36), and we are told that he speaks not *to eugenian his agenre dehter*, but *to þam abbode þe wæs his agen dohtor*. Similarly, in response to the accusation, the Otho scribe records the rebuttal not of *eugenia* and *heo*, but of *se abbod* and *he*; Melantia's servants falsely accuse not *eugenia* but *se abbod* (38), and the narrator says that they all lied against not *eugenian* but *þone abbod*.

The question is, then, why the Otho scribe felt the need to make these changes. The pronouns clearly do not obscure Eugenia's identity from the audience; it is made explicit in the phrase *to þam abbode þe wæs his agen dohtor*. The effect these changes do have is to postpone the use of Eugenia's name and the use of feminine pronouns until the climactic moment when she finally reveals her true identity, which is represented first, narratorially, in the words *Hwæt ða eugenia seo æþele fæmne | cwæð* and then with the description of the act which provides physical proof of the validity of her speech: how *heo* 'she' tears her clothes and reveals the unequivocal sign of femininity, *hyre breost*. More than mere rhetorical effect, however, we may suspect that behind this textual strategy lies a dynamic of wider significance.

As discussed in the Introduction, Thomas Laqueur has argued that medieval attitudes to gender relied on a 'one-sex model', where women were seen as defective versions of men, and Carol Clover applies this model to Old Norse literature to hypothesize a fluid gender continuum, where old men and effeminate men can be seen as 'not-men' along with most women and children, but where some exceptional women can attain the social status of 'man' through their strength of character. One might ask, then, whether the scribe views Eugenia in her role

---

[19] Skeat, *Ælfric's Lives of Saints*, I, pp. 32–40, lines 117–260. On the Julius and Otho manuscripts, see vol. II, pp. vii–xiii and xv–xvii (based on Humphrey Wanley, *Librorum Veterum Septentrionalium Catalogus*, in George Hickes, *Linguarum Veterum Septentrionalium Thesaurus*, Oxford, 1705). See also Ker §177, pp. 224–9 (for Otho B. x, dated by Ker as s. XI[1]); §162, pp. 206–10 (for Julius E. vii, dated by Ker as s. XI in.).

as abbot as a 'social man'—that is, has she progressed in his eyes from the status of not-man to man because she has successfully left behind the attributes of her female nature and taken on the attributes of a positive (because male) nature? She could then be seen as leaving this behind when she is forced to reaffirm her femininity by baring her breasts, the unequivocal sign of femaleness. Although this is a possible reading of the episode, however, it has the unfortunate effect of taking the focus away from Eugenia's act of transvestism, and I want now to replace the focus on this act for reasons I shall now outline.

Marjorie Garber, in her book *Vested Interests: Cross-Dressing and Cultural Anxiety*, shows that the dominant critical desire has been to look through and beyond the transvestite figure in literature, and argues that we need to take account of the various kinds of cultural work that this figure can perform.[20] In her terms, then, rather than look *through* the transvestite Eugenia to attempt to determine whether s/he is *really* a man or *really* a woman, we may ask whether the scribe is not emphasizing (perhaps even revelling in) the ambiguity of her appearance, the very fact that she is a woman dressed as a man. The approach we take to these questions deeply affects our reading of the entire episode, and how we view other peculiarities of lexis and thematic motif, as we shall see. However, I want to start with the related question of how we view the attraction of Melantia to the disguised Eugenia and the rhetorical work that Eugenia's stark repudiation of the widow's advances may be deemed to perform.

When we are told that the widow comes *to þam wlytegan mædene* 'to the beautiful maiden', thinking that she is *cniht* 'a boy' (32), do we see the lecherous desires, of which the audience is clearly meant to disapprove, as same- or other-sex oriented? The choice of the term *cniht* is interesting, for not only does it assert that Melantia thinks she desires a male person, it also provides a rationale for the mistake: even though Eugenia is beardless and presumably has a higher-pitched voice than would be normal for an abbot, this can be explained by the presumption of youth and incomplete sexual maturity. Nevertheless, the fact that she is indeed feeling and expressing desire for another woman may perhaps colour the way that Ælfric describes her lust. We are told that Melantia is *yfele eall afylled* 'filled with evil' and *mid bysmorfullum geþance* 'with shameful intent'; she has *sweartan geþohtas* 'dark thoughts' and is *seo myltestre* 'the whore' who tempts Eugenia to *bismorlicum hæmede* 'shameful adultery'. One may ask whether Ælfric here has in his mind the learned Latin discourse of the sodomite which he so carefully avoids explicitly invoking in his texts for lay audiences. Eugenia's retort is said to be to Melantia's *sceande* 'shame' (and causes her to be *micclum ofsceamod* 'greatly ashamed'), showing a preponderance of words in the semantic field of shame and disgrace, and the saint's speech continues the associations with blackness and darkness that we saw in the phrase *sweartan geþohtas*, even though

[20] See Marjorie Garber, *Vested Interests: Cross-Dressing and Cultural Anxiety*. London: Penguin, 1992, *passim* and esp. p. 9.

Ælfric does not explicitly play on the etymology of Melantia's name.[21] Melantia is *þeostra gefæra* 'companion of darkness' and *mid sweartnysse afylled* 'filled with blackness', and the speech culminates in the statement that she is the devil's *fætels*, meaning 'vessel' in a metaphorical sense, but containing the more literal senses of 'bag' or 'sack' which might carry a more appropriate association with the abject, also expressed later in Eugenia's revelation that for Christ's love, she despised her family and earthly desires *swa swa meox* 'like filth' (effectively, 'a piece of shit'). The potential link to Sodom is strengthened by the punishment that Melantia receives—not at earthly hands, but via a divine over-ruling of earthly mercy—we are not specifically told that she is consumed in the conflagration that destroys her household, but after this point Melantia vanishes from the narrative, and the vision of fire coming down from heaven and obliterating a house is surely reminiscent of the fire and brimstone which consumes Sodom in the Genesis account, which, as we have seen, is linked by Ælfric and others in in-house religious writings to same-sexuality and other forms of non-procreative sexuality. It is therefore not enough to see Melantia as 'undisguised woman at her moral worst, contrasting with de-sexed Eugenia' (Szarmach, 'Ælfric's Women Saints', p. 151), for the analysis above indicates that Ælfric is raising the spectre of sodomitic lust, for the clerical element in his audience, at least, although the spectre is not delineated enough to lead the innocent astray.

There is a further question we may ask, however, which is what contemporary Anglo-Saxon audiences might have got out of the Life, and there are a couple of peculiar observations in the text which hint at some unexpected possibilities. Why, for instance, when Melantia offers her body and her property to Eugenia, does Ælfric have her utter as a parting shot the opinion that it would not be *unrihtwisnysse ætforan gode* 'unrighteousness before God' if Eugenia *wifes bruce and blysse on life* 'enjoyed a wife and happiness in this life'? Having a wife is here equated with earthly happiness, and it is important to remember that Melantia thinks at this point that Eugenia is an abbot, and thus sworn to celibacy. It is relevant too that many laypeople and even many priests questioned the necessity of monastic celibacy. Indeed the contemporary ordinances concerning married priests indicate that many clerics ignored the rule of celibacy.[22] Here, then, this topical argument (with which Ælfric explicitly and vehemently disagreed elsewhere) is placed in the mouth of a clearly evil character, and rebutted sternly by the saint as *olecunge* 'flattery, blandishment'. If we look closer, though, we may think that particularly here, Ælfric has a dual audience in mind, and is directing some of the details in the text at his monastic and clerical colleagues. For instance,

---

[21] Compare Gopa Roy, 'A Virgin Acts Manfully', p. 18.

[22] See Joyce Tally Lionarons, 'Napier Homily L: Wulfstan's Eschatology at the Close of his Career', in *Wulfstan, Archbishop of York: The Proceedings of the Second Alcuin Conference*, ed. Matthew Townend. Studies in the Early Middle Ages, 10. Turnhout: Brepols, 2004, pp. 413–28 at p. 420; and in the same volume, Malcolm Godden, 'The Relations of Wulfstan and Ælfric: A Reassessment', pp. 353–74, at p. 373.

why should Eugenia say that Melantia is *galnysse ontendnyss* 'incitement to lust'? Ælfric would presumably not have countenanced any idea that she was genuinely tempted by desire for the widow. Rather, Eugenia voices the exemplary response for an abbot or monk in a similar situation.

This focus on the potential audiences of the text opens up a rich variety of possible responses to the Life, at some of which Ælfric would surely have been horrified. On one level, the idea of a monk identifying with Eugenia is unproblematic—she is, after all, represented as being asexual and occupying a man's role for much of the poem, just as monks should be asexual beings in a man's role.[23] Catherine Cubitt concurs that virgin martyrs are 'powerful emblems of the monastic life'. However, although as she points out they are 'embedded in a text whose concerns are entirely dictated by men' (p. 13), this slippage of gender identity also raises a range of erotic potentialities—from the erotic potential of same-sex attraction between women, to that of the possible presence of women in monasteries (both of which can be disavowed, of course, on the grounds that Eugenia is a saint and, as such, exceptional).[24] However, the fact that Eugenia is thought by Melantia to be a *cniht* 'boy' also raises another erotic potentiality, namely the idea that other monks, possibly younger monks or novices, may be sexually attractive. The preceding chapter showed the anxieties around this subject within monastic settings, and the way that texts like *The Phoenix* both sublimate and control same-sex eroticism and also problematize other-sex-oriented sexuality. The erotic potential of seeing Eugenia, the object of sexual desire, as a beautiful boy within the monastery is both increased and disavowed by the explicit description of her as *wlytegan mædene* 'beautiful maiden', as with the scene where she bares her breast. There the double sense of *mannum uncuð* implies both that Eugenia is hidden from people in general and 'unknown to men' specifically in the sexual sense. Moreover, *wærlices hades* in the same passage can carry the connotations not only of manly raiment, but also of the garb of a manly or manlike holy order, or a manly or manlike condition or nature. Gender here becomes both troubled and troubling to the careful reader.

This chapter has explored a complex sexual and gender dynamic in Ælfric's saints' lives and sought to bring out his contradictory constructions of same-sex relations. Texts such as the Life of the Forty Soldiers and Ælfric's account of the Maccabees construct homosocial desire as natural and use it to reinforce their ideological message, although there are hints in the use of terms such as *eargian* that even this male military intimacy may have created an authorial

[23] Indeed, as the famous 'Easter play' of the *Regularis concordia* shows, monks might even enact the roles of women in religious ritual. The text gives detailed 'stage directions' for the four monks involved and makes it clear that: 'Now these things are done in imitation of the angel seated on the tomb and of the women coming with perfumes to anoint the body of Jesus.' Symons, *Regularis Concordia*, ch. 5, §51, p. 49.

[24] For a powerful and productive use of the concepts of cross-gender identification and disavowal, see Carol Clover, *Men, Women, and Chainsaws: Gender in the Modern Horror Film*. Princeton: Princeton University Press, 1992.

anxiety, which the spectre of cowardice associated with substandard masculinity and sexuality may serve to assuage. Intra-gender bonds are replaced by homo-social bonds in religious as well as military contexts, and a homosocial dynamic of conversion was observed in the Lives of Crysanthus and Daria, Julian and Basilissa, and Agatha. However, the anxieties that the monastic setting produced around gender and sexuality were evinced in the complexities of the interpersonal dynamic created by Ælfric in the Life of Eugenia. The next chapter explores further this dynamic in works by Anglo-Saxon authors potentially less orthodox in their convictions than the abbot of Eynsham.

10

Unorthodox Desire:
The Anonymous *Life of Euphrosyne*
and the *Colloquies* of Ælfric Bata

The previous chapter ended with an extended discussion of Ælfric's Life of the transvestite saint Eugenia and the complex and contradictory gender dynamic observable in that text. A very similar dynamic can be seen in another saint's life, edited by Skeat in the *Lives of Saints*, but probably not in fact by Ælfric: the Life of Euphrosyne (Skeat XXXIII).[1] Because of the transvestism in the narrative, it is indeed commonly discussed in conjunction with the Life of Eugenia, and as Szarmach says in his discussion of this Life, many elements of the plot (such as the use of disguise, the aid of servants) are typical in tales of lovers thwarting unwanted marriages.[2] However, here the lover is Christ, and the aim is not conjugal bliss but the celibate life.

THE ANONYMOUS *LIFE OF EUPHROSYNE*

The Life begins with the introduction of Paphnutius, a man from Alexandria who is not only *eallum mannum leof and wurð* 'dear to and honoured by all men' but who also maintains God's commandments zealously (334). He marries a woman of his own rank who is also *mid eallum wurðfullum þeawum gefylled* 'filled with all honourable virtues', yet this seemingly ideal marriage of virtuous partners is blighted by barrenness. Paphnutius is filled with sorrow because he has no heir to whom he can leave his possessions, and his nameless wife prays continually to God for a child to end her husband's sorrow, while he himself travels far and wide to find a man of God who *his gewilnunga gefultumian mihte* 'might fulfil his desires' (336). He comes at last to a very great monastery and after a sizeable donation becomes very friendly with the abbot and brothers. Hearing

---

[1] See Hugh Magennis, 'Contrasting Features in the Non-Ælfrician Lives in the Old English *Lives of Saints*', *Anglia* 104 (1986), 316–48. On the Life's Latin source, see his 'On the Sources of Non-Ælfrician Lives in the Old English *Lives of Saints*, with Reference to the Cotton-Corpus Legendary', *Notes and Queries* NS 230 (1985), 292–9.

[2] Paul E. Szarmach, 'St. Euphrosyne: Holy Transvestite', in Szarmach, *Holy Men and Holy Women*, pp. 353–65, at p. 356.

his desire for a child, the abbot has compassion and prays on Paphnutius's behalf to God, who grants *heora begra bene and forgeaf him ane dohtor*. Here, the second pronoun is ambiguous—God hears the prayer of both of them (*heora begra*), but it is not clear whether he gives only Paphnutius a daughter (*him*, dative singular) or the two of them together a daughter (*him*, dative plural). As Szarmach points out, although the latter interpretation is a biological impossibility, the joint fatherhood of abbot and nobleman later becomes a 'thematic reality' for these 'father figures' (p. 356). Thus, even before Euphrosyne's life properly begins, themes of physical and spiritual fatherhood are raised, which as we shall see are reworked and complicated by the end of the Life, where Euphrosyne becomes in effect the spiritual father to her own biological father.

Euphrosyne's mother dies when she is 12 years old and thus she is instructed by her father, amazing him and everyone else by her wisdom, so much so that many are attracted by her virtues and ask to marry her, one of whom, wealthier and worthier than the others, is accepted by Paphnutius as a suitable husband for his daughter. When Euphrosyne is 18, her father takes her to the abbot who had prayed for her conception and asks for his blessing on this woman whom he calls *þone wæstm þinra gebeda* 'the fruit of your prayers'. The bride-to-be remains at the monastery for a week, listening to the brothers' songs and conversation, and wonders at their lifestyle, saying:

Eadige synd þas weras þe on þisse worulde syndon englum gelice, and þurh þæt begitað þæt ece lif.   (338)

Blessed are those men who in this world are like angels, and through that obtain eternal life.

This observation is not elaborated upon at this juncture. However, Euphrosyne has clearly taken the blessed nature of celibacy to heart, and, although she sees it as a property of *weras* 'men' and not *menn* 'people', she is unwilling to allow her gender to be a barrier to adopting this lifestyle for herself. About a year after her visit to the monastery, it is the abbot's ordination day and he sends a monk to invite Paphnutius to the celebration. Euphrosyne calls the monk to her and asks various questions about the monastic life he leads, then reveals that she would like to turn to such a life, were she not afraid of being disobedient to her father *se for his idlum welum me wile to were geþeodan* 'who because of his empty wealth wishes to join me to a man' (338). And here the double sense of *wer* as 'man, husband' becomes significant. She wishes, rather than to take a *wer* 'husband', to join the company of *weras* 'men' who, like angels, do not marry. The reply of the monk brings out this rich irony, as he counsels her not to let any man *þinne lichaman besmite* 'defile your body' or give her beauty (*wlite*) to any reproach (*hospe*) (340). Rather he advises *bewedde þe sylfe criste* 'wed yourself to Christ' who can give her a heavenly kingdom rather than transient wealth—and the means of doing this is to disguise herself secretly as a monk so as to escape her impending marriage.

Paphnutius returns home and is taken by the monk to the abbot's ordination-day celebration, but Euphrosyne sends a servant to bring another monk to her. She explains her situation again in the same terms, and again worries about being disobedient to her father, presumably to reassure the audience that the saint is not undermining family values in any frivolous way. However, the brother quotes Christ's teaching that his disciples must be prepared to forsake parents and family, and at Euphrosyne's request cuts off her hair and invests her in the monastic habit, then returns home praising God. There is clearly some problem with the transmission of the text here, for Euphrosyne is then said to worry that if she goes to *fæmnena mynstre* 'a monastery for women' (342) her father will look for and find her there; therefore she decides to go to a *wera mynstre* 'monastery for men' and the text claims that it is at this point that she removes her female clothing (*wiflican gegyrlan*) and puts on a man's (*werlicum*), which makes a nonsense of the previous paragraph unless we assume an initial disguise as a nun, followed by a change of plan and subsequent disguise as a monk. However, Euphrosyne then goes to the very monastery her father had visited, claiming to be a *eunuchus* 'eunuch' from the king's household who wishes to take up the monastic life. Somewhat surprisingly, the abbot does not recognize the daughter of the man with whom he celebrated his ordination-day the night before, and he welcomes the self-styled eunuch in, ironically terming him *min bearn* 'my child' (344). Euphrosyne names herself as Smaragdus, and from here on the narrator of the Life calls her either by this name or by the relevant male pronoun, and this practice creates an interesting gender dynamic, particularly in terms of the reception of Smaragdus by the other monks. It is worth quoting the episode at length:

Þa forþam se sylfe smaragdus wæs wlitig on ansyne, swa oft swa ða broðra comon to cyrcan, þonne besende se awyrgeda gast mænigfealde geþohtas on heora mod and wurdon þearle gecostnode þurh his fægernysse, and hi þa æt nyxtan ealle wurdon astyrode wið þone abbod forþam swa wlitigne man into heora mynstre gelædde, and he þa gecigde smaragdum to him and cwæð: 'Min bearn þiu ansyn is wlitig and þissum broðrum cymð micel hryre for heora tyddernyssum. nu wille ic þæt þu sitte þe sylf on þire cytan and singe þær þine tida and þe þærinne gereorde. nelle ic þeh þæt þu ahwider elles ga,' and he þa bebead agapito þæt he gegearwode æne emptige cytan and smaragdum þider inne gelædde. (344)

Then because the same Smaragdus was beautiful of face, as often as the brothers came to church, then the accursed spirit sent various thoughts into their minds and they were severely tempted by his beauty, and they then at last all became angry with the abbot for bringing so beautiful a person into their monastery, and he then called Smaragdus to him and said: 'My child, your face is beautiful and great ruin comes to these brothers because of their weakness. Now I wish you to remain by yourself in your cell and sing your hours there and eat in there. I do not wish, though, that you go elsewhere,' and he then instructed Agapitus so that he prepared an empty cell and led Smaragdus inside there.

Of this passage, Szarmach merely speculates: 'Are these temptations homo-sexual—one wonders, the temptation is *purh HIS fægernesse*—or heterosexual? Or is the OE author simply toying—metaphysically, so to speak—with the sexual theme?'[3] He makes no further comment, but his question is indeed productive.

Clearly, within the overall context of the narrative, this episode brings out the importance of chastity—in a sense it does not matter whether the temptation is felt for a woman or a man. It could be said, however, that the abbot and the brothers see their temptation as sexual desire for a member of the same gender—after all the narrator refers to Euphrosyne exclusively as Smaragdus, or *he*. This is certainly Allen Frantzen's view: he thinks that the desire is 'homosexual' and that the episode reveals this as a subtext of the Life which the transvestite motif seeks to obscure.[4] Nevertheless, the dynamic is more complex than this—and certainly more complex than Szarmach's heterosexual-homosexual binary would suggest. To see Smaragdus as a member of the same gender as the other monks is to ignore two factors. Firstly, we must remember that, internally within the narrative, Smaragdus has designated himself as a eunuch, a castrated man. Andrew Scheil emphasizes the importance of this in a richly illuminating article entitled 'Somatic Ambiguity and Masculine Desire in the Old English Life of Euphrosyne'.[5] Invoking Laqueur's one-sex model, he sees the eunuch as 'a liminal creature, the embodiment of alterity' and argues that 'the beautiful eunuch disrupts the monastic community because of his somatic ambiguity' (352). He argues both that the monks' anger represents erotic desire 'redirected as anger or rivalry' in a way 'typical of homosocial situations', and also that it is directed at 'the plasticity of the male body represented by Smaragdus' (354). Again, the text is not quite as simple as Scheil's approach suggests: we are not told that the monks other than the abbot know that Smaragdus is a eunuch; they blame the abbot for bringing *swa wlitigne man* 'so beautiful a person' into the monastery, not specifying the gender, so the monks may see Smaragdus either as a young man or as a eunuch. Nevertheless, it is indeed possible to argue that the brothers in the narrative are relating to a member of one who both is and is not of their gender.

Secondly, and crucially, Frantzen's straightforward assumption that Smaragdus is of the same gender as the other monks also ignores the fact that, externally to the narrative, the audience is continually kept aware of the fact that this is a

---

[3] Szarmach, 'St. Euphrosyne', p. 358.

[4] Frantzen, 'When Women Aren't Enough', 466.

[5] Andrew P. Scheil, 'Somatic Ambiguity and Masculine Desire in the Old English Life of Euphrosyne', *Exemplaria* 11 (1999), 345–61. Scheil's article takes an approach similar to my own approach to the transvestite saints, but as the discussion below indicates, it differs in several respects, and particularly in my argument about the way that the diverse potential audiences of the text need to be taken into consideration.

woman dressed as a man. Therefore, just as the brothers within the narrative are relating to a man who is not a man, so too the audience outside the narrative is aware that this both is and is not a man—it is a man on the level of clothing, behaviour, and spiritual/social status, but it is nevertheless a biological woman. A couple of inferences follow from these points, namely that in this monastic context both same-sex and other-sex temptation is possible and is not entirely distinguishable—the emphasis is on the fact that Smaragdus is *wlitig on ansyne*; the abbot confirms that *þiu ansyn is wlitig*. The beauty is not seen as Smaragdus's fault—as in some patristic texts, women are held culpable if they allow men to see their beauty and thus cause them to sin[6]—but it nevertheless causes his separation from the rest. His otherness, whether that is seen to be his gender or lack of gender, in effect separates him from his peers.

We may wonder with whom the audience may be expected to identify at this point, and the answer is surely with the tempted monks—particularly, of course, for those in the audience who were monks. The lesson, then, is to separate oneself from the source of temptation—in effect, to demonize or at least marginalize the other. However, for some in the audience there was surely the potential, in identifying with the tempted monks, to enjoy the erotic charge of the idea of women being a disguised presence in the monastery (as we saw with Eugenia above), or of other monks being attractive, both of which can be disavowed on the grounds that Smaragdus is actually a woman and a saint and therefore exceptional.

We might stop at this point, at the point of individual audience members' reactions to the interpersonal relations depicted in this Life. However, this would be to ignore another dimension to the text, which is the simultaneous function of raising and allaying anxiety about the monastic way of life, and the nature of clerics in general.[7] Returning to Laqueur's one-sex model discussed above, clerics—although clearly physically men—may be seen in social terms as 'not-men' and thus akin to women, since they do not take part in the activities which are part of the socially constructed definition of men: fighting, engendering offspring. However, they are also more-than-men, since they transcend earthly gender and prefigure the ideal state of asexuality in heaven. Euphrosyne-Smaragdus, as a transvestite saint, perfectly captures this dual status and represents a site on which the anxieties this anomalous state inspires can be both centred and worked through. The resolution of the narrative may attempt to reaffirm biological binaries, but the course of the narrative has effectively destabilized notions of

---

[6] For such views and a discussion of medieval misogyny more generally, see R. Howard Bloch, *Medieval Misogyny and the Invention of Western Romantic Love*. Chicago: University of Chicago Press, 1989.

[7] Compare Scheil's view that this text reveals unresolved issues and 'the unconscious ideological stresses of the community' (360). My argument is not that Euphrosyne-Smaragdus lays bare 'the potentially erotic component of homosociality' (361), but that it reveals anxieties about the nature of the monk himself and the implications of the radical Christian revisioning of gender and sexuality, as explored below.

gender in a way that provides rich potential for multiple audience identifications. There are signs within the narrative, however, that this gender dynamic is not only fascinating but also disquieting and raises problems which the narrative closure does not quite resolve. In this reading of Euphrosyne-Smaragdus, then, the monk becomes a tranvestite figure, dressed in the garb of a woman, associated by the range of activities he pursues with women more than men. We might thus invoke Judith Butler and Marjorie Garber to read the monk as a figure always already in drag, whose appearance insistently provokes the question of what is under his habit, and the fear that perhaps (like Eugenia and Euphrosyne) there is nothing at all.

Both this text and Ælfric's Life of Eugenia contain within them destabilizing elements which work against the ideology they seek to propound. For instance, we are told when Eugenia is asked to become abbot that she became *mycclum hohful | hu heo æfre wæras wissian sceolde* 'very anxious how she was ever to guide men' (32). Szarmach sees this as a realistic note of a natural worry (Eugenia's 'reaction to the burdens of office is human and real', p. 149), but this surely rather reminds the reader of the Pauline dictum that women may not teach or lead men (1 Timothy 2: 9–15). It seems difficult to state whether this awareness of the unorthodox position in which Eugenia is placed represents an anxiety about the implications of the narrative, or rather fits in with the working of the other Pauline dictum in the text which states that in Christ there is neither male nor female (Galatians 3: 28).[8] Do we see Eugenia as a man in social terms and therefore able to lead and teach men? And what does this imply for the status of women generally? It seems unlikely from Ælfric's other writings that he would wish other women to take Eugenia as their example and dress and behave as men.

Similarly there is an emphasis in the anonymous Life of Euphrosyne on the fact that she is behaving as and indeed in some sense is a man in social terms. When Paphnutius her father comes to the deathbed of Smaragdus, he reproaches the abbot for promising that he will see the daughter who has been lost to him for thirty-eight years. Smaragdus asks him to wait for three days, and when that day comes, we are told:

Ða onget smaragdus, se ær wæs eufrosina gehaten, þæt se dæg wæs to becumen hire geleorednysse. Þa cwæð heo to him: 'God ælmihtig hæfð wel gedihtod min earme lif and gefylled minne willan þæt ic moste þone ryne mines lifes werlice ge-endian. (352)

Then Smaragdus, who had been called Euphrosyne, perceived that the day of her departure had come. Then she said to him: 'God Almighty has arranged my poor life well and fulfilled my desire that I could end the course of my life manfully.'

---

[8] We may note also that Eugenia's initial impulse towards conversion is aroused by the teaching of *paules þæs mæran ealles manncynnes lareowes* 'Paul the famous teacher of all humankind' (26).

It is only at this point, where Smaragdus is poised to reveal his biological sex and relation to his father, that the narrator returns to using female pronouns. The term *werlice* 'in a manly way, like a man' is in juxtaposition to the term *ryne* 'course' which is often used of the flow of water or blood and strengthens the sense of Euphrosyne's rejection of her female physicality, which includes of course menstruation. The term is repeated in the abbot's speech when he sees Euphrosyne's corpse and asks her to pray to God for him and the other monks that they may come *werlice* to heaven and to communion with Christ and the saints. This sense of gender reversal is echoed in the reversal of the father-daughter relationship, when Paphnutius enters the monastery and lives in the same cell Euphrosyne-Smaragdus had inhabited until his death and is buried beside the daughter who became his spiritual father.

However, there is more to the representation of the saint's death than this. Great emphasis is placed in the text on the fact that Paphnutius waits three days before the revelation. Smaragdus has already given him a heavy clue as to his identity, since he tells him to remember how God revealed to the patriarch Jacob his son Joseph whom he had likewise mourned as if he were dead. Since the Genesis account of Joseph plays similarly on disguise and secret identities, Paphnutius might have anticipated that his spiritual adviser may not be all he seems. The three sentences which follow this advice mention the time period of three days a total of four times in close proximity:

'ac ic bidde þe þæt þu þrym dagum me ne forlæte.' Pafnuntius þa anbidode þara þreora daga fæc, þus cweðende: 'weninga god him hæfð be me sum þing onwrigen', and on þam þryddan dæge cwæð he to him, 'Ic anbidode broðor þas þry dagas'. (352)

'but I ask you that you do not leave me for three days.' Paphnutius then waited for the interval of three days, saying thus: 'perhaps God has revealed something to him about me', and on the third day he said to him, 'I have waited, brother, these three days'.

It seems probable that this emphasis would bring to mind the most significant three days of the Christian tradition—the time between Christ's death and resurrection, when as the Creed has it 'on the third day he rose again in accordance with the scriptures'. Euphrosyne-Smaragdus is thus not merely acting on the example of Joseph, but her/his self-revelation is bound up with the central mystery of the Christian faith, where Christ, who took on human flesh (clothing?) and subjected his divine nature to all human infirmity to the extent of undergoing physical death on the cross, dies into new life, and the triumphant reassertion of the divinity he has possessed all the time. Seen in this light, the fluid gender dynamic is undermined by the implication that Smaragdus has, after all, all along always been the woman Euphrosyne. There is indeed perhaps not just a sense of wonder in the reaction of the monks to the discovery of Euphrosyne's physical sex. We are told that *þa hi ða onfundon þæt heo wæs wifhades man, þa wuldrodan hi on god* 'when they discovered that she was a person of womanhood, then they gloried in God' (354). They may be mindful of the abbot's prayer that they may all come to heaven manfully like Euphrosyne-Smaragdus, but they are also perhaps relieved and glad that their troublesome attraction was not to another monk, but to a woman. It seems significant that just after this a monk who was *anegede* 'one-eyed' is healed by kissing and touching the holy corpse— this restoration of vision, so often associated in Christian texts with both physical and moral (in)sight, bears an ambiguous relation to this figure whose female nature was concealed from their sight for so long.

In the monks' anxiety over their attraction to Smaragdus-Euphrosyne, the anonymous Life brings to the fore some of the anxieties inherent in same-sex communities which remain latent in Ælfric's Lives, and it indicates why Ælfric was perhaps right (on his own terms) to be anxious about open discussion of same-sexuality. Ælfric was clearly anxious about invoking the learned Sodom discourse in texts written for lay people, despite the overtones in some of his texts (and the potential transgressive appropriation of his texts against his presumed intentions). To construct homosocial desire as praiseworthy and integral to faithful Christian living and male-female desire as something to be shunned, in the absence of an explicit Sodom discourse, creates a rather ambiguous discourse of sexuality.[9] The separation of religious communities into male and female homosocial communities paradoxically both destabilizes gender conceptually, in the sense that celibacy is exhorted for men and women and an asexual ideal is held up, and also emphasizes the gender binary on a very physical and visual level. Invoking Laqueur's differentiation of one-sex or two-sex models of gender, we may in fact see these two models uneasily coexisting, in an ambiguous dynamic which creates anxiety in the author and presumably the audience. This anxiety is visible in the various veiled allusions to stigmatized same-sexuality which may seek to curtail the extent to which gender and other-oriented sexuality can be undermined. This picture is complicated (reflecting further anxieties) by the transvestite saints lives, which both uphold and undermine the gender binary in their depictions of women who are both women and not women, men and not men—whose biological nature conflicts with their gender identity, a gender identity which is not stable itself, and which may reflect anxieties about the nature of clerics. Further complicating this scenario are the concepts of disavowed pleasure and identification on the part of some in the audiences of these texts, as they enjoyed or appropriated parts of the texts which deal with sexuality, whether that is male-female, same-sex, or both simultaneously in the figure of the transvestite. The complexities of this dynamic are both frustrating and rewarding, and rely to a large extent on the necessity clearly felt by Ælfric to avoid explicitly invoking the learned discourse of Sodom.

---

[9] Indeed, that Ælfric was uneasy about the dangers of wholly abjecting male-female desire, and felt the need to maintain a place for Christian marriage, is indicated by his addition to the Life of Æðelðryð, as shown in Peter Jackson, 'Ælfric and the Purpose of Christian Marriage: A Reconsideration of the *Life of Æthelthryth*, lines 120–30', *Anglo-Saxon England* 29 (2000), 235–60.

It is in fact probable, however, that a relaxed attitude to such matters is in fact more representative of attitudes in general to sexuality in many religious contexts, as we can see if we look at a work by one of Ælfric's pupils, known as Ælfric Bata, which exhibits what seems to be a relatively pragmatic attitude to same-sex relations. Of course, it is not possible to see this text as a window onto the monastic world—it is discourse, not a genuine reflection of lived reality. Nevertheless, the sentiments expressed provide a clear indication that Ælfric in this matter, as in many others, had a far more strict attitude than many of his contemporaries.

THE *COLLOQUIES* OF ÆLFRIC BATA AND SAME-SEX DESIRE IN THE MONASTERY

Little is known about Ælfric Bata, except his status as pupil of Ælfric of Eynsham, and his authorship of three Latin colloquies for schoolboys, preserved in a single manuscript, consisting of a rewriting of his teacher's *Colloquy* and two longer dialogues which are the ones discussed here: the *Colloquia* and the *Colloquia difficiliora* (so-called because of the recondite language it employs).[10] Ælfric Bata was writing some time around the turn of the millennium, that is, shortly after his former teacher Ælfric wrote his *Lives of Saints*. However, the style and tone of the two authors could not be more different. David Porter characterizes Bata's collection as a set of 'dramatic skits in monastic settings' and credits its author with

an outré sense of humor delighting in the bizarre and fantastic. His fictional interlocutors, usually schoolmasters and oblates, abuse one another with the sharpest invective, verbal self-defence is elaborated with the finest sophistry, and drinking and drunkenness are depicted in minute detail.[11]

Although, as stressed above, one might not want to go as far as Porter in seeing the *Colloquies* as 'monastic childhood come alive' (2), since fictional elements of the texts cannot easily be distinguished from sociohistorical fact, still it seems fair to concur that Bata's texts support the idea that 'Benedictine writers exaggerated the standards of monastic behavior while ignoring [laxity] among Anglo-Saxon monks' (13). Porter details this relaxed attitude mainly in relation to drunkenness. However, here I shall concentrate on the evidence for a relaxed or pragmatic

---

[10] For an edition with facing-page translation of the *Colloquies*, see *Anglo-Saxon Conversations: The Colloquies of Ælfric Bata*, ed. Scott Gwara; trans. David W. Porter. Woodbridge: Boydell Press, 1997. The introduction to this edition provides the most up-to-date overview of the context, nature, and content of the texts. However, Porter has been strongly criticized for 'overreading' and undue speculation: see the review by Anthony E. Farnham in *Speculum* 75 (2000), 188–9, and the comments below.

[11] Gwara, *Anglo-Saxon Conversations*, p. 1.

attitude to expressions of same-sexuality or situations in which such expressions were likely to occur.

Conventional expressions of homosocial bonds are closely juxtaposed with examples of behaviour which starkly diverge from that prescribed by the Benedictine Rule. For instance, Colloquy 7 ends with one boy lending another his ball and stick to play a game, which generosity occasions the response:

Modo habeo sensatum, quod meus es amicus, et ego propter hoc uolo te amare recte et optime in bona amicitia et non ficta.   (94)

Now I've realized that you're my friend and because of that I want to love you sincerely and well in true and honest friendship.

However, in the following Colloquy, a junior brother is encouraged to eat and drink immoderately by a senior brother (98), and in Colloquies 9 and 10, this laxity extends to potentially sexualized situations.

Colloquy 9 begins with an older monk asking a boy (*fratercule mi*) to go with him to the toilet and expressing astonishment when the boy says that he dare not go without his master's permission (98). When asked, however, the master replies:

Licet bene, karissime amice. Vadat tecum libenter. Fili mi, surge, et accipe lucernam unam, et unam candelam accende, et porta uobiscum, et sic uade secum ministrans ei in omnibus in latrina, et sterne lectulum eius, et ficones uel calciamenta illius trahe foras, et ei humili deuotione oboedi in omnibus quamdiu secum eris modo, et ueni postea huc ad me et ad tuos socios quando totum hoc habes perfectum.

He certainly may, dearest friend. He may freely go with you. My son, get up and take a lamp, light a candle and carry it with you. Go with him, taking care of everything for him in the latrine, and make his bed and pull off his shoes or footwear. Obey him in every way with humble devotion as long as you're with him. Afterwards when you've finished all this, come here to me and your mates.

This situation, freely countenanced by the master and similar to that described in Colloquy 10, is in stark contrast to the stipulation of the *Regularis concordia* §8: *Nec ad obsequium priuatum quempiam illorum…obtentu solum deducere praesumant* '[Not on any excuse] shall any monk presume to take with him a young boy alone for any private purpose'.[12] When the boy returns, he thanks God that the monk is resting in bed, and is offered a drink because he is so tired from his errand (101). He drinks a wine jug to the bottom and agrees that he is *unus fortis glutto et multus edax lupus* 'a healthy strong glutton and a great ravening wolf', swearing *per meam rasam barbam et per meum caluum caput* 'by my shaven beard and my bald head'. His interlocutor then replies: *Non est caluus sed crispus et crinitus pulchre* 'You're not bald—your hair is beautifully long and curly!' and the boy responds with equanimity *Quicquid tu uis, hoc ero ego.*

---

[12] Cited and translated in Gwara, *Anglo-Saxon Conversations*, p. 99.

Non curo omnino 'Whatever you want, that I'll be! I don't care at all.' Porter shows that this scene brings together two passages of the *Etymologiae* of Isidore of Seville, which was a popular text in Anglo-Saxon England. The first relates to the passage just quoted, and concerns the gender ambiguity of actors. The second, however, is more explicitly sexual, for when the boy utters a paean to the drinking horn he has been brought, the term for horn chosen, *cornu*, playfully associates the drinking of alcohol with oral sex:

Cornu bibere uolo. Cornu habere debeo, cornu tenere...Cum cornu uiuere, cornu quoque iacere uolo et dormire, nauigare, equitare et ambulare et laborare atque ludere... (102)

I want to drink from the horn. I ought to have the horn, to hold the horn...I want to live with the horn, to lie with the horn and sleep, to sail, ride, walk, work and play with the horn...[13]

It is hard to imagine Ælfric of Eynsham countenancing the sexual ambiguities rife in this text, or approving of the special relationship between the master and his favourite student, *meus dilectus puer et meus amantissimus amicus* 'my most beloved boy and dearest friend' (140), a talented 12-year-old whose ability and behaviour is compared favourably with the 15-year-old being criticized.[14] Similarly inappropriate or unorthodox situations can be found in Colloquy 20, where a father asks a boy to kiss him before he leaves on a trip, but reluctantly accepts the boy's refusal, or Colloquy 23, where a boy shaves and washes a monk in his bath.

It seems unnecessary to speculate with Porter on whether Bata was 'homosexual' or not (p. 14, n. 29), since a principle of this book has been that homosexuality (in opposition to heterosexuality) is not a helpful concept in this period. However, looking to the wider issue, can we take the *Colloquies* as evidence that Bata was involved or complicit in, or at least tolerant of, same-sex activity within the monastery? Perhaps, but only with caution. The activities described above are not recommended in the text as normative, nor are they claimed to be representative of actual monastic life. At the end of the *Colloquies*, the master tells the boys that in the foregoing conversations *iocus cum sapientiae loquelis et uerbis inmixtus est et sepe coniunctus* 'joking is often mixed and joined with wise words and sayings' (170). There follows a strict moralizing condemnation of gluttony, lechery, and other bestial passions, exhorting the boys to live as true Christians, who *caste et sobrie uiuant* 'live chastely and soberly' (172). It would therefore be possible to argue that Bata creates these fictional scenarios only to condemn them viciously as a sting in the tail of his collection, making his readers complicit in these sins only to open their eyes to their need for repentance. Nevertheless, this idea is open to the same objections as there are to a straightforward acceptance of

---

[13] See Gwara, *Anglo-Saxon Conversations*, notes 70 and 72 (pp. 101 and 103) on Isidore.
[14] Compare Gwara, *Anglo-Saxon Conversations*, p. 14

the 'palinodes' of Andreas de Capellanus's *On the Art of Courtly Love* or Chaucer's *Troilus and Criseyde*. The final rejection does not negate what has come before, at least in the eyes of many readers.[15] I would suggest instead that it would be more natural to see Colloquy 29 as voicing the official view which Bata should be taking, and the preceding colloquies as reflecting a more tolerant and pragmatic approach to monastic life which was adopted in practice by many clerics, including most likely Bata himself.[16] This possibility has far-reaching implications, since it suggests that the Benedictine Reform may have had limited effects even on the clergy as far as interpersonal relations were concerned, despite Ælfric's impressive contacts and influence. Certainly, it provides a voice for alternative and less orthodox attitudes to same-sex relations, even if, ultimately, the text condemns them.

CONCLUDING REMARKS

This book has argued for the importance of examining all kinds of same-sex relations in the Anglo-Saxon period and revisiting well-known texts and issues from a different perspective. From the first chapter, which emphasized the need to avoid cultural assumptions, whether about male-female or male-male relationships, and the paramount place of homosocial bonds in Old English literature, we moved into Part II's investigation of same-sex acts and identities in a range of ethnographic, penitential, and theological texts. Although Tacitus claims the Germanic tribes despised effeminacy, various other Classical authors strongly associate Germanic and Celtic tribes with same-sex activity, and this was explained using the concept of *ergi* and *níð* in Old Norse literature and arguments that only passivity and receptivity in same-sex acts were stigmatized. The same attitude seems likely to have been characteristic of Anglo-Saxon secular society, and some traces survive in the literature of what may have been a less developed concept of *ergi* among the Anglo-Saxons.

None of the Anglo-Saxon law-codes mentions same-sex acts, but it is strongly prohibited in penitential texts. Interestingly, however, the Old English penitentials introduce what seems to be a separate category of participant in same-sex activity, the *bædling*, and it was tentatively suggested that it might represent

[15] The question of how to read the ending(s) of *Troilus* is of course an almost hopelessly vexed one. For a concise overview of scholarly attitudes, see Barry Windeatt, *Oxford Guides to Chaucer: Troilus and Criseyde*. Oxford: Clarendon Press, 1992, pp. 310–13.

[16] It has been suggested that the byname *bata* may imply its referent was of stout appearance, or even had a propensity for drinking heavily. If this were the case, then it would provide support for the idea that the author was effectively covering his back with the moralizing palinode against anticipated criticisms from stricter colleagues. See Gösta Tengvik, 'Old English Bynames', *Nomina Germania* 4 (1938), 287–8; though cf. Tracey-Anne Cooper, 'Basan and Bata—The Occupational Surnames of two Pre-Conquest Monks of Canterbury', available at <http://www.kentarchaeology.ac/authors/012.pdf> [accessed 10 March 2008].

someone who was seen as a biological man, but with a social status as not-man because of an exclusive preference for the passive role in same-sex intercourse. The two chapters on Sodom in Latin and vernacular texts showed that the Old Testament city and its inhabitants were not uniformly associated with same-sex acts, or even sexual acts, except within in-house clerical writings, and even here there is a range of associations.

Part II expanded the focus to homosocial bonds in Old English literature in order to explore the range of associations for same-sex intimacy and their representation in literary texts. In *Genesis A*, same-sex acts were seen to function as part of a wider sexual-gender dynamic, where normative homosocial bonds were praised but all forms of unsanctioned sexual desire presented as destructive. A range of attitudes is present in heroic literature, from the *Beowulf*-poet's ambivalence about the value of homosocial bonds to the *Maldon*-poet's disgust for cowardice which he equates with effeminacy and opposes to the normative bonds between lord and retainer. In contrast the poet of *The Dream of the Rood* revalues passivity as heroic in his sexualized rendering of the crucifixion, and this paved the way for an exploration of the associations of and tensions concerning homosocial bonds in poetry and prose for a mixed lay and clerical audience. From the same-sex sexless procreation of *The Phoenix*, to the heroic homosociality and same-sex conversion dynamic of Ælfric's *Lives of Saints*, we saw a productive tension about the Christian revaluation of gender and the anxiety this sparked around same-sex intimacy. In both Ælfric's Life of Eugenia and the anonymous *Life of Euphrosyne* these anxieties do not mitigate against a range of erotic potentialities, and, as we have seen, Ælfric Bata's more relaxed attitude to same-sex relations may more accurately represent the general feeling than the hyper-orthodox strictures of his teacher.

It is important to recognize the range of attitudes to same-sex acts available in this period, from unambiguous condemnation and an anxiety to eradicate them to tolerant amusement and even ignorance that they were sinful. We must take into account when building up a picture of how Old English literature displays or seeks to mould Anglo-Saxon sociocultural attitudes not only the paucity of the surviving material, but also the fact that the bulk of what survives is probably more representative of what religious orthodoxy deemed worthy to survive than of what was actually produced during the Anglo-Saxon period. Ælfric may be vastly over-represented in the extant Old English corpus, but this surely does not accurately reflect the period. Much material which would throw light on Anglo-Saxon attitudes to male-male intimacy and sexuality has doubtless been lost through censorship and accident. We are left with traces in what texts survive, some of which go against religious orthodoxy, and with what inferences can be made from the anxieties and tensions displayed in orthodox religious texts. Indeed, although many of those texts stigmatize male-male sexuality, there is nevertheless the potential for audiences to read transgressively between the lines or against the grain. It is impossible to regain a full sense of Anglo-Saxon attitudes to same-sex activity, but the probable scenario is one of tolerance and even a lack of stigma as long as such activity is not exclusive or passive. This is particularly likely to have been the case in secular contexts, and even in clerical and monastic contexts, depending on the specific local environment and its proximity or resistance to the Benedictine Reforms.

It seems likely that, along with much else, one of the worries of the Benedictine Reformers was same-sex intimacy. The *Regularis concordia*, for instance, shows the influence of the Benedictine Rule's concern to keep monks from being alone with younger novices and oblates.[17] However, as yet this surfaced mainly in hints and anxieties and not the strident denunciations which characterize the efforts of Peter Damian and other would-be reformers of the eleventh and twelfth centuries. These writers paved the way for an increasing intolerance of same-sex acts, latched onto for reasons of political expedience by church and state officials and beginning a cycle of periods of relative tolerance and vicious persecution.[18] The evidence shows, of course, that this did not stop people engaging in relations with others of the same sex, and in fact the persecution may have aided a counter-discourse and the beginnings of a counter-culture in the molly houses of Renaissance England.[19] Whether this, not to mention the much later formation of a homosexual pathology and subsequently identity based largely on gender inversion, was a good thing is difficult to say. There is plenty of evidence that lack of labels and rigid identities in fact gives people a greater fluidity of sexual boundaries than is the case in societies and periods where it is deemed important to label and categorize one's sexual identity. Many men in Western society today are trying to regain a sense of the manifoldness and fluidity of sexual identity, for good or ill. Even more are lamenting the poverty of their interpersonal relationships and their inability to form close male friendships. One suspects Anglo-Saxon writers such as the author of the Exeter Book Maxim quoted at the outset of this book could have told present-day Western men a lot about male intimacy, if they had first understood their manifest problem with it.

During the course of this book's argument, it has inevitably raised more questions than it has answered. It has also come up against several under-researched issues which remain *desiderata* for further study. How do views of same-sex relations differ in religious and secular texts? To what extent did clerical prohibitions against intra-gender sexual acts impact upon secular society? How far did literary constructs of sexuality impact upon contemporary perceptions of sexuality? To what extent can we see actual sexual practices or concerns reflected

---

[17] Compare Chapter 8, p. 169 above.

[18] See Boswell, *Christianity, Social Tolerance, and Homosexuality*, and Jordan, *Invention of Sodomy*, *passim*. One wonders whether an anxiety about male intimacy and masculinity, generated at least partly by the Benedictine Reform and associated with monasticism and the complex gender dynamic of medieval Christianity, may not have laid the groundwork for subsequent articulations of the abstract discourse of sodomy. This, however, must await another study.

[19] See the essays in Gerard and Hekma, *Pursuit of Sodomy*, Alan Bray, *Homosexuality in Renaissance England, with a new Afterword*. New York: Columbia University Press, 1995.

in the literature of the period? How far have heterosexist assumptions affected modern critical accounts of homosocial and other bonds in the literature? How does the monastic repudiation of intergender sexuality affect religious constructions of same-sex relations? How far was the burgeoning religious discourse of sodomy, particularly in the later period, known to secular society? All these topics are touched on in this book but far from exhausted. There is a great danger for us as critics that, in omitting to ask certain questions of Anglo-Saxon material, in being too willing to accept the status quo indicated by the extant corpus, in uncritically importing invisible (because normative) heterosexist assumptions in our reading, that we will misrepresent the diversity and complexity that a more nuanced approach to issues of gender and sexuality suggests may be more genuinely characteristic of the period.

Bibliography

Allott, Stephen, *Alcuin of York: His Life and Letters*. York: William Sessions, 1974.

Anderson, Earl R., 'Old English Poets and their Latin Sources: Iconicity in *Caedmon's Hymn* and the *Phoenix*', in *The Motivated Sign: Iconicity in Language and Literature 2*, ed. Olga Fischer and Max Nänny. Amsterdam: Benjamins, 2001, pp. 109–32.

Anderson, James E., '*Deor, Wulf and Eadwacer*, and *The Soul's Address*: How and Where the Old English Exeter Book Riddles Begin', in *The Old English Elegies: New Essays in Criticism and Research*, ed. Martin Green. London and Toronto: Associated University Presses, 1983, pp. 204–30.

Anlezark, Daniel, 'An Ideal Marriage: Abraham and Sarah in Old English Literature', *Medium Ævum* 69 (2000), 187–210.

—— *Water and Fire: The Myth of the Flood in Anglo-Saxon England*. Manchester: Manchester University Press, 2006.

Anon., [review of Szarmach, '*Ælfric's Women Saints: Eugenia*'] *Old English Newsletter* 25 (1992), 56.

—— [Report of a meeting of the Cambridge Philological Society (Friday, 8 December 1893)], *The Academy: A Weekly Review of Literature, Science, and Art* no. 1129 (Saturday, 23 December 1893), p. 572, col. 3.

—— [Report of a meeting of the Cambridge Philological Society (Friday, 8 December 1893)], *The Athenaeum* No. 3451, 16 December [18]93, p. 853, col. 3 to p. 854 col. 1.

—— trans., *Morals on the Book of Job, By S. Gregory the Great, the First Pope of that Name*. 3 vols. Oxford: John Henry Parker, 1845.

Aquinas, Thomas, *Summa Theologiae: Latin Text and English Translation, Introductions, Notes, Appendices, and Glossaries*, trans. Thomas Gilby et al. 61 vols. London: Eyre & Spottiswoode, 1964–80.

Bailey, Derrick Sherwin, *Homosexuality and the Western Christian Tradition*. London: Longmans, Green, 1955.

Baker, Peter S., 'The Ambiguity of *Wulf and Eadwacer*', *Studies in Philology* 78 (1981), 39–51.

Bambas, Rudolph C., 'Another View of the Old English *Wife's Lament*', *JEGP* 62 (1963), 303–9.

Bankert, Dabney Anderson, 'Reconciling Family and Faith: Ælfric's *Lives of Saints* and Domestic Dramas of Conversion', in Hall, *Via Crucis*, pp. 138–57.

Barnard, Leslie William, trans., *The First and Second Apologies. St. Justin Martyr*. Ancient Christian Writers, 56. New York: Paulist Press, 1997.

Bately, Janet M., 'The Literary Prose of King Alfred's Reign: Translation or Transformation?' Inaugural Lecture in the Chair of English Language and Medieval Literature at University of London King's College, 4 March 1980, reprinted in Szarmach, *Old English Prose*, pp. 3–27.

—— ed., *The Old English Orosius*. EETS SS 6. London: Oxford University Press, 1980.

Beckman, Nat., 'Ignavi et imbelles et corpore infames', *Arkiv för nordisk filologi* 52 (1936), 78–81.

Belanoff, Patricia, 'Women's Songs, Women's Language: *Wulf and Eadwacer* and *The Wife's Lament*', in Damico and Olsen, *New Readings on Women*, pp. 193–203.

Bernard, G. W., *The King's Reformation: Henry VIII and the Remaking of the English Church*. New Haven: Yale University Press, 2005.

Bethurum, Dorothy, ed., *The Homilies of Wulfstan*. Oxford: Clarendon Press, 1957.

Biggs, Frederick M., '*Beowulf* and Some Fictions of the Geatish Succession', *Anglo-Saxon England* 32 (2003), 55–77.

—— 'The Politics of Succession in *Beowulf* and Anglo-Saxon England', *Speculum* 80 (2005), 709–41.

Björn K. Þórólfsson and Guðni Jónsson, eds, *Vestfirðinga sǫgur*. Íslenzk fornrit VI. Reykjavík: Hið íslenzka fornritafélag, 1943.

Blake, N. F., 'The Battle of Maldon', *Neophilologus* 49 (1965), 332–45.

—— 'Some Problems of Interpretation and Translation in the OE *Phoenix*', *Anglia* 80 (1962), 50–62.

—— ed., *The Phoenix*. Manchester: Manchester University Press, 1964, rev. Exeter: Exeter University Press, 1990.

Bloch, R. Howard, *Medieval Misogyny and the Invention of Western Romantic Love*. Chicago: University of Chicago Press, 1989.

Bolton, W. F., *Alcuin and Beowulf: An Eighth-Century View*. London: Edward Arnold, 1979.

Boswell, John, 'Revolutions, Universals, and Sexual Categories', in *Hidden from History: Reclaiming the Gay and Lesbian Past*, ed. Martin Duberman, Martha Vicinus, and George Chauncey, Jr. London: Meridian, 1989, pp. 17–36.

—— *Christianity, Social Tolerance and Homosexuality: Gay People in Western Europe from the Beginning of the Christian Era to the Fourteenth Century*. Chicago: University of Chicago Press, 1980.

Boyle, Andrew, 'The Hare in Myth and Reality: A Review Article', *Folklore* 84 (1973), 313–26.

Bradley, Henry '[review of Morley's *English Writers*]', *The Academy* 33 (1888), 197.

Bradley, S. A. J., ed. and trans., *Anglo-Saxon Poetry*. London: Everyman, 1982.

Bray, Alan, *Homosexuality in Renaissance England, with a New Afterword*. New York: Columbia University Press, 1995.

Brecht, Bertolt, *The Life of Galileo*, trans. Desmond I. Vesey. London: Methuen, 1963.

Bremmer, Jan, 'An Enigmatic Indo-European Rite: Paederasty', *Arethusa* 13 (1980), 279–98.

—— 'Avunculate and Fosterage', *Journal of Indo-European Studies* 4 (1976), 65–78.

Bremmer, Jr, Rolf H., 'The Importance of Kinship: Uncle and Nephew in "Beowulf" ', *Amsterdamer Beiträge zur älteren Germanistik* 15 (1980), 21–38.

Brooke, Stopford A., *English Literature from the Beginning to the Norman Conquest*. rev. edn. London: Macmillan, 1898.

Bugge, John, 'The Virgin Phoenix', *Mediaeval Studies* 38 (1976), 332–50.

Bullough, Vern L., 'The Sin against Nature and Homosexuality', in *Sexual Practices and the Medieval Church*, ed. Vern L. Bullough and James Brundage. Buffalo, NY: Prometheus Books, 1982, pp. 55–71.

Bullough, Vern L., 'Transvestites in the Middle Ages: A Sociological Analysis', *American Journal of Sociology* 79 (1974), 1381–94; repr. with modifications in *Sexual Practices and the Medieval Church*, ed. Vern L. Bullough and James Brundage. Buffalo, NY, 1982, pp. 43–54.

——and James A. Brundage, eds, *Handbook of Medieval Sexuality*. New York: Garland, 1996.

Burgess, Glenn, and Steven F. Kruger, eds, *Queering the Middle Ages*. Minnesota: University of Minnesota Press, 2001.

Burgwinkle, William E., *Sodomy, Masculinity, and Law in Medieval Literature: France and England, 1050–1230*. Cambridge: Cambridge University Press, 2004.

Bury, R. G., *Sextus Empiricus*. 4 vols. London: Heinemann, 1976.

Cadden, Joan, 'Sciences/Silences: The Natures and Languages of "Sodomy" in Peter of Abano's *Problemata* Commentary', in Lochrie et al., *Constructing Medieval Sexualities*, pp. 40–57.

——*Meanings of Sex Difference in the Middle Ages: Medicine, Science, and Culture*. Cambridge: Cambridge University Press, 1993.

Calder, D. G., 'The Vision of Paradise: A Symbolic Reading of the Old English *Phoenix*', *Anglo-Saxon England* 1 (1972), 167–81.

Campbell, Alistair, *Old English Grammar*. Oxford: Clarendon Press, 1959.

Campbell, Jackson J., 'Learned Rhetoric in Old English Poetry', *Modern Philology* 63 (1966), 189–201.

Canuteson, John, 'The Crucifixion and the Second Coming in *The Dream of the Rood*', *Modern Philology* 66 (1969), 293–7.

Cascarino, Tony, 'Boys being boys in the dressing-room helps to keep homosexuality in football's closet', *The Times*, 13 February 2006.

Cazier, Pierre, ed., *Isidorus Hispalensis Sententiae*. CCSL, CXI. Turnhout: Brepols, 1998.

Charles, R. H., trans., *The Testaments of the Twelve Patriarchs*. London: Adam and Charles Black, 1908.

Chickering, Jr, Howell D., trans., *Beowulf: A Dual-Language Edition*. New York: Anchor Books, 1977.

Clark, David, 'Creating a Tradition: Dying with One's Lord in *The Battle of Maldon* and its Analogues' (forthcoming).

——'Revisiting *Gísla saga*: Sexual Themes and the Heroic Past', *JEGP* 106 (2007), 492–515.

——'Relaunching the Hero: The Case of Scyld and Beowulf Re-opened', *Neophilologus* 90 (2006), 621–42.

——'Undermining and En-Gendering Vengeance: Distancing and Anti-Feminism in the *Poetic Edda*', *Scandinavian Studies* 77 (2005), 173–200.

——'Vengeance and the Heroic Ideal in Old English and Old Norse Literature' (unpublished doctoral thesis, University of Oxford, 2003).

Clark Hall, John R., *A Concise Anglo-Saxon Dictionary*. Toronto: University of Toronto Press, 1984.

Clayton, Mary, 'Homiliaries and Preaching in Anglo-Saxon England', *Peritia* 4 (1985), 207–42; corrected reprint in Szarmach, *Old English Prose*, pp. 151–98.

Clemoes, P. A. M., 'The Chronology of Ælfric's Works', in *The Anglo-Saxons: Studies in Some Aspects of their History and Culture presented to Bruce Dickins*, ed. Peter Clemoes. London: Bowes & Bowes, 1959, pp. 212–47.

—— *Interactions of Thought and Language in Old English Poetry*. Cambridge Studies in Anglo-Saxon England, 12. Cambridge: Cambridge University Press, 1995.

—— ed., *Ælfric's Catholic Homilies: The First Series, Text*. EETS SS 17, Oxford: Oxford University Press, 1997.

Clover, Carol J., 'Regardless of Sex: Men, Women, and Power in Early Northern Europe', *Speculum* 68 (1993), 365–88.

—— *Men, Women, and Chainsaws: Gender in the Modern Horror Film*. Princeton, NJ: Princeton University Press, 1992.

—— 'Hildigunnr's lament', in *Structure and Meaning in Old Norse Literature: New Approaches to Textual Analysis and Literary Criticism*, ed. John Lindow et al. Odense: Odense University Press, 1986, pp. 141–83.

Coates, Richard, 'Middle English *badde* and Related Puzzles', *North-Western European Language Evolution* 11 (1988), 91–104.

Cohen, Jeffrey Jerome, and Bonnie Wheeler, eds, *Becoming Male in the Middle Ages*. New York: Garland, 1997.

Coleman, Peter, *Christian Attitudes to Homosexuality*. London: SPCK, 1980.

Conner, Patrick W., 'Exeter's Relics, Exeter's Books', in *Essays on Anglo-Saxon and Related Themes in Memory of Lynne Grundy*, ed. Jane Roberts and Janet Nelson. London: King's College London Centre for Late Antique & Medieval Studies, 2000, pp. 117–56.

—— *Anglo-Saxon Exeter: A Tenth-Century Cultural History*. Woodbridge: Boydell Press, 1993.

Cook, Albert S., *The Old English Elene, the Phoenix and the Physiologus*. New Haven: Yale University Press, 1919.

—— and Chauncey B. Tinker, eds, *Select Translations from Old English Poetry*. Boston, MA: Ginn, 1926.

Cooper, Janet, ed., *The Battle of Maldon: Fiction and Fact*. London: Hambledon Press, 1993.

Cooper, Tracey-Anne, 'Basan and Bata—The Occupational Surnames of two Pre-Conquest Monks of Canterbury', available at <http://www.kentarchaeology.ac/authors/012.pdf> [accessed 10 March 2008].

Cornelius, Regina, ed., *Die altenglische Interlinearversion zu "De vitiis et peccatis" in der Hs. British Library, Royal 7 C. iv: Textausgabe mit Kommentar und Glossar*. Europäische Hochschulschriften: Reihe 14, Angel-sächsische Sprache und Literatur, 296. Frankfurt am Main: Peter Lang, 1995, pp. 164–81.

Crawford, S. J., ed., *The Old English Version of the Heptateuch*. EETS 160. London: Oxford University Press, 1922; repr. with additions by N. R. Ker, 1969.

Creed, Robert P., 'The Art of the Singer: Three Old English Tellings of the Offering of Isaac', in Creed, *Old English Poetry*, pp. 69–92.

—— ed., *Old English Poetry: Fifteen Essays*. Providence, RI: Brown University Press, 1967.

Cross, J. E., 'Oswald and Byrhtnoth: A Christian Saint and a Hero who is Christian', *English Studies* 46 (1965), 93–109.

—— 'The Conception of the Old English *Phoenix*', in Creed, *Old English Poetry*, pp. 129–52.

Crossley-Holland, Kevin, trans., and Bruce Mitchell, ed., *The Battle of Maldon and Other Old English Poems*. London: Macmillan, 1965.

Cubitt, Catherine, 'Virginity and Misogyny in Tenth- and Eleventh-Century England', *Gender and History* 12 (2000), 1–32.

Curry, Jane L., 'Approaches to a Translation of the Anglo-Saxon *The Wife's Lament*', *Medium Ævum* 35 (1966), 187–98.

Damico, Helen, and Alexandra Hennessey Olsen, eds, *New Readings on Women in Old English Literature*. Bloomington, IN: Indiana University Press, 1990.

—— and John Leyerle, eds, *Heroic Poetry in the Anglo-Saxon Period: Studies in Honor of Jess B. Bessinger, Jr.* Studies in Medieval Culture, 32. Kalamazoo, MI: Medieval Institute Publications, 1993.

Davidson, Clifford, 'Erotic "Women's Songs" in Anglo-Saxon England', *Neophilologus* 59 (1975), 451–62.

Davis, Henry, trans., *St. Gregory the Great. Pastoral Care*. London: Longmans, Green & Co., 1950.

Dendle, Peter, *Satan Unbound: The Devil in Old English Narrative Literature*. Toronto: University of Toronto Press, 2001.

Desmond, Marilyn, 'The Voice of Exile: Feminist Literary History and the Anonymous Anglo-Saxon Elegy', *Critical Inquiry* 16 (1990), 573–90.

Dewing, H. B., *Procopius*. 6 vols. London: Heinemann, 1919.

Dinshaw, Carolyn, *Getting Medieval: Sexualities and Communities, Pre-and Post Modern*. Durham: Duke University Press, 1999.

Doane, A. N., ed., *Genesis A: A New Edition*. Madison: University of Wisconsin Press, 1978.

Dockray-Miller, Mary, 'Beowulf's Tears of Fatherhood', *Exemplaria* 10 (1998), 1–28.

—— 'The Feminized Cross of *The Dream of the Rood*', *Philological Quarterly* 76 (1997), 1–18.

Doignon, J., ed., *Sancti Hilarii Pictaviensis Episcopi Tractatus super Psalmos*. CCSL 61. Turnhout: Brepols, 1997.

Donahue, James J., '"Of this I can make no sense": *Wulf and Eadwacer* and the Destabilization of Meaning', *Medieval Forum* 4 (2004), [no page numbers], <http://www.sfsu.edu/~medieval/Volume4/Donahue.html> [accessed 10 March 2008].

Donovan, Leslie A., 'The Gendered Body as Spiritual Problem and Spiritual Answer in the Lives of Women Saints', in eadem, *Women Saints' Lives in Old English Prose*. Cambridge: Brewer, 1999, pp. 121–34.

Dragland, S. L., 'Monster-Man in *Beowulf*', *Neophilologus* 61 (1977), 606–18.

Drijvers, H. J. W., trans., *The Book of the Laws of Countries: Dialogue on Fate of Bardaiṣan of Edessa*. Assen, Netherlands: Van Gorcum, 1965.

Dynes, Wayne R., ed., *Encyclopedia of Homosexuality*. 2 vols. London: St James Press, 1990.

Dyson, R. W., ed. and trans., *Augustine. The City of God against the Pagans*. Cambridge: Cambridge University Press, 1998.

Earl, James W., '[review of Klinck, *Old English Elegies*]', *Speculum* 69 (1994), 1196–8.

Eco, Umberto, *Art and Beauty in the Middle Ages*, trans. Hugh Bredin. New Haven: Yale University Press, 1986.

Edelstein, L., and I. G. Kidd, eds, *Posidonius*. 3 vols. Cambridge: Cambridge University Press, 1972–99.

Ehwald, Rudolf, ed., *Aldhelmi Opera*. MGH Auctorum Antiquissimorum, XV. Berlin: Weidmann, 1919.

Einar Ól. Sveinsson, ed., *Brennu-Njáls saga*. Íslenzk fornrit XII. Reykjavík: Hið íslenzka fornritafélag, 1954.

Eliason, Norman E., 'Beowulf, Wiglaf, and the Wægmundings', *Anglo-Saxon England* 7 (1978), 95–105.

—— 'On *Wulf and Eadwacer*', in *Old English Studies in Honour of John C. Pope*, ed. Robert B. Burlin and Edward B. Irving, Jr. Toronto: University of Toronto Press, 1974, pp. 225–34.

Emerton, Ephraim, *The Letters of Saint Boniface*. New York: Octagon Books, 1973.

Enright, Michael J., *Lady with a Mead Cup: Ritual, Prophecy and Lordship in the European Warband from La Tène to the Viking Age*. Blackrock, Co. Dublin: Four Courts Press, 1996.

Evans, George Ewart, and David Thomson, *The Leaping Hare*. London: Faber and Faber, 1972.

Fairweather, Janet, *Liber Eliensis: A History of the Isle of Ely from the Seventh Century to the Twelfth, Compiled by a Monk of Ely in the Twelfth Century*. Woodbridge: Boydell Press, 2005.

Fanning, Steven, 'Tacitus, *Beowulf*, and the *Comitatus*', in *Haskins Society Journal* 9 (1997), 17–38.

Fiske, Adele M., *Friends and Friendship in the Monastic Tradition*. CIDOC Cuaderno, 51. Cuernavaca, Mexico: Centro Intercultural de Documentacion, 1980.

Fitzpatrick, Mary Cletus, ed. and trans., *Lactanti De Ave Phoenice: with Introduction, Text, Translation, and Commentary*. Philadelphia: University of Pennsylvania Press, 1933.

Foucault, Michel, *The Use of Pleasure: The History of Sexuality, Volume 2*, trans. Robert Hurley. Harmondsworth: Penguin, 1985.

Fowler, Roger, 'A Late Old English Handbook for the Use of a Confessor', *Anglia* 83 (1965), 1–34.

Fox, Samuel, ed. and trans., *King Alfred's Anglo-Saxon Version of Boethius De Consolatione Philosophiæ*. Cited from the repr. of the 1864 edn. New York: AMS Press, 1970.

Fradenburg, Louise, and Carla Freccero, eds, *Premodern Sexualities*. New York: Routledge, 1996.

Frank, Roberta, 'The Ideal of Men Dying with their Lord in *The Battle of Maldon*: Anachronism or *nouvelle vague?*' in *People and Places in Northern Europe 500–1600: Essays in Honour of Peter Hayes Sawyer*, ed. Ian Wood and Niels Lund. Woodbridge: Boydell Press, 1991; repr. 1996, pp. 95–106.

Frantzen, Allen, *Before the Closet: Same-Sex Love from Beowulf to Angels in America*. Chicago: University of Chicago Press, 1998.

—— 'Bede and Bawdy Bale: Gregory the Great, Angels, and the "Angli" ', in *Anglo-Saxonism and the Construction of Social Identity*, ed. Allen J. Frantzen and John D. Niles. Gainesville: University Press of Florida, 1997, pp. 17–39.

—— 'Between the Lines: Queer Theory, the History of Homosexuality, and Anglo-Saxon Penitentials', *Journal of Medieval and Early Modern Studies* 26 (1996), 255–96.

—— 'When Women Aren't Enough', *Speculum* 68 (1993), 445–71.

—— *The Literature of Penance in Anglo-Saxon England*. New Brunswick, NJ: Rutgers University Press, 1983.

Frantzen, Allen, and Douglas Moffat, eds, *The Work of Work: Servitude, Slavery, and Labor in Medieval England*. Glasgow: Cruithne Press, 1994.

Fremantle, W. H., trans., *The Principle Works of St. Jerome*. Select Library of Nicene and Post-Nicene Fathers, 2nd ser., vol. VI, Oxford: Parker, 1893.

Frese, Dolores Warwick, '*Wulf and Eadwacer*: The Adulterous Woman Reconsidered', in Damico and Olsen, *New Readings on Women*, pp. 273–91.

Frey, Leonard H., 'Exile and Elegy in Anglo-Saxon Christian Epic Poetry', *JEGP* 62 (1963), 293–302.

Fulk, R. D., 'Male Homoeroticism in the Old English *Canons of Theodore*', in Pasternack and Weston, *Sex and Sexuality*, pp. 1–34.

Gameson, Richard, 'The Origin of the Exeter Book of Old English Poetry,' *Anglo-Saxon England* 25 (1996), 135–85.

—— and Fiona Gameson [review of Conner, *Anglo-Saxon Exeter*], *Notes and Queries* 42 (1995), 228–30.

Garber, Marjorie, *Vested Interests: Cross-Dressing and Cultural Anxiety*. London: Penguin, 1992.

Garde, Judith N., *Old English Poetry in Medieval Christian Perspective: A Doctrinal Approach*. Cambridge: Brewer, 1991.

Gerard, Kent, and Gert, Hekma, eds, *The Pursuit of Sodomy: Male Homosexuality in the Renaissance and Enlightenment Europe*. New York: Haworth, 1989.

Gilbert, Jane, 'Gender and Sexual Transgression', in *A Companion to the* Gawain-*Poet*, ed. Derek Brewer and Jonathan Gibson. Cambridge: Brewer, 1997, pp. 53–69.

Girsch, Elizabeth Stevens, 'Metaphorical Usage, Sexual Exploitation, and Divergence in the Old English Terminology for Male and Female Slaves', in Frantzen and Moffat, *The Work of Work*, pp. 30–54.

Gneuss, Helmut, *Handlist of Anglo-Saxon Manuscripts: A List of Manuscripts and Manuscript Fragments Written or Owned in England up to 1100*. MRTS 241. Tempe, AZ: Arizona Center for Medieval and Renaissance Studies, 2001.

—— *English Language Scholarship: A Survey and Bibliography from the Beginnings to the End of the Nineteenth Century*. MRTS, 125. New York: MRTS, 1996, pp. 8–13.

—— 'The Study of Language in Anglo-Saxon England' (The Toller Memorial Lecture 1989), *Bulletin of the John Rylands University Library of Manchester* 72 (1990), 3–32.

—— '*The Battle of Maldon* 89: Byrhtnoð's *ofermod* Once Again', *Studies in Philology* 73 (1976), 117–37.

Godden, Malcolm, 'The Relations of Wulfstan and Ælfric: A Reassessment', in Townend, *Wulfstan, Archbishop of York*, pp. 353–74.

—— 'The Trouble with Sodom: Literary Responses to Biblical Sexuality', *Bulletin of the John Rylands University Library of Manchester* 77 (1995), 97–119.

—— ed., *Ælfric's Catholic Homilies. Introduction, Commentary and Glossary*. EETS SS 18. Oxford: Oxford University Press, 2000.

—— ed., *Ælfric's Catholic Homilies: The Second Series, Text*. EETS SS 5. London: Oxford University Press, 1979.

Goldsmith, Margaret, *The Mode and Meaning of Beowulf*. London: Athlone Press, 1970.

Gollancz, Israel, 'Wulf and Eadwacer: An Anglo-Saxon Monodrama in Five Acts', *The Athenaeum* No. 3452, 23 December [18]93, p. 883, col. 3.

Jacquart, Danielle, and Claude Thomasset, *Sexuality and Medicine in the Middle Ages*, trans. Matthew Adamson. Cambridge: Polity Press, 1988.

Jaeger, Stephen C., *Ennobling Love: In Search of a Lost Sensitivity*. Philadelphia: University of Pennsylvania Press, 1999.

—— 'L'amour des rois: structure sociale d'une forme de sensibilité aristocratique', *Annales* 46 (1991), 547–71.

Jaffé, Philipp, ed., *Monumenta Alcuiniana*. Berlin: Weidmann, 1873.

Jankuhn, Hans, 'Archäologische Bemerkungen zur Glaubwürdigkeit des Tacitus in der Germania', *Nachrichten der Akademie der Wissenschaften in Göttingen*, Philologisch-historische Klasse; Jahrg. 1966, 409–26.

Jochens, Jenny, *Old Norse Images of Women*. Philadelphia: University of Pennsylvania Press, 1996.

Johansson, Warren, and William A. Percy, 'Homosexuality', in Bullough and Brundage, *Handbook of Medieval Sexuality*, pp. 155–89.

Jones, Alexander, ed., *Jerusalem Bible*. Standard Edition. London: Dartman, Longman & Todd, 1966.

Jones, Charles W., 'Some Introductory Remarks on Bede's Commentary on Genesis', *Sacris Erudiri* 19 (1969–70), 115–98.

—— *Bedæ Venerabilis Opera. Pars 2, Opera Exegetica*. CCSL, 118–21. Turnhout, Belgium: Brepols, 1960–83.

Jones, Horace Leonard, *The Geography of Strabo*. 8 vols. London: Heinemann, 1923.

Jordan, Mark D., *The Invention of Sodomy in Christian Theology*. Chicago: University of Chicago Press, 1997.

Kabir, Ananya Jahanara, *Paradise, Death and Doomsday in Anglo-Saxon Literature*. Cambridge: Cambridge University Press, 2001.

Kantrowitz, Joanne Spencer, 'The Anglo-Saxon *Phoenix* and Tradition', *Philological Quarterly* 43 (1964), 1–13.

Karkov, Catherine E., *Text and Picture in Anglo-Saxon England: Narrative Strategies in the Junius 11 Manuscript*. Cambridge: Brewer, 2001.

Karras, Ruth Mazo, *Sexuality in Medieval Europe: Doing unto Others*. New York: Routledge, 2005.

—— *From Boys to Men: Formations of Masculinity in Late Medieval Europe*. Philadelphia: University of Pennsylvania Press, 2003.

—— 'Desire, Descendants, and Dominance: Slavery, the Exchange of Women, and Masculine Power', in Frantzen and Moffat, *The Work of Work*, pp. 16–29.

Kaske, Robert E., 'A Poem of the Cross in the Exeter Book: "Riddle 60" and "The Husband's Message"', *Traditio* 23 (1967), 41–71.

Katz, Jonathan Ned, ' "Homosexual" and "Heterosexual": Questioning the Terms', in *Sexualities: Identities, Behaviors, and Society*, ed. Michael S. Kimmel and Rebecca F. Plante. Oxford University Press, 2004, pp. 44–6.

—— *The Invention of Heterosexuality*. New York: Plume, 1996.

Kay, Richard, *Dante's Swift and Strong: Essays on Inferno XV*. Lawrence: Regents Press of Kansas, 1978.

Keiser, Elizabeth E., *Courtly Desire and Medieval Homophobia: The Legitimation of Sexual Pleasure in Cleanness and Its Contexts*. New Haven: Yale University Press, 1997.

Kelly, Richard J., ed. and trans., *The Blickling Homilies. Edition and Translation*. London: Continuum, 2003.

Ker, N. R., *Catalogue of Manuscripts Containing Anglo-Saxon*. Oxford: Clarendon Press, 1957.

Kidd, I. G., *Posidonius. II. The Commentary: (i) Testimonia and Fragments 1–149*. Cambridge: Cambridge University Press, 1988.

Kindschi, L., 'The Latin-Old English Glossaries in Plantin-Moretus MS. 32 and British Museum MS. Additional 32246' (unpublished doctoral thesis, Stanford University, 1955).

Klaeber, Fr., ed., *Beowulf and the Fight at Finnsburg*. 3rd edn. Boston: Heath, 1950.

Klein, Stacy S., *Ruling Women: Queenship and Gender in Anglo-Saxon Literature*. Notre Dame, IN: University of Notre Dame Press, 2006.

Klinck, Anne L., 'Animal Imagery in "Wulf and Eadwacer" and the Possibilities of Interpretation', *Papers in Language and Literature* 23 (1987), 3–26.

—— ed., *The Old English Elegies: A Critical Edition and Genre Study*. Montreal: McGill-Queen's University Press, 1992.

Kolve, V. A., 'Ganymede/*Son of Getron*: Medieval Monasticism and the Drama of Same-Sex Desire', *Speculum* 73 (1998), 1014–67.

Kuefler, Matthew, *The Manly Eunuch: Masculinity, Gender Ambiguity, and Christian Ideology in Late Antiquity*. Chicago: University of Chicago Press, 2001.

Lapidge, Michael, and Michael Herren, trans., *Aldhelm: The Prose Works*. Cambridge: Brewer, 1979.

—— and James L. Rosier, trans., *Aldhelm: The Poetic Works*. Cambridge: Brewer, 1985.

Laqueur, Thomas, *Making Sex: Body and Gender from the Greeks to Freud*. Cambridge, MA: Harvard University Press, 1990.

Lees, Clare A., 'Engendering Religious Desire: Sex, Knowledge, and Christian Identity in Anglo-Saxon England', *Journal of Medieval and Early Modern Studies* 27 (1997), 17–45.

—— 'Men and *Beowulf*', in Lees, *Medieval Masculinities*, pp. 129–48.

—— 'The "Sunday Letter" and the "Sunday Lists"', *Anglo-Saxon England* 14 (1985), 129–51.

—— ed., *Medieval Masculinities: Regarding Men in the Middle Ages*. Minnesota: University of Minnesota Press, 1994.

Leneghan, Francis, ' "That Was a Good King": *Beowulf* and its Prologue' (unpublished doctoral thesis, Trinity College, Dublin, 2005).

Lewis, C. S., *The Allegory of Love: A Study in Medieval Tradition*. Oxford: Oxford University Press, 1936.

Liddell, Henry George, and Robert Scott, *A Greek-English Lexicon*, rev. Henry Stuart Jones et al. Oxford: Clarendon Press, 1968.

Lionarons, Joyce Tally, 'Napier Homily L: Wulfstan's Eschatology at the Close of his Career', in Townend, *Wulfstan, Archbishop of York*, pp. 413–28.

Liuzza, R. M., ed., *The Poems of MS Junius 11: Basic Readings*. London: Routledge, 2002.

Lochrie, Karma, *Heterosyncrasies: Female Sexuality When Normal Wasn't*. Minnesota: University of Minnesota Press, 2005.

—— James A. Schultz, and Peggy McCracken, eds, *Constructing Medieval Sexuality*. Minneapolis: University of Minnesota Press, 1997.

Logeman, H., 'Anglo-Saxonica Minora', *Anglia* 11 (1888), 97–120.

Lubac, Henri de, *Medieval Exegesis, Vol. 1: The Four Senses of Scripture*, trans. Mark Sebanc. Edinburgh: Clark, 1998.

Lucas, Angela M., 'The Narrator of "The Wife's Lament"', *Neuphilologische Mitteilungen* 70 (1969), 282–97.

Lutz, Tom, *Crying: The Natural and Cultural History of Tears*. London: Norton, 1999.

McCann, Justin, trans., *The Rule of St Benedict*. London: Sheed and Ward, 1952, 1976.

McGuire, Brian Patrick, *Friendship and Community: The Monastic Experience 350–1250*. Cistercian Studies Series, 95. Kalamazoo, MI: Cistercian Publications, 1958.

McHugh, Michael P., trans., *Saint Ambrose: Seven Exegetical Works*. Fathers of the Church, 65. Washington, DC: Catholic University of America Press, 1972.

MacLean, G. E., ed., *Ælfric's A-S version of Alcuini Interrogationes Sigewulfi in Genesin*, in *Anglia* 6 (1883), 425–73 and *Anglia* 7 (1884), 1–59.

Mackie, W. S., ed., *The Exeter Book. Part II: Poems IX–XXXII*. EETS OS 194. Oxford: Oxford University Press, 1934.

Magennis, Hugh, 'Ælfric's *Lives of Saints* and Cotton Julius E.vii: Adaptation, Appropriation and the Disappearing Book', in *Imagining the Book*, ed. Stephen Kelly and John J. Thompson. Turnhout: Brepols, 2005, pp. 99–109.

—— 'Warrior Saints, Warfare, and the Hagiography of Ælfric of Eynsham', *Traditio* 56 (2001), 27–51.

—— ' "No Sex Please, We're Anglo-Saxons"? Attitudes to Sexuality in Old English Prose and Poetry', *Leeds Studies in English* 26 (1995), 1–27.

—— 'Contrasting Features in the Non-Ælfrician Lives in the Old English *Lives of Saints*', *Anglia* 104 (1986), 316–48.

—— 'On the Sources of Non-Ælfrician Lives in the Old English *Lives of Saints*, with Reference to the Cotton-Corpus Legendary', *Notes and Queries* NS 230 (1985), 292–9.

Mandel, Jerome, *Alternative Readings in Old English Poetry*. New York: Peter Lang, 1987.

Marcus, Sharon, *Between Women: Friendship, Desire, and Marriage in Victorian England*. Princeton: Princeton University Press, 2007.

Matter, E. Ann, 'My Sister, My Spouse: Woman-Identified Women in Medieval Christianity', in *The Boswell Thesis: Essays on 'Christianity, Social Tolerance, and Homosexuality'*, ed. Matthew Kuefler. Chicago: University of Chicago Press, 2006, pp. 152–66.

Meulengracht Sørensen, Preben, *The Unmanly Man: Concepts of Sexual Defamation in Early Northern society*, trans. Joan Turville-Petre. Odense: Odense University Press, 1983.

Migne, J.-P., ed., *Patrologia Graeca*, 2nd ser. 166 vols. Paris: Migne, 1857–66.

—— ed., *Patrologia Latina*. 221 vols. Paris: Migne, 1844–91.

Miller, William Ian, 'Choosing the Avenger: Some Aspects of the Bloodfeud in Medieval Iceland and England', *Law and History Review* 1 (1983), 159–204.

Mitchell, Bruce, 'The Narrator of *The Wife's Lament*: Some Syntactical Problems Reconsidered', *Neuphilologische Mitteilungen* 73 (1972), 222–34.

Moore, Gareth, *A Question of Truth: Christianity and Homosexuality*. London: Continuum, 2003.

Morris, R., ed., *The Blickling Homilies of the Tenth Century*. 3 vols., EETS 58, 63, 73, 1874–80; repr. in 1 vol. 1967.

Muir, Bernard J., ed., *A Digital Facsimile of Oxford, Bodleian Library, MS. Junius 11*. Software: Nick Kennedy. Oxford: Bodleian Library, 2004. CD-ROM.

Muir, Bernard J., ed., *The Exeter Anthology of Old English Poetry: An Edition of Exeter Dean and Chapter MS 3501*. 2nd rev. edn. 2 vols. Exeter: Exeter University Press, 2000.

Murray, Jacqueline, 'Twice Marginal and Twice Invisible: Lesbians in the Middle Ages', in Bullough and Brundage, *Handbook of Medieval Sexuality*, pp. 191–222.

—— ed., *Conflicted Identities and Multiple Masculinities: Men in the Medieval West*. New York: Garland, 1999.

Murray, Stephen O., *Homosexualities*. Chicago: University of Chicago Press, 2000.

Napier, A., 'Contributions to Old English Literature 1: An Old English Homily on the Observance of Sunday', in [W. P. Ker and A. S. Napier], eds, *An English Miscellany Presented to Dr. Furnivall in Honour of his Seventy-Fifth Birthday*. Oxford: Clarendon Press, 1901, pp. 355–62.

—— 'Altenglische Kleinigkeiten', *Anglia* 11 (1888), 1–10.

—— ed., *Wulfstan. Sammlung der ihm zugeschriebenen Homilien nebst Untersuchungen über ihre Echtheit. Pt. I: Text und Varianten*. Sammlung Englischer Denkmäler in kritischen Ausgaben, 4. Berlin: Weidmann, 1883.

Nash, Daphne, 'Reconstructing Poseidonios' Celtic Ethnography: Some Considerations', *Britannia* 7 (1976), 111–26.

Niles, John D., *Old English Enigmatic Poems and the Play of the Texts*. Studies in the Early Middle Ages, 13. Turnhout: Brepols, 2006.

North, Richard, 'Getting to Know the General in "The Battle of Maldon"', *Medium Ævum* 60 (1991), 1–15.

O'Donnell, Katherine, and Michael O'Rourke, eds, *Love, Sex, Intimacy, and Friendship between Men, 1550–1800*. New York: Palgrave Macmillan, 2003.

Oldfather, C. H., *Diodorus of Sicily*. 12 vols. London: Heinemann, 1939.

Oliphaunt, Robert T., ed., *The Harley Latin-Old English Glossary* [British Library MS Harley 3376]. The Hague: Mouton, 1966.

—— 'Conspicuous Heroism: Abraham, Prudentius, and the Old English Verse *Genesis*', in *Heroes and Heroines in Medieval English Literature*, ed. Leo Carruthers. Cambridge: Brewer, 1994, pp. 45–58.

Orchard, Andy, *Pride and Prodigies: Studies in the Monsters of the 'Beowulf'-Manuscript*. Cambridge: Cambridge University Press, 1995.

Osborn, Marijane, 'Norse Ships at Maldon: The Cultural Context of *æschere* in the Old English Poem "The Battle of Maldon"', *Neuphilologische Mitteilungen* 104 (2003), 261–80.

—— 'Reading the "Animals" of *Wulf and Eadwacer* with Hrabanus Maurus', *Medievalia et Humanistica* 29 (2003), 27–49.

—— 'The Text and Context of *Wulf and Eadwacer*', in *The Old English Elegies: New Essays in Criticism and Research*, ed. Martin Green. London and Toronto: Associated University Prees, 1983, pp. 174–89.

Pasternack, Carol, and Lisa M. C. Weston, eds, *Sex and Sexuality in Anglo-Saxon England: Essays in Memory of Daniel Gillmore Calder*. MRTS 277. Tempe, AZ: Arizona Center for Medieval and Renaissance Studies, 2004.

Patten, Faith, 'Structure and Meaning in *The Dream of the Rood*', *English Studies* 49 Tempe, A2: (1968), 385–401.

Petersen, Helle Falcher, '*The Phoenix*: The Art of Literary Recycling', *Neuphilologische Mitteilungen* 101 (2000), 375–86.

Places, Édouard des, ed. and trans., *Eusèbe de Césarée. La Préparation évangélique*. Paris: Cerf, 1980.

Pope, John C., ed., *Homilies of Ælfric. A Supplementary Collection* . . . 2 vols. EETS 259 & 260. London: Oxford University Press, 1967–8.

Porter, David W., ed. and trans., *Excerptiones de Prisciano: The Source for Ælfric's Latin-Old English Grammar*. Cambridge: Brewer, 2002.

Price, Arnold H., 'The Role of the Germanic Warrior Club in the Historical Process: A Methodological Exposition', *Miscellanea mediaevalia* 12 (1980), 558–65.

Priebsch, R., 'The Chief Sources of Some Anglo-Saxon Homilies', *Otia Merseiana* 1 (1899), 129.

Pugh, Tison, *Queering Medieval Genres*. New York: Palgrave Macmillan, 2005.

Rabinowitz, Nancy Sorkin, 'Introduction' in *Among Women: From the Homosocial to the Homoerotic in the Ancient World*, ed. Nancy Sorkin Rabinowitz and Lisa Auanger. Austin: University of Texas Press, 2002, pp. 1–33.

Raith, Josef, ed., *Die altenglische Version des Halitgar'schen Bussbuches (sog. Poenitentiale Pseudo-Ecgberti)*. Bibliothek der angelsächsischen Prosa, 13. Hamburg: Henri Grand, 1933.

Ray, Roger, 'What do we Know about Bede's Commentaries?' *Recherches de théologie ancienne et médiévale* 49 (1982), 5–20.

Raymond, Irving Woodworth, trans., *Seven Books of History against the Pagans. The Apology of Paulus Orosius*. New York: Columbia University Press, 1936.

Renoir, Alain, 'A Reading Context for *The Wife's Lament*', in *Anglo-Saxon Poetry: Essays in Appreciation of John C. McGalliard*, ed. Lewis E. Nicholson and Dolores Warwick Frese. Notre Dame, IN: University of Notre Dame Press, 1975, pp. 224–41.

—— '*Wulf and Eadwacer*: A Non-Interpretation', in *Franciplegius: Medieval and Linguistic Studies in Honor of Francis Peabody Magoun, Jr.*, ed. Jess B. Bessinger, Jr and Robert P. Creed. New York: New York University Press, 1965, pp. 147–63.

Richards, Jeffrey, *Sex, Dissidence and Damnation: Minority Groups in the Middle Ages*. London: Routledge, 1991.

Rives, J. B., *Tacitus. Germania*. Oxford: Clarendon Press, 1999.

Robbins, F. E., *Ptolemy. Tetrabiblos*. London: Heinemann, 1980.

Robinson, Fred C., 'Literary Dialect in *Maldon* and the Casley Transcript', in idem, *The Tomb of Beowulf*, pp. 138–9.

—— 'Some Aspects of the *Maldon* Poet's Artistry', in idem, *The Tomb of Beowulf*, pp. 122–37.

—— *The Tomb of Beowulf, and Other Essays*. Oxford: Blackwell, 1993.

Rolfe, John C., *Ammianus Marcellinus*. 3 vols. London: Heinemann, 1958.

Rousseau, G. S., [Review of Sedgwick, *Between Men*], *The Pursuit of Sodomy: Male Homosexuality in the Renaissance and Enlightenment Europe*, ed. Kent Gerard and Gert Hekma. New York: Haworth, 1989, pp. 515–29.

Rowland, Beryl, 'Animal Imagery and the Pardoner's Abnormality', *Neophilologus* 48 (1964), 56–60.

Roy, Gopa, 'A Virgin Acts Manfully: Ælfric's *Life of St Eugenia* and the Latin Versions', *Leeds Studies in English* NS 23 (1992), 1–27.

Rupp, Leila J., 'Toward a Global History of Same-Sex Sexuality', *Journal of the History of Sexuality* 10 (2001), 287–302.

Saunders, Trevor J., *Aristotle. Politics. Books I and II*. Oxford: Clarendon Press, 1995.

Sayers, William, '*æschere* in *The Battle of Maldon*: Fleet, Warships' Crews, Spearmen, or Oarsmen?' *Neuphilologische Mitteilungen* 107 (2006), 199–205.

Schaefer, Kenneth G., 'An Edition of Five Old English Homilies for Palm Sunday, Holy Saturday, and Easter Sunday' (unpublished dissertation, University of Columbia, 1972), pp. 249–59.

Scheil, Andrew P., 'Somatic Ambiguity and Masculine Desire in the Old English Life of Euphrosyne', *Exemplaria* 11 (1999), 345–61.

Schmidt, Ludwig, *Die Ostgermanen*. 2nd edn. Munich: Beck, 1941; repr. (unaltered) 1969.

Schneider, Catherine, *[Quintilien]. Le soldat de Marius (Grandes déclamations, 3)*. Cassino: Edizioni dell'Università degli Studi di Cassino, 2004.

Schrader, Richard J., *Old English Poetry and the Genealogy of Events*. East Lansing: Colleagues Press, 1993.

Schultz, James A., 'Heterosexuality as a Threat to Medieval Studies', *Journal of the History of Sexuality* 15 (2006), 14–29.

Scott, Peter Dale, 'Alcuin's *Versus de Cuculo*: The Vision of Pastoral Friendship', *Studies in Philology* 62 (1965), 510–30.

Scragg, D. G., 'The Corpus of Vernacular Homilies and Prose Saints' Lives before Ælfric', *Anglo-Saxon England* 8 (1979), 223–77.

—— ed., *The Vercelli Homilies and Related Texts*. EETS 300. Oxford: Oxford University Press, 1992.

—— ed., *The Battle of Maldon, AD 991*. Oxford: Blackwell, 1991.

Sedgwick, Eve Kosofsky, *Epistemology of the Closet*. Berkeley: University of California Press, 1990.

—— *Between Men: English Literature and Male Homosocial Desire*. New York: Columbia University Press, 1985.

Skeat, Walter W., ed., *The Holy Gospels in Anglo-Saxon, Northumbrian, and Old Mercian Versions...* Cambridge: Cambridge University Press, 1871–87.

—— ed., *Ælfric's Lives of Saints, Being A Set of Sermons on Saints' Days formerly observed by the English Church*. EETS OS 76 & 82 (vol. I) and 94 & 114 (vol. II), London: Trübner, 1966.

Spindler, Robert, *Das altenglische Bussbuch (sog. Confessionale Pseudo-Egberti)*. Leipzig: Tauchnitz, 1934.

Stafford, Pauline, 'Kinship and Women in the World of *Maldon*: Byrhtnoth and His Family', in Cooper, *The Battle of Maldon*, pp. 225–35.

Stanley, Eric Gerald, 'Heroic Aspects of the Exeter Book Riddles', in *Prosody and Poetics in the Early Middle Ages: Essays in Honour of C. B. Hieatt*, ed. M. J. Toswell. Toronto: University of Toronto Press, 1995, pp. 197–218.

Stehling, Thomas, trans., *Medieval Latin Love Poems of Male Love and Friendship*. New York: Garland, 1984.

Stevens, Martin, 'The Narrator of *The Wife's Lament*', *Neuphilologische Mitteilungen* 69 (1968), 72–90.

Stevick, R. D., 'Mathematical Proportions and Symbolism in *The Phoenix*', *Viator* 11 (1980), 95–121.

Stryker, William G., ed., 'The Latin-Old English Glossary in MS. Cotton Cleopatra A. III' (unpublished doctoral thesis, Stanford University, 1951).

Swan, Mary, and Elaine Treharne, eds, *Rewriting Old English in the Twelfth Century*. Cambridge Studies in Anglo-Saxon England, 30. Cambridge: Cambridge University Press, 2000.

Sweet, Henry, ed. and trans., *King Alfred's West-Saxon Version of Gregory's Pastoral Care*. EETS OS 45. London: Oxford University Press, 1871.

Syme, Ronald, *Tacitus*. Oxford: Clarendon Press, 1958.

Symons, Thomas, trans., *Regularis concordia Anglicae nationis monachorum sanctimonialiumque: The Monastic Agreement of the Monks and Nuns of the English Nation*. London: Nelson, 1953.

Szarmach, Paul E., 'St. Euphrosyne: Holy Transvestite', in Szarmach, *Holy Men and Holy Women*, pp. 353–65.

—— 'Ælfric's Women Saints: Eugenia', in Damico and Olsen, *New Readings on Women*, pp. 146–57.

—— 'Three Versions of the Jonah Story: An Investigation of Narrative Technique in Old English Homilies', *Anglo-Saxon England* 1 (1972), 183–92.

—— ed., *Old English Prose: Basic Readings*. New York: Garland, 2000.

—— ed., *Holy Men and Holy Women: Old English Prose Saints' Lives and Their Contexts*. New York: State University of New York Press, 1996.

Tengvik, Gösta, 'Old English Bynames', *Nomina Germania* 4 (1938), 287–8.

Thelwall, S., 'A Strain of Sodom', in *Ante-Nicene Fathers: The Writings of the Fathers down to A.D. 325*, ed. Alexander Roberts and James Donaldson, rev. A. Cleveland Coxe. 10 vols. Peabody, MA: Hendrickson, 1994, vol. IV, X.2.

Thorpe, Benjamin, ed. and trans., *Codex Exoniensis: A Collection of Anglo-Saxon Poetry*. London: Society of Antiquaries, 1842.

Tierney, J. J., 'The Celtic Ethnography of Posidonius', *Proceedings of the Royal Irish Academy* 60C (1960), 189–275.

Too, Yun Lee, 'The Appeal to the Senses in the Old English *Phoenix*', *Neuphilologische Mitteilungen* 91 (1990), 229–42.

Topsell, Edward, *The Historie of Four-footed Beasts*. London, 1607.

Tougher, Shaun, 'Holy Eunuchs! Masculinity and Eunuch Saints in Byzantium', in *Holiness and Masculinity in the Middle Ages*, eds. P. H. Cullum and Katherine J. Lewis. Toronto: University of Toronto Press, 2004, pp. 93–108.

—— 'Images of Effeminate Men: The Case of Byzantine Eunuchs', in *Masculinity in Medieval Europe*, ed. D. M. Hadley. London: Longman, 1999, pp. 89–100.

—— ed., *Eunuchs in Antiquity and Beyond*. London: Classical Press of Wales, 2002.

Townend, Matthew, ed., *Wulfstan, Archbishop of York: The Proceedings of the Second Alcuin Conference*. Studies in the Early Middle Ages, 10. Turnhout: Brepols, 2004.

Treharne, E. M., ed., *The Old English Life of St Nicholas with the Old English Life of St Giles*. Leeds Texts and Monographs New Series 15. Leeds: Leeds Studies in English, 1997.

Upchurch, Robert K., *Ælfric's Lives of the Virgin Spouses*. Exeter: University of Exeter Press, 2007.

—— 'Virgin Spouses as Model Christians: The Legend of Julian and Basilissa in Ælfric's *Lives of Saints*', *Anglo-Saxon England* 34 (2005), 197–217.

—— 'The Legend of Chrysanthus and Daria in Ælfric's *Lives of Saints*', *Studies in Philology* 101 (2004), 250–69.

Vogüé, Adalbert de, ed., and Paul Antin, trans., *Grégoire le Grand. Dialogues*. 3 vols. Paris: Cerf, 1978–80.

Walker-Pelkey, Faye, '*Frige hwæt ic hatte*: "The Wife's Lament" as Riddle', *Papers on Language and Literature* 28 (1992), 242–66.

Ward, Donald J., 'The Threefold Death: An Indo-European Trifunctional Sacrifice?' in *Myth and Law among the Indo-Europeans: Studies in Indo-European Comparative Mythology*, ed. Jaan Puhvel. Berkeley: University of California Press, 1970, pp. 123–42.

Weiser-Aall, Lily, 'Zur Geschichte der altgermanischen Todesstrafe und Friedlosigkeit', *Archiv für Religionswissenschaft* 30 (1933), 209–27.

Welldon, J. E. C., *The Politics of Aristotle*. London: Macmillan, 1901.

Whatley, E. Gordon, '*Pearls before Swine*: Ælfric, Vernacular Hagiography, and the Lay Reader', in Hall, *Via Crucis*, pp. 158–84.

Widengren, Geo, *Der Feudalismus im alten Iran: Männerbund, Gefolgswesen, Feudalismus in der iranischen Gesellschaft im Hinblick auf die indogermanischen Verhältnisse*. Cologne: Westdeutscher Verlag, 1969.

Windeatt, Barry, *Oxford Guides to Chaucer: Troilus and Criseyde*. Oxford: Clarendon Press, 1992.

Woolf, Rosemary, 'The Ideal of Men Dying with their Lord in the *Germania* and in *The Battle of Maldon*', *Anglo-Saxon England* 5 (1976), 63–81.

Wormald, Patrick, 'Archbishop Wulfstan and the Holiness of Society', in idem, *Legal Culture in the Early Medieval West: Law as Text, Images and Experience*. London: Hambledon, 1999, pp. 225–51.

Wright, Thomas L., 'Hrothgar's Tears', *Modern Philology* 65 (1967), 39–44.

Yerkes, David, 'The Old Norse and Old English Prose Accounts of the Phoenix', *Journal of English Linguistics* 17 (1984), 24–8.

Young, Antonia, *Women Who Become Men: Albanian Sworn Virgins*. Oxford: Oxford University Press, 2000.

Zacher, Samantha, 'The Source of Vercelli VII: An Address to Women', in *New Readings on the Vercelli Book*, ed. Andy Orchard and Samantha Zacher. Toronto: University of Toronto Press (forthcoming).

Zeikowitz, Richard, *Homoeroticism and Chivalry: Discourses of Male Same-Sex Desire in the Fourteenth Century*. New York: Palgrave Macmillan, 2003.

Zettel, Patrick H., 'Saints' Lives in Old English: Latin Manuscripts and Vernacular Accounts: Ælfric', *Peritia* 1 (1982), 17–37.

Zimmermann, Odo John, trans., *Saint Gregory the Great. Dialogues*. Washington, DC: Catholic University of America Press, 1959.

Zupitza, Julius, ed., *Aelfrics Grammatik und Glossar. Text und Varianten*. 4th, unaltered edn. with an introduction by Helmut Gneuss. Hildesheim: Weidmann, 2003.

Index

Printed and bound by CPI Group (UK) Ltd, Croydon, CR0 4YY